& My Brothers

Volume 5

Hari Tokeino

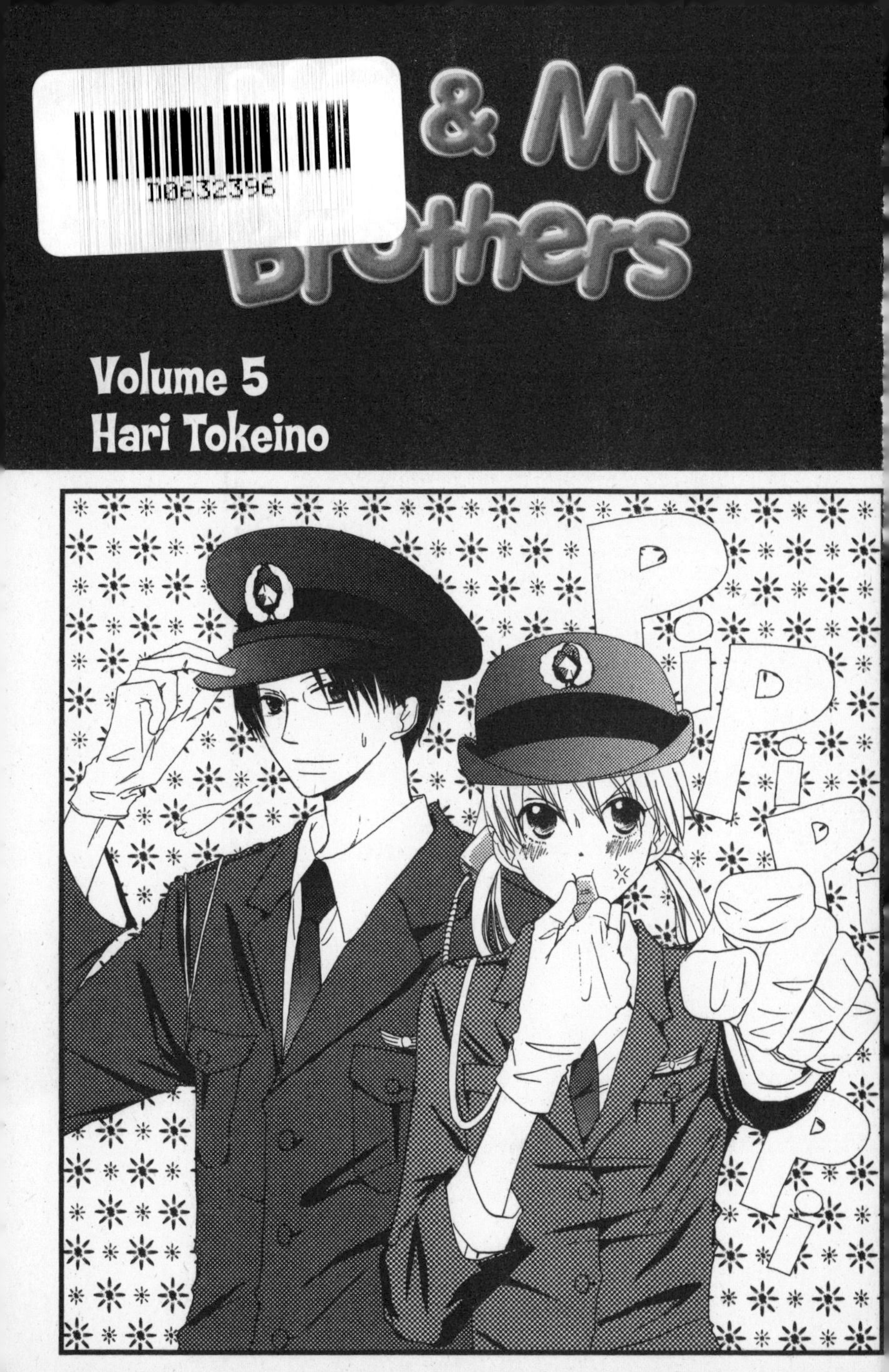
PiPiPiPi

Me & My Brothers Volume 5
Created by Hari Tokeino

Translation - Haruko Furukawa
English Adaptation - Joel Black
Retouch and Lettering - Star Print Brokers
Production Artist - Michael Paolilli
Graphic Designer - Monalisa De Asis

Editor - Hyun Joo Kim
Digital Imaging Manager - Chris Buford
Pre-Production Supervisor - Vicente Rivera, Jr.
Production Specialist - Lucas Rivera
Managing Editor - Vy Nguyen
Art Director - Al-Insan Lashley
Editor-in-Chief - Rob Tokar
Publisher - Mike Kiley
President and C.O.O. - John Parker
C.E.O. and Chief Creative Officer - Stu Levy

A  Manga

TOKYOPOP and are trademarks or registered trademarks of TOKYOPOP Inc.

TOKYOPOP Inc.
5900 Wilshire Blvd. Suite 2000
Los Angeles, CA 90036

E-mail: info@TOKYOPOP.com
Come visit us online at www.TOKYOPOP.com

ISBN: 978-1-4278-0229-3

First TOKYOPOP printing: September 2008
10 9 8 7 6 5 4 3 2 1
Printed in the USA

Me & My Brothers

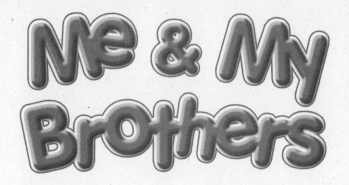

Volume 5
Hari Tokeino

TOKYOPOP®

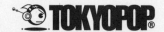

HAMBURG // LONDON // LOS ANGELES // TOKYO

Contents

CHARACTERS PROFILE

ME & MY BROTHERS

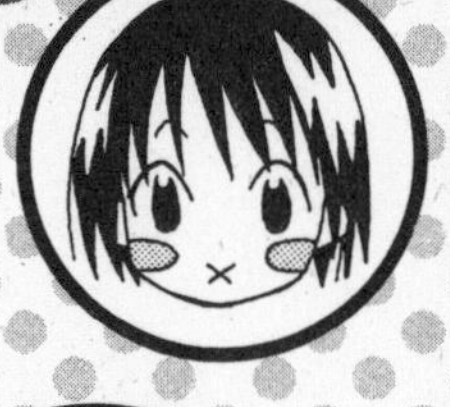

SAKURA MIYASHITA:
THE YOUNGEST. IN 10TH GRADE. THE ONLY GIRL IN THE MIYASHITA FAMILY. SHE IS NOT BLOOD RELATED TO HER FOUR BROTHERS.

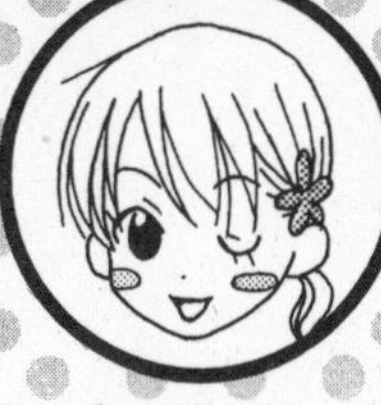

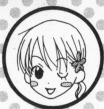

MASASHI MIYASHITA:
THE ELDEST. ROMANCE NOVELIST. ACCORDING TO HIM, HE SOUNDS LIKE A WOMAN BECAUSE OF HIS JOB. HE'S THE LEADER OF THE FOUR SAKURA-SPOILERS.

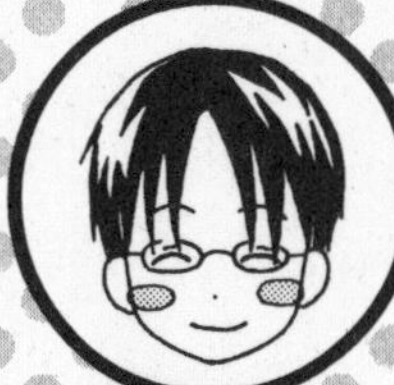

TAKASHI MIYASHITA:
THE 2ND BROTHER. TEACHER. HE TEACHES JAPANESE AT SAKURA'S SCHOOL. HE'S A GENTLEMAN.

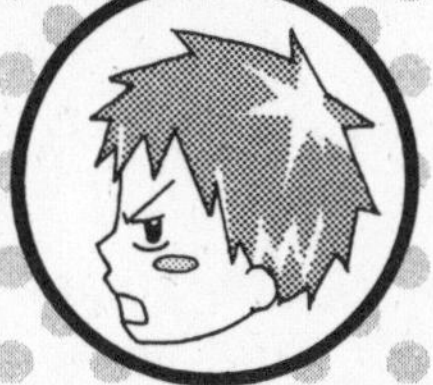

TSUYOSHI MIYASHITA:
THE 3RD BROTHER. FULL-TIME PART-TIMER. HE HAS A DIRTY MOUTH, BUT IS ACTUALLY SHY.

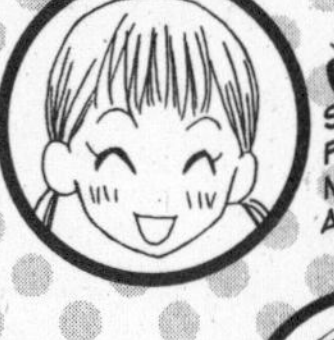

NAKA-CHAN:
SAKURA'S BEST FRIEND. HER FAMILY NAME IS TANAKA. A CHEERFUL GIRL.

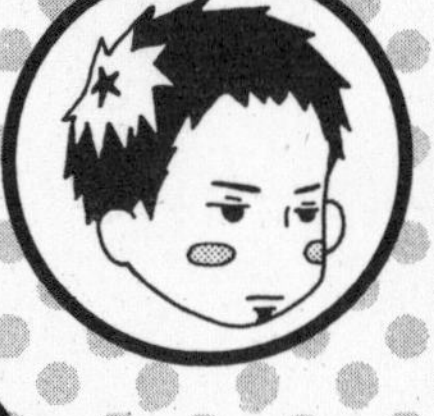

TAKESHI MIYASHITA:
THE 4TH BROTHER. NOW IN COLLEGE. HE LOOKS OLD, BUT HE'S THE YOUNGEST OF FOUR BROTHERS. HE'S QUIET AND LOVES PLANTS.

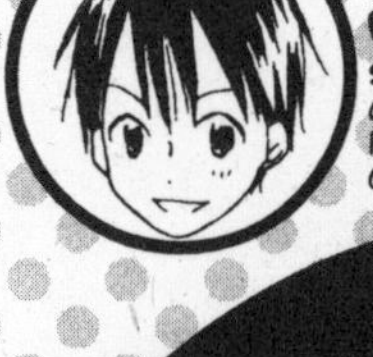

SUZUKI-KUN:
SAKURA'S CLASSMATE. DOES HE HAVE A CRUSH ON SAKURA?

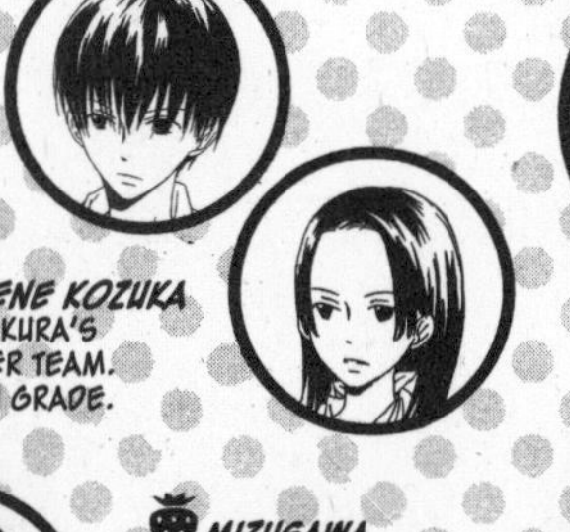

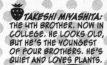

NANA & NENE KOZUKA
THE TWINS IN SAKURA'S SCHOOL SOCCER TEAM. BOTH IN THE 11TH GRADE.

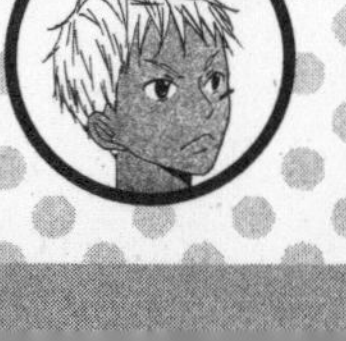

MIZUSAWA
IN THE 10TH GRADE. A SELF-PROCLAIMED BULLS-EYE AIM.

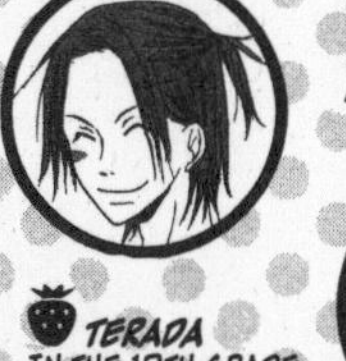

TERADA
IN THE 12TH GRADE. CAPTAIN OF THE SOCCER TEAM.

STORY

SAKURA LOST HER PARENTS WHEN SHE WAS 3 AND WAS RAISED BY HER GRANDMOTHER. THEN, WHEN SAKURA WAS 14, HER GRANDMOTHER PASSED AWAY. SHE WAS ALL ALON UNTIL FOUR STEPBROTHERS SHOWED UP! THE STEPBROTHE ARE FROM SAKURA'S FATHER'S FIRST MARRIAGE. WHILE HE STEPBROTHERS' FATHER HAD RAISED SAKURA AS HIS OWN SAKURA'S BIRTH FATHER IS ACTUALLY HER MOTHER'S EX-BOYFRIEND. EVEN THOUGH THE BROTHERS HAVE NO BLOO CONNECTION TO SAKURA, AFTER 11 YEARS OF SEPARATIO THEY STARTED TO LIVE TOGETHER! WHEN WE LAST LEFT OFF, SAKURA HAD STARTED HIGH SCHOOL AND AGREED TO BE THE TEMPORARY MANAGER FOR THE SOCCER TEAM.

Thanks !!

MIKAMI CHITO SAMA
KONDOU SAMA

&

YOU !!!

HARI.

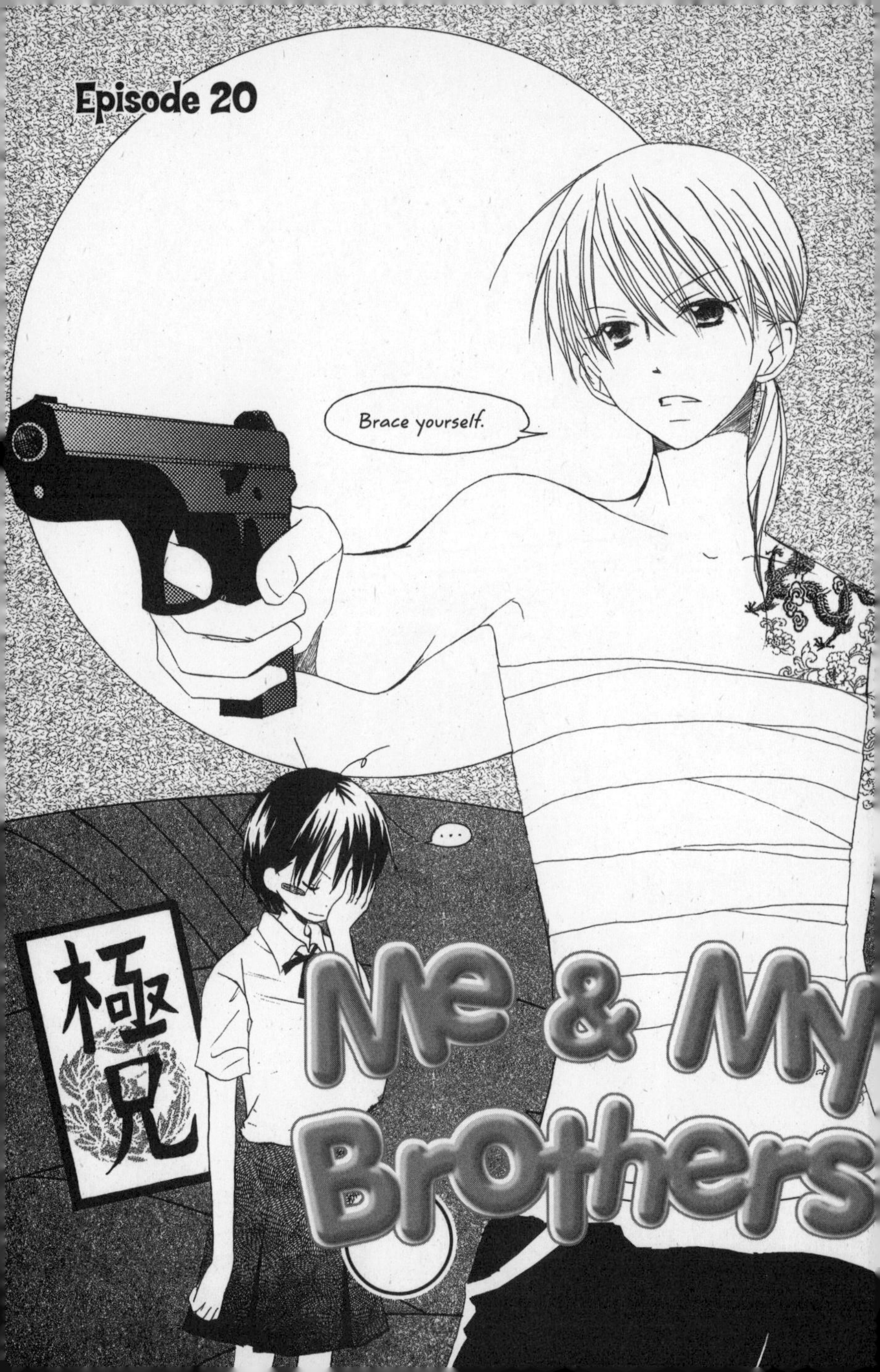
Episode 20
Brace yourself.
...
極兄
Me & My Brothers

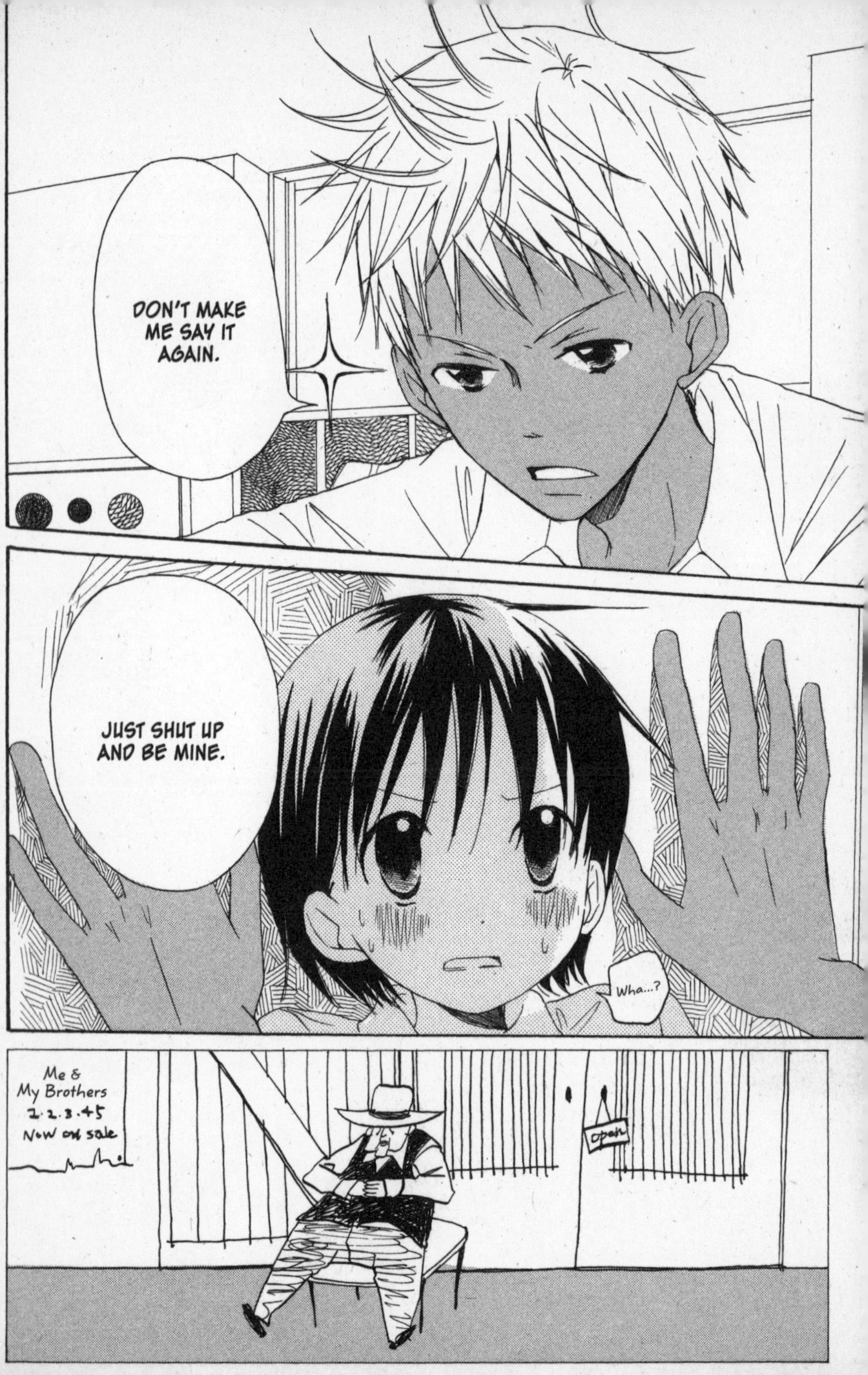
DON'T MAKE ME SAY IT AGAIN.
JUST SHUT UP AND BE MINE.
Wha...?
Me & My Brothers 1·2·3·4·5 Now on sale
open

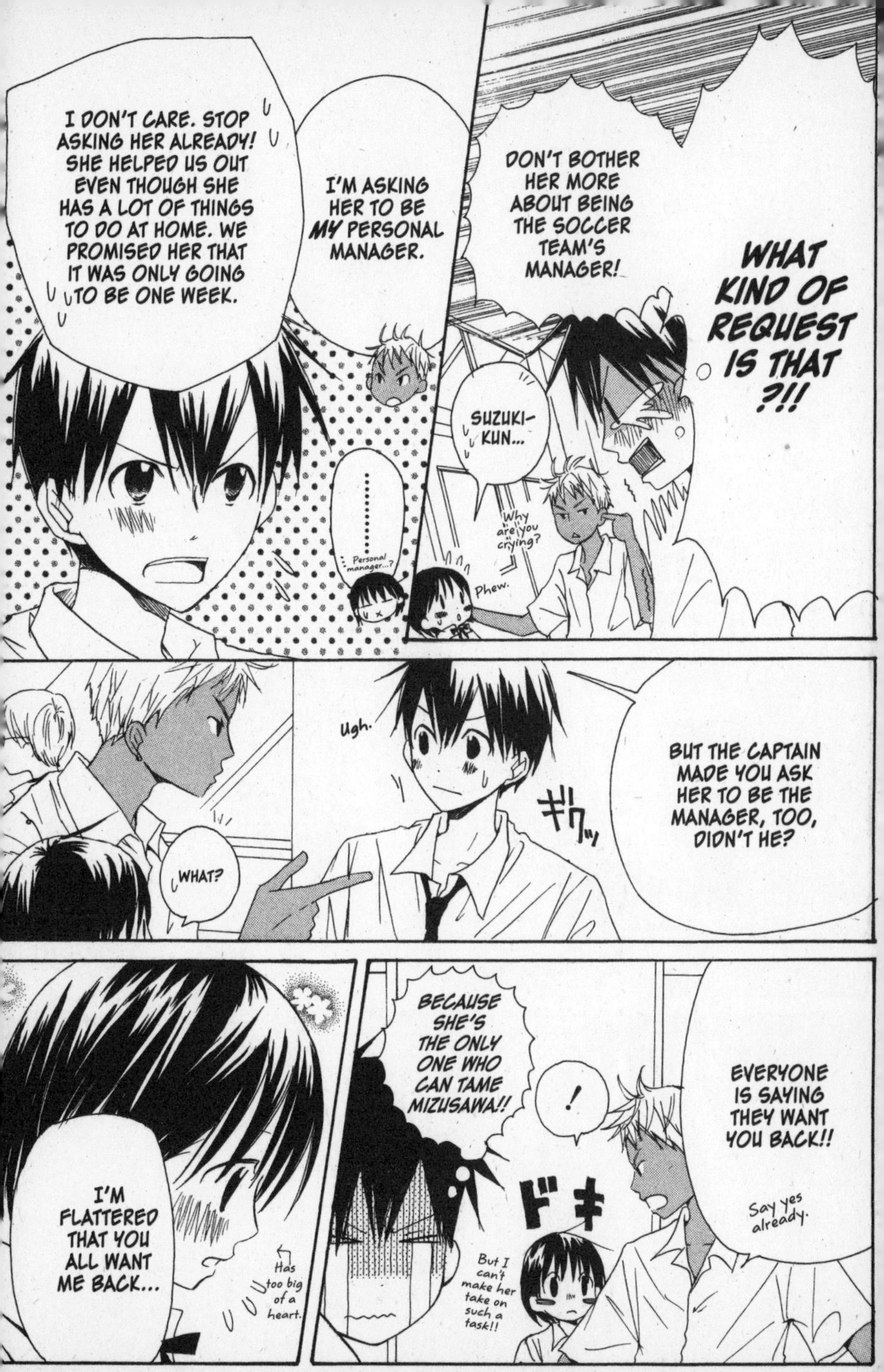
WHAT KIND OF REQUEST IS THAT ?!!
DON'T BOTHER HER MORE ABOUT BEING THE SOCCER TEAM'S MANAGER!
SUZUKI-KUN...
Why are you crying?
Phew.
I'M ASKING HER TO BE MY PERSONAL MANAGER.
I DON'T CARE. STOP ASKING HER ALREADY! SHE HELPED US OUT EVEN THOUGH SHE HAS A LOT OF THINGS TO DO AT HOME. WE PROMISED HER THAT IT WAS ONLY GOING TO BE ONE WEEK.
......
Personal manager...?
BUT THE CAPTAIN MADE YOU ASK HER TO BE THE MANAGER, TOO, DIDN'T HE?
ギクッ
Ugh.
WHAT?
EVERYONE IS SAYING THEY WANT YOU BACK!!
Say yes already.
!
BECAUSE SHE'S THE ONLY ONE WHO CAN TAME MIZUSAWA!!
ドキ
But I can't make her take on such a task!!
I'M FLATTERED THAT YOU ALL WANT ME BACK...
Has too big of a heart.

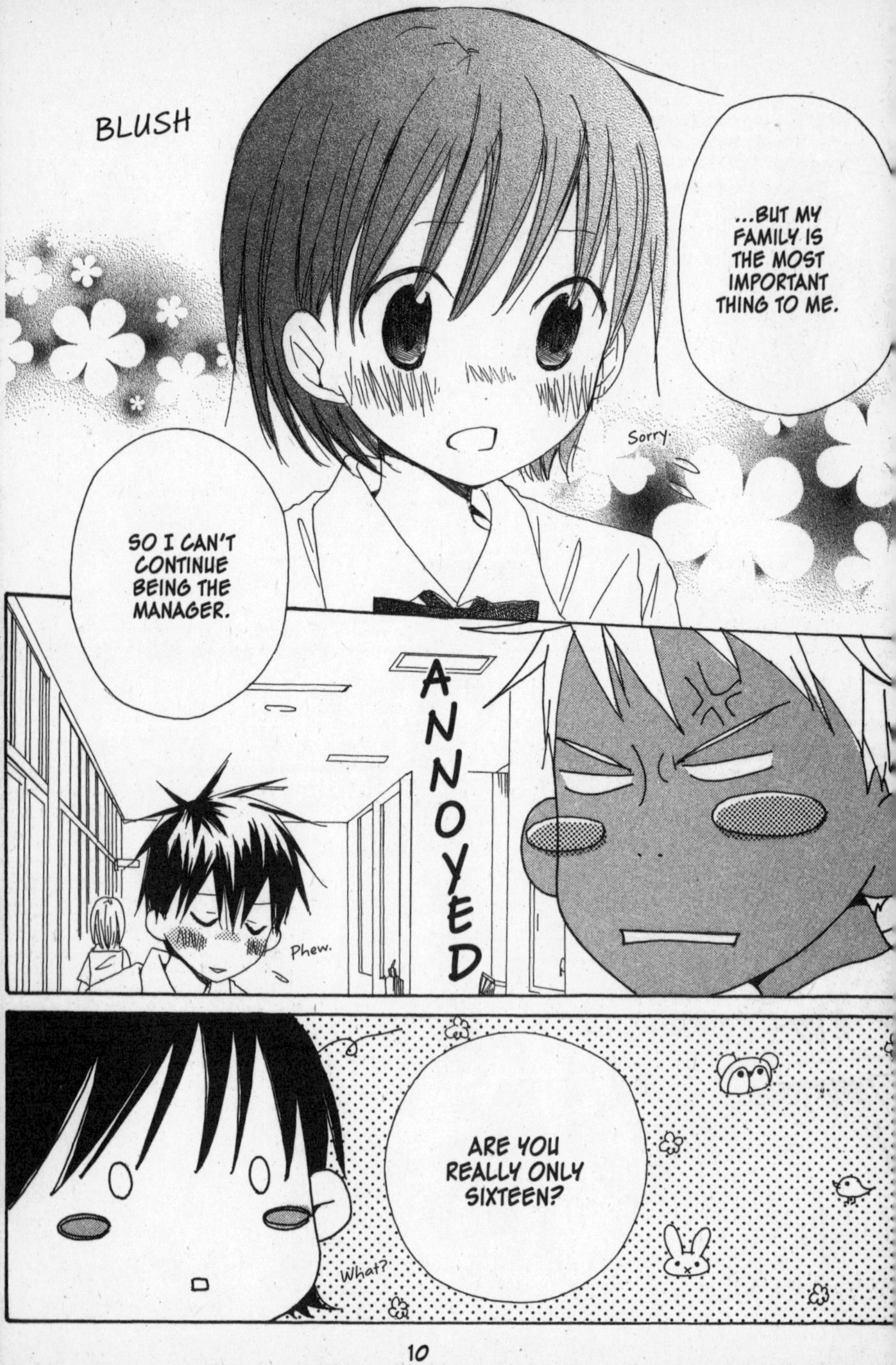
...BUT MY FAMILY IS THE MOST IMPORTANT THING TO ME.
BLUSH
Sorry.
SO I CAN'T CONTINUE BEING THE MANAGER.
ANNOYED
Phew.
ARE YOU REALLY ONLY SIXTEEN?
What?

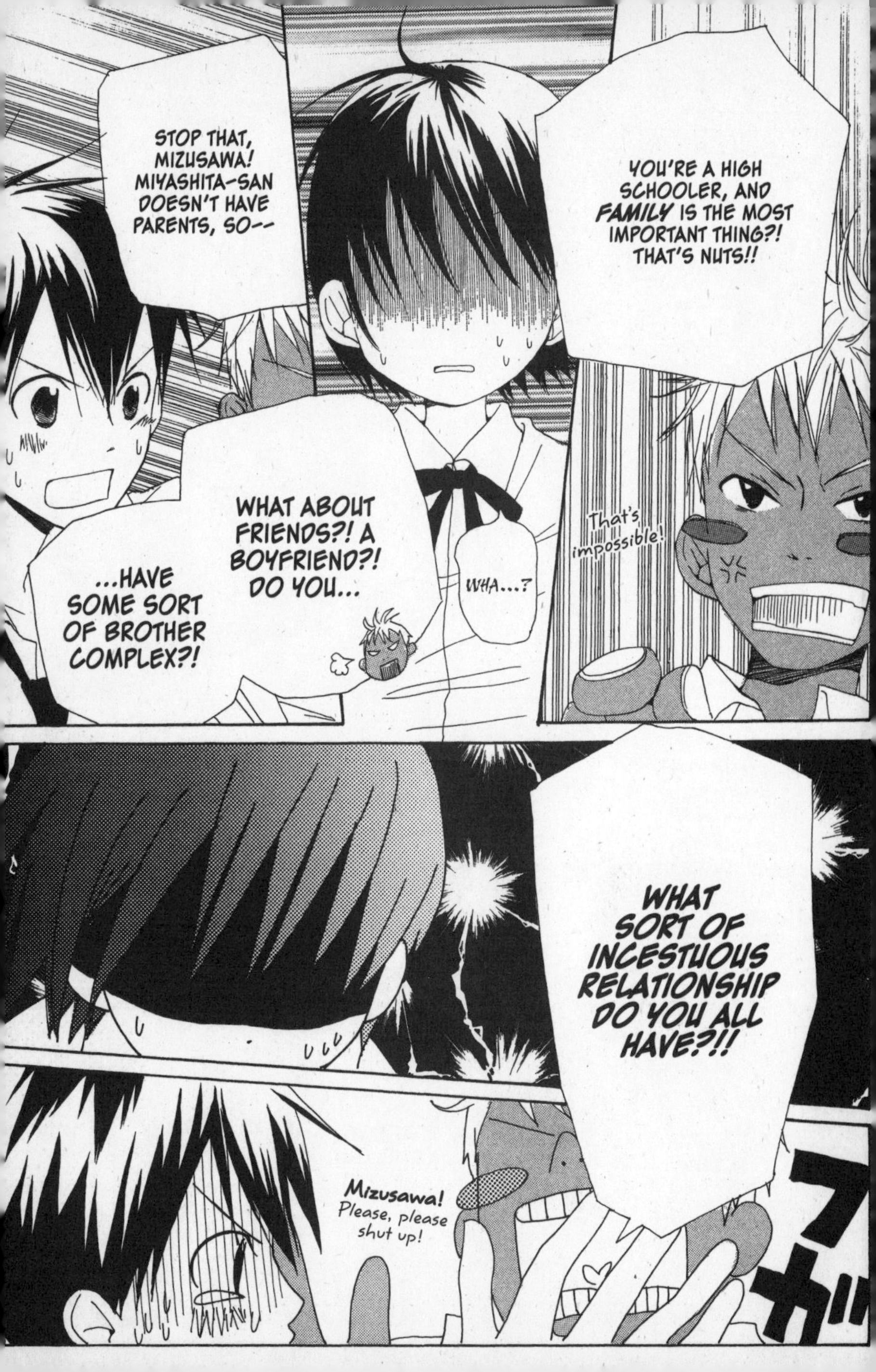
YOU'RE A HIGH SCHOOLER, AND FAMILY IS THE MOST IMPORTANT THING?! THAT'S NUTS!!
That's impossible!
STOP THAT, MIZUSAWA! MIYASHITA-SAN DOESN'T HAVE PARENTS, SO--
WHAT ABOUT FRIENDS?! A BOYFRIEND?! DO YOU...
...HAVE SOME SORT OF BROTHER COMPLEX?!
WHA...?
WHAT SORT OF INCESTUOUS RELATIONSHIP DO YOU ALL HAVE?!!
Mizusawa! Please, please shut up!

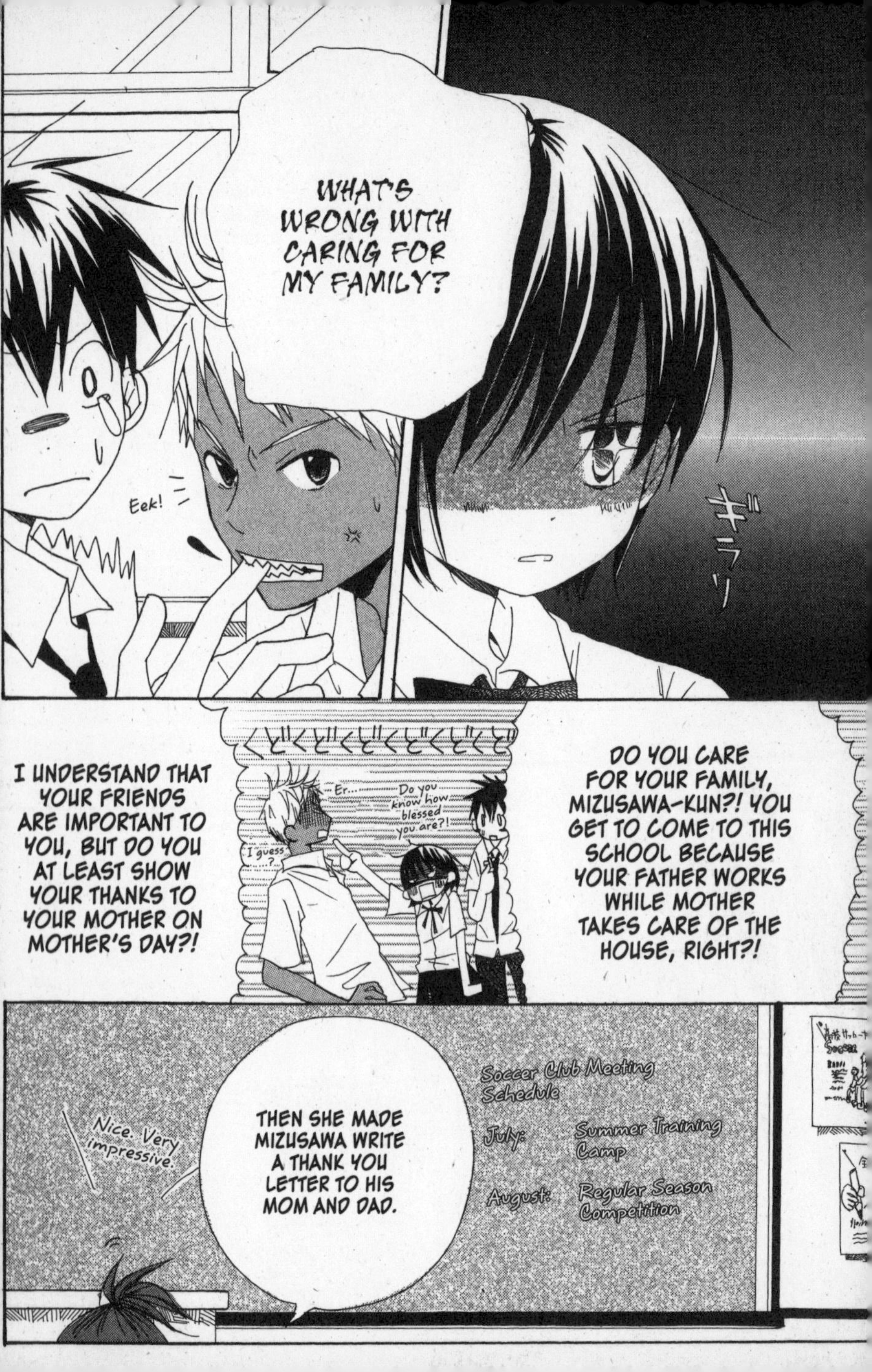
WHAT'S WRONG WITH CARING FOR MY FAMILY?
ギラッ
Eek!
DO YOU CARE FOR YOUR FAMILY, MIZUSAWA-KUN?! YOU GET TO COME TO THIS SCHOOL BECAUSE YOUR FATHER WORKS WHILE MOTHER TAKES CARE OF THE HOUSE, RIGHT?!
くどくどくどくどくど
Do you know how blessed you are?!
Er...
I guess...?
I UNDERSTAND THAT YOUR FRIENDS ARE IMPORTANT TO YOU, BUT DO YOU AT LEAST SHOW YOUR THANKS TO YOUR MOTHER ON MOTHER'S DAY?!
Soccer Club Meeting Schedule
July: Summer Training Camp
August: Regular Season Competition
THEN SHE MADE MIZUSAWA WRITE A THANK YOU LETTER TO HIS MOM AND DAD.
Nice. Very impressive.

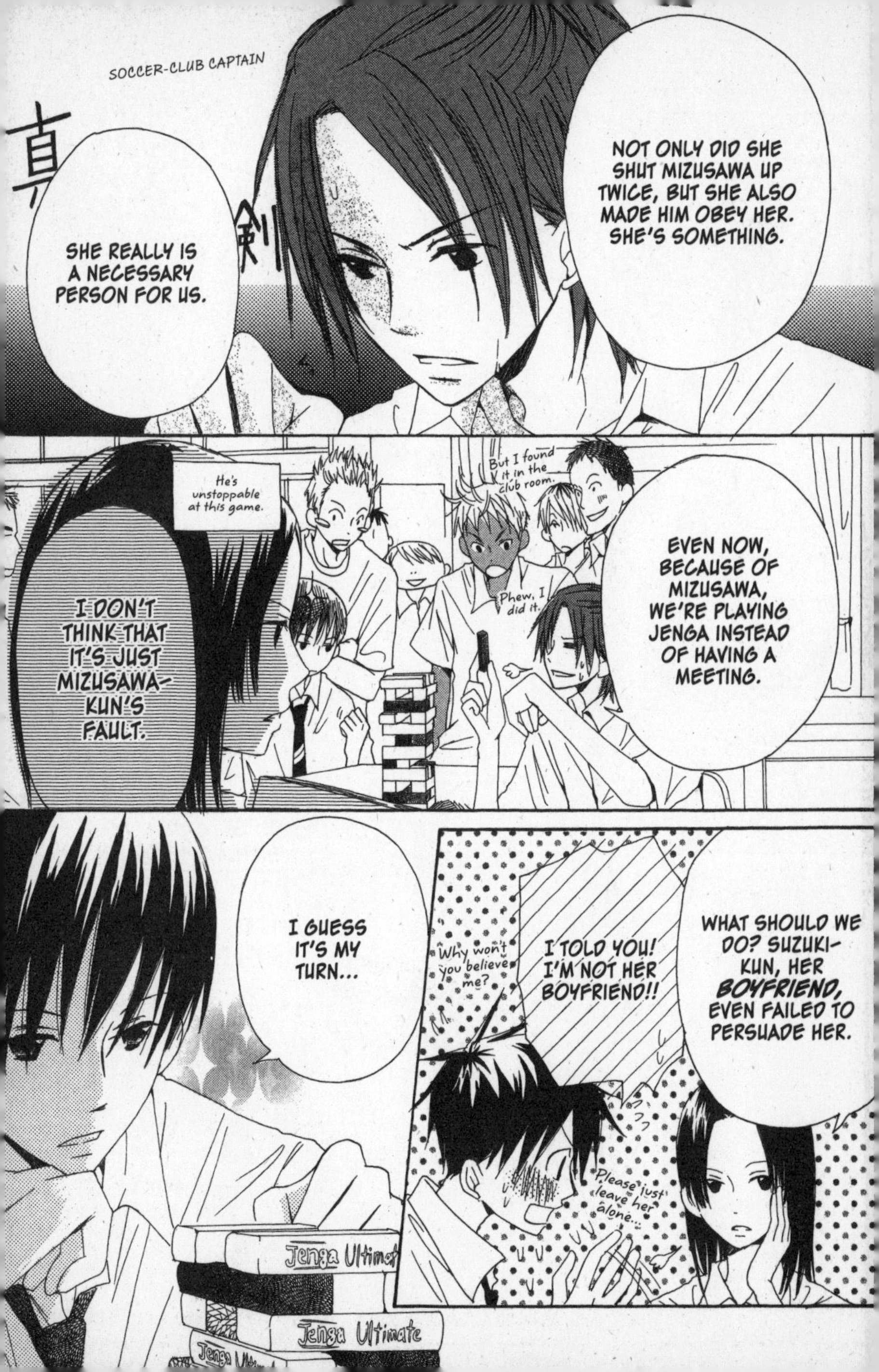
SOCCER-CLUB CAPTAIN
NOT ONLY DID SHE SHUT MIZUSAWA UP TWICE, BUT SHE ALSO MADE HIM OBEY HER. SHE'S SOMETHING.
真剣
SHE REALLY IS A NECESSARY PERSON FOR US.
EVEN NOW, BECAUSE OF MIZUSAWA, WE'RE PLAYING JENGA INSTEAD OF HAVING A MEETING.
But I found it in the club room.
Phew, I did it.
He's unstoppable at this game.
I DON'T THINK THAT IT'S JUST MIZUSAWA-KUN'S FAULT.
WHAT SHOULD WE DO? SUZUKI-KUN, HER *BOYFRIEND*, EVEN FAILED TO PERSUADE HER.
I TOLD YOU! I'M NOT HER BOYFRIEND!!
Why won't you believe me?
Please just leave her alone...
I GUESS IT'S MY TURN...
Jenga Ultimate

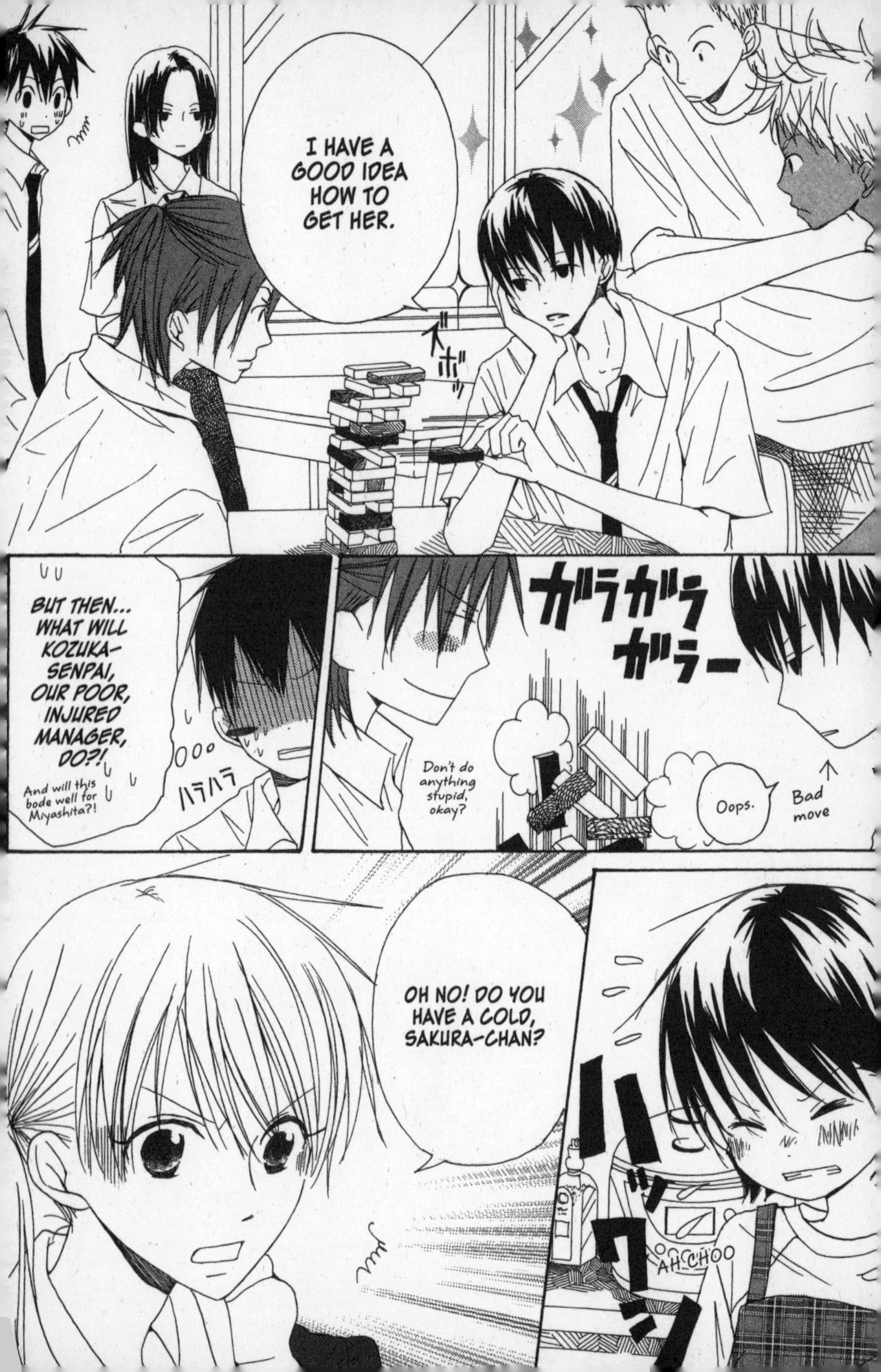

I HAVE A GOOD IDEA HOW TO GET HER.
ズボッ
ガラガラガラー
Oops.
↑ Bad move
Don't do anything stupid, okay?
BUT THEN... WHAT WILL KOZUKA-SENPAI, OUR POOR, INJURED MANAGER, DO?!
ハラハラ
And will this bode well for Miyashita?!
AH-CHOO
OH NO! DO YOU HAVE A COLD, SAKURA-CHAN?

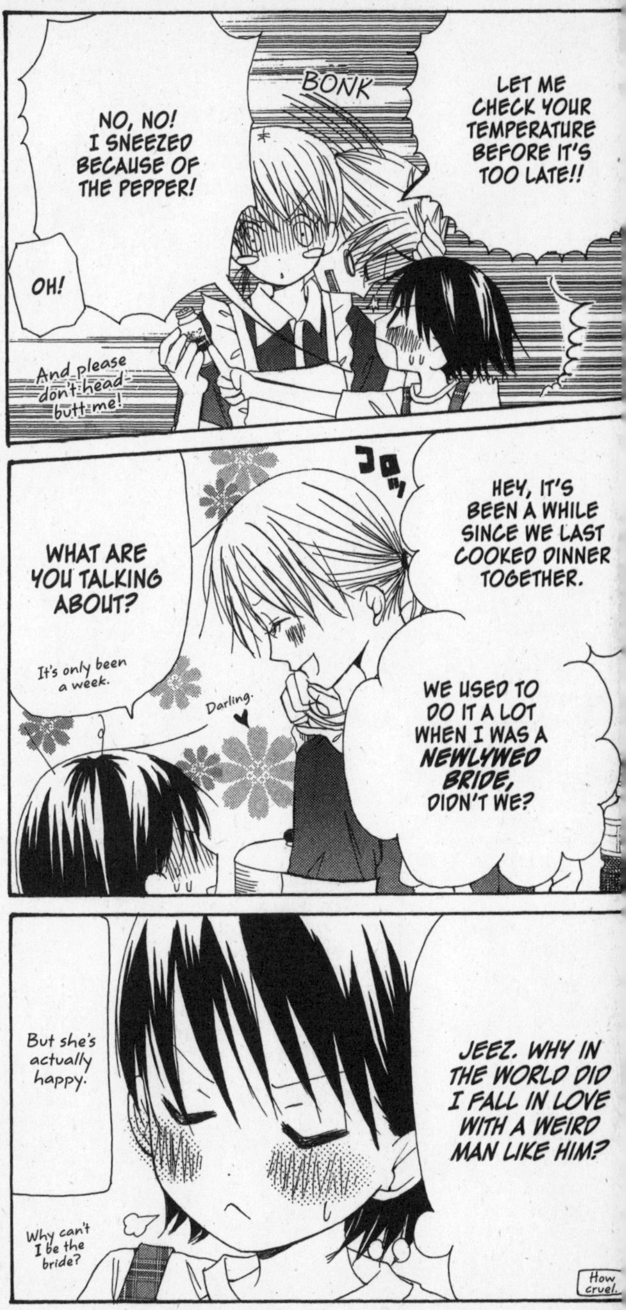
LET ME CHECK YOUR TEMPERATURE BEFORE IT'S TOO LATE!!
BONK
NO, NO! I SNEEZED BECAUSE OF THE PEPPER!
OH!
And please don't head-butt me!
HEY, IT'S BEEN A WHILE SINCE WE LAST COOKED DINNER TOGETHER.
WE USED TO DO IT A LOT WHEN I WAS A NEWLYWED BRIDE, DIDN'T WE?
Darling.
WHAT ARE YOU TALKING ABOUT?
It's only been a week.
JEEZ. WHY IN THE WORLD DID I FALL IN LOVE WITH A WEIRD MAN LIKE HIM?
How cruel.
But she's actually happy.
Why can't I be the bride?

1

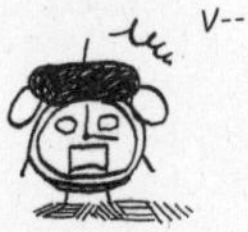
V--

Volume 5?!

Hi, this is the fifth volume. How did I make it this far?! I've impressed myself! So the series has come to the fifth volume... Good work, me. Gasp! No, no!! I should thank the readers!! I'm annoying, aren't I? Sorry... Anyway, I'm really happy that the series has made it this far. Thanks!

Me & My Chicks

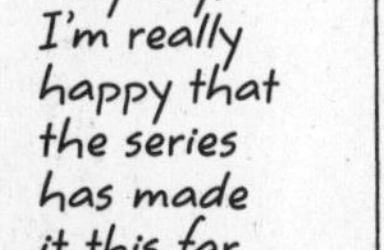
Hiyokochan to Issyo.

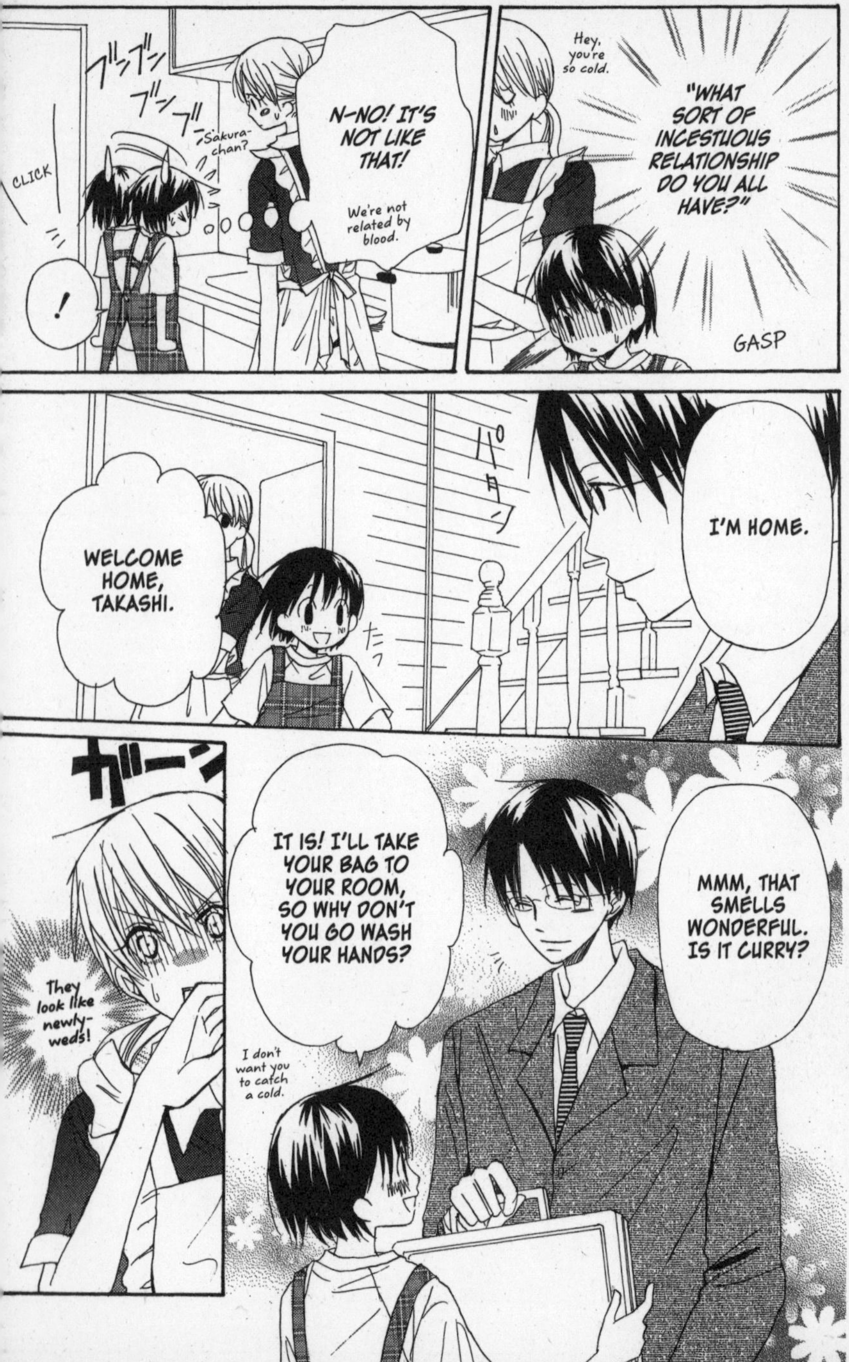
Hey, you're so cold.
"WHAT SORT OF INCESTUOUS RELATIONSHIP DO YOU ALL HAVE?"
GASP
N-NO! IT'S NOT LIKE THAT!
We're not related by blood.
Sakura-chan?
CLICK
!
I'M HOME.
WELCOME HOME, TAKASHI.
MMM, THAT SMELLS WONDERFUL. IS IT CURRY?
IT IS! I'LL TAKE YOUR BAG TO YOUR ROOM, SO WHY DON'T YOU GO WASH YOUR HANDS?
I don't want you to catch a cold.
They look like newly-weds!

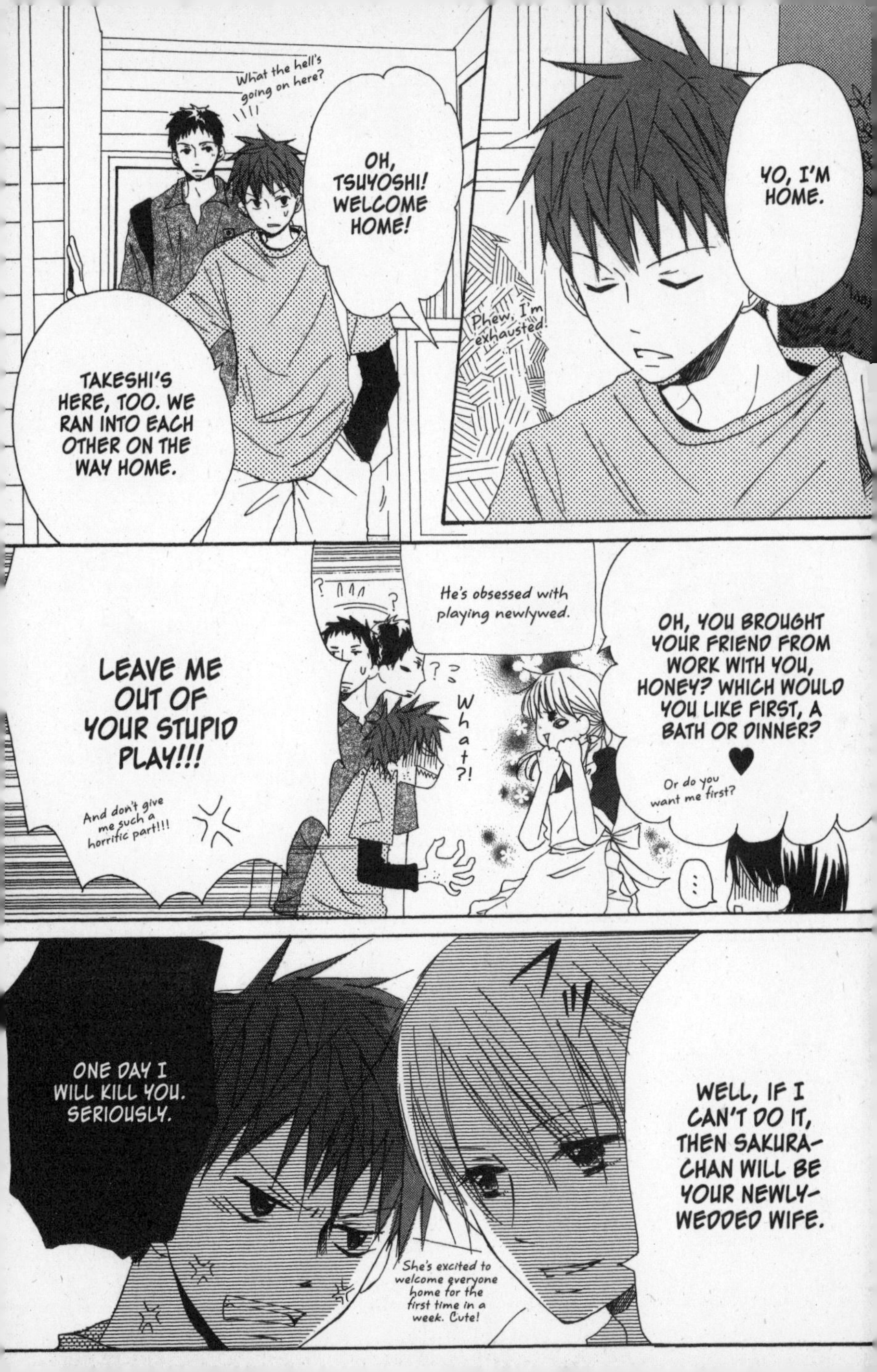
YO, I'M HOME.
Phew, I'm exhausted!
OH, TSUYOSHI! WELCOME HOME!
What the hell's going on here?
TAKESHI'S HERE, TOO. WE RAN INTO EACH OTHER ON THE WAY HOME.
OH, YOU BROUGHT YOUR FRIEND FROM WORK WITH YOU, HONEY? WHICH WOULD YOU LIKE FIRST, A BATH OR DINNER? ♥
Or do you want me first?
...
He's obsessed with playing newlywed.
What?!
LEAVE ME OUT OF YOUR STUPID PLAY!!!
And don't give me such a horrific part!!!
WELL, IF I CAN'T DO IT, THEN SAKURA-CHAN WILL BE YOUR NEWLY-WEDDED WIFE.
She's excited to welcome everyone home for the first time in a week. Cute!
ONE DAY I WILL KILL YOU. SERIOUSLY.

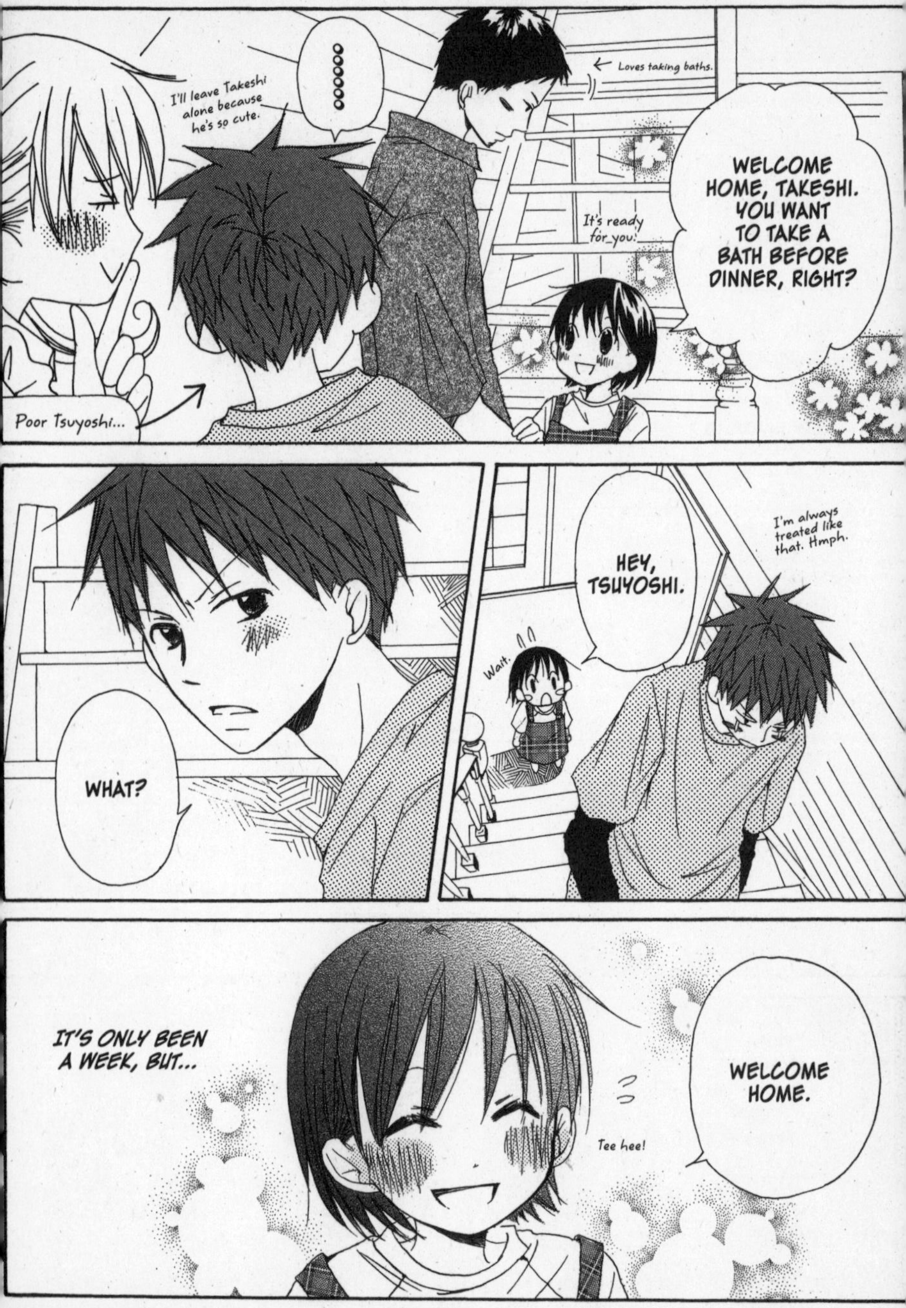
Loves taking baths.
WELCOME HOME, TAKESHI. YOU WANT TO TAKE A BATH BEFORE DINNER, RIGHT?
It's ready for you!
......
I'll leave Takeshi alone because he's so cute.
Poor Tsuyoshi...
I'm always treated like that. Hmph.
HEY, TSUYOSHI.
Wait.
WHAT?
WELCOME HOME.
Tee hee!
IT'S ONLY BEEN A WEEK, BUT...

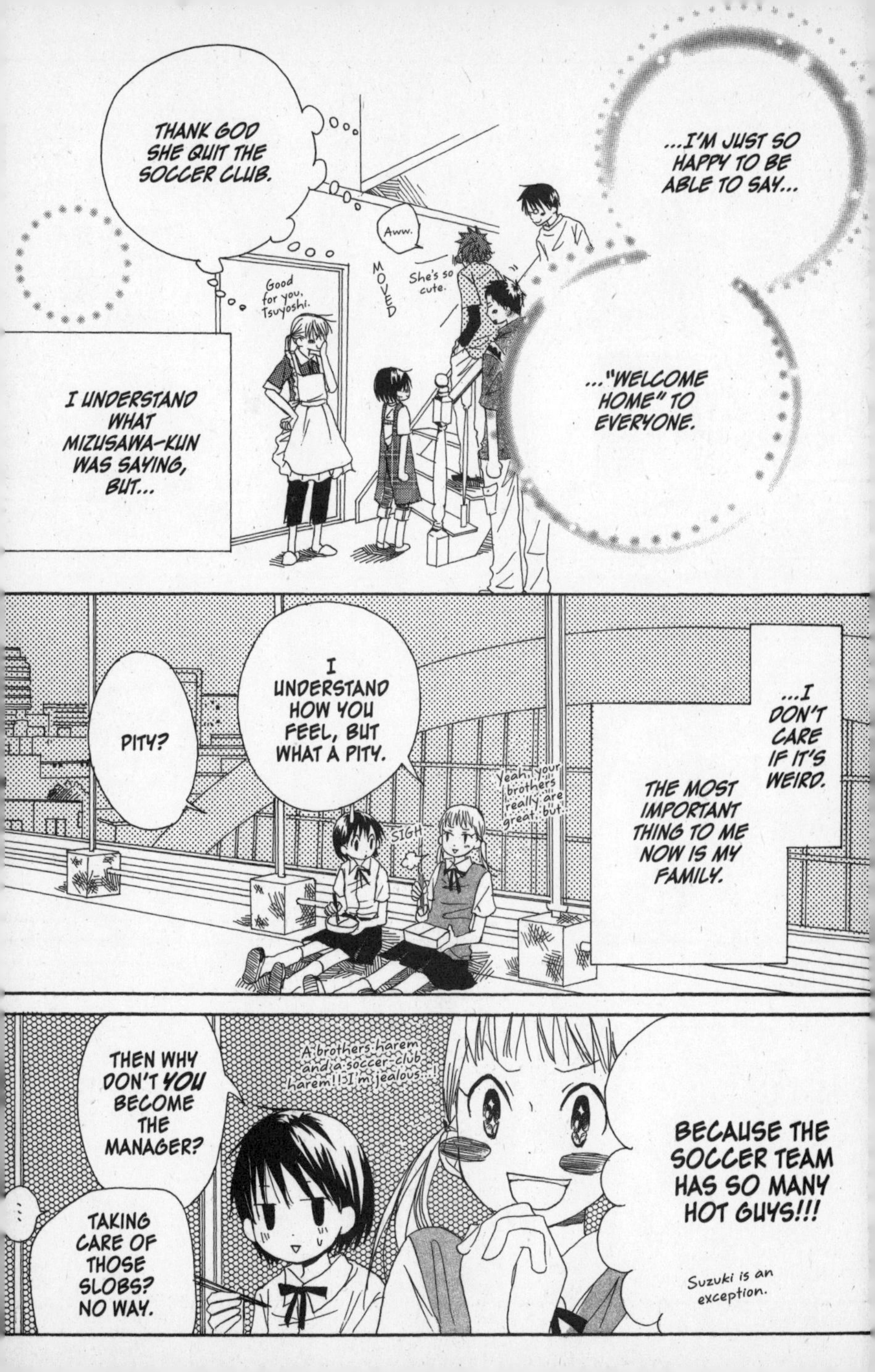
...I'M JUST SO HAPPY TO BE ABLE TO SAY...
..."WELCOME HOME" TO EVERYONE.
Aww.
She's so cute.
MOVED
THANK GOD SHE QUIT THE SOCCER CLUB.
Good for you, Tsuyoshi.
I UNDERSTAND WHAT MIZUSAWA-KUN WAS SAYING, BUT...
...I DON'T CARE IF IT'S WEIRD.
THE MOST IMPORTANT THING TO ME NOW IS MY FAMILY.
Yeah, your brothers really are great, but...
I UNDERSTAND HOW YOU FEEL, BUT WHAT A PITY.
SIGH
PITY?
BECAUSE THE SOCCER TEAM HAS SO MANY HOT GUYS!!!
Suzuki is an exception.
A brothers harem and a soccer-club harem!! I'm jealous...!
THEN WHY DON'T YOU BECOME THE MANAGER?
...
TAKING CARE OF THOSE SLOBS? NO WAY.

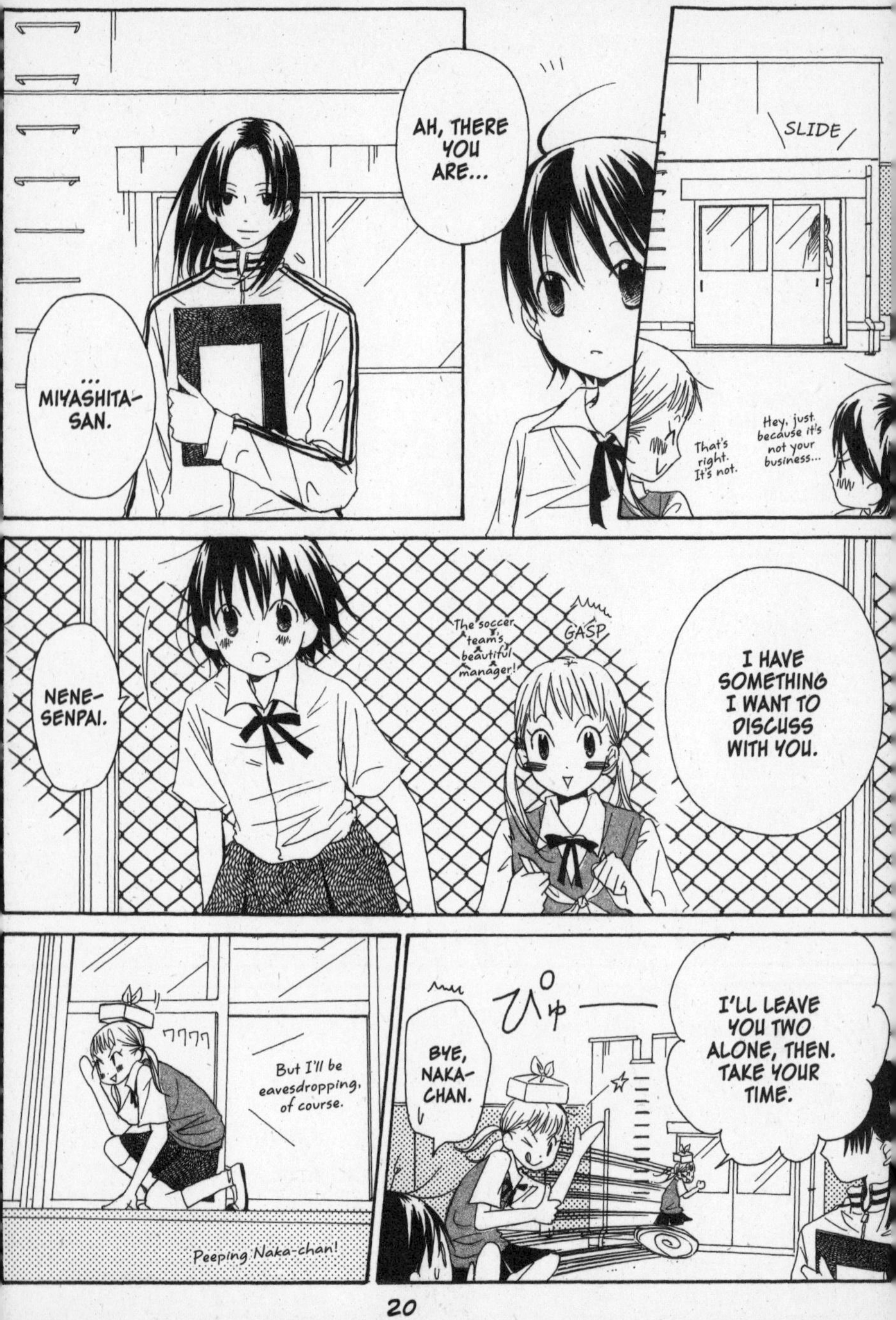
SLIDE
AH, THERE YOU ARE...
Hey, just because it's not your business...
That's right. It's not.
... MIYASHITA-SAN.
I HAVE SOMETHING I WANT TO DISCUSS WITH YOU.
GASP
The soccer team's beautiful manager!
NENE-SENPAI.
I'LL LEAVE YOU TWO ALONE, THEN. TAKE YOUR TIME.
ぴゅ
BYE, NAKA-CHAN.
But I'll be eavesdropping, of course.
Peeping Naka-chan!

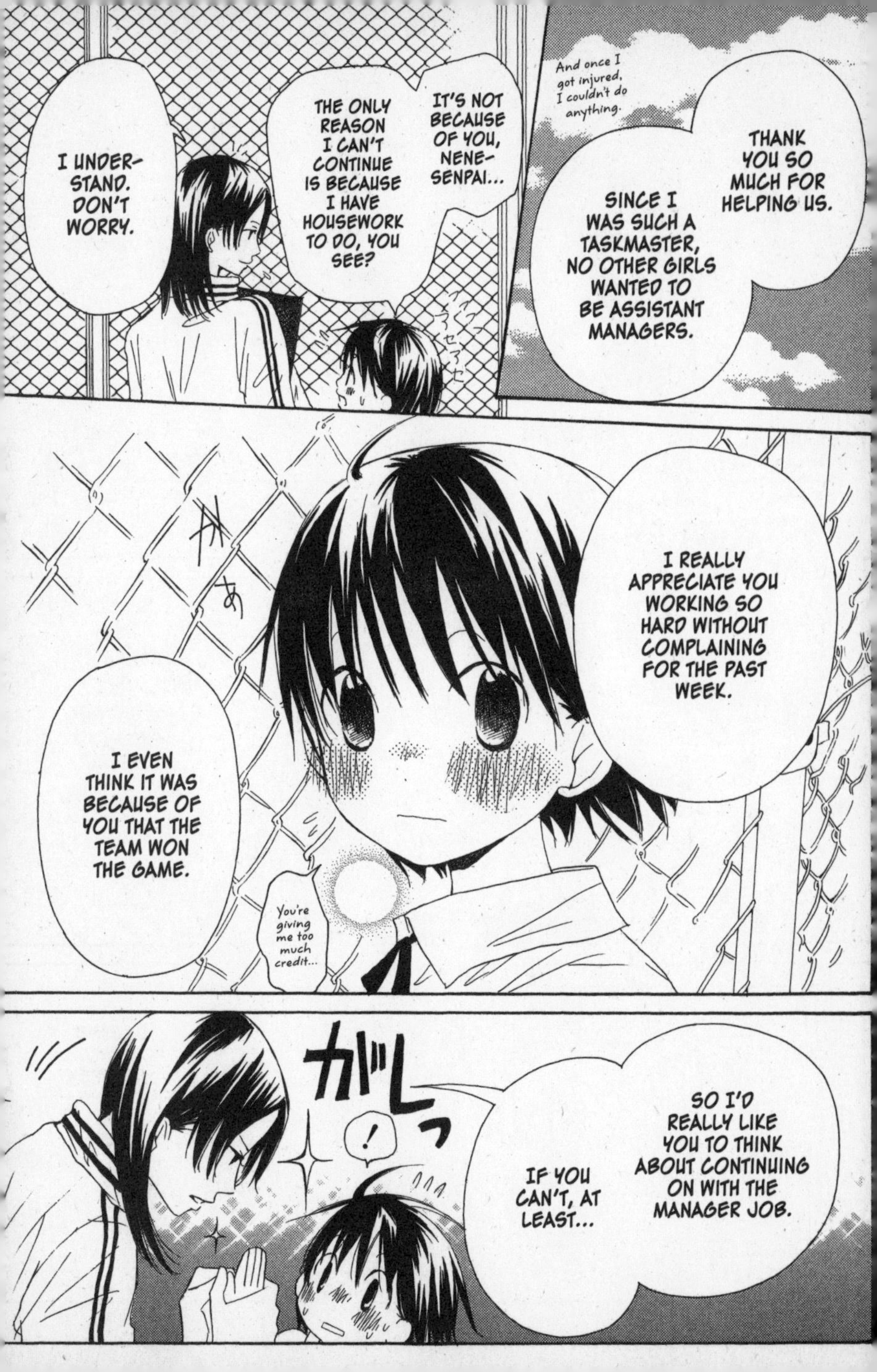
THANK YOU SO MUCH FOR HELPING US.
SINCE I WAS SUCH A TASKMASTER, NO OTHER GIRLS WANTED TO BE ASSISTANT MANAGERS.
And once I got injured, I couldn't do anything.
IT'S NOT BECAUSE OF YOU, NENE-SENPAI...
THE ONLY REASON I CAN'T CONTINUE IS BECAUSE I HAVE HOUSEWORK TO DO, YOU SEE?
I UNDER-STAND. DON'T WORRY.
I REALLY APPRECIATE YOU WORKING SO HARD WITHOUT COMPLAINING FOR THE PAST WEEK.
I EVEN THINK IT WAS BECAUSE OF YOU THAT THE TEAM WON THE GAME.
You're giving me too much credit...
!
SO I'D REALLY LIKE YOU TO THINK ABOUT CONTINUING ON WITH THE MANAGER JOB.
IF YOU CAN'T, AT LEAST...

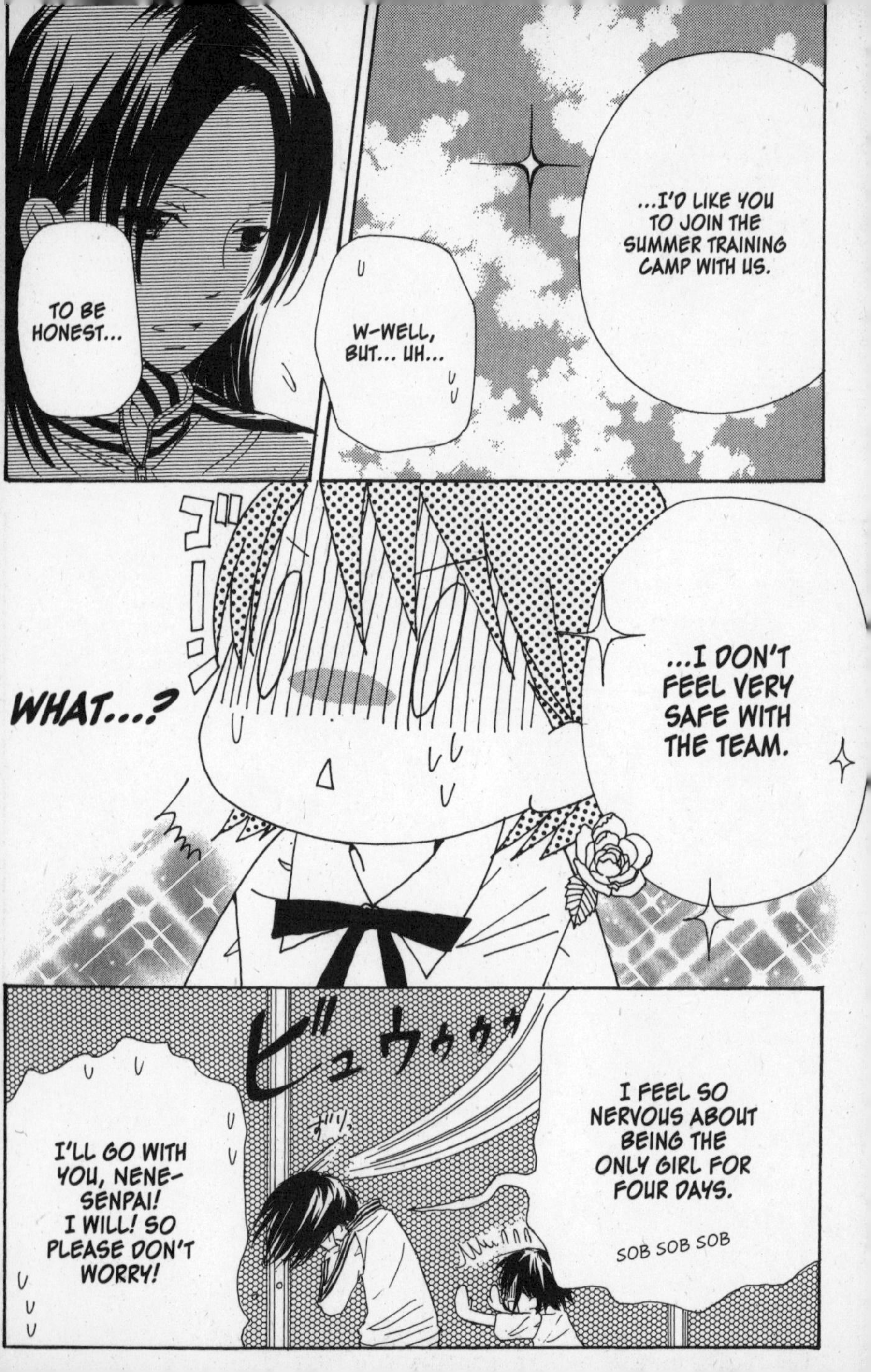
...I'D LIKE YOU TO JOIN THE SUMMER TRAINING CAMP WITH US.
W-WELL, BUT... UH...
TO BE HONEST...
...I DON'T FEEL VERY SAFE WITH THE TEAM.
ゴーン
WHAT...?
ビュウウウウ
I FEEL SO NERVOUS ABOUT BEING THE ONLY GIRL FOR FOUR DAYS.
SOB SOB SOB
I'LL GO WITH YOU, NENE-SENPAI! I WILL! SO PLEASE DON'T WORRY!

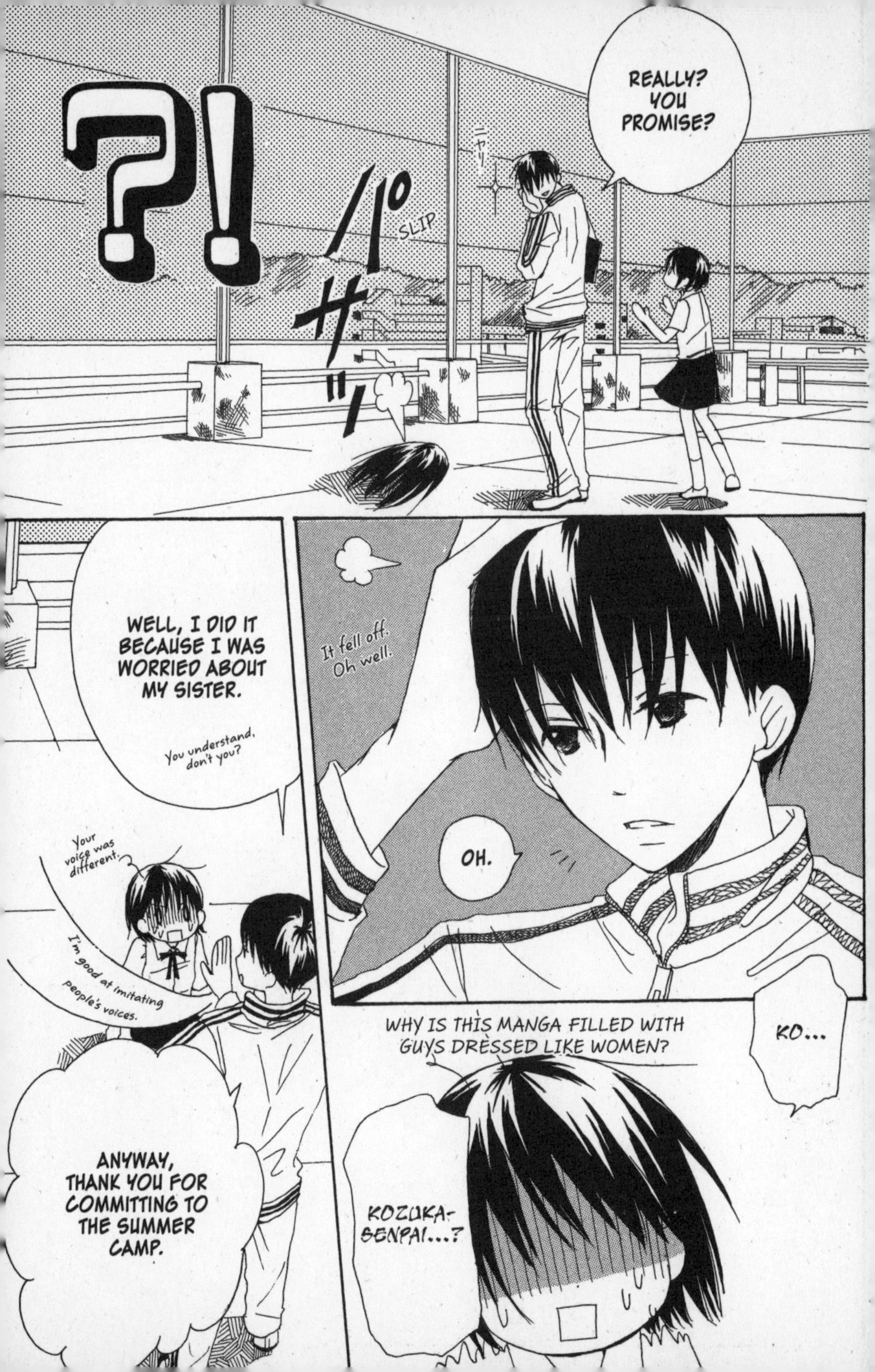
REALLY? YOU PROMISE?
ニヤリ
パサッ
SLIP
?!
It fell off. Oh well.
OH.
KO...
WHY IS THIS MANGA FILLED WITH GUYS DRESSED LIKE WOMEN?
KOZUKA-SENPAI...?
WELL, I DID IT BECAUSE I WAS WORRIED ABOUT MY SISTER.
You understand, don't you?
Your voice was different.
I'm good at imitating people's voices.
ANYWAY, THANK YOU FOR COMMITTING TO THE SUMMER CAMP.

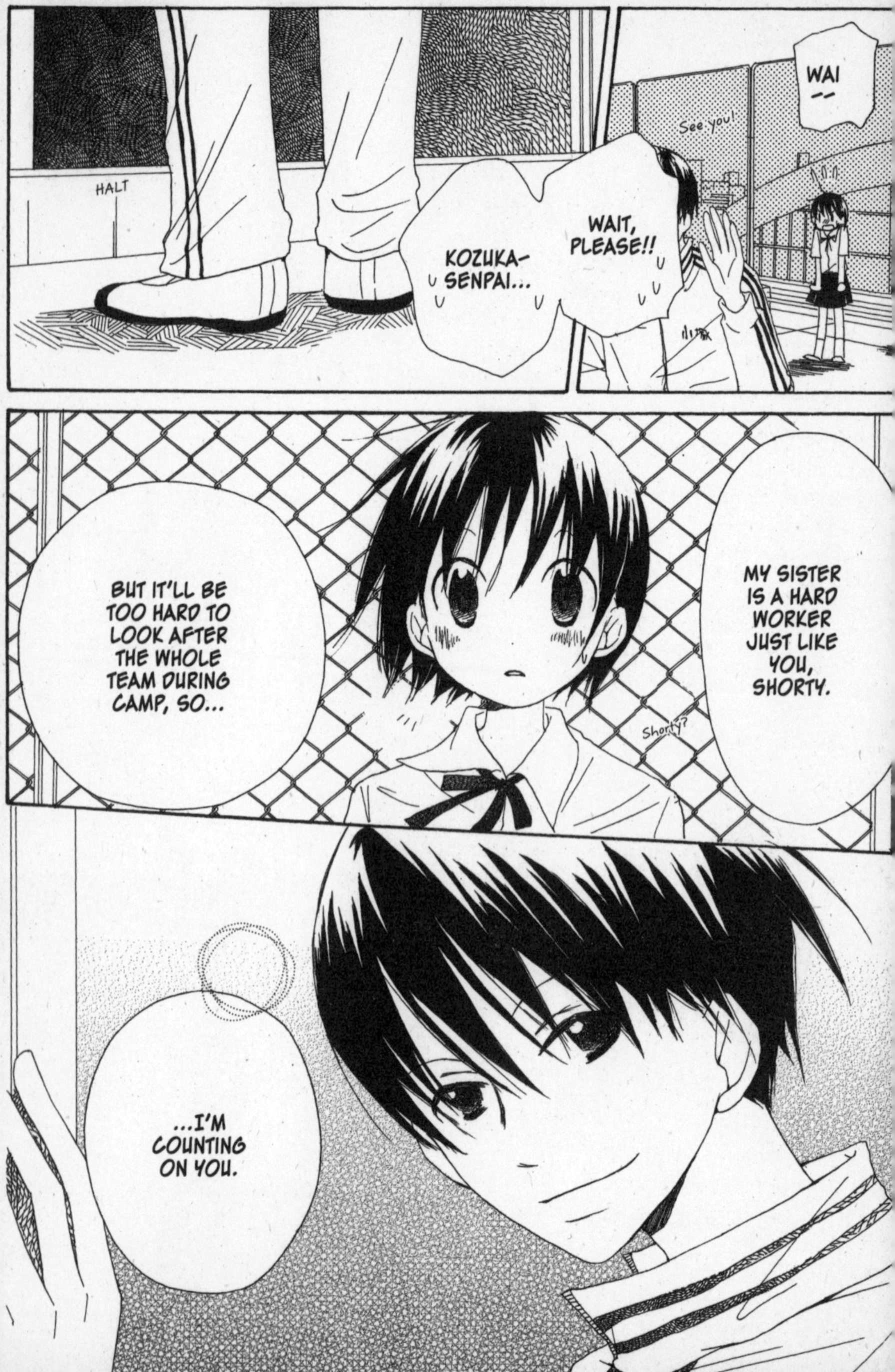
WAI --
See you!
WAIT, PLEASE!!
KOZUKA-SENPAI...
HALT
MY SISTER IS A HARD WORKER JUST LIKE YOU, SHORTY.
Shorty?
BUT IT'LL BE TOO HARD TO LOOK AFTER THE WHOLE TEAM DURING CAMP, SO...
...I'M COUNTING ON YOU.

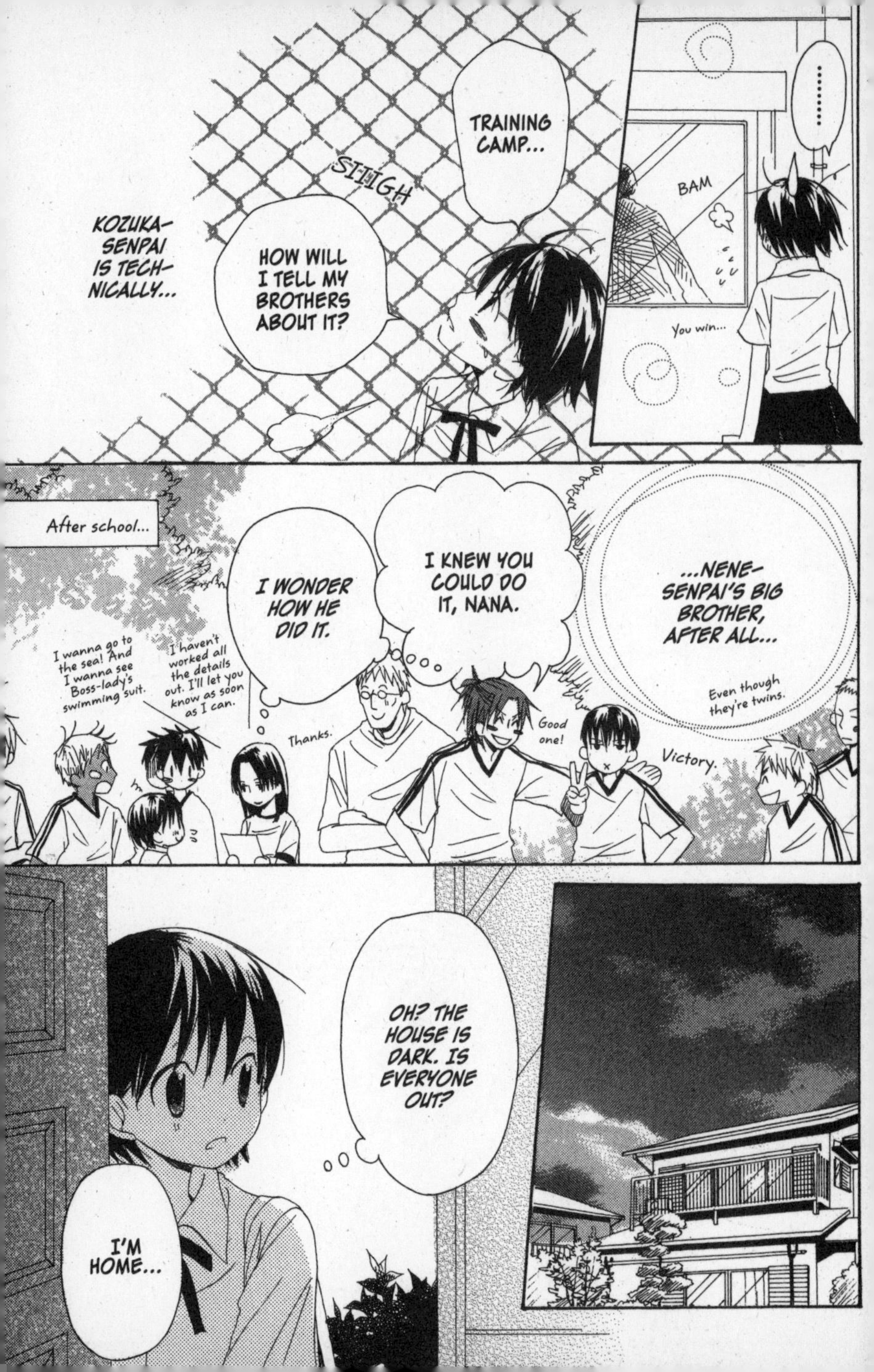
......
BAM
You win...
TRAINING CAMP...
SIIIGH
HOW WILL I TELL MY BROTHERS ABOUT IT?
KOZUKA-SENPAI IS TECHNICALLY...
After school...
...NENE-SENPAI'S BIG BROTHER, AFTER ALL...
Even though they're twins.
Victory.
Good one!
I KNEW YOU COULD DO IT, NANA.
I WONDER HOW HE DID IT.
Thanks.
I haven't worked all the details out. I'll let you know as soon as I can.
I wanna go to the sea! And I wanna see Boss-lady's swimming suit.
OH? THE HOUSE IS DARK. IS EVERYONE OUT?
I'M HOME...

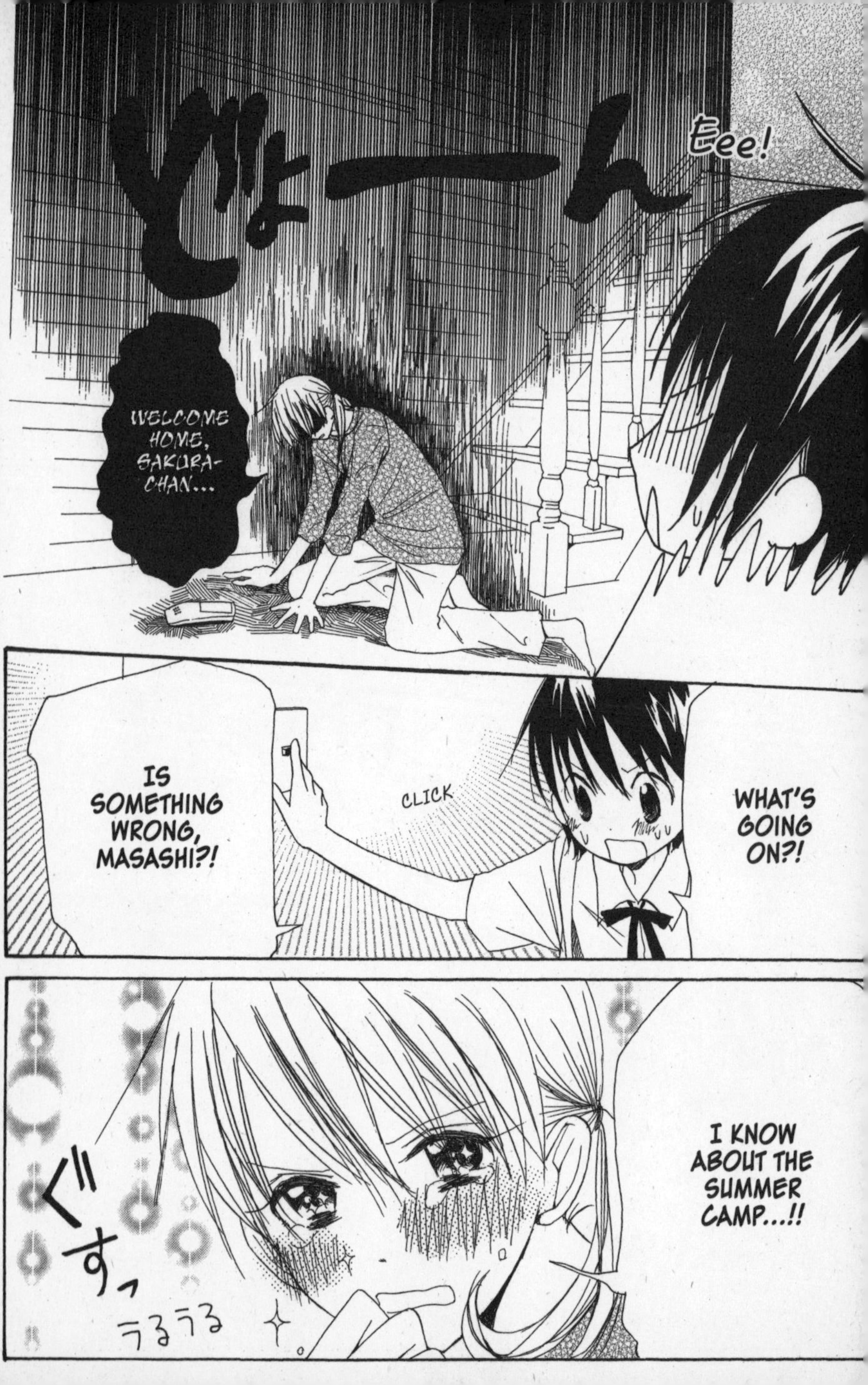
Eee!
どよーん
WELCOME HOME, SAKURA-CHAN...
WHAT'S GOING ON?!
CLICK
IS SOMETHING WRONG, MASASHI?!
I KNOW ABOUT THE SUMMER CAMP...!!
ぐすっ
うるうる

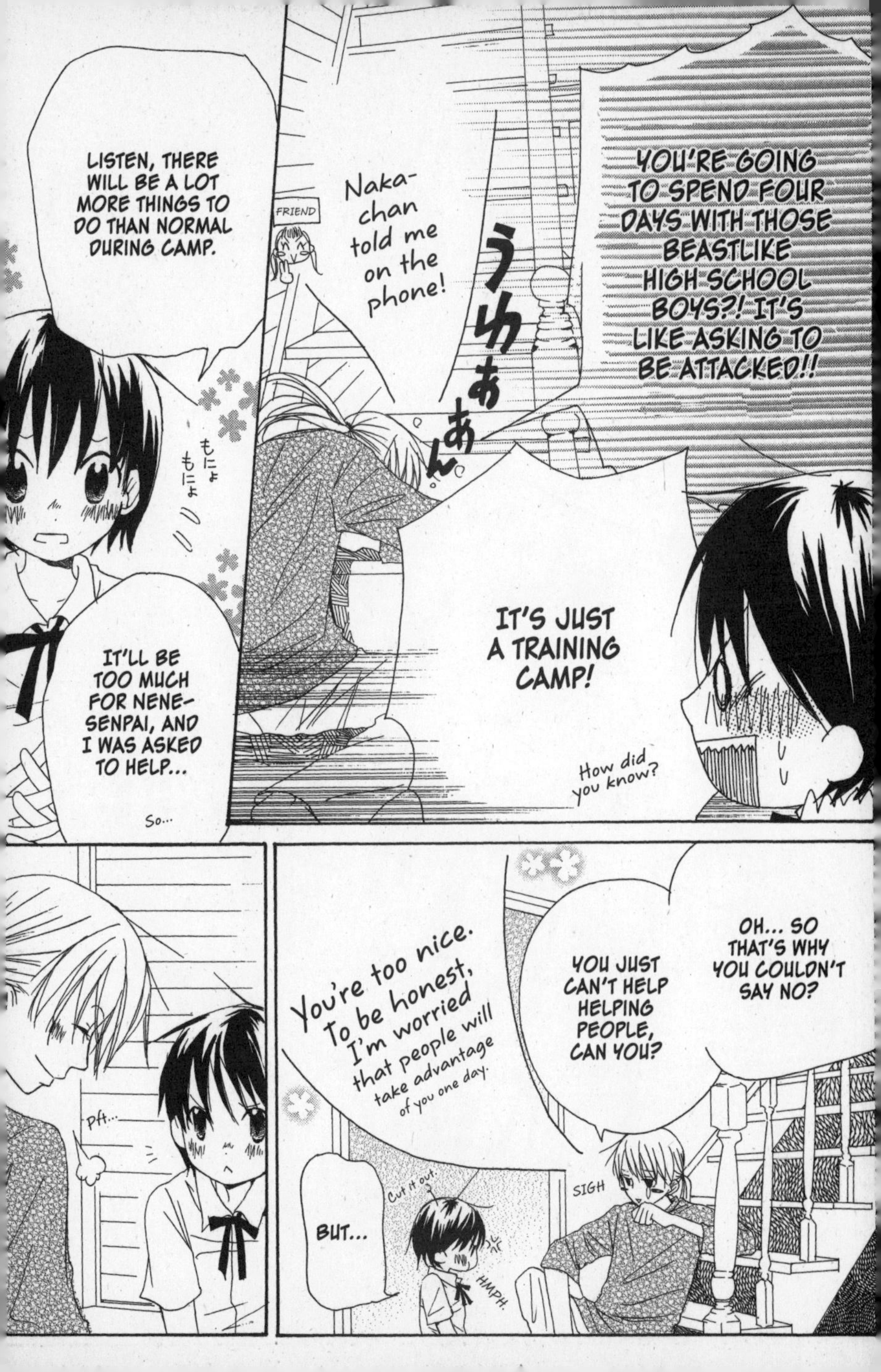
YOU'RE GOING TO SPEND FOUR DAYS WITH THOSE BEASTLIKE HIGH SCHOOL BOYS?! IT'S LIKE ASKING TO BE ATTACKED!!
うゅぁあん
Naka-chan told me on the phone!
FRIEND
IT'S JUST A TRAINING CAMP!
How did you know?
LISTEN, THERE WILL BE A LOT MORE THINGS TO DO THAN NORMAL DURING CAMP.
もにょもにょ
IT'LL BE TOO MUCH FOR NENE-SENPAI, AND I WAS ASKED TO HELP...
So...
OH... SO THAT'S WHY YOU COULDN'T SAY NO?
YOU JUST CAN'T HELP HELPING PEOPLE, CAN YOU?
You're too nice. To be honest, I'm worried that people will take advantage of you one day.
SIGH
Cut it out.
BUT...
HMPH.
Pft...

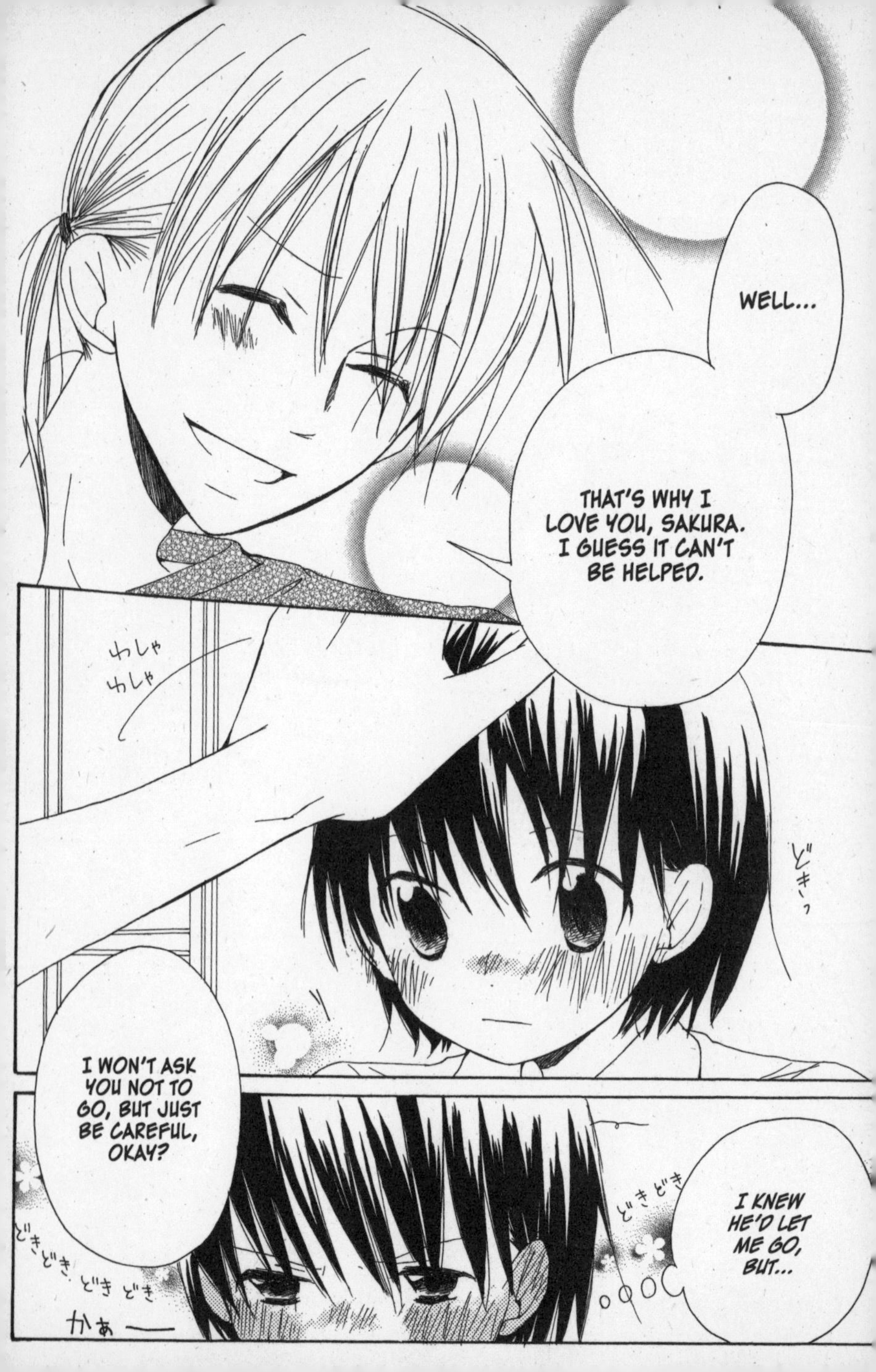
WELL...
THAT'S WHY I LOVE YOU, SAKURA. I GUESS IT CAN'T BE HELPED.
わしゃ わしゃ
どきっ
I KNEW HE'D LET ME GO, BUT...
どきどき
I WON'T ASK YOU NOT TO GO, BUT JUST BE CAREFUL, OKAY?
どきどき どきどき
かあー

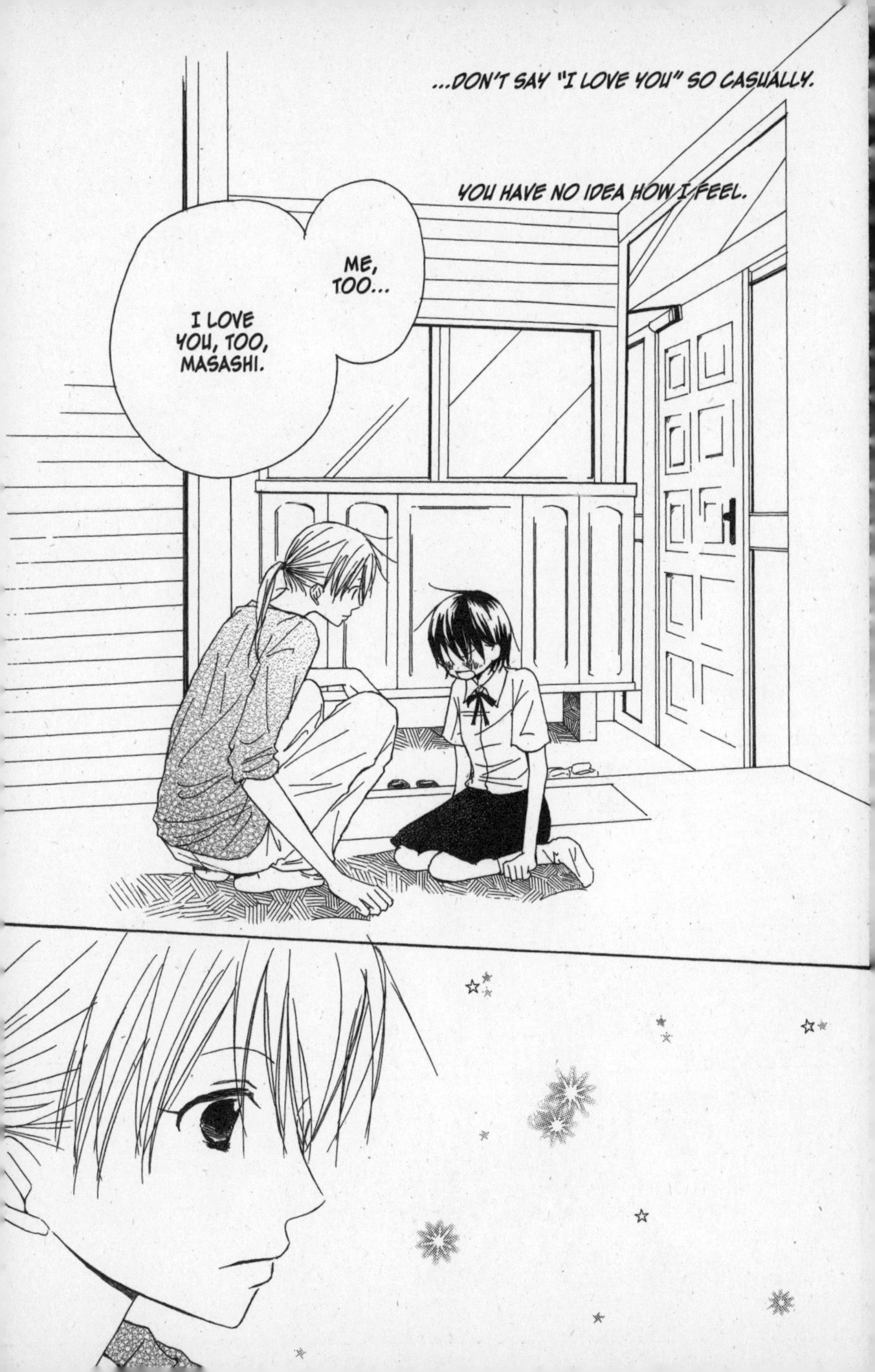
...DON'T SAY "I LOVE YOU" SO CASUALLY.
YOU HAVE NO IDEA HOW I FEEL.
ME, TOO...
I LOVE YOU, TOO, MASASHI.

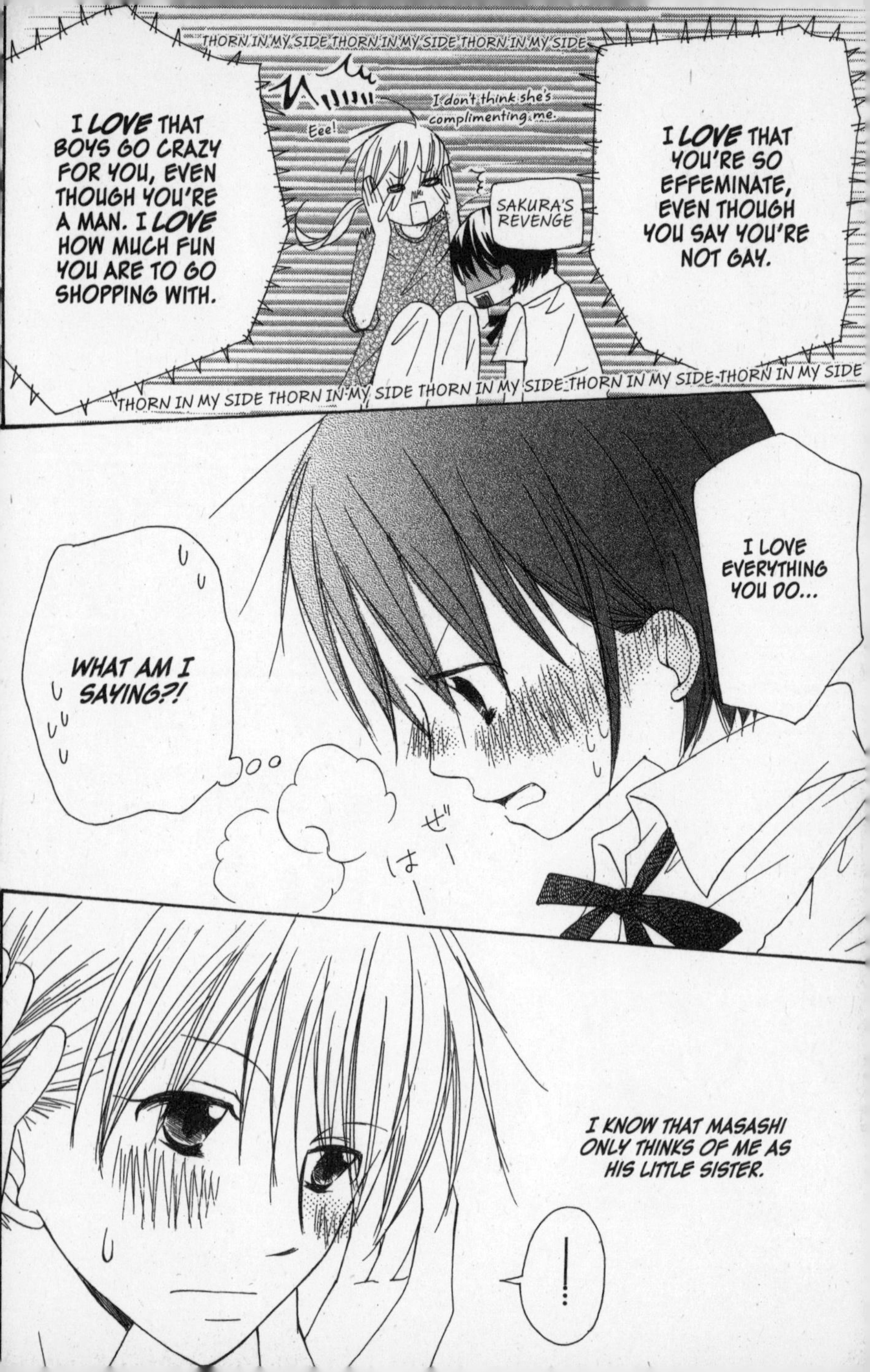
THORN IN MY SIDE THORN IN MY SIDE THORN IN MY SIDE
I LOVE THAT YOU'RE SO EFFEMINATE, EVEN THOUGH YOU SAY YOU'RE NOT GAY.
SAKURA'S REVENGE
I don't think she's complimenting me.
Eee!
I LOVE THAT BOYS GO CRAZY FOR YOU, EVEN THOUGH YOU'RE A MAN. I LOVE HOW MUCH FUN YOU ARE TO GO SHOPPING WITH.
THORN IN MY SIDE THORN IN MY SIDE THORN IN MY SIDE THORN IN MY SIDE
I LOVE EVERYTHING YOU DO...
WHAT AM I SAYING?!
ぜー
はー
I KNOW THAT MASASHI ONLY THINKS OF ME AS HIS LITTLE SISTER.
...!

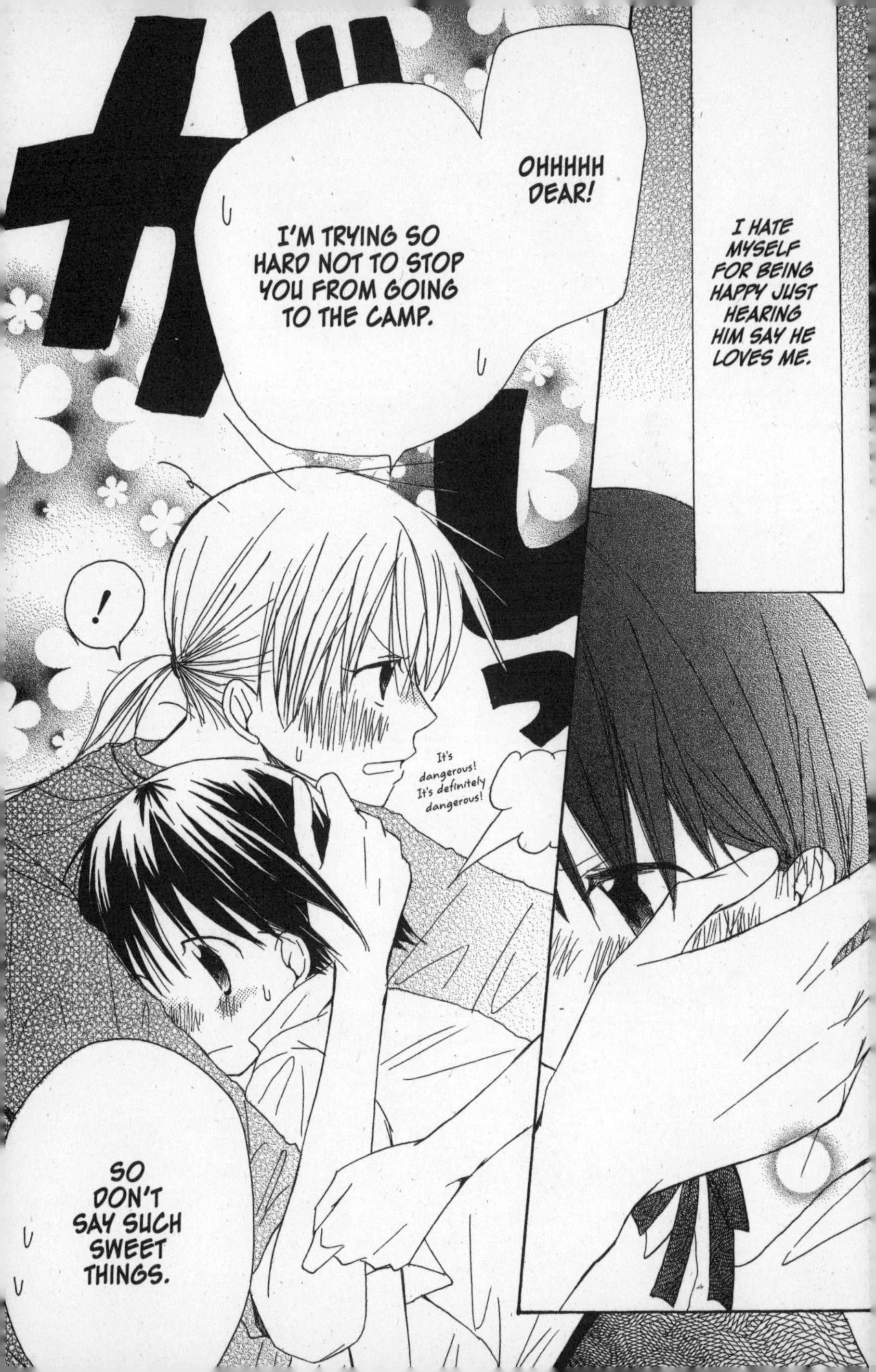
I HATE MYSELF FOR BEING HAPPY JUST HEARING HIM SAY HE LOVES ME.
OHHHHH DEAR!
I'M TRYING SO HARD NOT TO STOP YOU FROM GOING TO THE CAMP.
!
It's dangerous! It's definitely dangerous!
SO DON'T SAY SUCH SWEET THINGS.

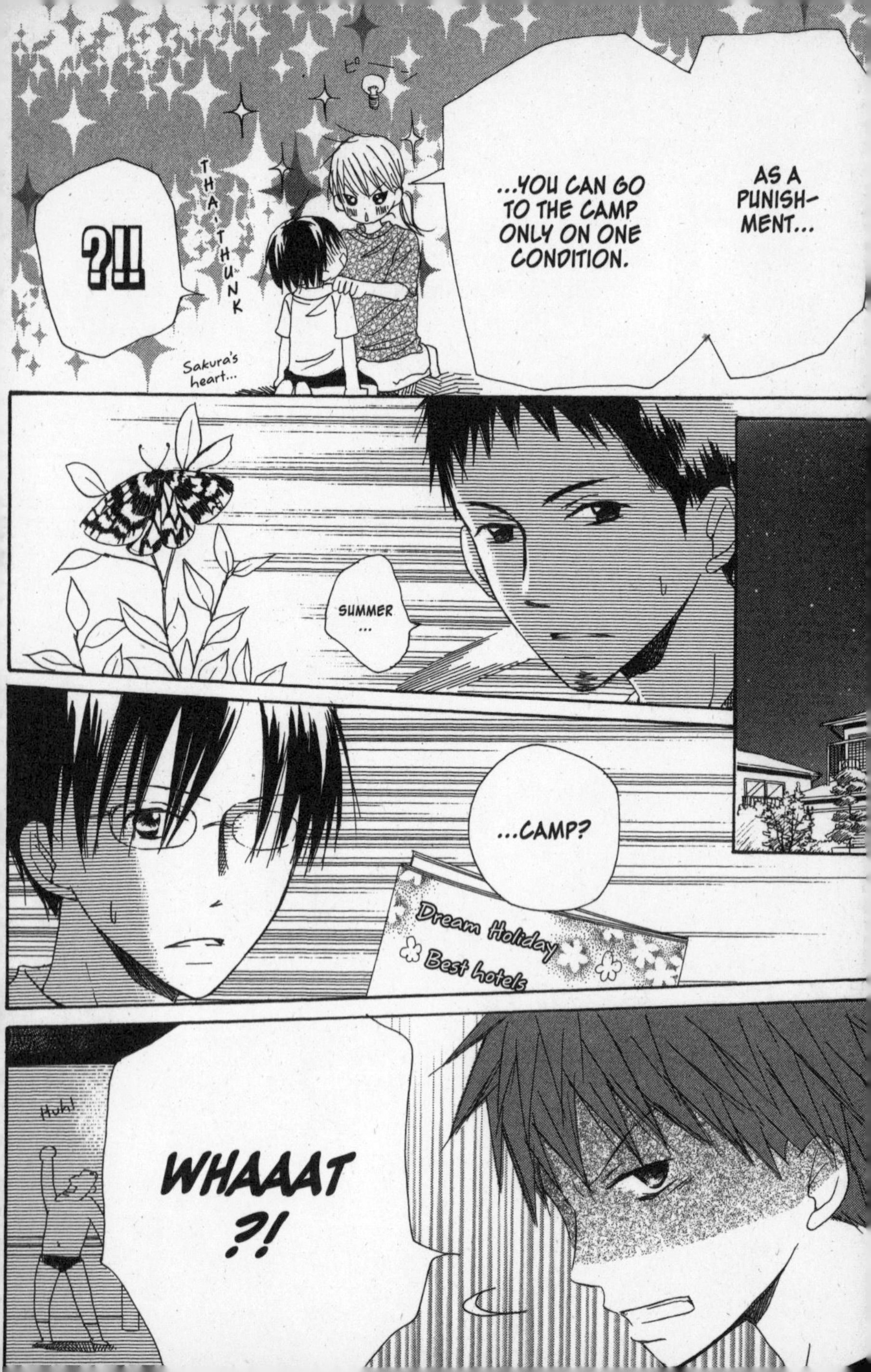
AS A PUNISH-
MENT...
...YOU CAN GO TO THE CAMP ONLY ON ONE CONDITION.
?!!
THA-THUNK
Sakura's heart...
SUMMER...
...CAMP?
Dream Holiday
Best hotels
WHAAAT?!
Huh!

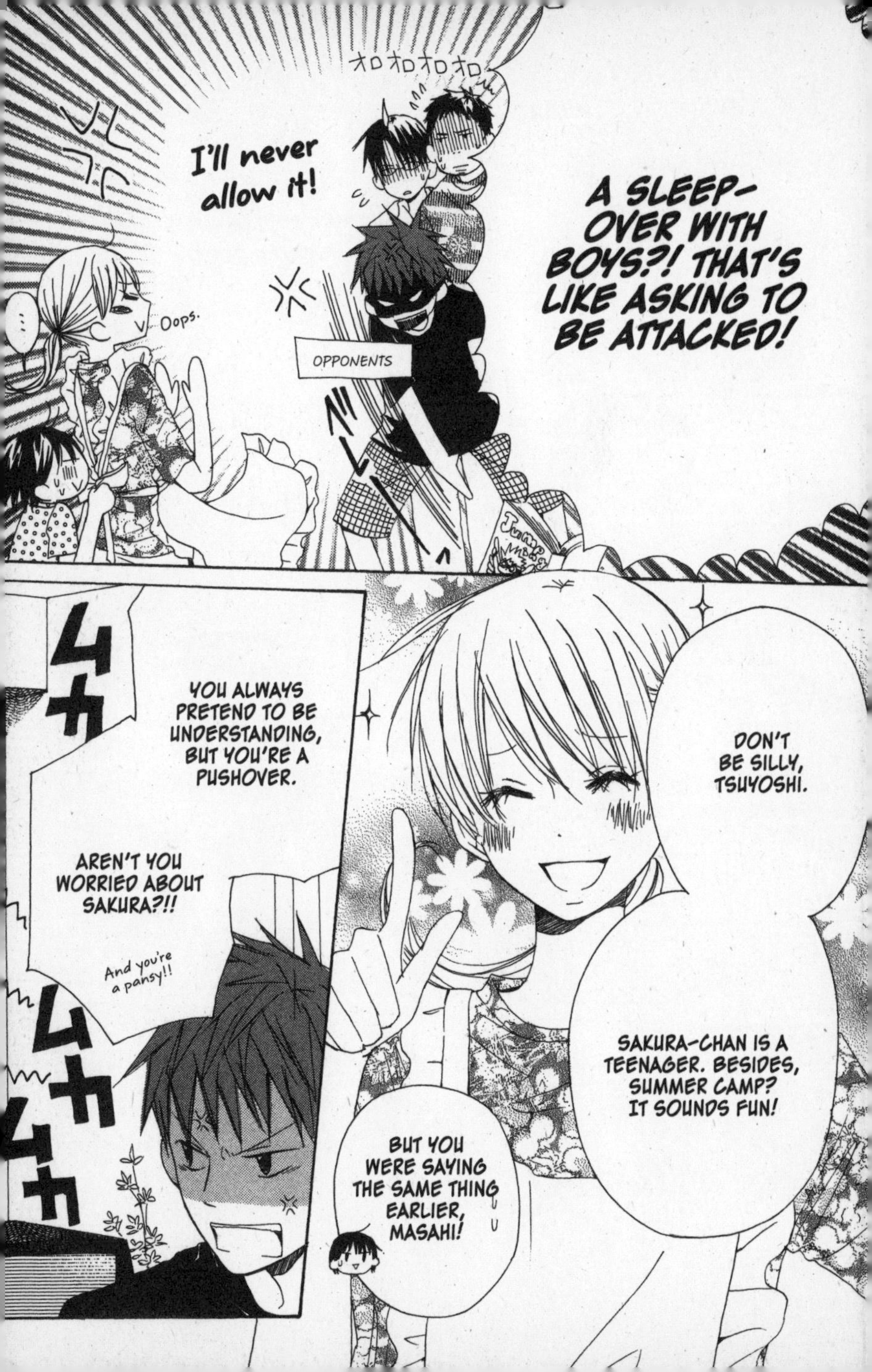
A SLEEP-OVER WITH BOYS?! THAT'S LIKE ASKING TO BE ATTACKED!
オロオロオロオロ
I'll never allow it!
OPPONENTS
Oops.
DON'T BE SILLY, TSUYOSHI.
SAKURA-CHAN IS A TEENAGER. BESIDES, SUMMER CAMP? IT SOUNDS FUN!
BUT YOU WERE SAYING THE SAME THING EARLIER, MASAHI!
YOU ALWAYS PRETEND TO BE UNDERSTANDING, BUT YOU'RE A PUSHOVER.
AREN'T YOU WORRIED ABOUT SAKURA?!!
And you're a pansy!!

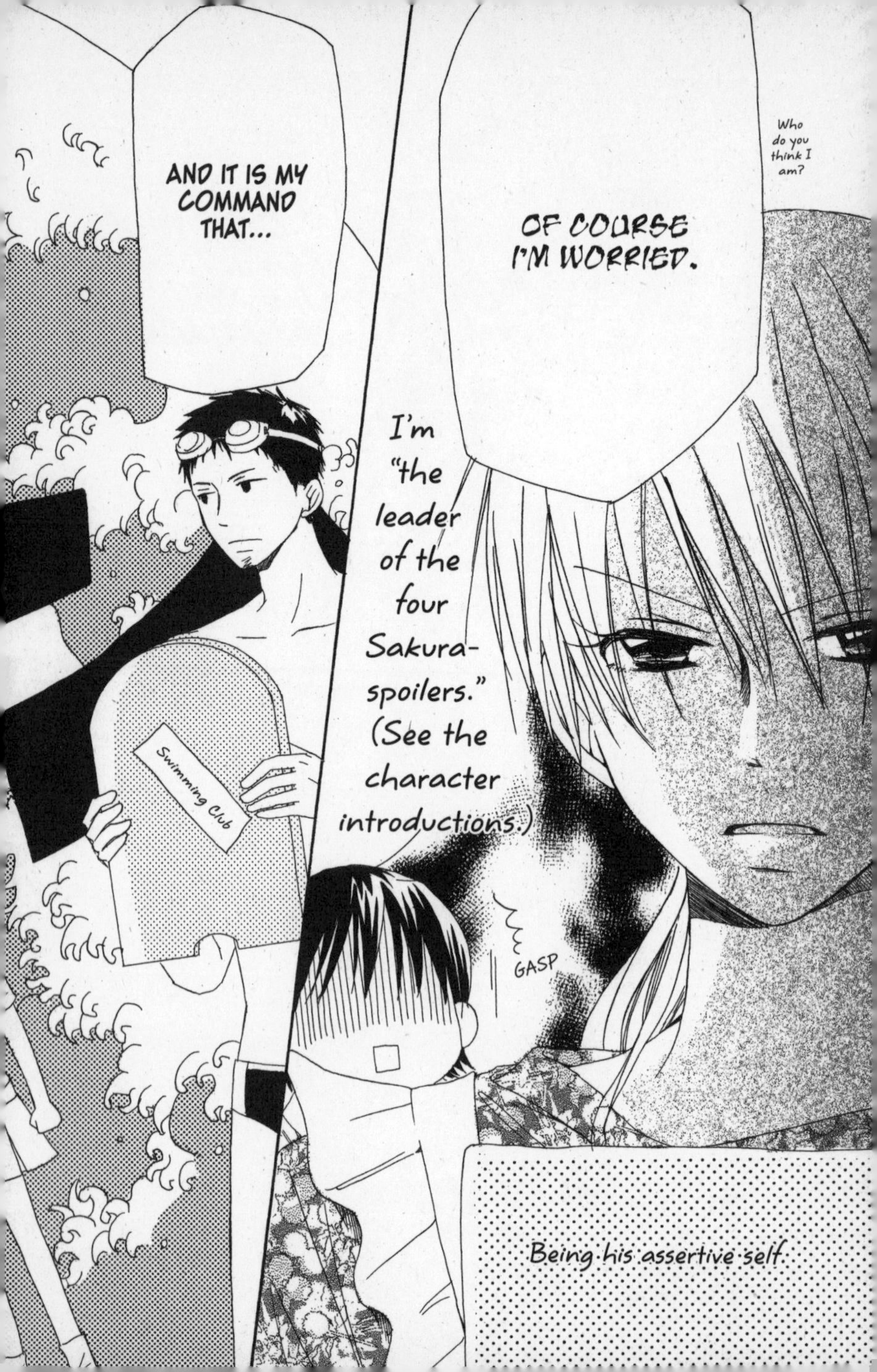
Who do you think I am?
OF COURSE I'M WORRIED.
I'm "the leader of the four Sakura-spoilers." (See the character introductions.)
GASP
Being his assertive self
AND IT IS MY COMMAND THAT...
Swimming Club

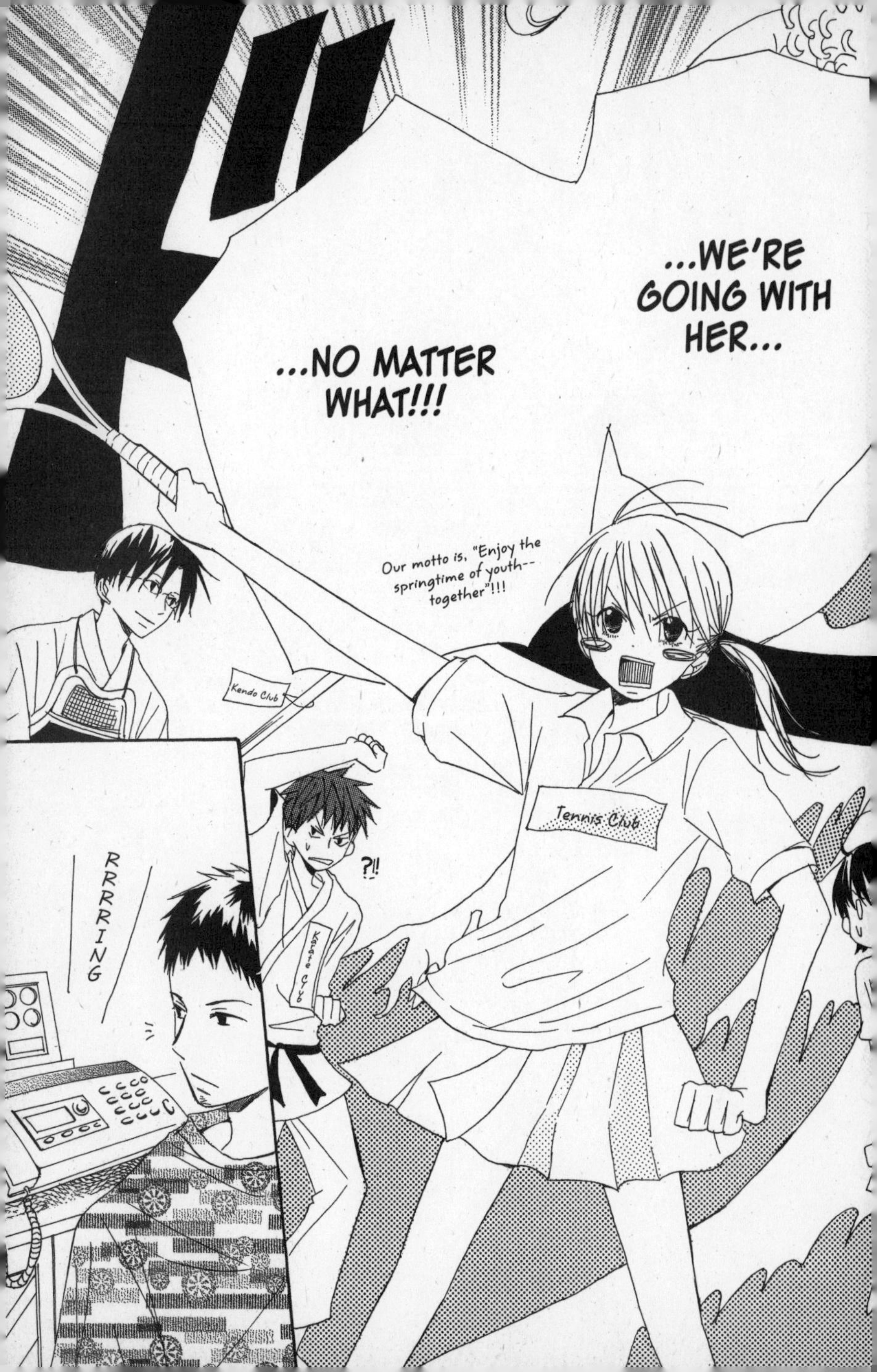
...WE'RE GOING WITH HER...
...NO MATTER WHAT!!!
Our motto is, "Enjoy the springtime of youth--together"!!!
Tennis Club
Kendo Club
?!!
Karate Club
RRRRING

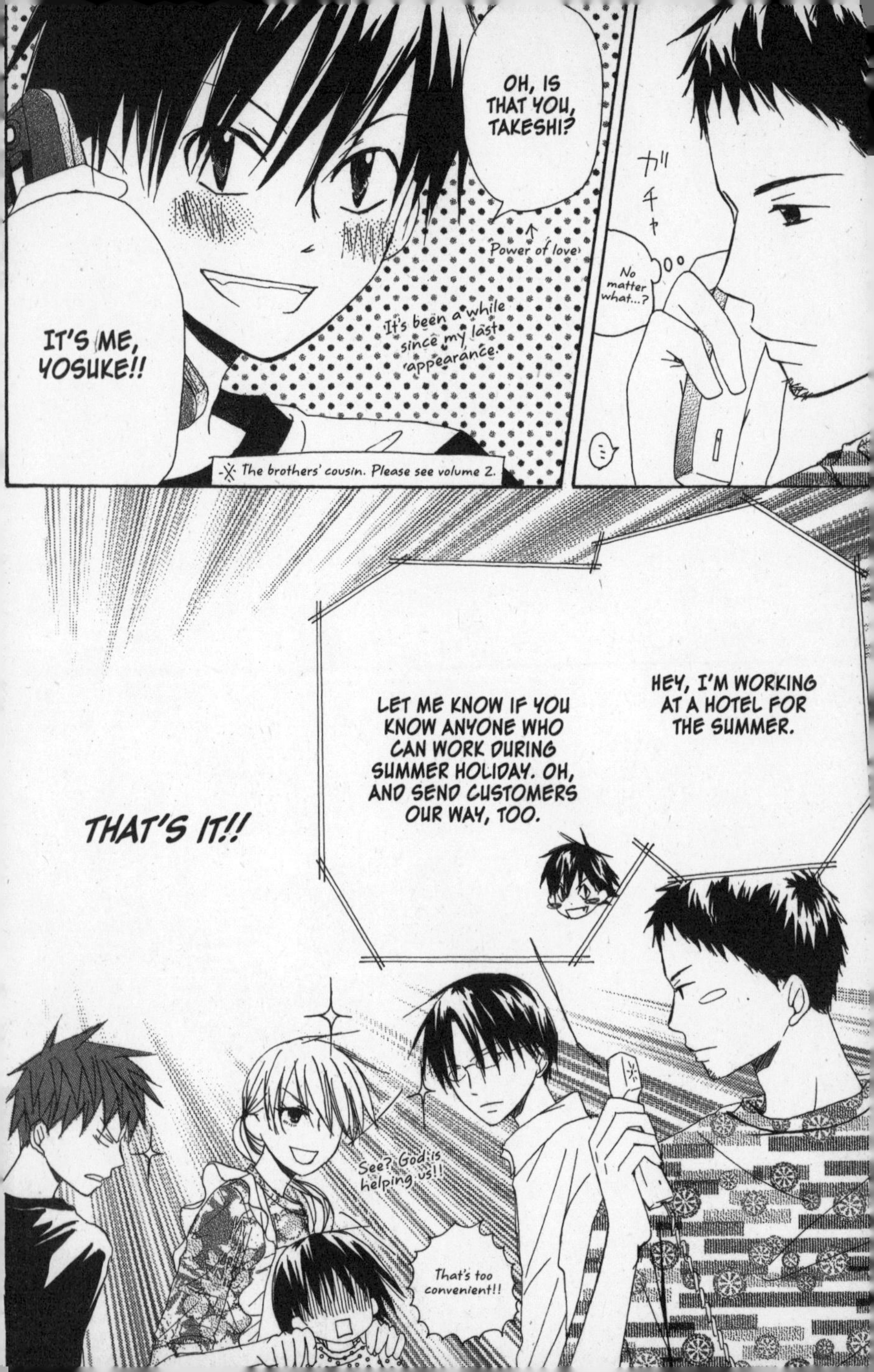
ガチャ
No matter what...?
OH, IS THAT YOU, TAKESHI?
Power of love
It's been a while since my last appearance.
IT'S ME, YOSUKE!!
※ The brothers' cousin. Please see volume 2.
HEY, I'M WORKING AT A HOTEL FOR THE SUMMER.
LET ME KNOW IF YOU KNOW ANYONE WHO CAN WORK DURING SUMMER HOLIDAY. OH, AND SEND CUSTOMERS OUR WAY, TOO.
THAT'S IT!!
See? God is helping us!!
That's too convenient!!

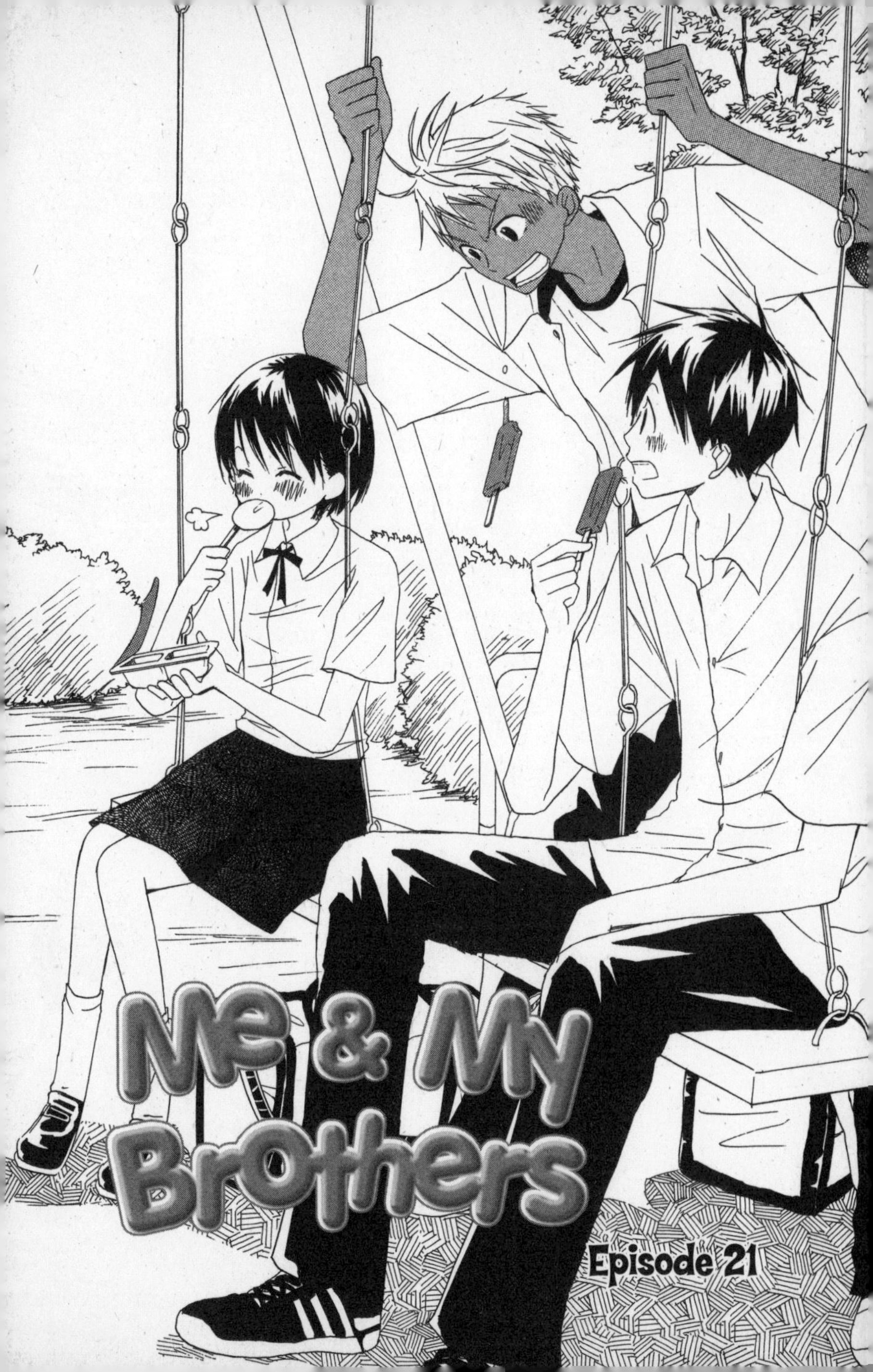
Me & My Brothers
Episode 21

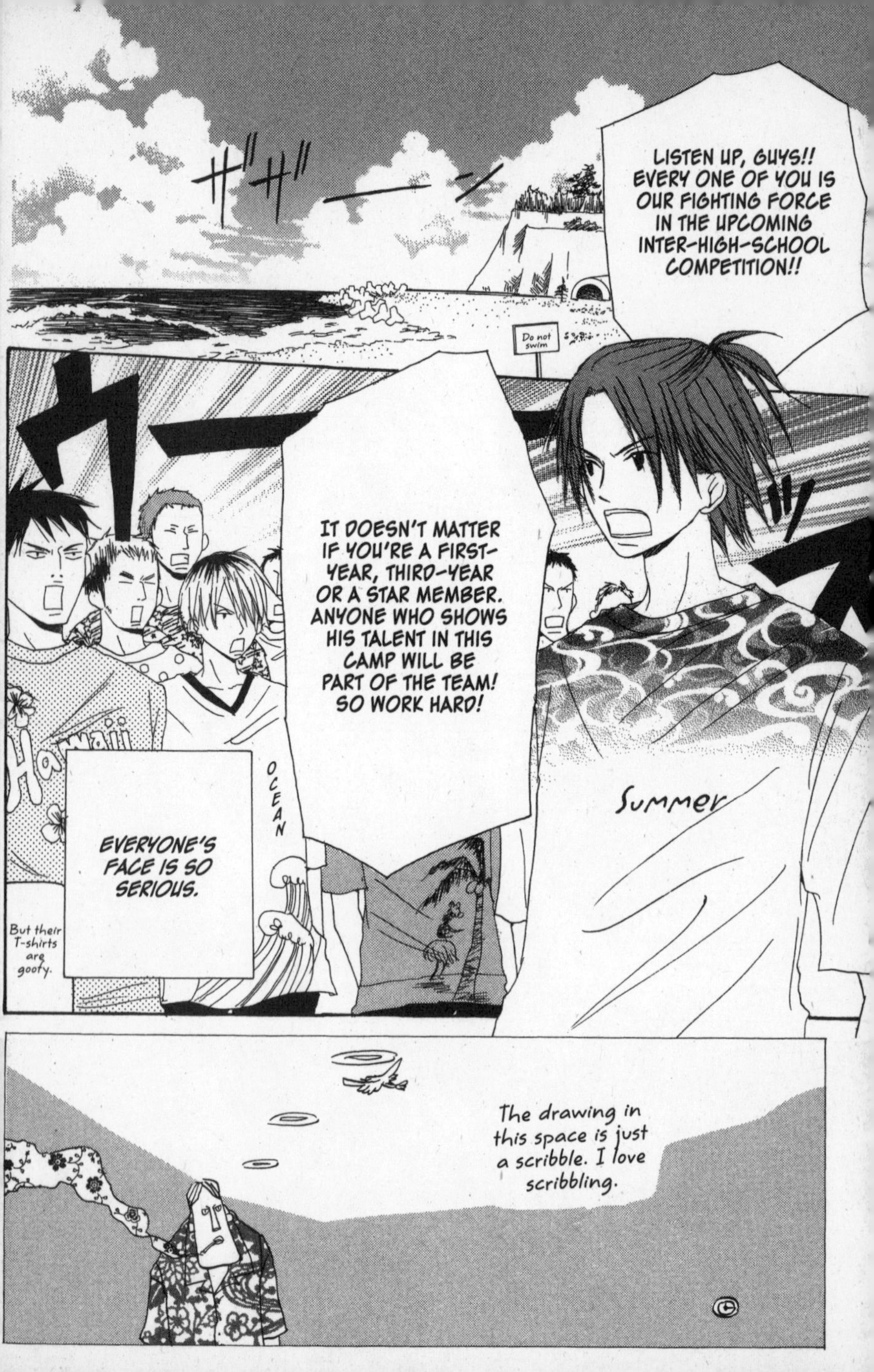
LISTEN UP, GUYS!! EVERY ONE OF YOU IS OUR FIGHTING FORCE IN THE UPCOMING INTER-HIGH-SCHOOL COMPETITION!!
Do not swim
IT DOESN'T MATTER IF YOU'RE A FIRST-YEAR, THIRD-YEAR OR A STAR MEMBER. ANYONE WHO SHOWS HIS TALENT IN THIS CAMP WILL BE PART OF THE TEAM! SO WORK HARD!
Summer
OCEAN
EVERYONE'S FACE IS SO SERIOUS.
But their T-shirts are goofy.
The drawing in this space is just a scribble. I love scribbling.

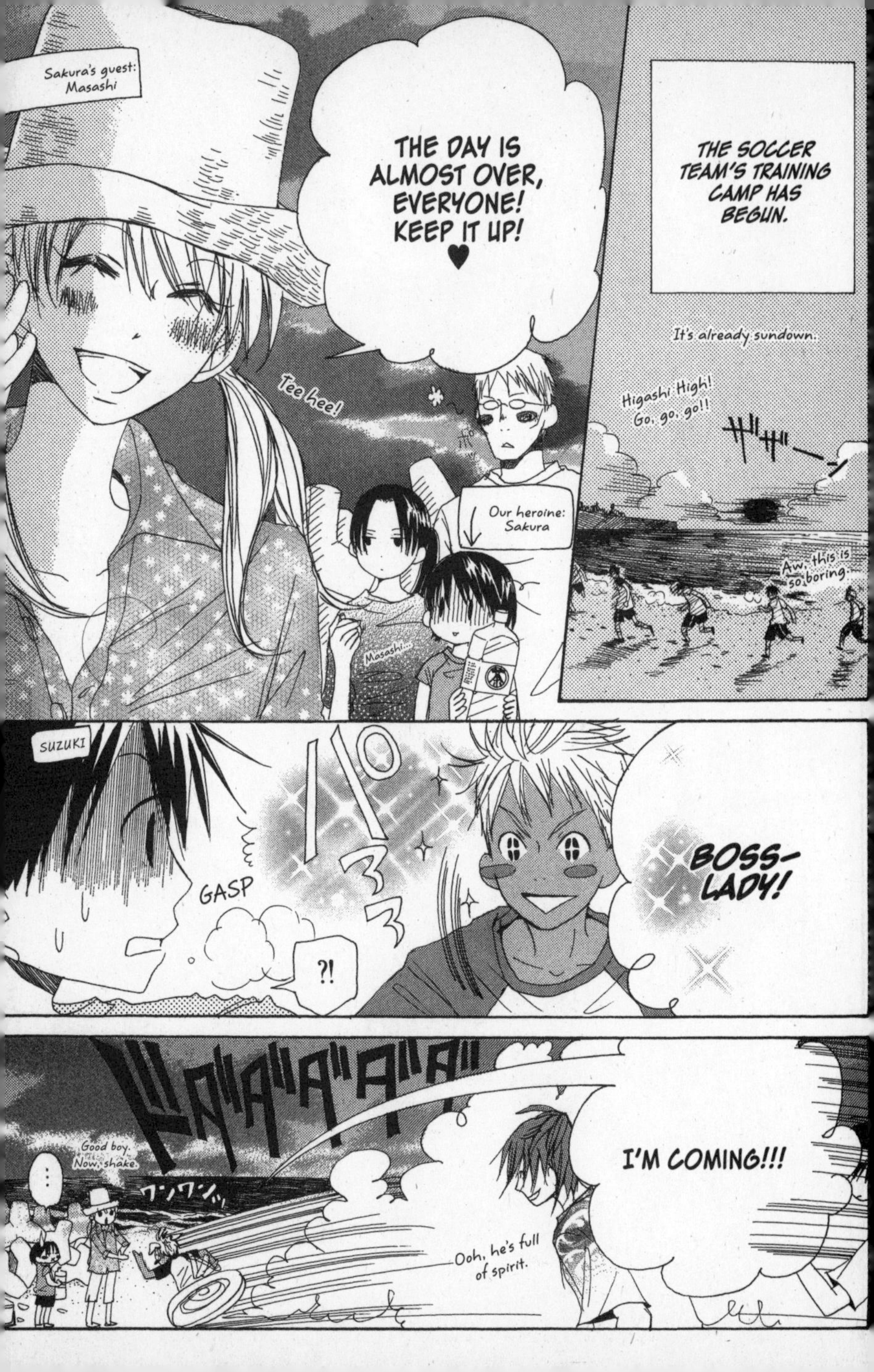
THE SOCCER TEAM'S TRAINING CAMP HAS BEGUN.
It's already sundown.
Higashi High! Go, go, go!!
Aw, this is so boring.
Sakura's guest: Masashi
THE DAY IS ALMOST OVER, EVERYONE! KEEP IT UP! ♥
Tee hee!
Our heroine: Sakura
Masashi...
BOSS-LADY!
SUZUKI
GASP
?!
I'M COMING!!!
Ooh, he's full of spirit.
Good boy. Now, shake.
...
ワンワンッ

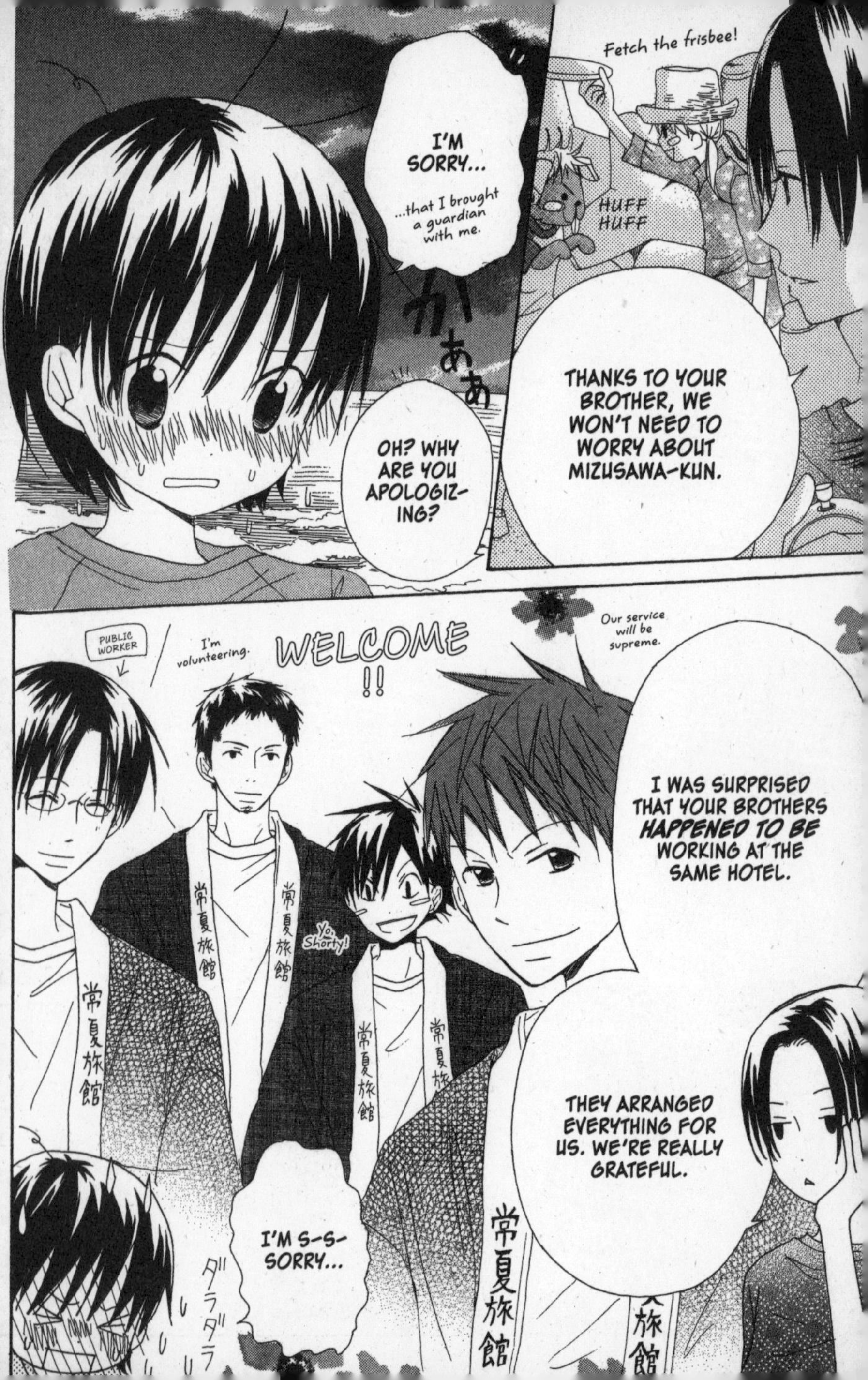
Fetch the frisbee!
HUFF HUFF
THANKS TO YOUR BROTHER, WE WON'T NEED TO WORRY ABOUT MIZUSAWA-KUN.
I'M SORRY...
...that I brought a guardian with me.
かあぁ
OH? WHY ARE YOU APOLOGIZ-ING?
Our service will be supreme.
I WAS SURPRISED THAT YOUR BROTHERS HAPPENED TO BE WORKING AT THE SAME HOTEL.
WELCOME !!
I'm volunteering.
PUBLIC WORKER
Yo, Shorty!
THEY ARRANGED EVERYTHING FOR US. WE'RE REALLY GRATEFUL.
I'M S-S-SORRY...
ダラダラ

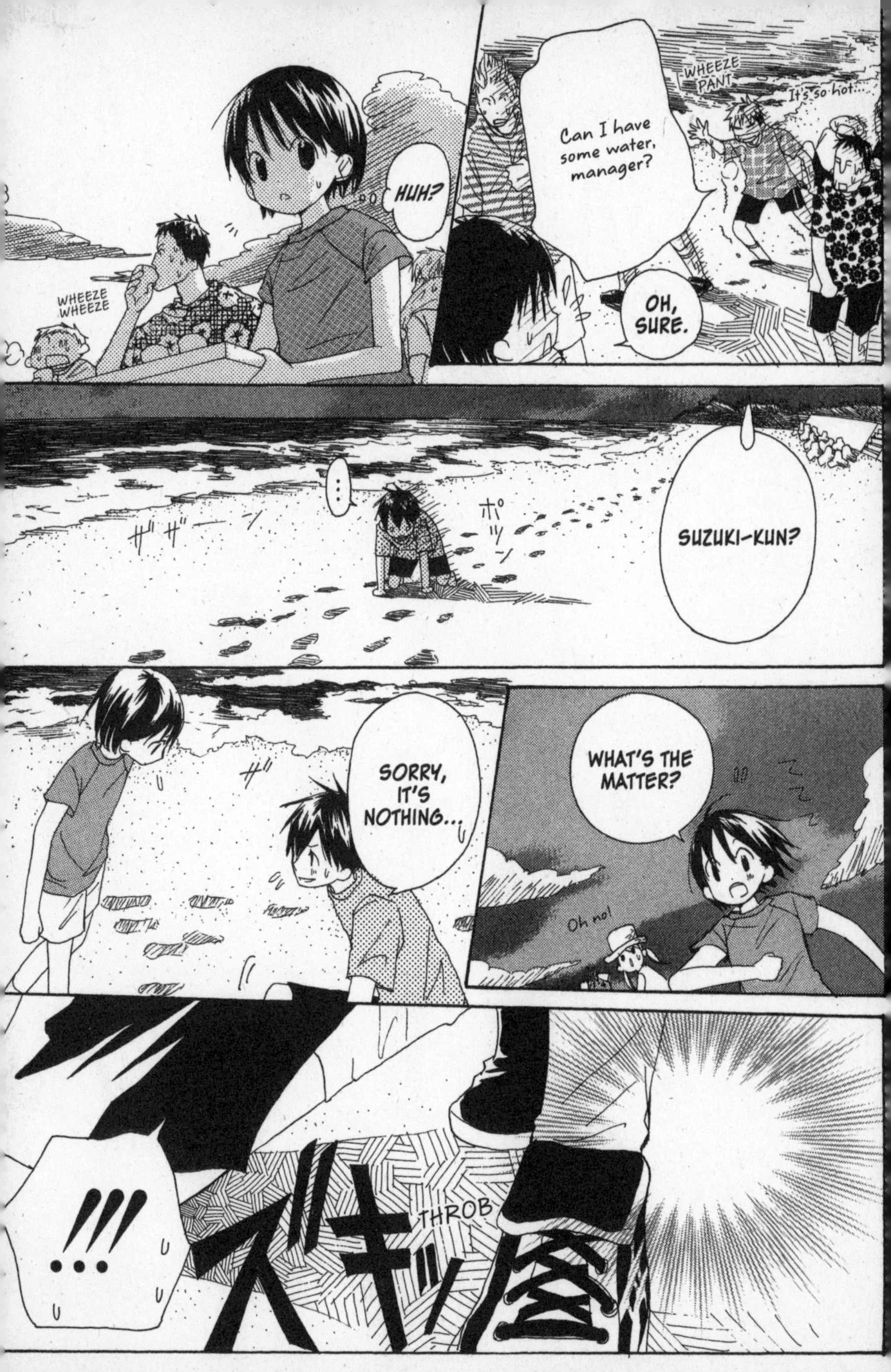
WHEEZE PANT
It's so hot...
Can I have some water, manager?
OH, SURE.
HUH?
WHEEZE WHEEZE
SUZUKI-KUN?
...
ポツーン
ザザーン
WHAT'S THE MATTER?
Oh no!
SORRY, IT'S NOTHING...
THROB
!!!...

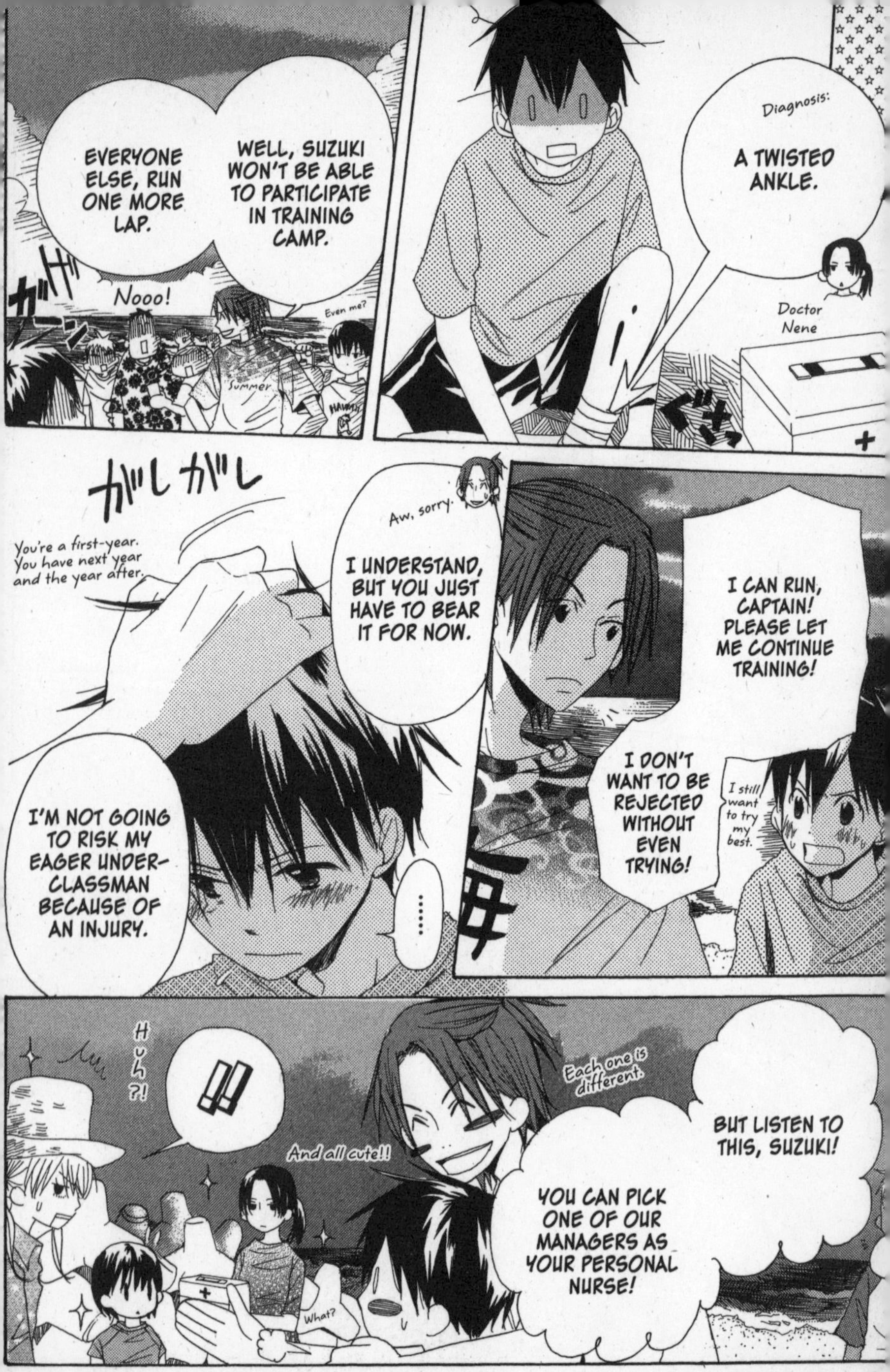
Diagnosis:
A TWISTED ANKLE.
Doctor Nene
WELL, SUZUKI WON'T BE ABLE TO PARTICIPATE IN TRAINING CAMP.
EVERYONE ELSE, RUN ONE MORE LAP.
Nooo!
Even me?
Summer
I CAN RUN, CAPTAIN! PLEASE LET ME CONTINUE TRAINING!
I DON'T WANT TO BE REJECTED WITHOUT EVEN TRYING!
I still want to try my best.
Aw, sorry.
I UNDERSTAND, BUT YOU JUST HAVE TO BEAR IT FOR NOW.
がしがし
You're a first-year. You have next year and the year after.
I'M NOT GOING TO RISK MY EAGER UNDER-CLASSMAN BECAUSE OF AN INJURY.
......
BUT LISTEN TO THIS, SUZUKI!
YOU CAN PICK ONE OF OUR MANAGERS AS YOUR PERSONAL NURSE!
Each one is different.
And all cute!!
!!
Huh?!
What?

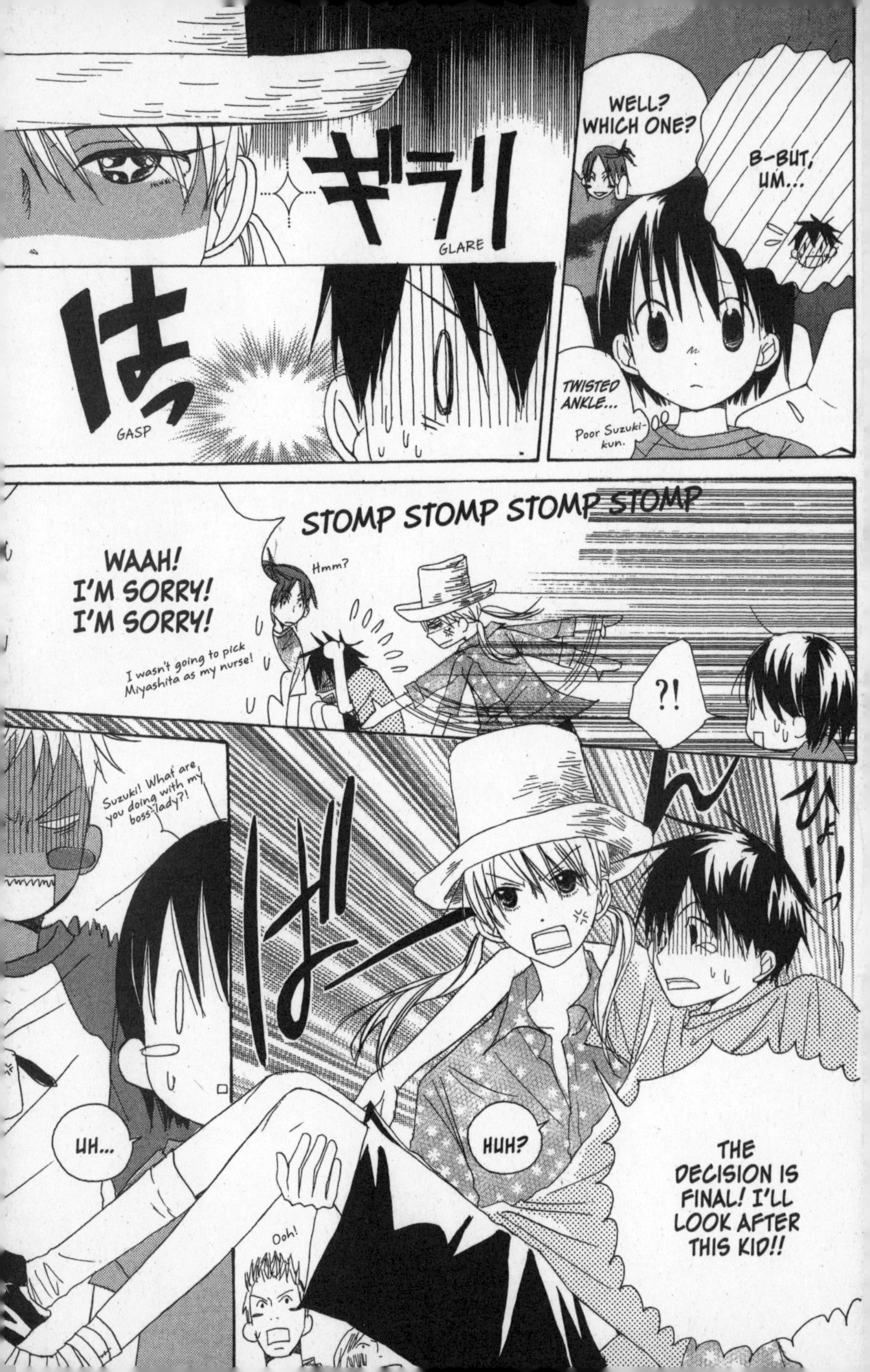
WELL? WHICH ONE?
B-BUT, UM...
TWISTED ANKLE...
Poor Suzuki-kun.
ギラリ
GLARE
はっ
GASP
STOMP STOMP STOMP STOMP
?!
Hmm?
WAAH! I'M SORRY! I'M SORRY!
I wasn't going to pick Miyashita as my nurse!
ひょいっ
THE DECISION IS FINAL! I'LL LOOK AFTER THIS KID!!
HUH?
ばっ
Suzuki! What are you doing with my boss-lady?!
UH...
Ooh!

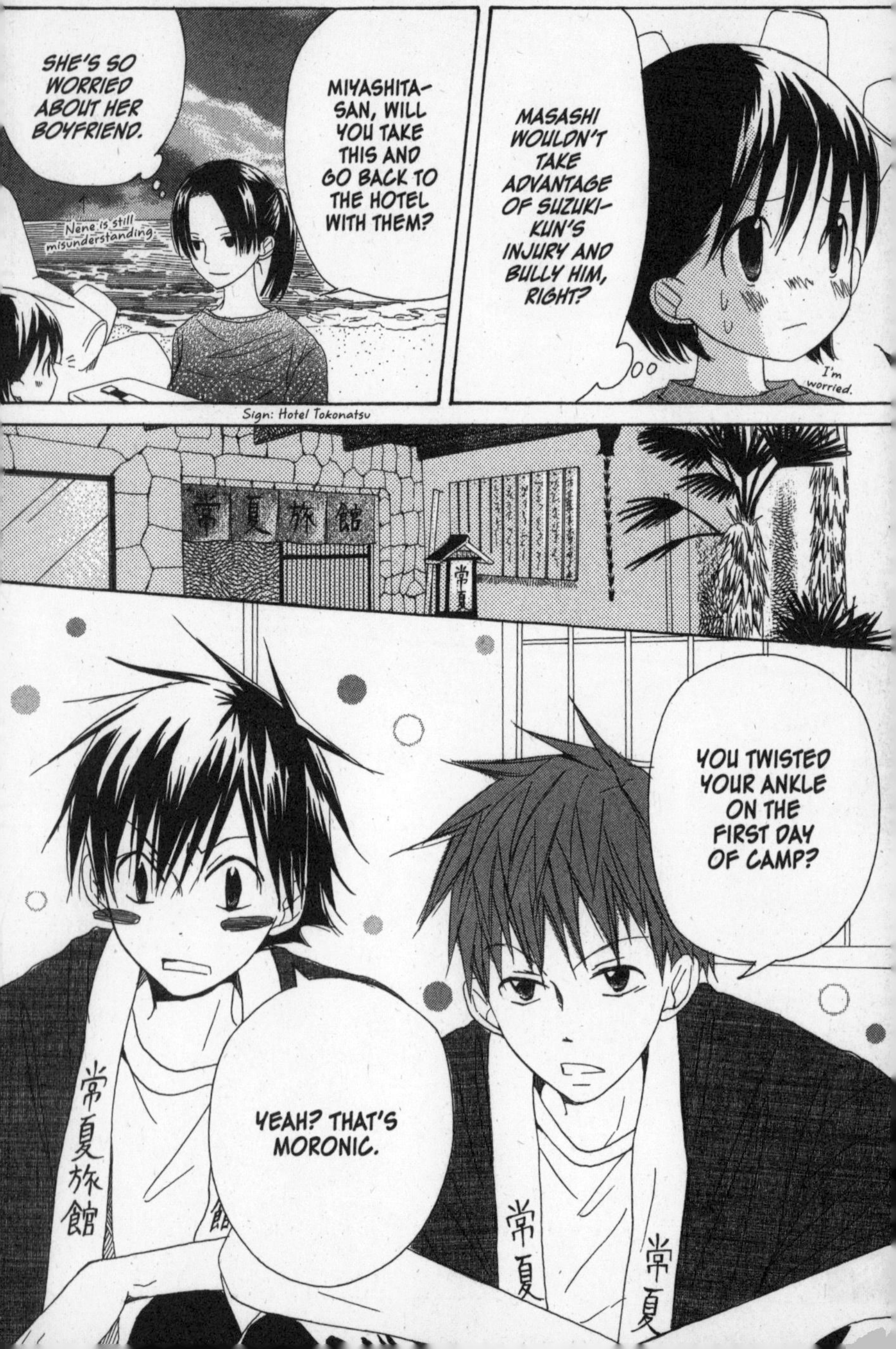
MASASHI WOULDN'T TAKE ADVANTAGE OF SUZUKI-KUN'S INJURY AND BULLY HIM, RIGHT?
I'm worried.
MIYASHITA-SAN, WILL YOU TAKE THIS AND GO BACK TO THE HOTEL WITH THEM?
SHE'S SO WORRIED ABOUT HER BOYFRIEND.
Nene is still misunderstanding.
Sign: Hotel Tokonatsu
常夏旅館
YOU TWISTED YOUR ANKLE ON THE FIRST DAY OF CAMP?
YEAH? THAT'S MORONIC.

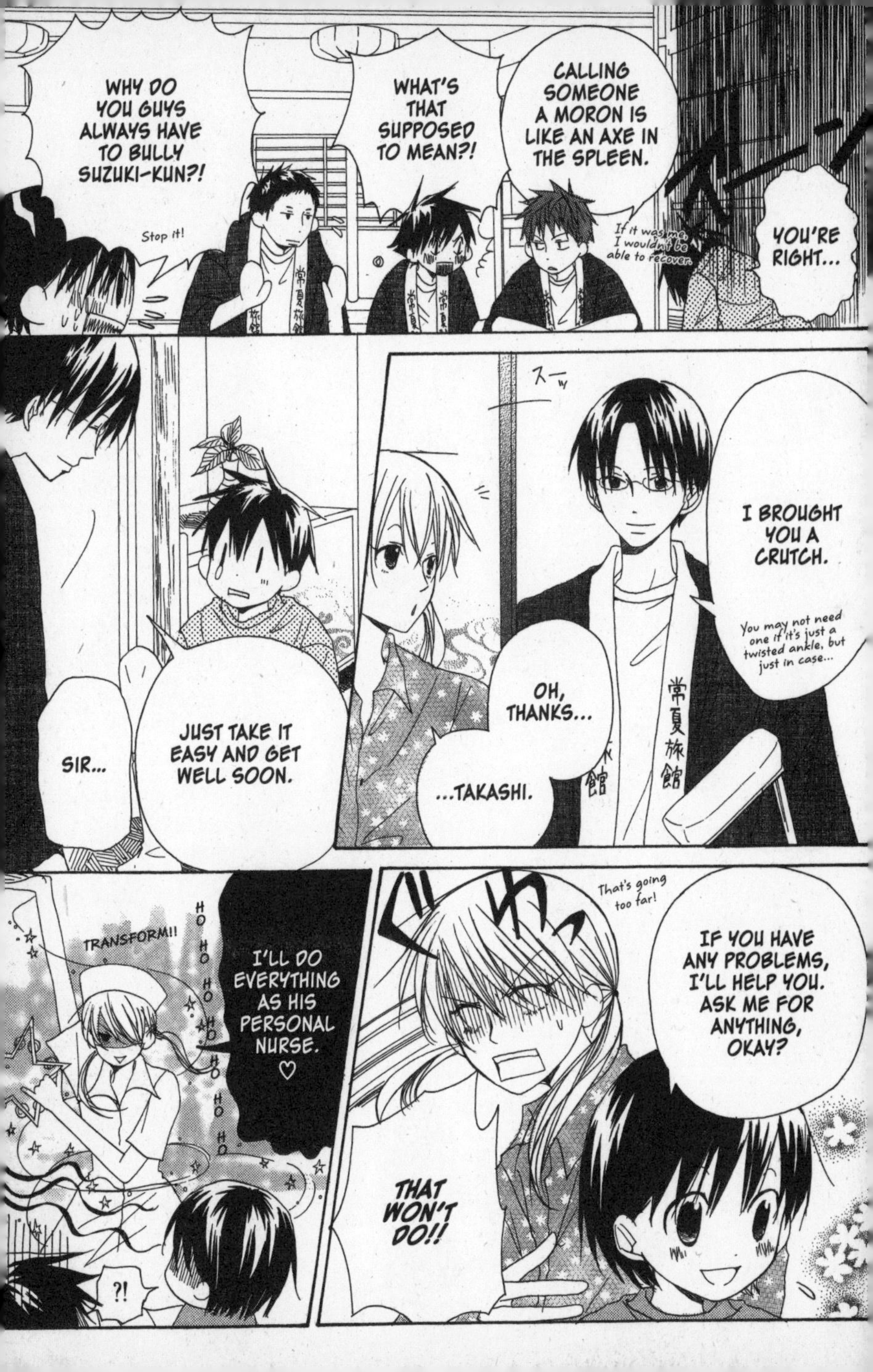
CALLING SOMEONE A MORON IS LIKE AN AXE IN THE SPLEEN.
YOU'RE RIGHT...
If it was me, I wouldn't be able to recover.
WHAT'S THAT SUPPOSED TO MEAN?!
WHY DO YOU GUYS ALWAYS HAVE TO BULLY SUZUKI-KUN?!
Stop it!
スー
I BROUGHT YOU A CRUTCH.
You may not need one if it's just a twisted ankle, but just in case...
OH, THANKS...
...TAKASHI.
JUST TAKE IT EASY AND GET WELL SOON.
SIR...
IF YOU HAVE ANY PROBLEMS, I'LL HELP YOU. ASK ME FOR ANYTHING, OKAY?
That's going too far!
THAT WON'T DO!!
I'LL DO EVERYTHING AS HIS PERSONAL NURSE. ♡
HO HO HO HO HO HO HO HO HO
TRANSFORM!!
?!

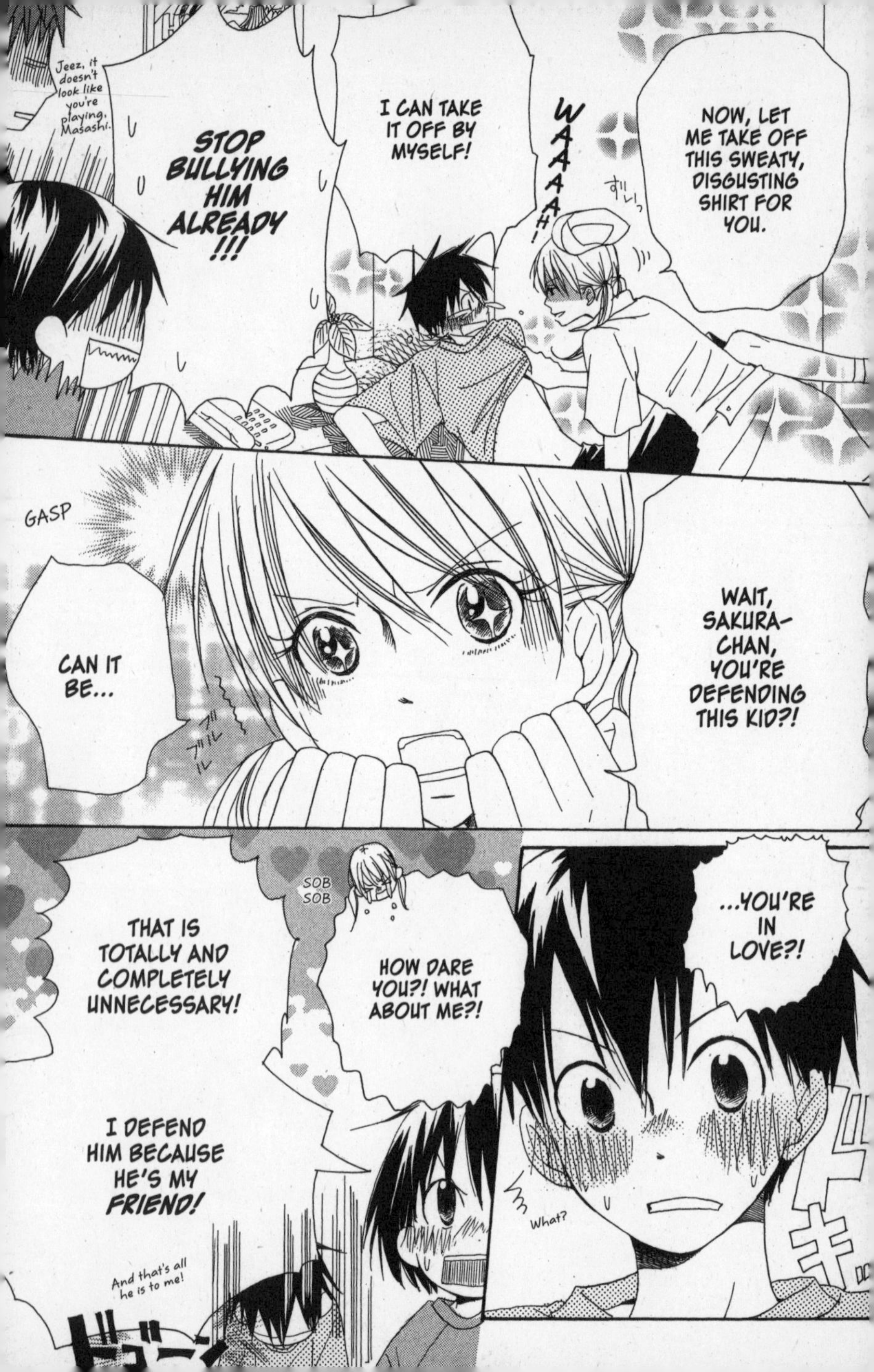
NOW, LET ME TAKE OFF THIS SWEATY, DISGUSTING SHIRT FOR YOU.
WAAAAAH!
I CAN TAKE IT OFF BY MYSELF!
STOP BULLYING HIM ALREADY!!!
Jeez, it doesn't look like you're playing, Masashi.
WAIT, SAKURA-CHAN, YOU'RE DEFENDING THIS KID?!
GASP
CAN IT BE...
...YOU'RE IN LOVE?!
What?
HOW DARE YOU?! WHAT ABOUT ME?!
SOB SOB
THAT IS TOTALLY AND COMPLETELY UNNECESSARY!
I DEFEND HIM BECAUSE HE'S MY FRIEND!
And that's all he is to me!

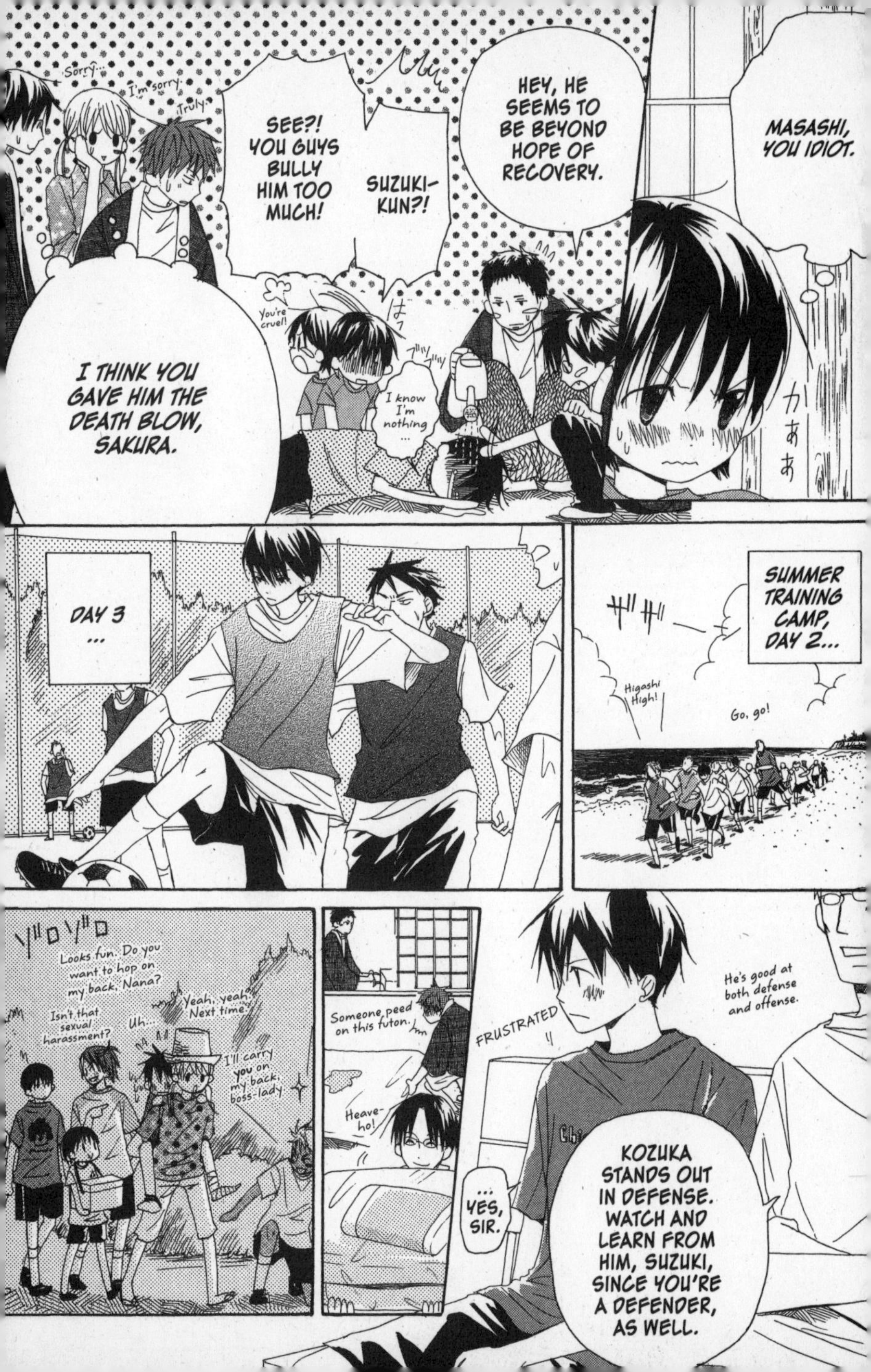
MASASHI, YOU IDIOT.
HEY, HE SEEMS TO BE BEYOND HOPE OF RECOVERY.
SUZUKI-KUN?!
SEE?! YOU GUYS BULLY HIM TOO MUCH!
Truly.
I'm sorry.
Sorry...
I know I'm nothing ...
You're cruel!
I THINK YOU GAVE HIM THE DEATH BLOW, SAKURA.
SUMMER TRAINING CAMP, DAY 2...
Go, go!
Higashi High!
DAY 3 ...
He's good at both defense and offense.
KOZUKA STANDS OUT IN DEFENSE. WATCH AND LEARN FROM HIM, SUZUKI, SINCE YOU'RE A DEFENDER, AS WELL.
FRUSTRATED
... YES, SIR.
Someone peed on this futon.
Heave-ho!
Looks fun. Do you want to hop on my back, Nana?
Yeah, yeah. Next time.
Uh...
Isn't that sexual harassment?
I'll carry you on my back, boss-lady.

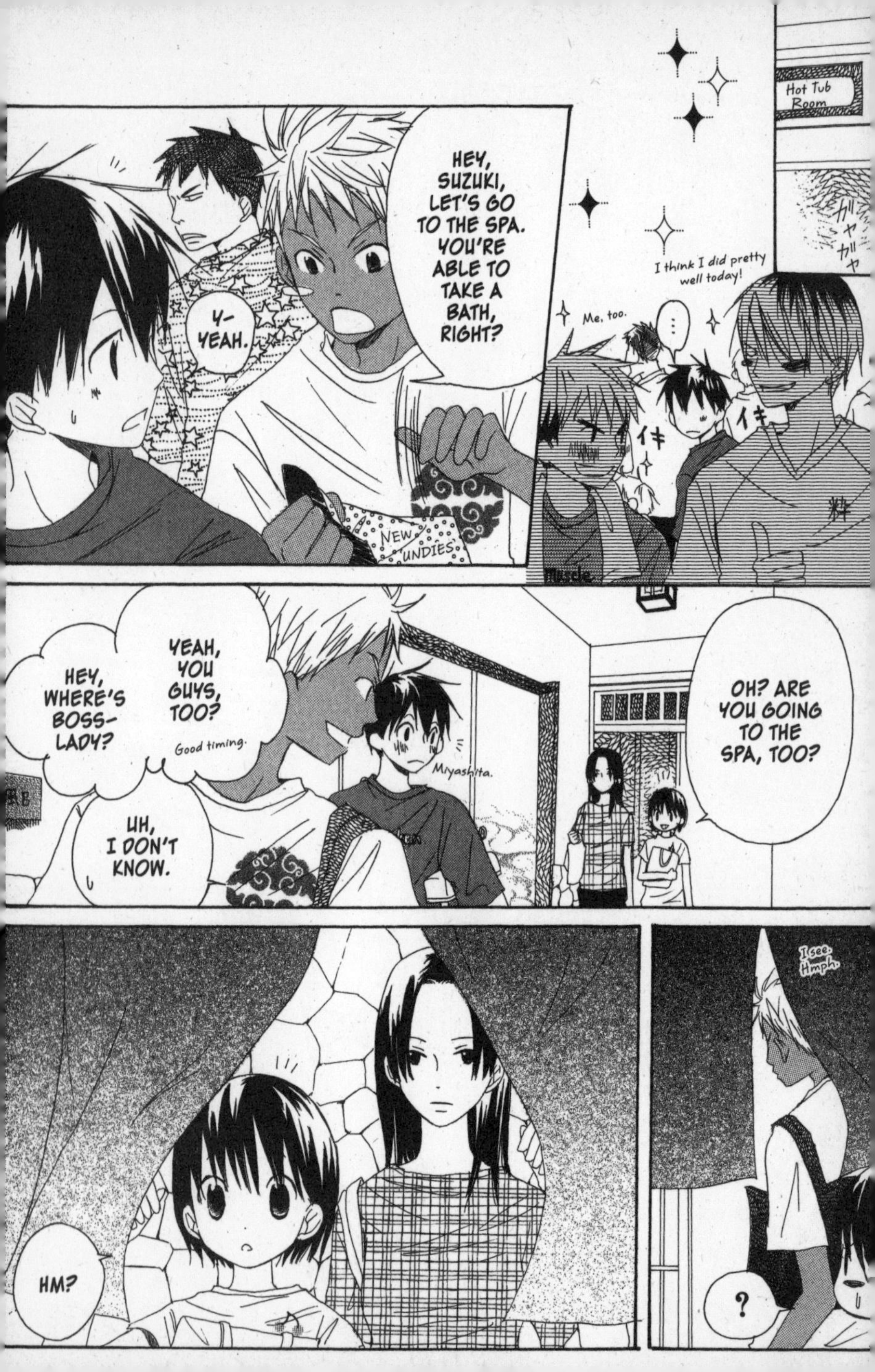
Hot Tub Room
ガヤガヤ
I think I did pretty well today!
Me, too.
…
イキ
イキ
Muscle
HEY, SUZUKI, LET'S GO TO THE SPA. YOU'RE ABLE TO TAKE A BATH, RIGHT?
Y-YEAH.
NEW UNDIES
OH? ARE YOU GOING TO THE SPA, TOO?
Miyashita.
YEAH, YOU GUYS, TOO?
Good timing.
HEY, WHERE'S BOSS-LADY?
UH, I DON'T KNOW.
I see. Hmph.
?
HM?

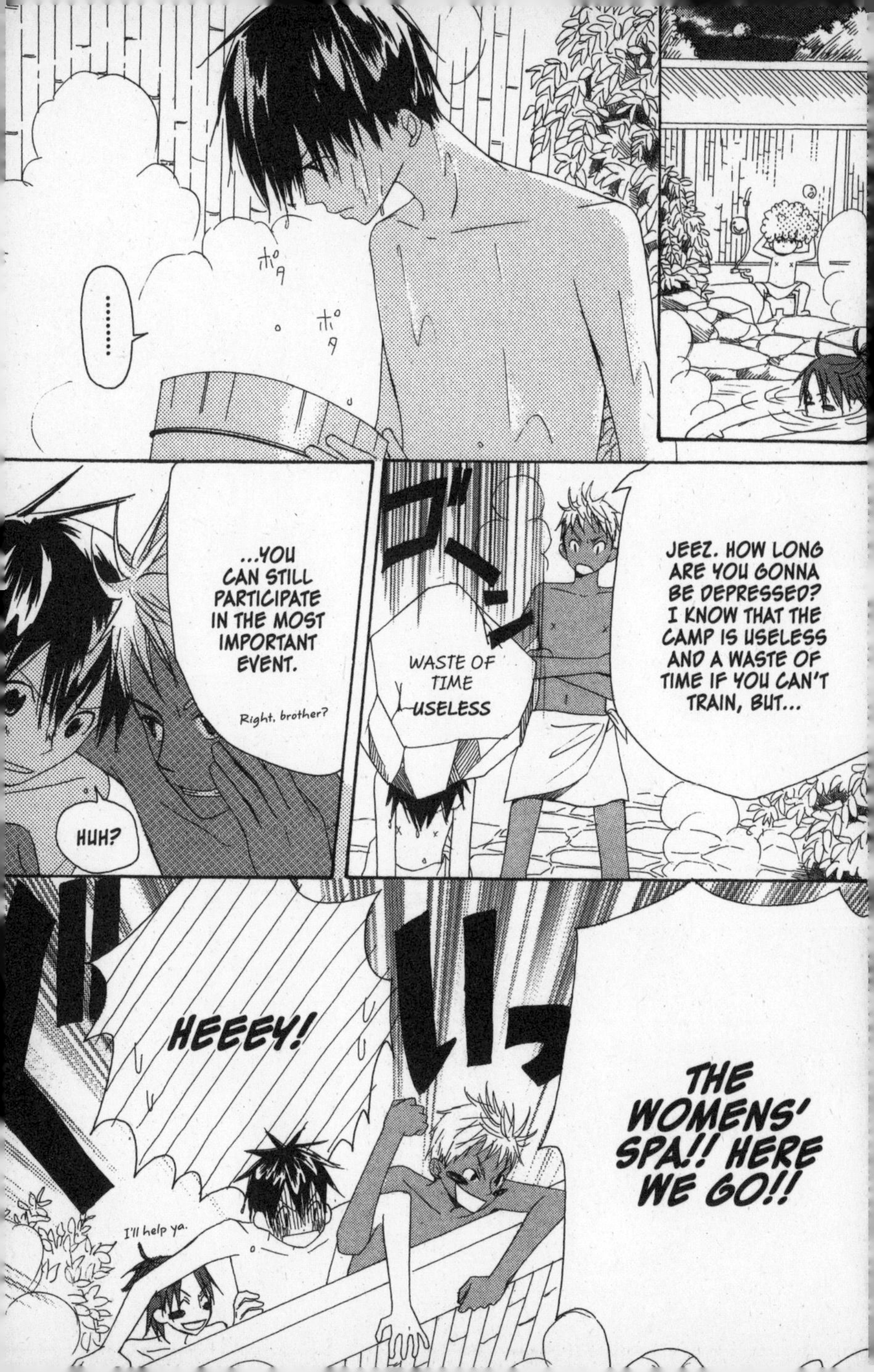
ポタ
ポタ
......
JEEZ. HOW LONG ARE YOU GONNA BE DEPRESSED? I KNOW THAT THE CAMP IS USELESS AND A WASTE OF TIME IF YOU CAN'T TRAIN, BUT...
WASTE OF TIME
USELESS
...YOU CAN STILL PARTICIPATE IN THE MOST IMPORTANT EVENT.
Right, brother?
HUH?
THE WOMENS' SPA!! HERE WE GO!!
HEEEY!
I'll help ya.

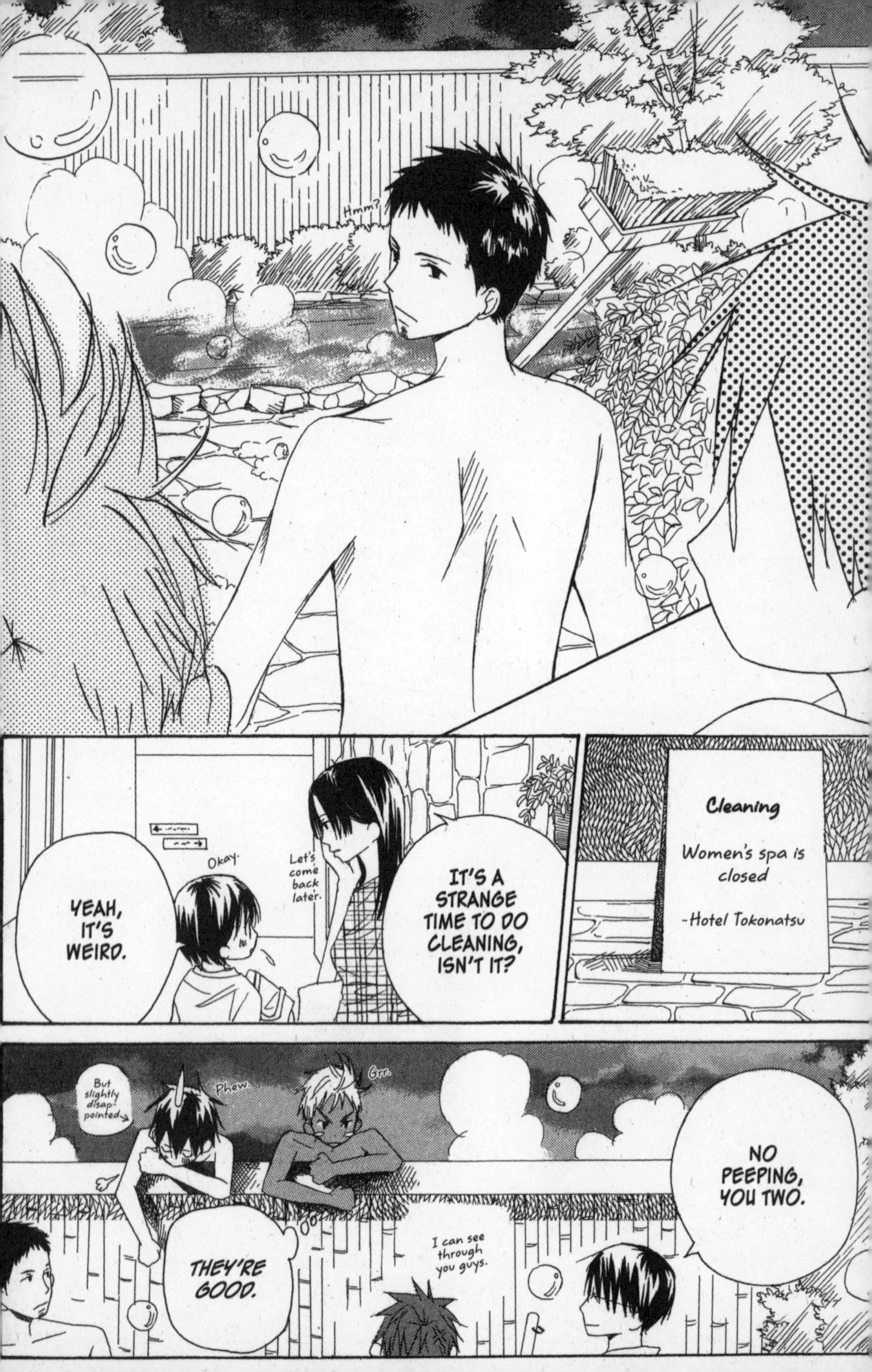
Hmm?
Cleaning
Women's spa is closed
-Hotel Tokonatsu
IT'S A STRANGE TIME TO DO CLEANING, ISN'T IT?
Let's come back later.
Okay.
YEAH, IT'S WEIRD.
NO PEEPING, YOU TWO.
Grr.
Phew.
But slightly disap-pointed
I can see through you guys.
THEY'RE GOOD.

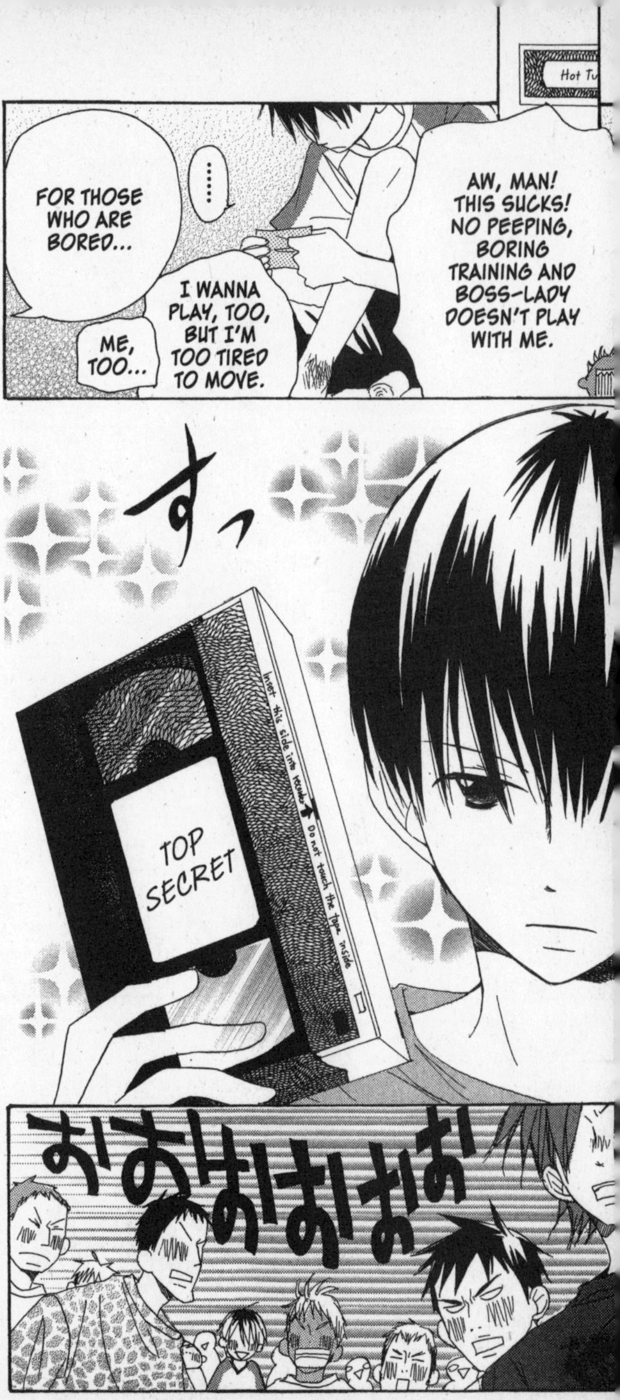
AW, MAN! THIS SUCKS! NO PEEPING, BORING TRAINING AND BOSS-LADY DOESN'T PLAY WITH ME.
......
FOR THOSE WHO ARE BORED...
I WANNA PLAY, TOO, BUT I'M TOO TIRED TO MOVE.
ME, TOO...
すっ
Do not touch the tape inside
TOP SECRET

2

Volume 5 is different from the other volumes. First, there's no short story. I don't know if it's a good thing or not, but straying from the usual makes me a bit nervous.

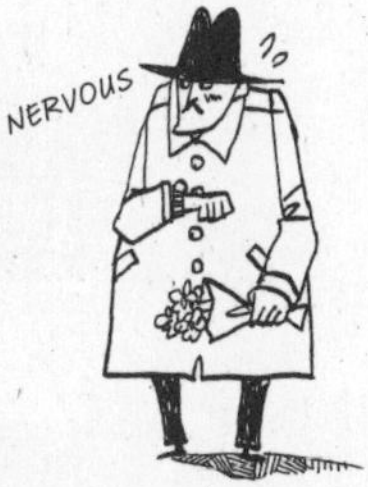
NERVOUS

Yes, sorry. This illustration has nothing to do with anything. But if I force a meaning into it, it'd be "romance." This shows that ***Me & My Brothers*** has changed from a family comedy to a brother love comedy. I hope it looks like a love comedy... I'm nervous.

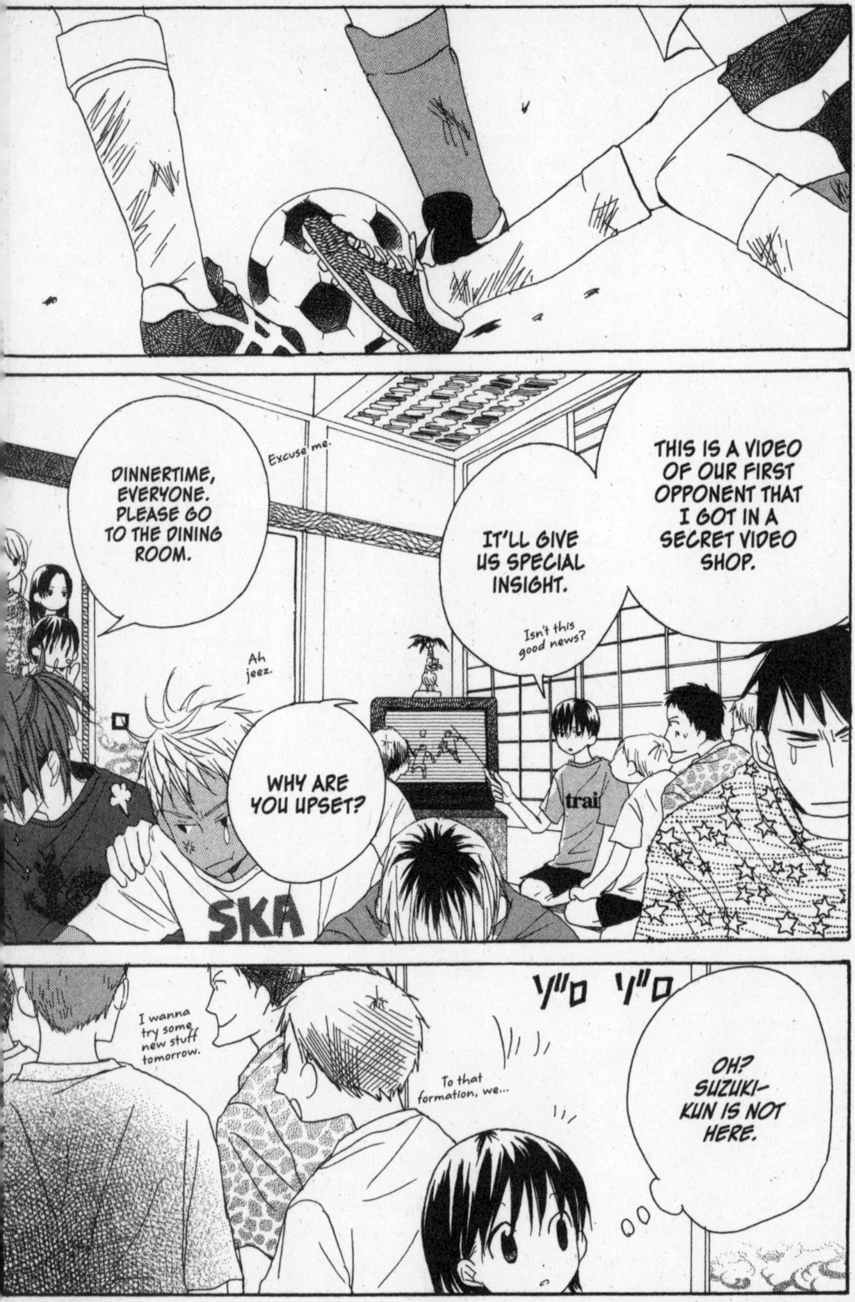
THIS IS A VIDEO OF OUR FIRST OPPONENT THAT I GOT IN A SECRET VIDEO SHOP.
IT'LL GIVE US SPECIAL INSIGHT.
Isn't this good news?
Excuse me.
DINNERTIME, EVERYONE. PLEASE GO TO THE DINING ROOM.
Ah jeez.
WHY ARE YOU UPSET?
ゾロ ゾロ
OH? SUZUKI-KUN IS NOT HERE.
To that formation, we...
I wanna try some new stuff tomorrow.

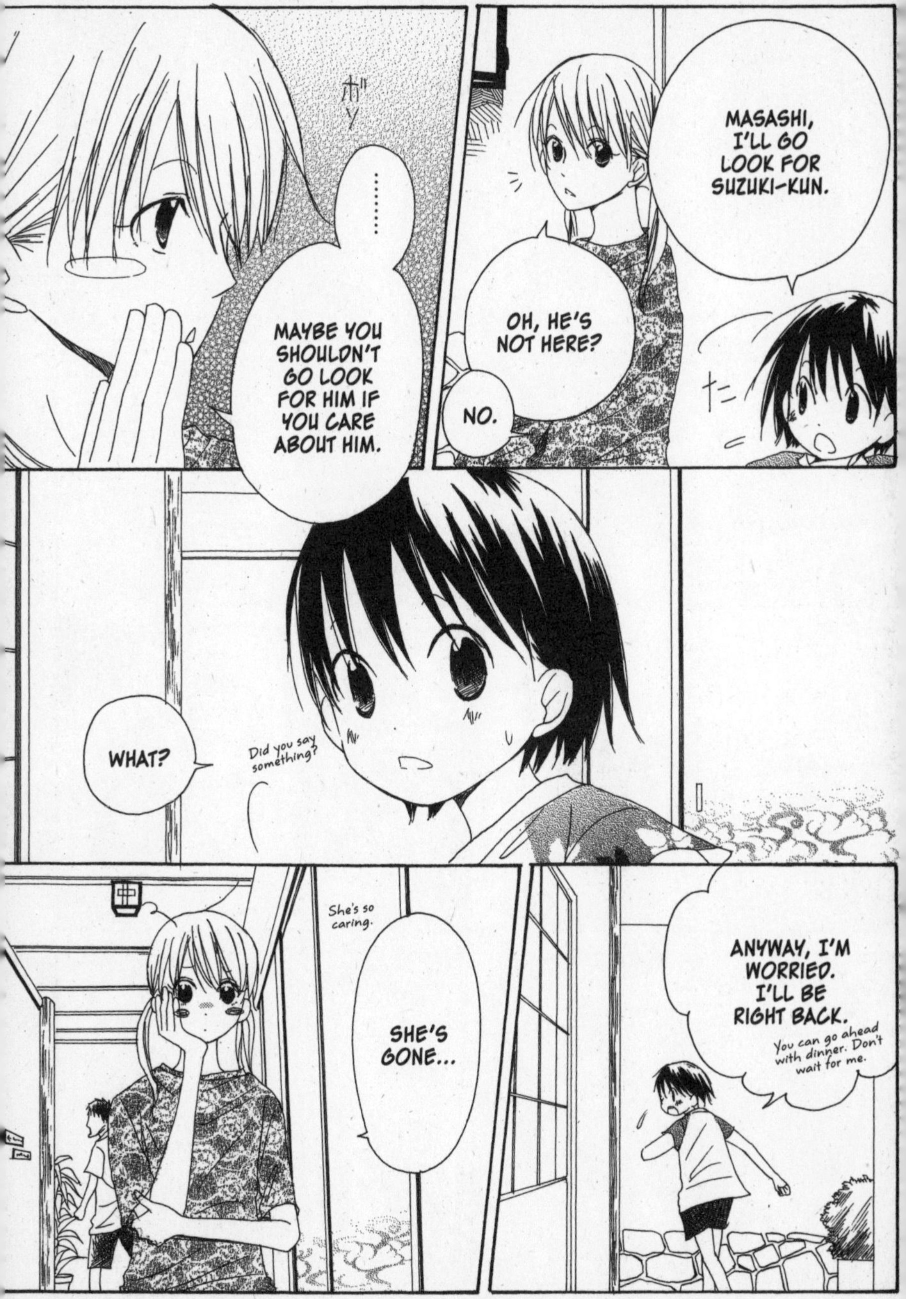
MASASHI, I'LL GO LOOK FOR SUZUKI-KUN.
OH, HE'S NOT HERE?
NO.
ボソ
......
MAYBE YOU SHOULDN'T GO LOOK FOR HIM IF YOU CARE ABOUT HIM.
WHAT?
Did you say something?
ANYWAY, I'M WORRIED. I'LL BE RIGHT BACK.
You can go ahead with dinner. Don't wait for me.
SHE'S GONE...
She's so caring.

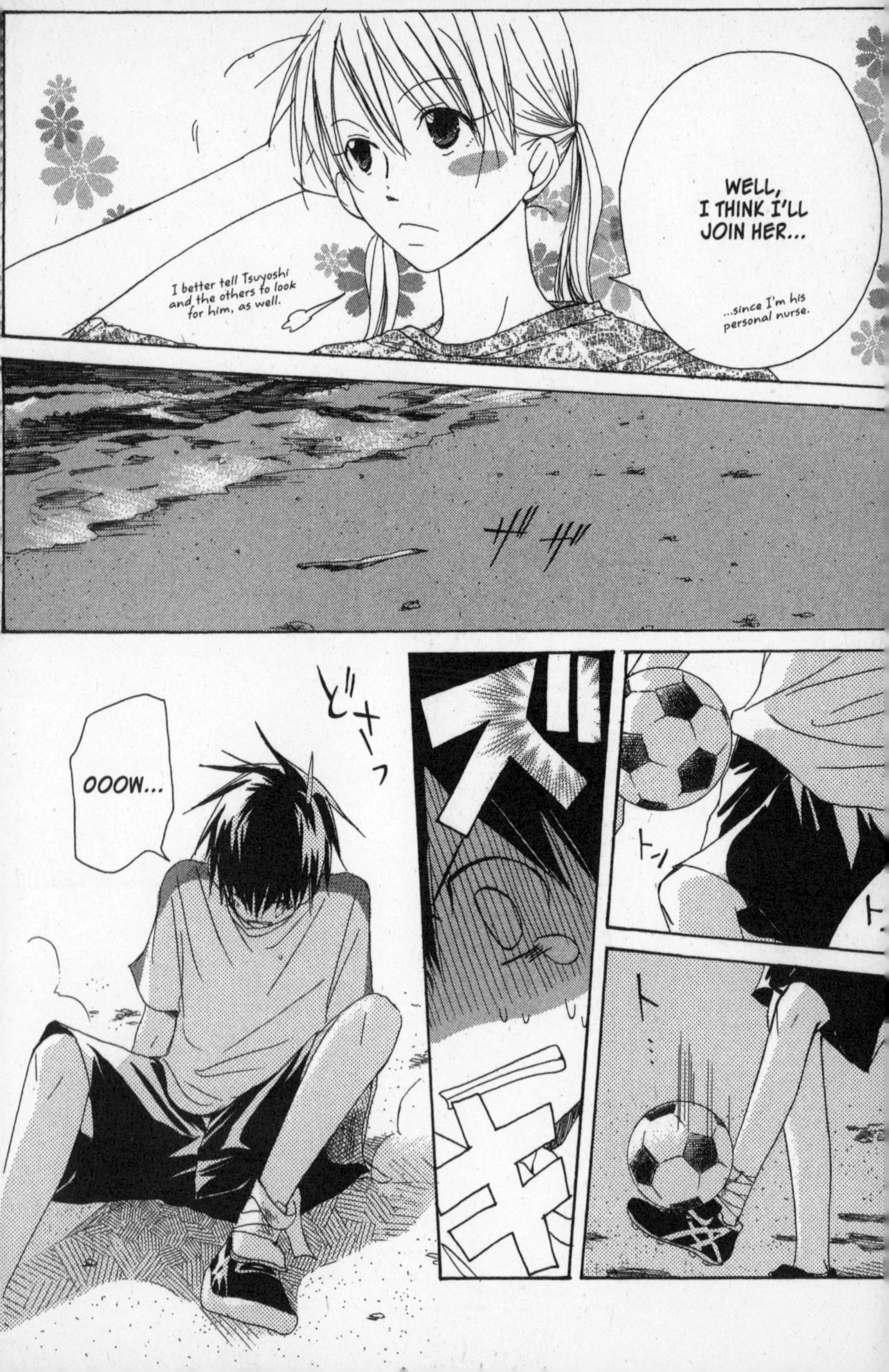
WELL, I THINK I'LL JOIN HER...
...since I'm his personal nurse.
I better tell Tsuyoshi and the others to look for him, as well.
OOOW...

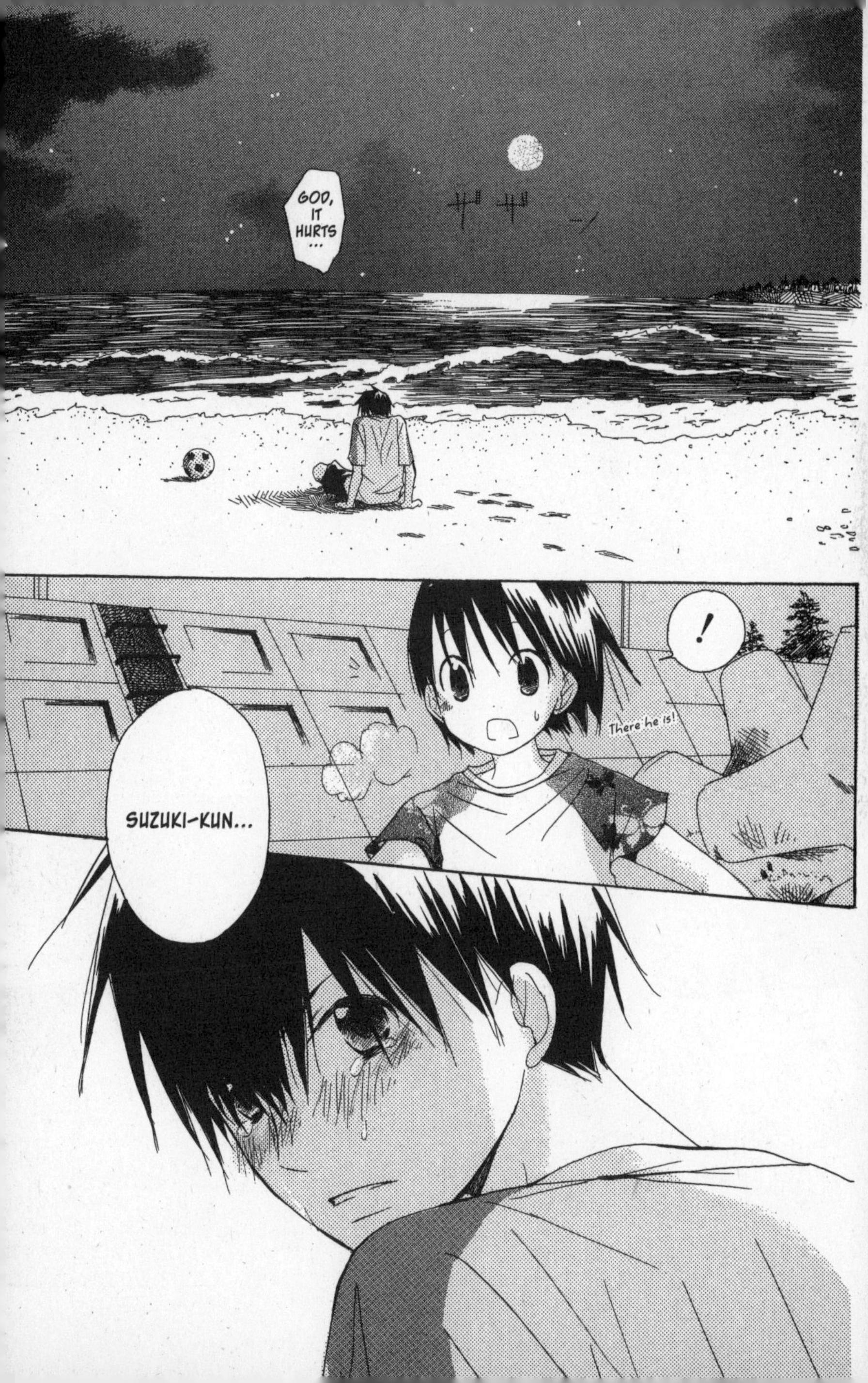
ザザーン
GOD, IT HURTS...
!
There he is!
SUZUKI-KUN...

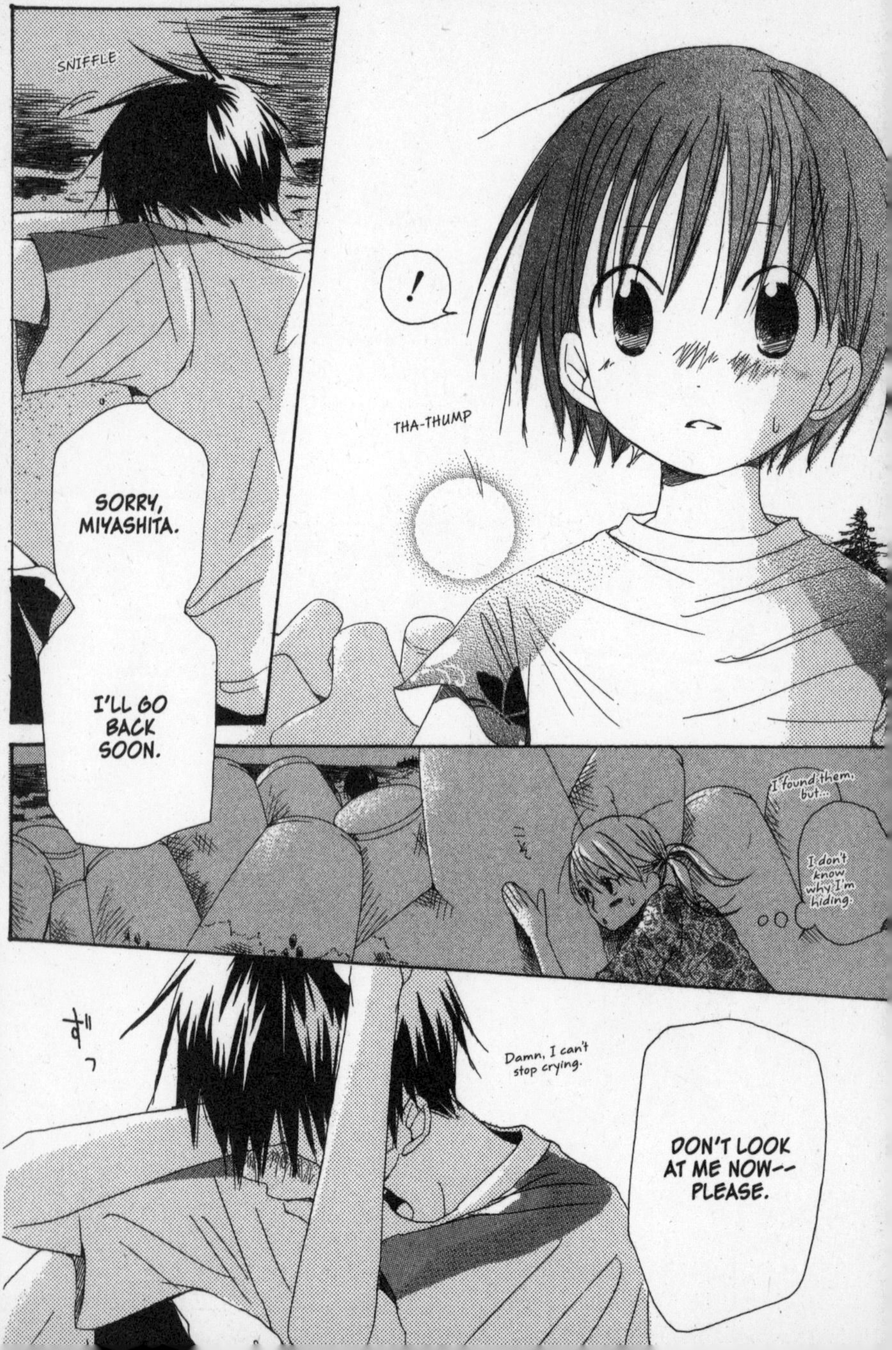
!
THA-THUMP
SNIFFLE
SORRY, MIYASHITA.
I'LL GO BACK SOON.
I found them, but...
I don't know why I'm hiding.
Damn, I can't stop crying.
DON'T LOOK AT ME NOW--PLEASE.
ずっ

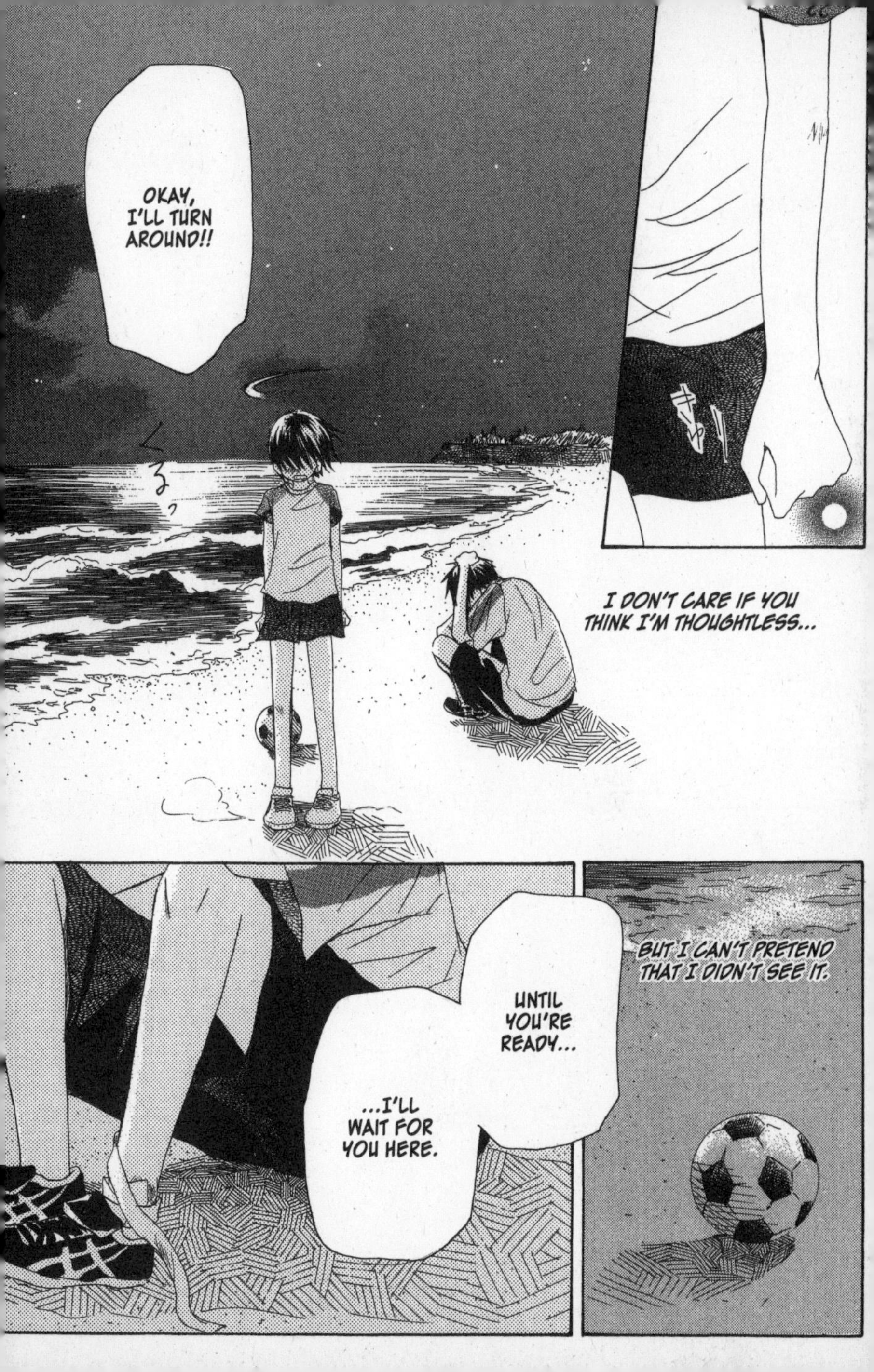
OKAY, I'LL TURN AROUND!!
I DON'T CARE IF YOU THINK I'M THOUGHTLESS...
BUT I CAN'T PRETEND THAT I DIDN'T SEE IT.
UNTIL YOU'RE READY...
...I'LL WAIT FOR YOU HERE.

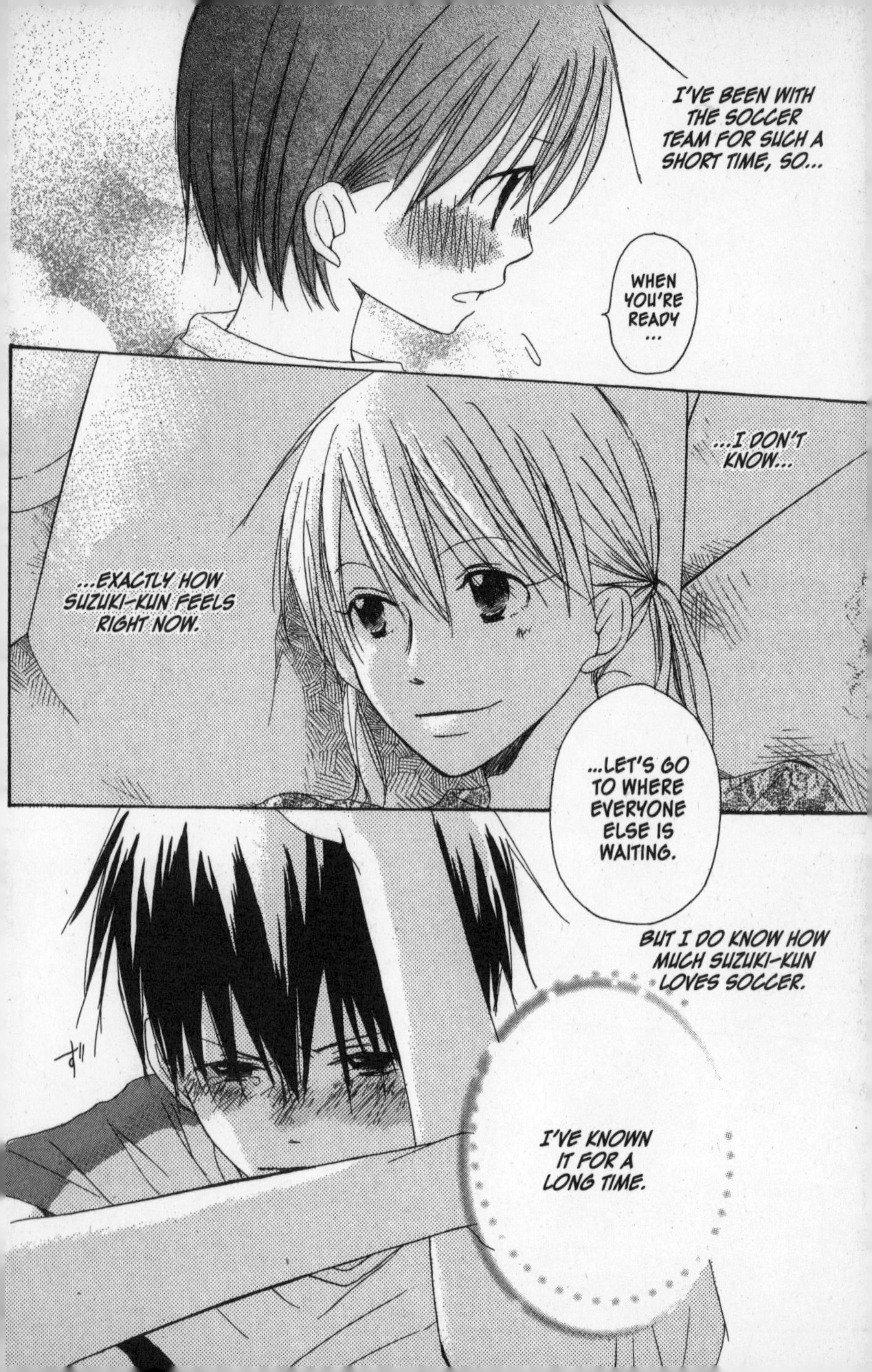
I'VE BEEN WITH THE SOCCER TEAM FOR SUCH A SHORT TIME, SO...
WHEN YOU'RE READY ...
...I DON'T KNOW...
...EXACTLY HOW SUZUKI-KUN FEELS RIGHT NOW.
...LET'S GO TO WHERE EVERYONE ELSE IS WAITING.
BUT I DO KNOW HOW MUCH SUZUKI-KUN LOVES SOCCER.
I'VE KNOWN IT FOR A LONG TIME.

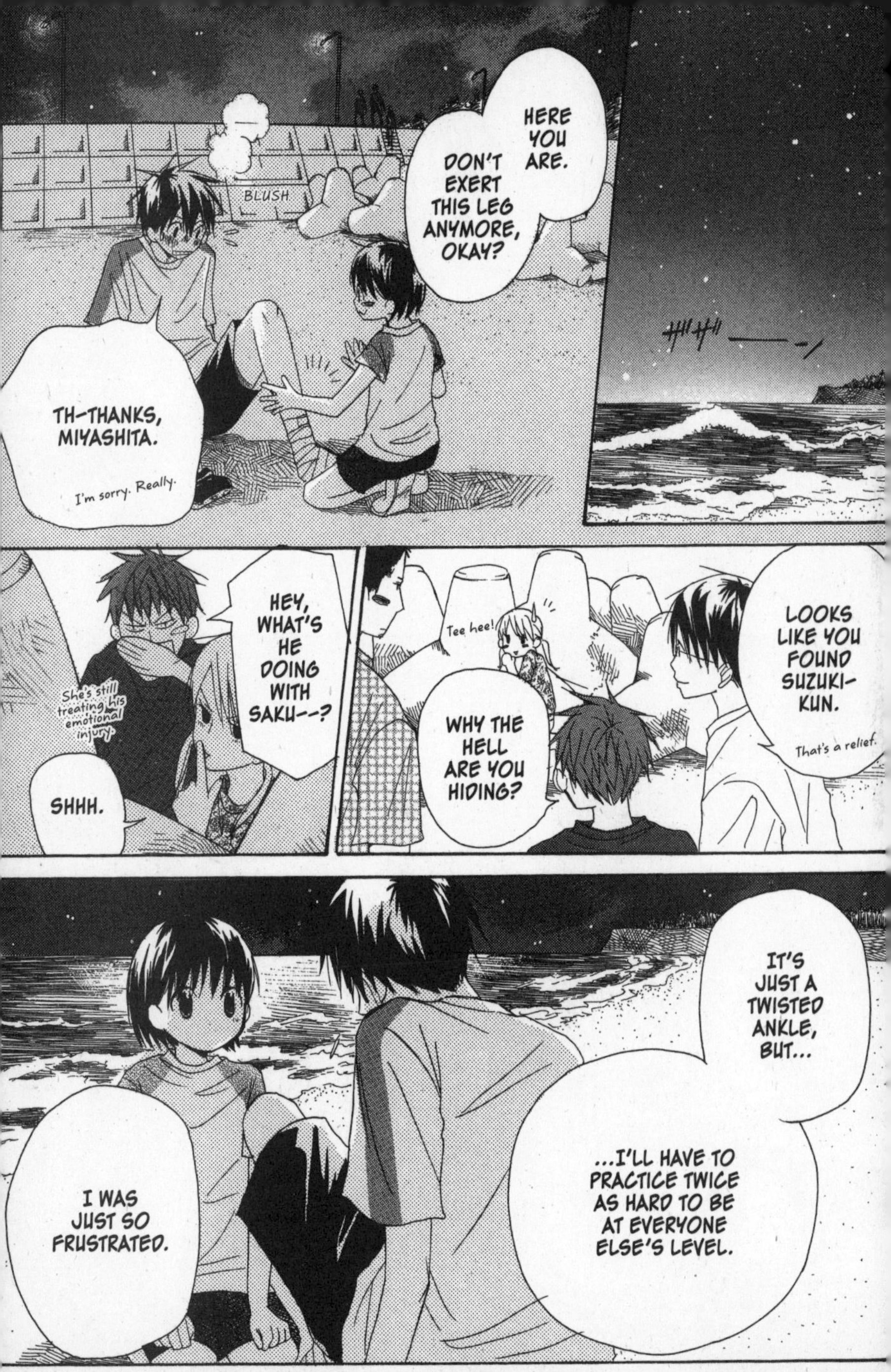
HERE YOU ARE.
DON'T EXERT THIS LEG ANYMORE, OKAY?
BLUSH
TH-THANKS, MIYASHITA.
I'm sorry. Really.
LOOKS LIKE YOU FOUND SUZUKI-KUN.
That's a relief.
Tee hee!
WHY THE HELL ARE YOU HIDING?
HEY, WHAT'S HE DOING WITH SAKU--?
She's still treating his emotional injury.
SHHH.
IT'S JUST A TWISTED ANKLE, BUT...
...I'LL HAVE TO PRACTICE TWICE AS HARD TO BE AT EVERYONE ELSE'S LEVEL.
I WAS JUST SO FRUSTRATED.

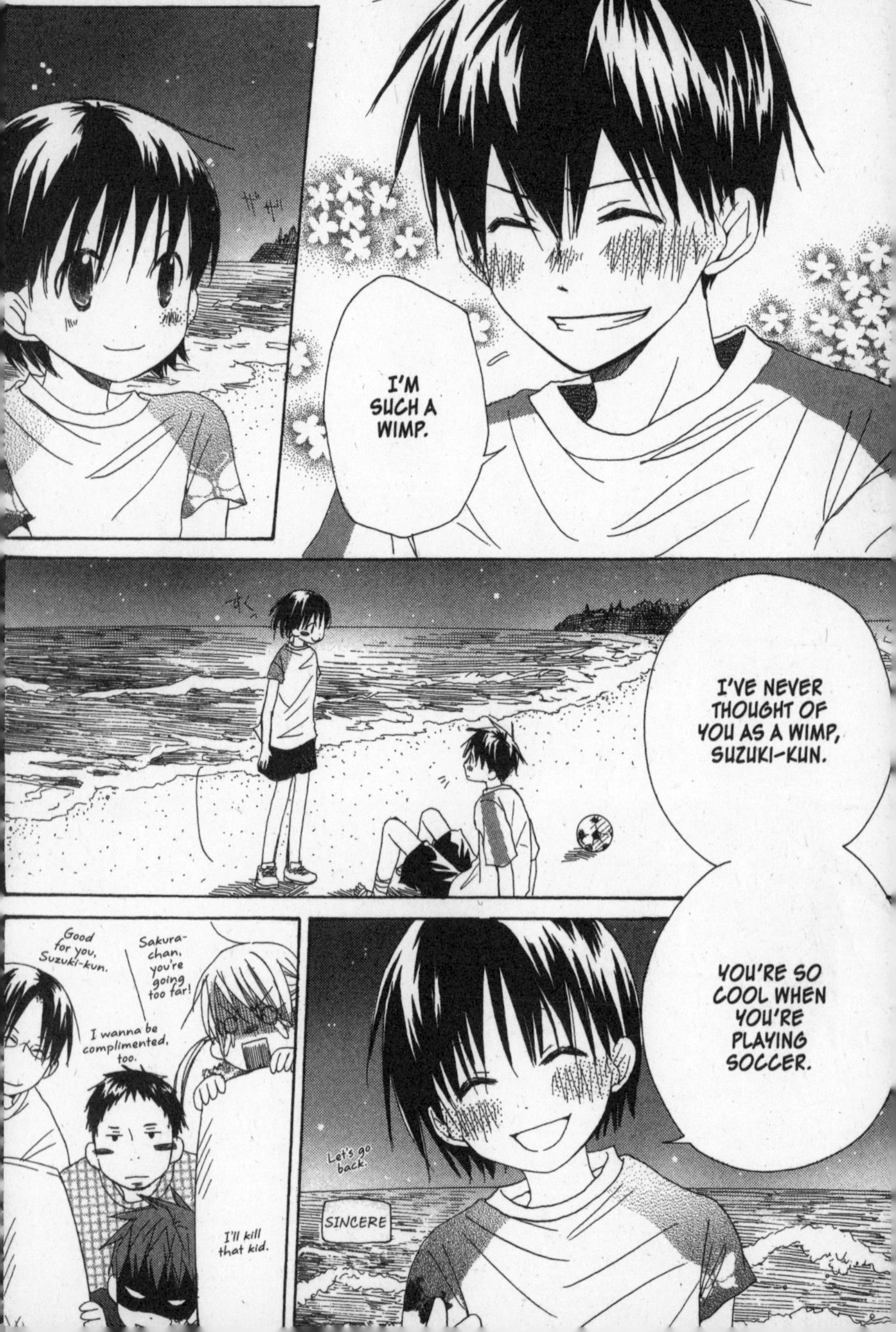
I'M SUCH A WIMP.
I'VE NEVER THOUGHT OF YOU AS A WIMP, SUZUKI-KUN.
YOU'RE SO COOL WHEN YOU'RE PLAYING SOCCER.
Let's go back.
SINCERE
Sakura-chan, you're going too far!
Good for you, Suzuki-kun.
I wanna be complimented, too.
I'll kill that kid.

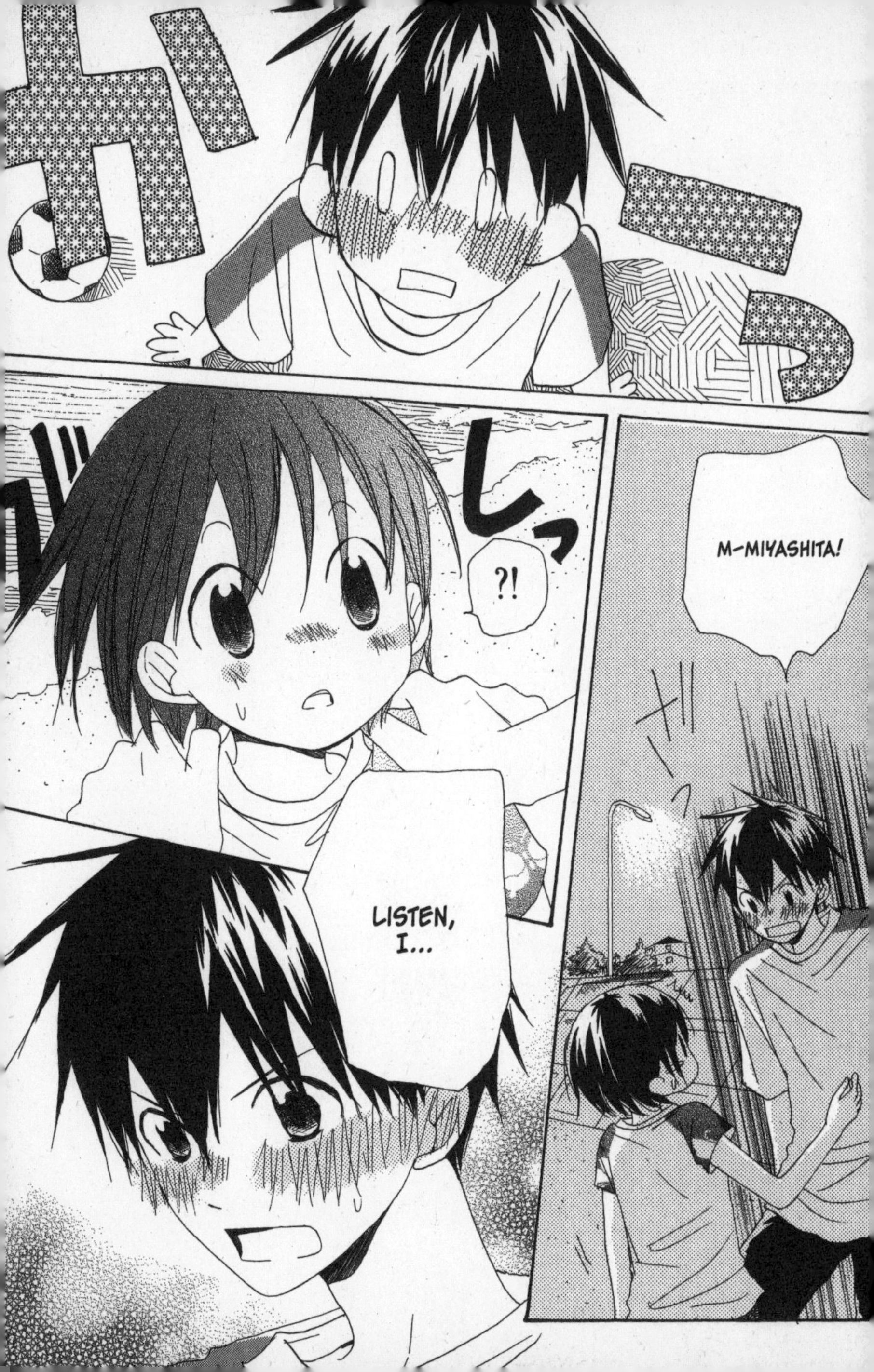
M-MIYASHITA!
?!
LISTEN, I...

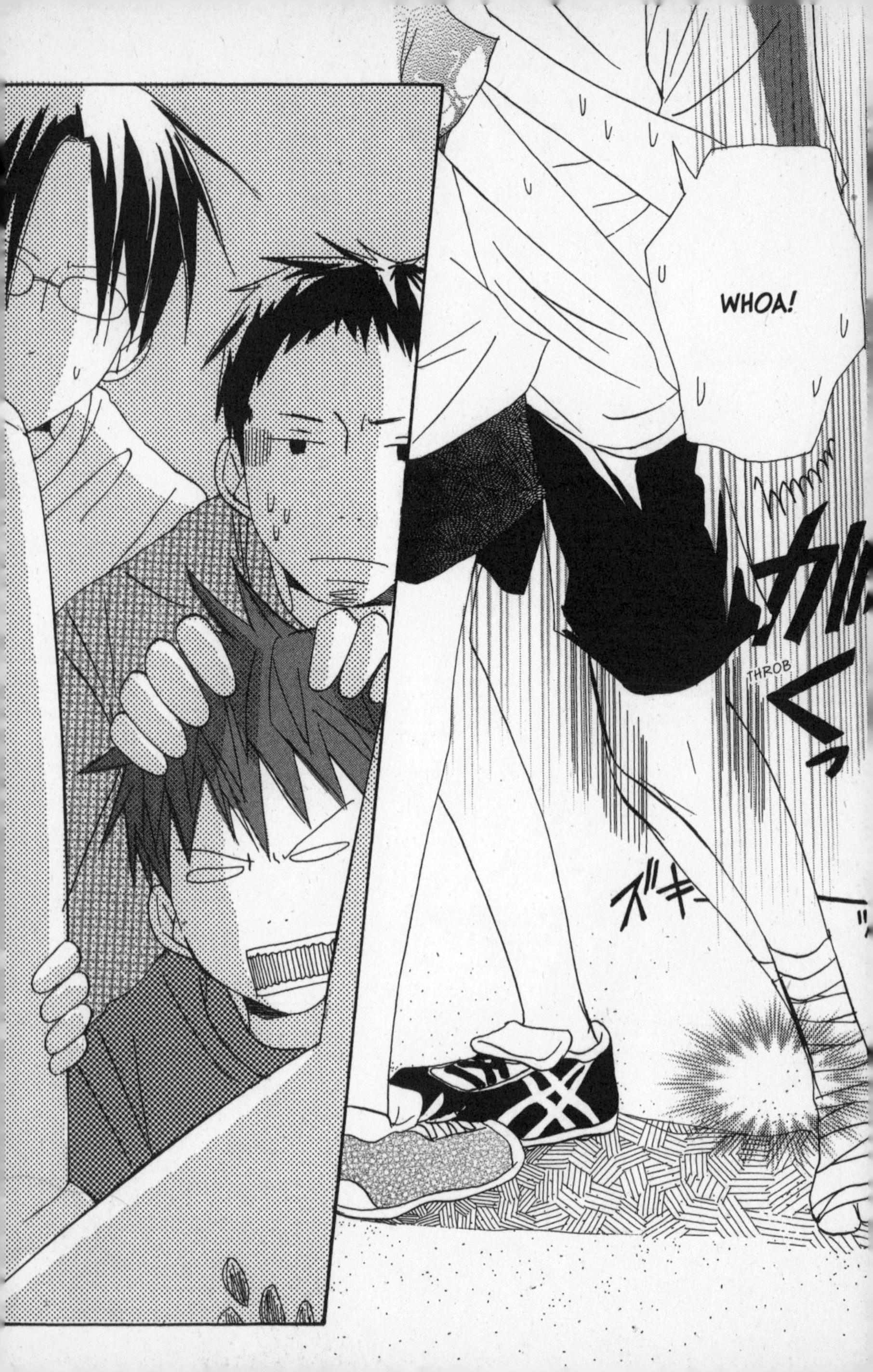
WHOA!
THROB

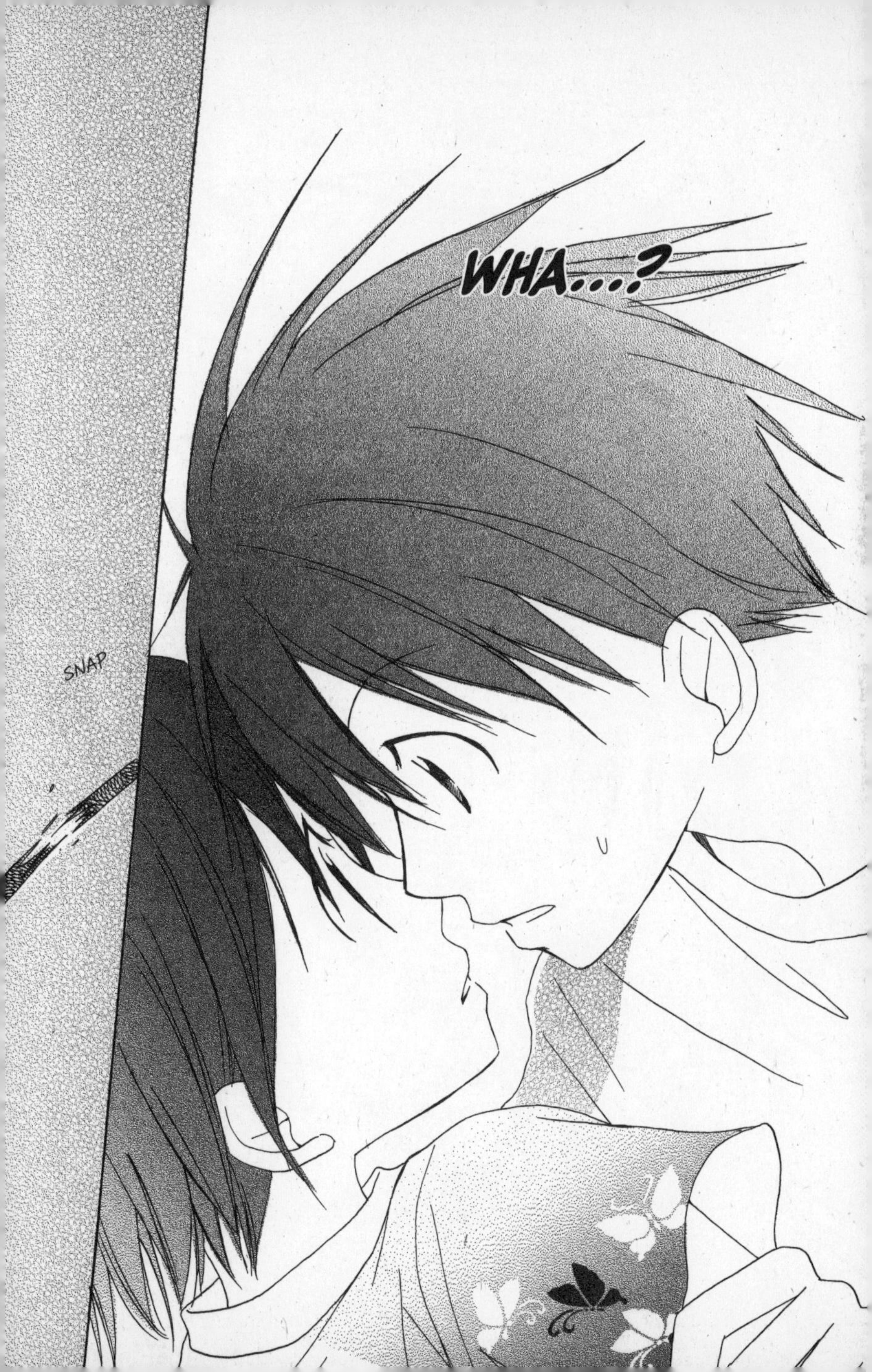
WHA...?
SNAP

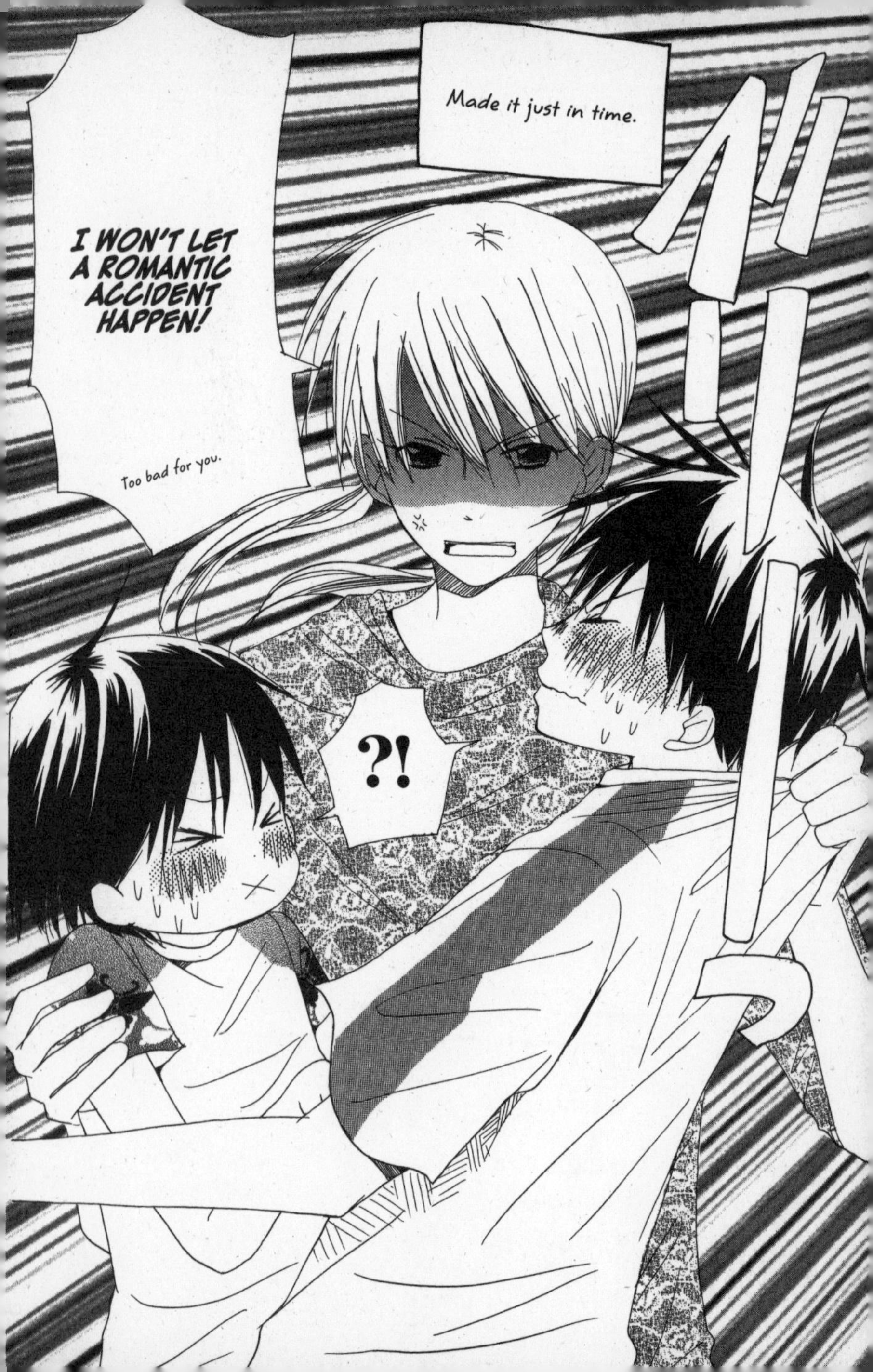
Made it just in time.
I WON'T LET A ROMANTIC ACCIDENT HAPPEN!
Too bad for you.
?!

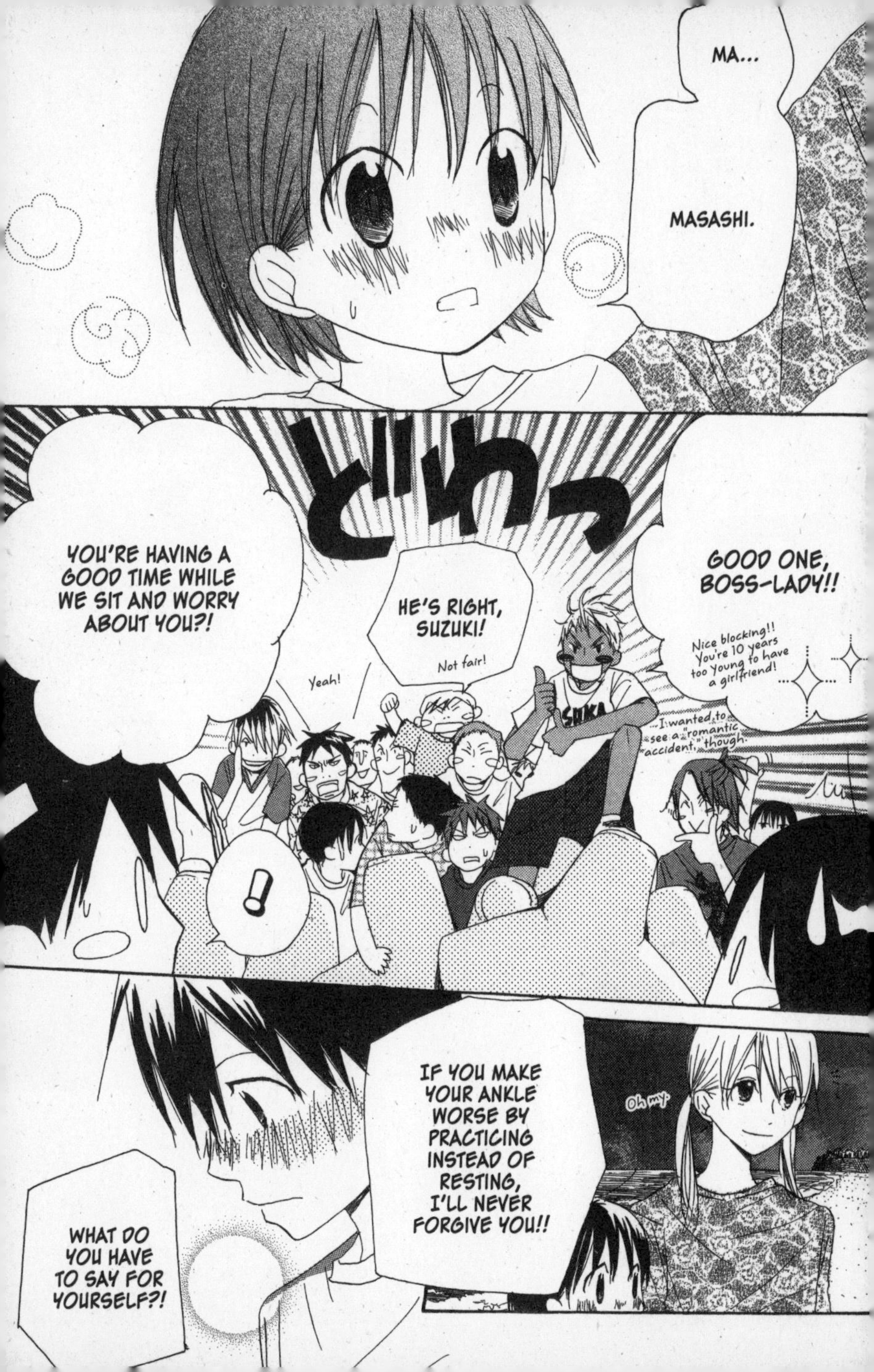
MA...
MASASHI.
GOOD ONE, BOSS-LADY!!
Nice blocking!! You're 10 years too young to have a girlfriend!
...I wanted to see a "romantic accident," though.
とりゃっ
HE'S RIGHT, SUZUKI!
Not fair!
Yeah!
YOU'RE HAVING A GOOD TIME WHILE WE SIT AND WORRY ABOUT YOU?!
!
Oh my.
IF YOU MAKE YOUR ANKLE WORSE BY PRACTICING INSTEAD OF RESTING, I'LL NEVER FORGIVE YOU!!
WHAT DO YOU HAVE TO SAY FOR YOURSELF?!

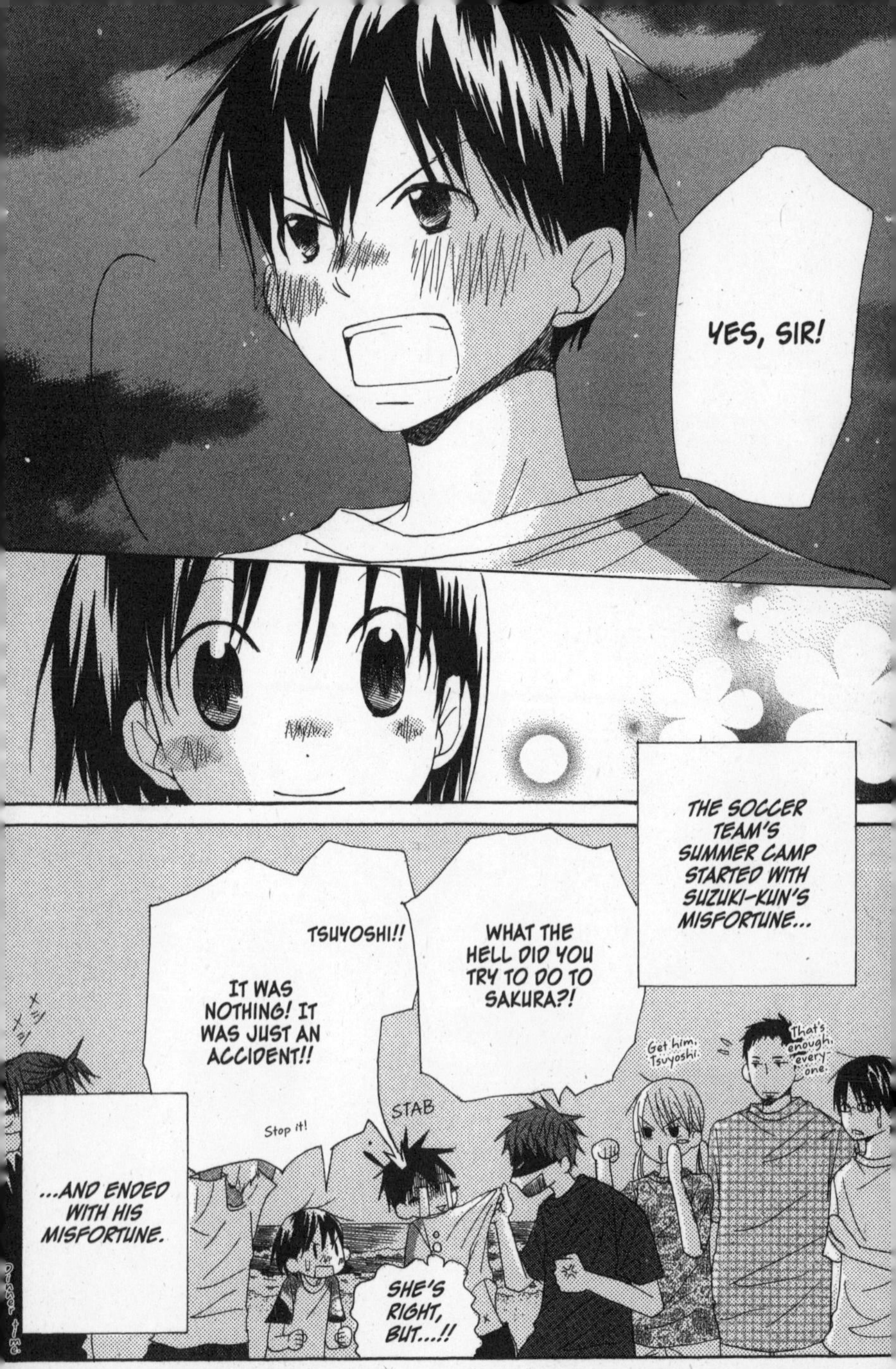
YES, SIR!
THE SOCCER TEAM'S SUMMER CAMP STARTED WITH SUZUKI-KUN'S MISFORTUNE...
WHAT THE HELL DID YOU TRY TO DO TO SAKURA?!
TSUYOSHI!!
IT WAS NOTHING! IT WAS JUST AN ACCIDENT!!
That's enough, every one.
Get him, Tsuyoshi.
STAB
Stop it!
SHE'S RIGHT, BUT...!!
...AND ENDED WITH HIS MISFORTUNE.
Dinner time

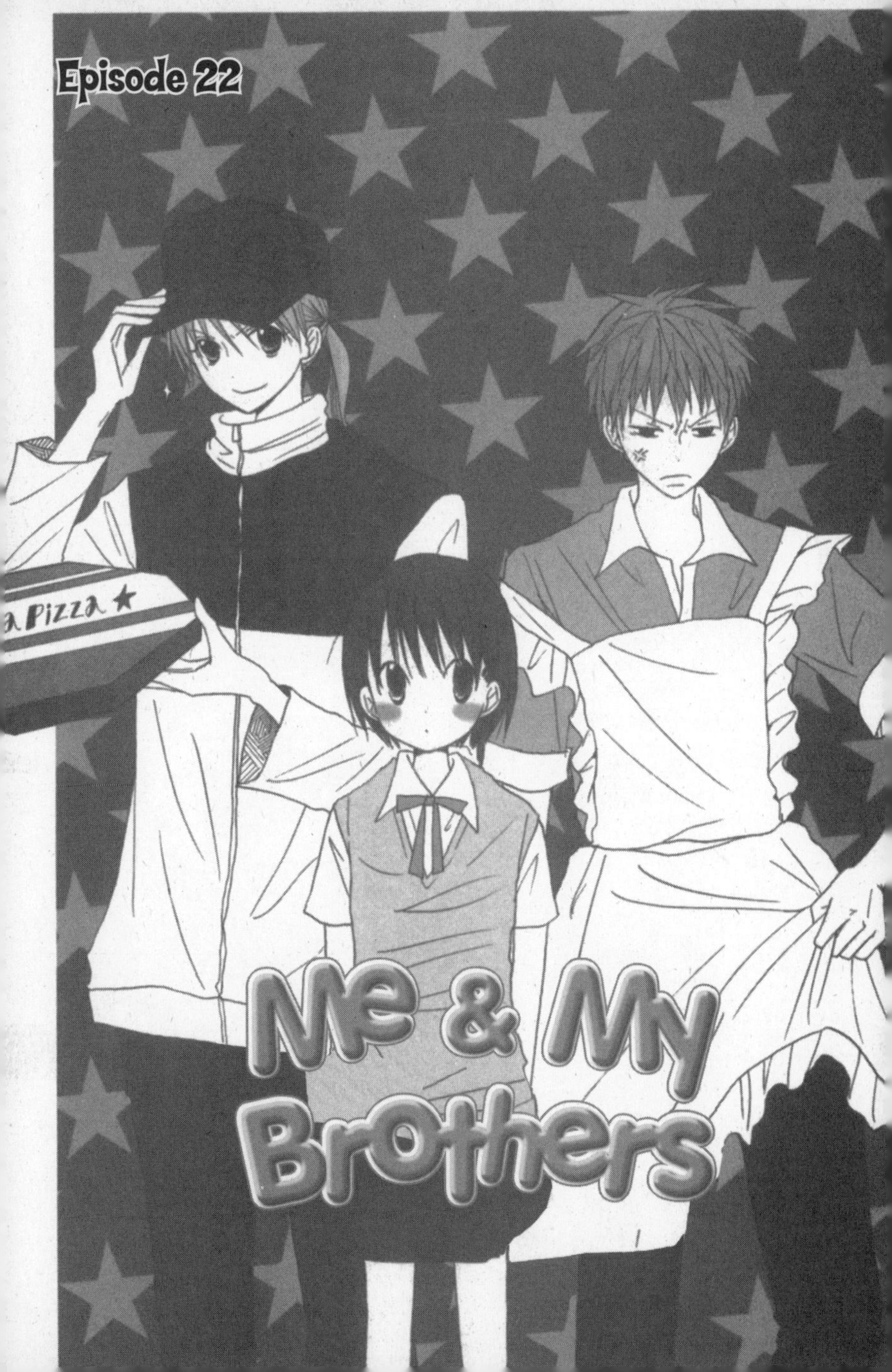
Episode 22
a Pizza ★
Me & My Brothers

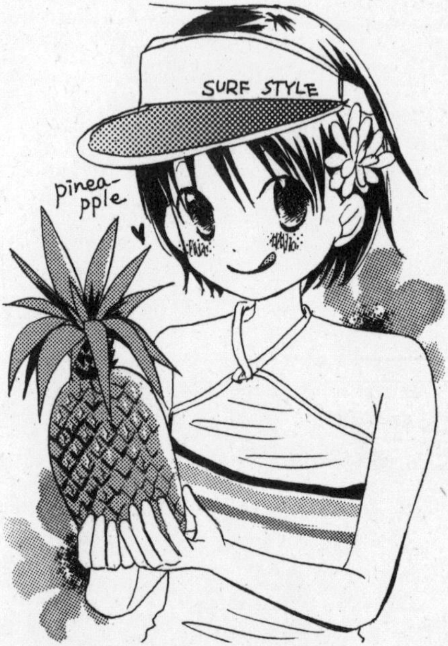
SURF STYLE
pinea-
pple

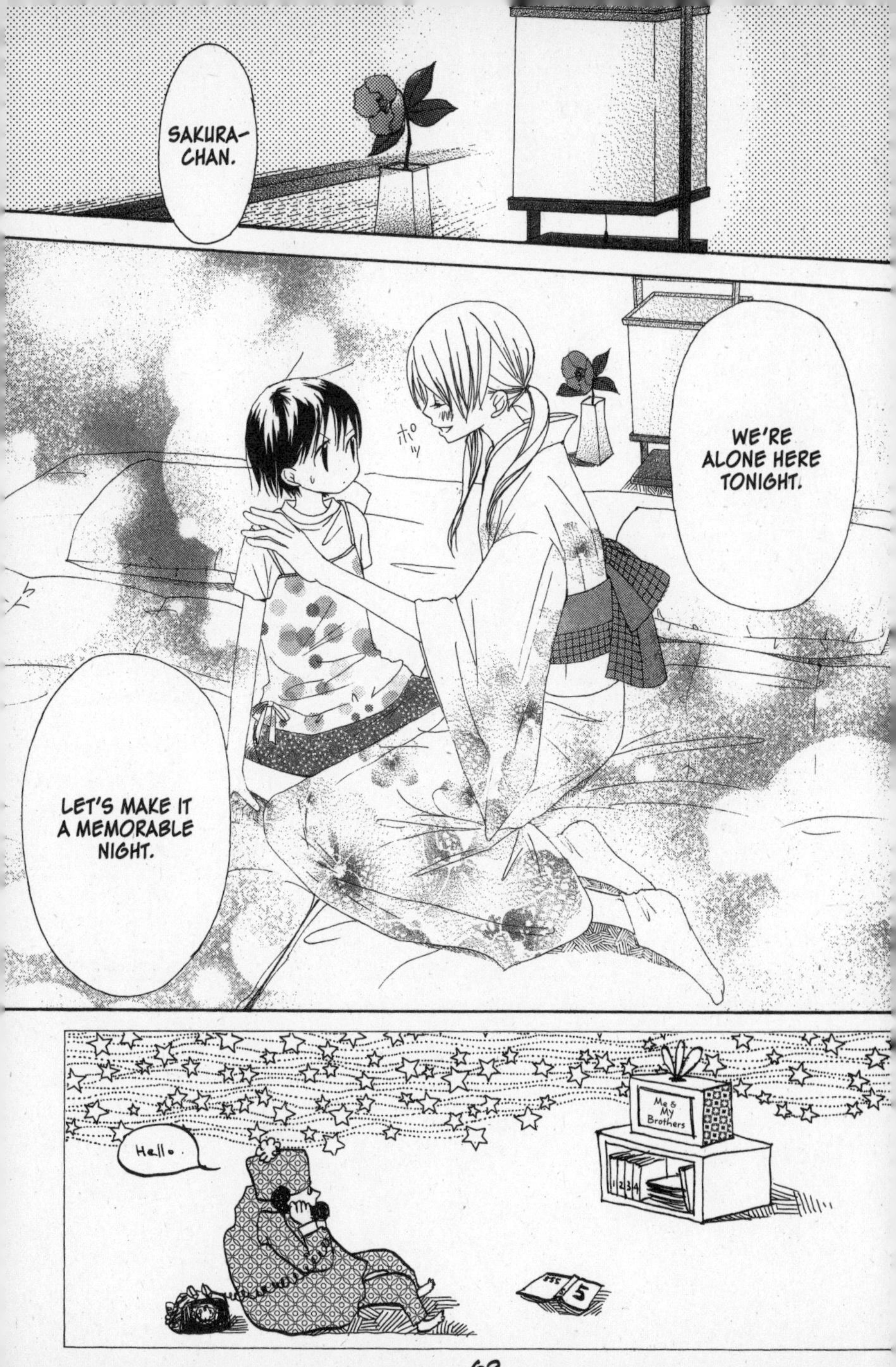
SAKURA-CHAN.
WE'RE ALONE HERE TONIGHT.
ポッ
LET'S MAKE IT A MEMORABLE NIGHT.
Hello..
Me & My Brothers
5

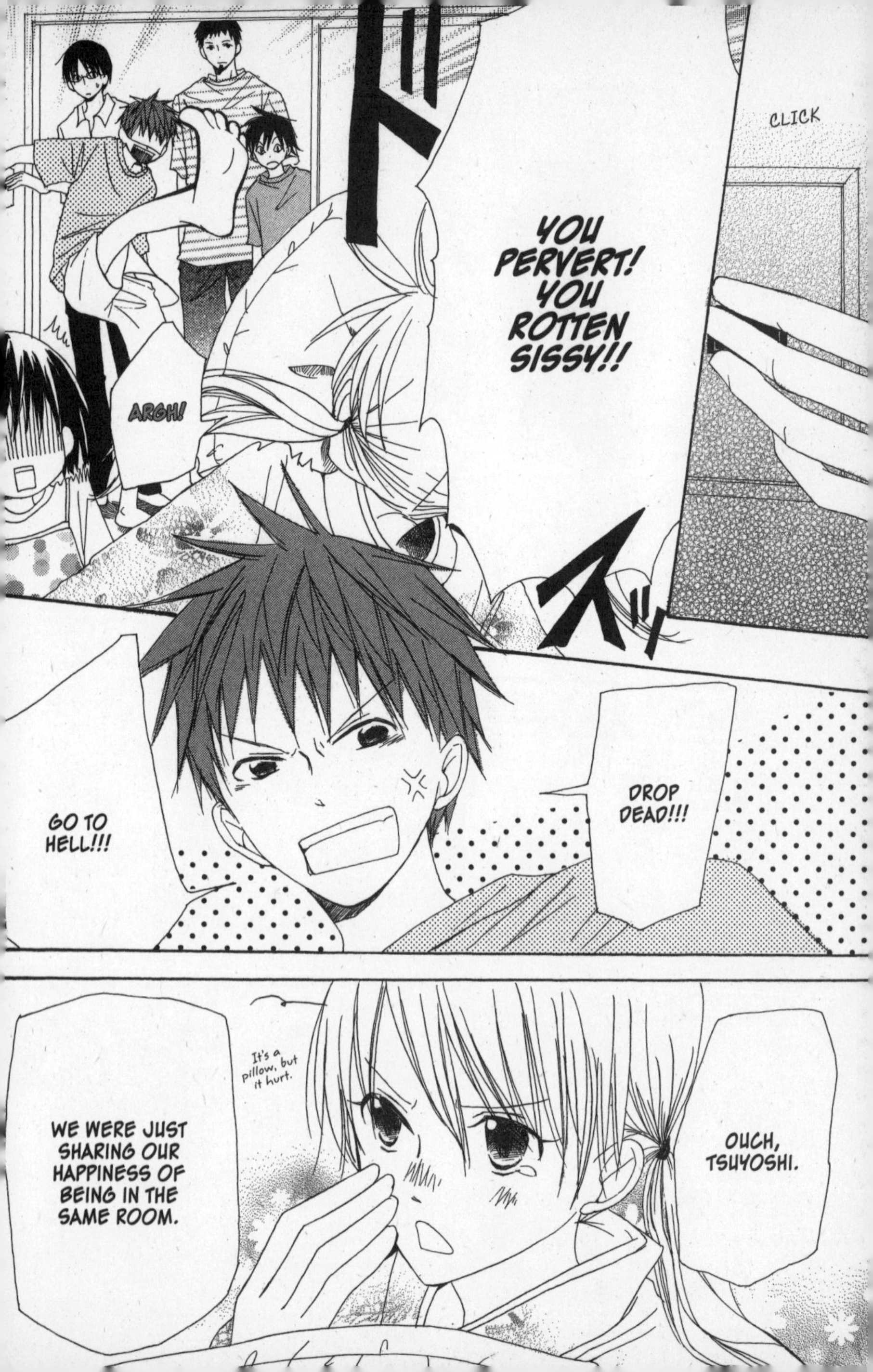
CLICK
YOU PERVERT! YOU ROTTEN SISSY!!
ド
ARGH!
DROP DEAD!!!
GO TO HELL!!!
OUCH, TSUYOSHI.
It's a pillow, but it hurt.
WE WERE JUST SHARING OUR HAPPINESS OF BEING IN THE SAME ROOM.

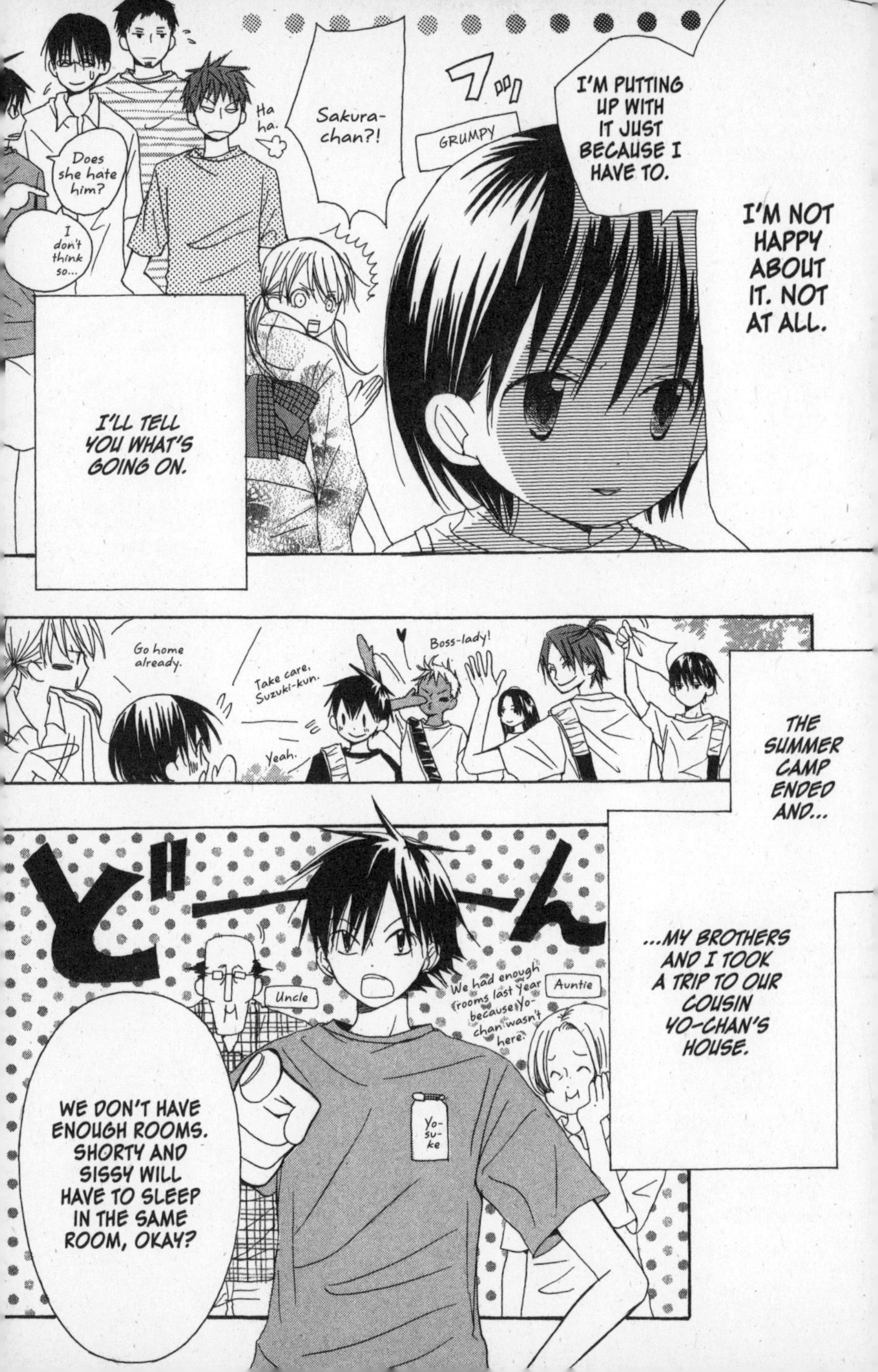
I'M PUTTING UP WITH IT JUST BECAUSE I HAVE TO.
I'M NOT HAPPY ABOUT IT. NOT AT ALL.
GRUMPY
Sakura-chan?!
Ha ha.
Does she hate him?
I don't think so...
I'LL TELL YOU WHAT'S GOING ON.
THE SUMMER CAMP ENDED AND...
Boss-lady!
Take care, Suzuki-kun.
Yeah.
Go home already.
...MY BROTHERS AND I TOOK A TRIP TO OUR COUSIN YO-CHAN'S HOUSE.
どーん
Auntie
We had enough rooms last year because Yo-chan wasn't here.
Uncle
Yo-suke
WE DON'T HAVE ENOUGH ROOMS. SHORTY AND SISSY WILL HAVE TO SLEEP IN THE SAME ROOM, OKAY?

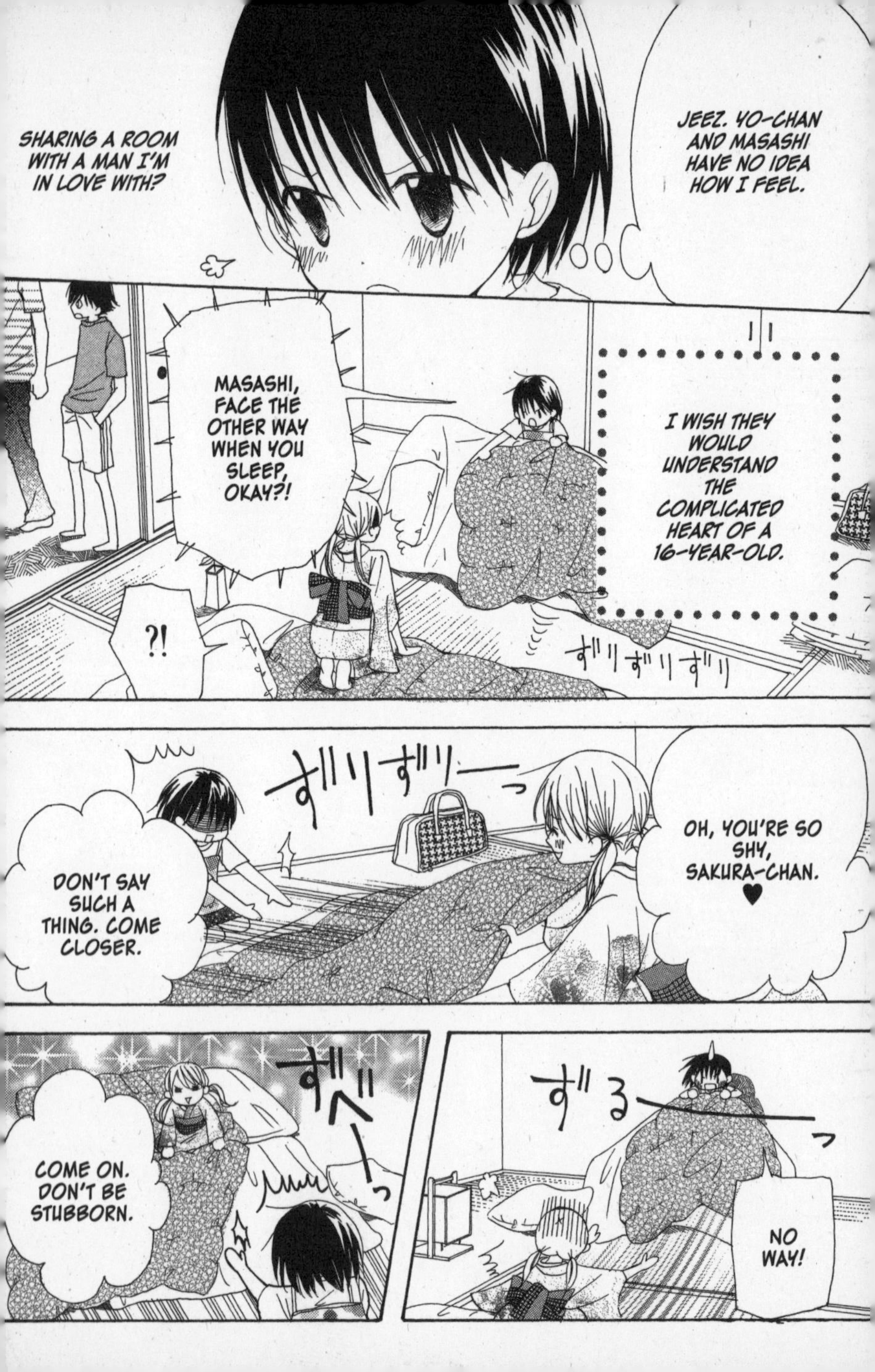

JEEZ. YO-CHAN AND MASASHI HAVE NO IDEA HOW I FEEL.
SHARING A ROOM WITH A MAN I'M IN LOVE WITH?
I WISH THEY WOULD UNDERSTAND THE COMPLICATED HEART OF A 16-YEAR-OLD.
ずりずりずり
MASASHI, FACE THE OTHER WAY WHEN YOU SLEEP, OKAY?!
?!
OH, YOU'RE SO SHY, SAKURA-CHAN. ♥
ずりりずりーっ
DON'T SAY SUCH A THING. COME CLOSER.
ずるーっ
NO WAY!
ずべーっ
COME ON. DON'T BE STUBBORN.

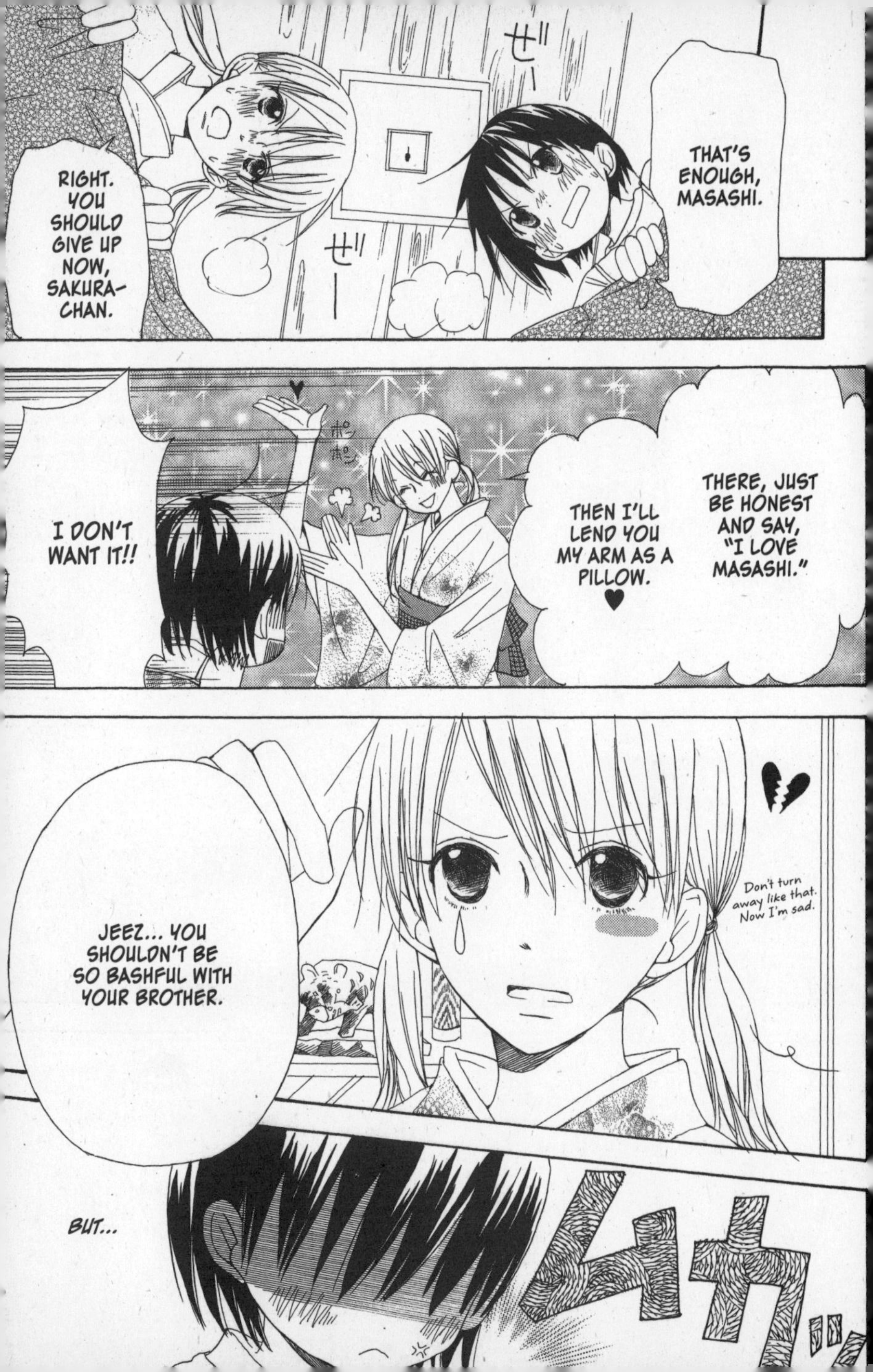
THAT'S ENOUGH, MASASHI.
RIGHT. YOU SHOULD GIVE UP NOW, SAKURA-CHAN.
THERE, JUST BE HONEST AND SAY, "I LOVE MASASHI."
THEN I'LL LEND YOU MY ARM AS A PILLOW. ♥
I DON'T WANT IT!!
Don't turn away like that. Now I'm sad.
JEEZ... YOU SHOULDN'T BE SO BASHFUL WITH YOUR BROTHER.
BUT...
ムカッ

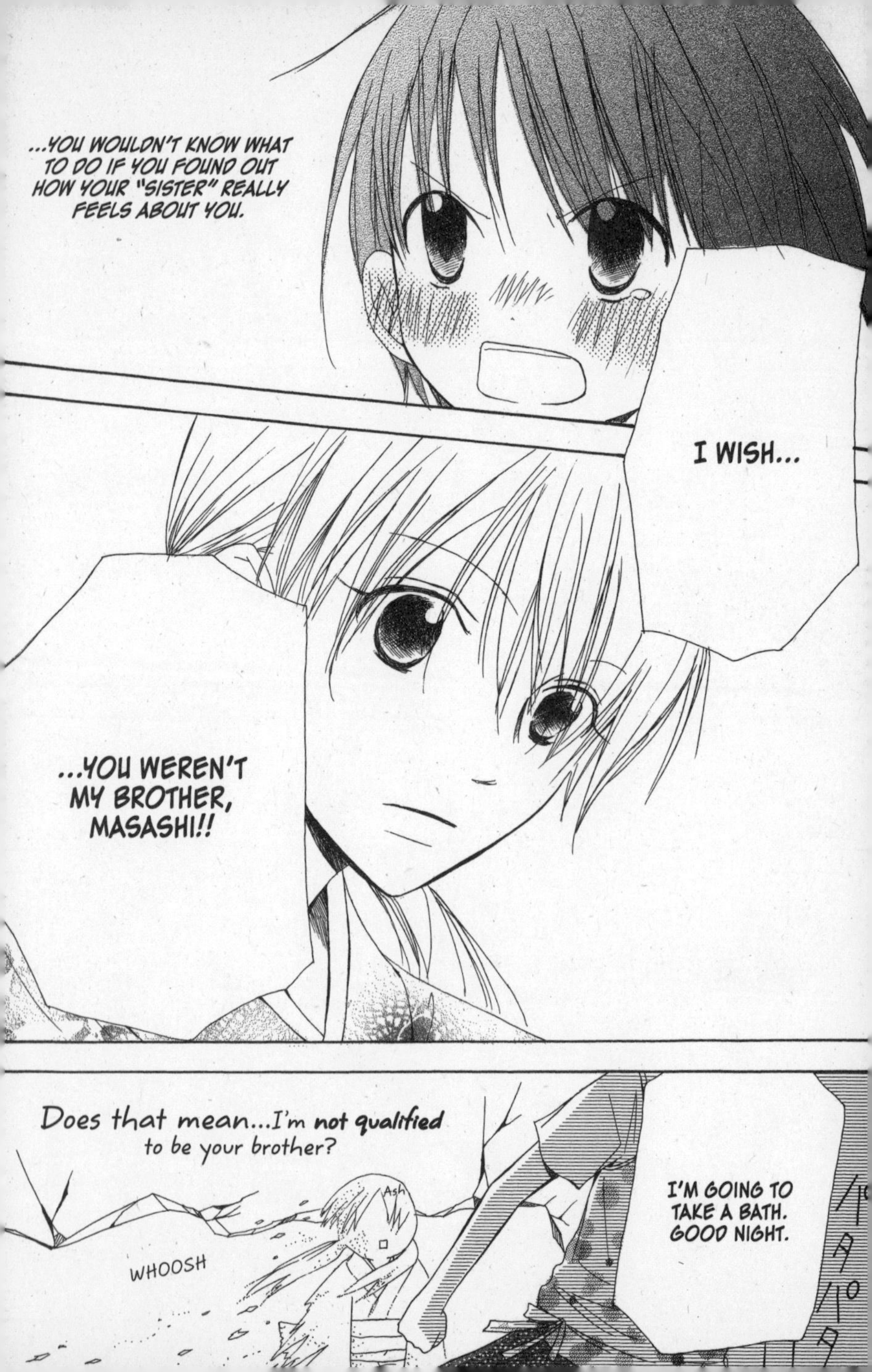
...YOU WOULDN'T KNOW WHAT TO DO IF YOU FOUND OUT HOW YOUR "SISTER" REALLY FEELS ABOUT YOU.
I WISH...
...YOU WEREN'T MY BROTHER, MASASHI!!
I'M GOING TO TAKE A BATH. GOOD NIGHT.
Does that mean...I'm **not qualified** to be your brother?
Ash
WHOOSH

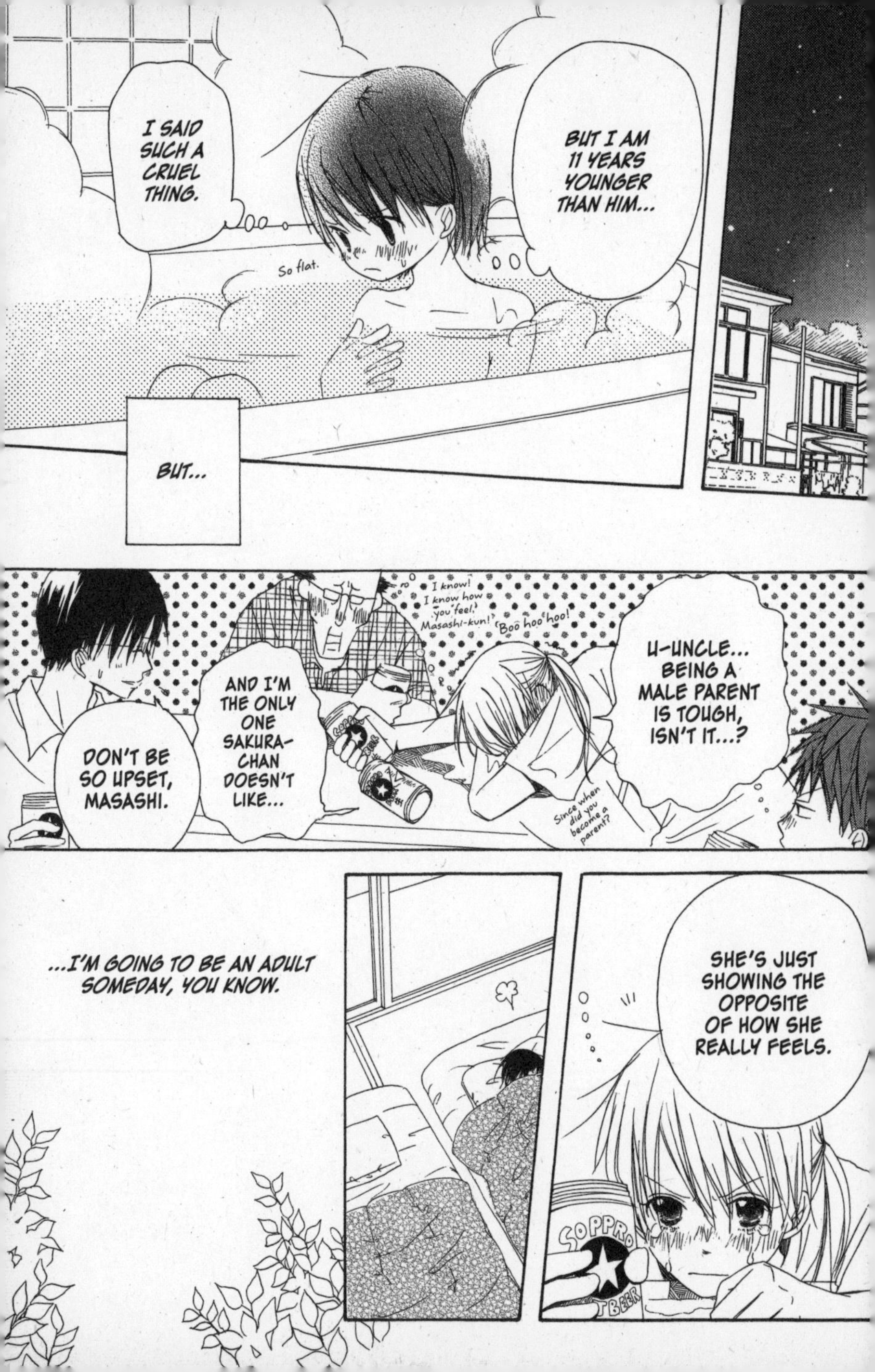
BUT I AM 11 YEARS YOUNGER THAN HIM...
I SAID SUCH A CRUEL THING.
So flat.
BUT...
U-UNCLE... BEING A MALE PARENT IS TOUGH, ISN'T IT...?
Since when did you become a parent?
Boo hoo hoo!
I know! I know how you feel, Masashi-kun!
AND I'M THE ONLY ONE SAKURA-CHAN DOESN'T LIKE...
DON'T BE SO UPSET, MASASHI.
SHE'S JUST SHOWING THE OPPOSITE OF HOW SHE REALLY FEELS.
...I'M GOING TO BE AN ADULT SOMEDAY, YOU KNOW.

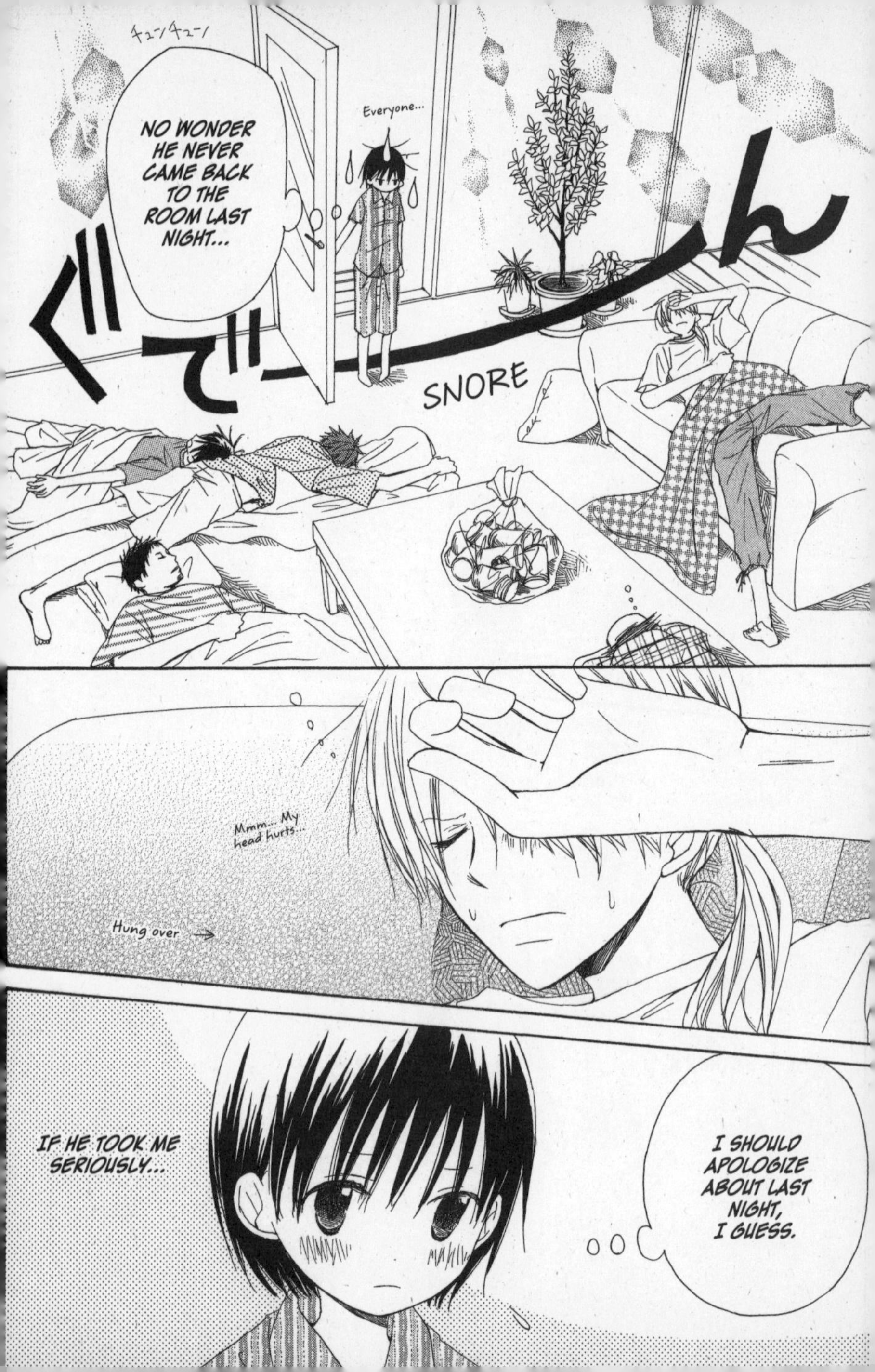

ぐでーーん
Everyone...
チュンチューン
NO WONDER HE NEVER CAME BACK TO THE ROOM LAST NIGHT...
SNORE
Mmm... My head hurts...
Hung over →
I SHOULD APOLOGIZE ABOUT LAST NIGHT, I GUESS.
IF HE TOOK ME SERIOUSLY...

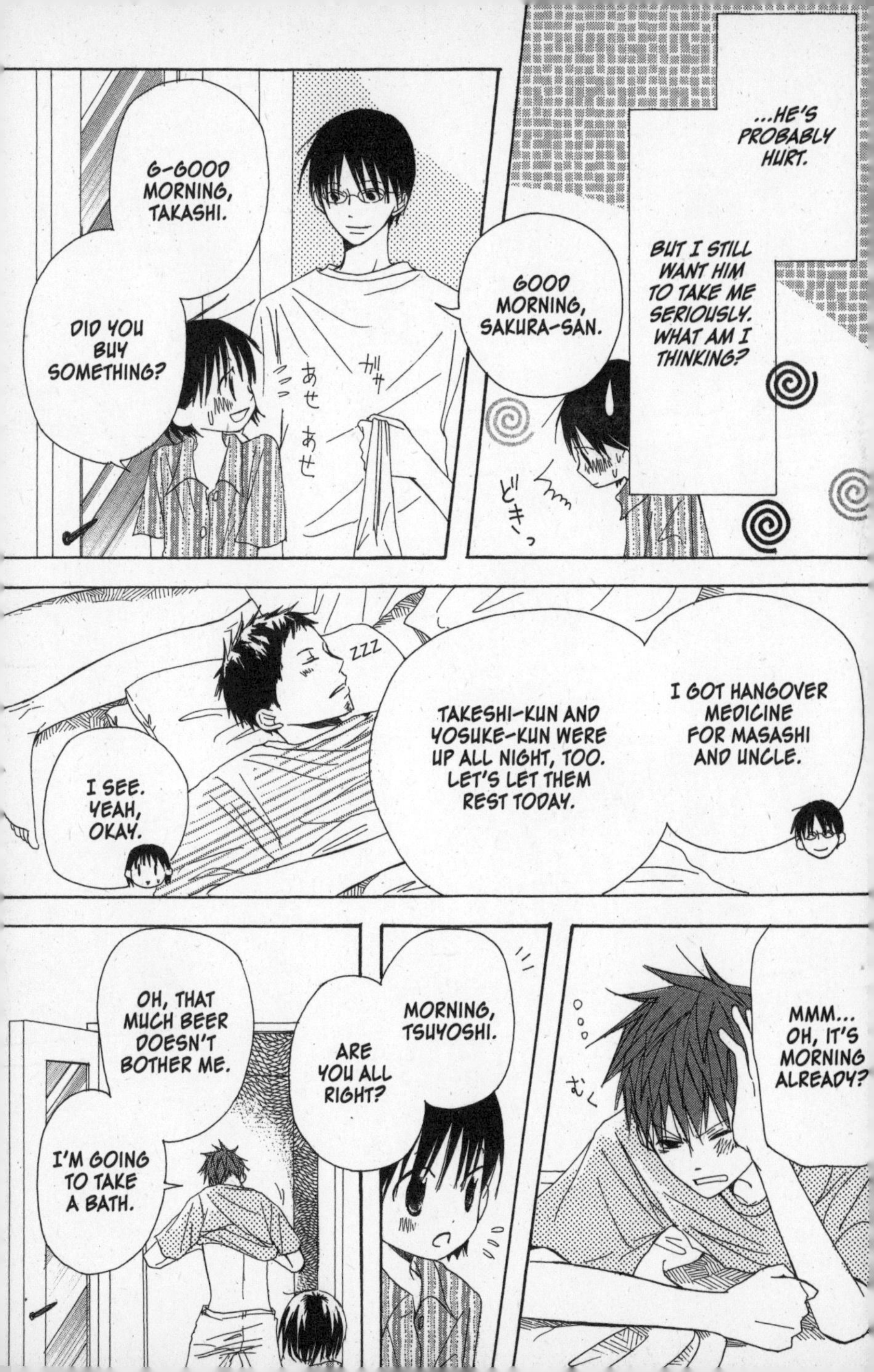
...HE'S PROBABLY HURT.
BUT I STILL WANT HIM TO TAKE ME SERIOUSLY. WHAT AM I THINKING?
どきっ
G-GOOD MORNING, TAKASHI.
GOOD MORNING, SAKURA-SAN.
ガサ
DID YOU BUY SOMETHING?
あせあせ
I GOT HANGOVER MEDICINE FOR MASASHI AND UNCLE.
TAKESHI-KUN AND YOSUKE-KUN WERE UP ALL NIGHT, TOO. LET'S LET THEM REST TODAY.
ZZZ
I SEE. YEAH, OKAY.
MMM... OH, IT'S MORNING ALREADY?
むく
MORNING, TSUYOSHI.
ARE YOU ALL RIGHT?
OH, THAT MUCH BEER DOESN'T BOTHER ME.
I'M GOING TO TAKE A BATH.

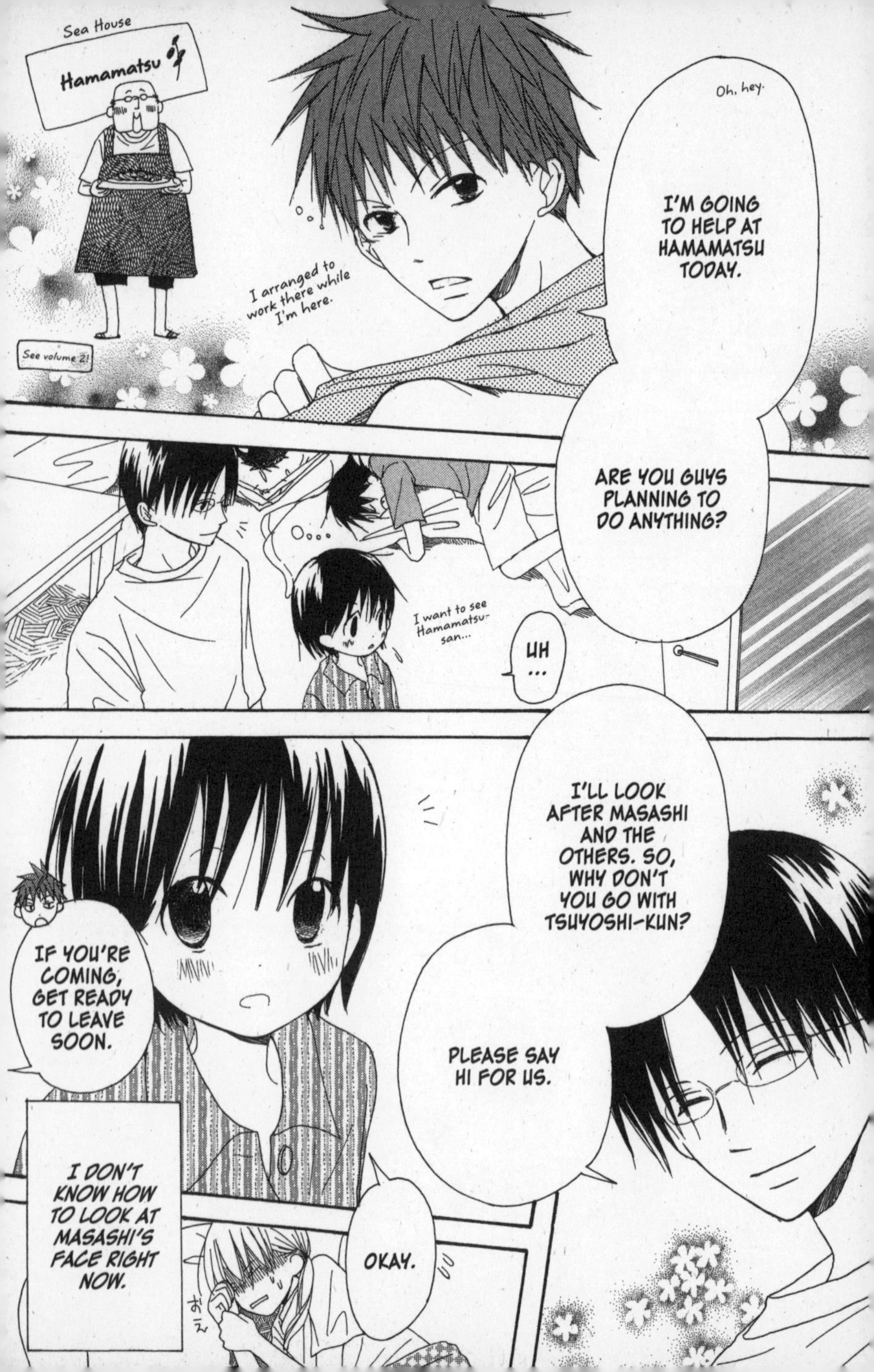
Oh, hey.
I'M GOING TO HELP AT HAMAMATSU TODAY.
I arranged to work there while I'm here.
Sea House
Hamamatsu
See volume 2!
ARE YOU GUYS PLANNING TO DO ANYTHING?
UH...
I want to see Hamamatsu-san...
I'LL LOOK AFTER MASASHI AND THE OTHERS. SO, WHY DON'T YOU GO WITH TSUYOSHI-KUN?
PLEASE SAY HI FOR US.
IF YOU'RE COMING, GET READY TO LEAVE SOON.
OKAY.
I DON'T KNOW HOW TO LOOK AT MASASHI'S FACE RIGHT NOW.

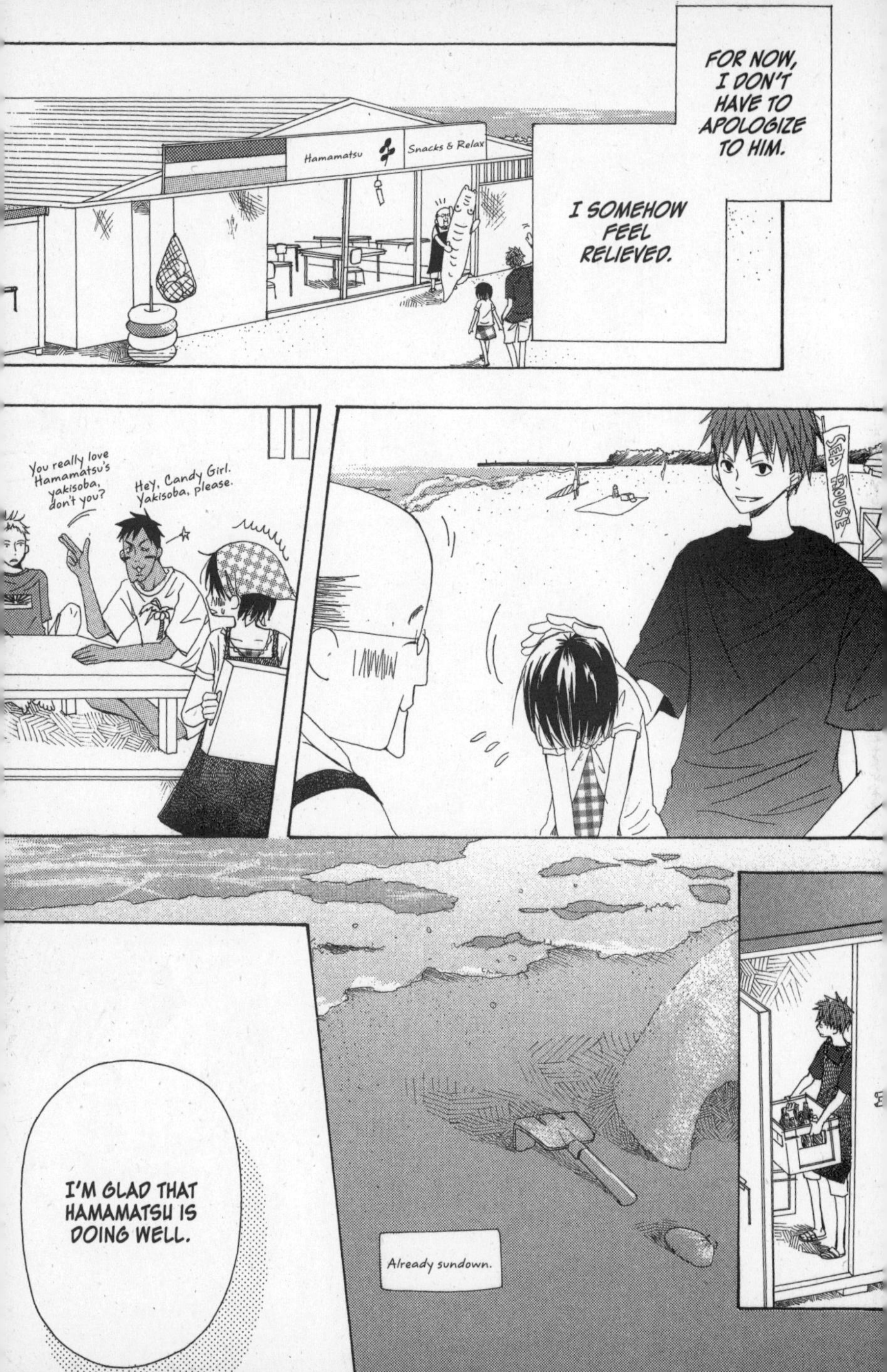
FOR NOW, I DON'T HAVE TO APOLOGIZE TO HIM.
I SOMEHOW FEEL RELIEVED.
Hamamatsu
Snacks & Relax
SEA HOUSE
Hey, Candy Girl. Yakisoba, please.
You really love Hamamatsu's yakisoba, don't you?
Already sundown.
I'M GLAD THAT HAMAMATSU IS DOING WELL.

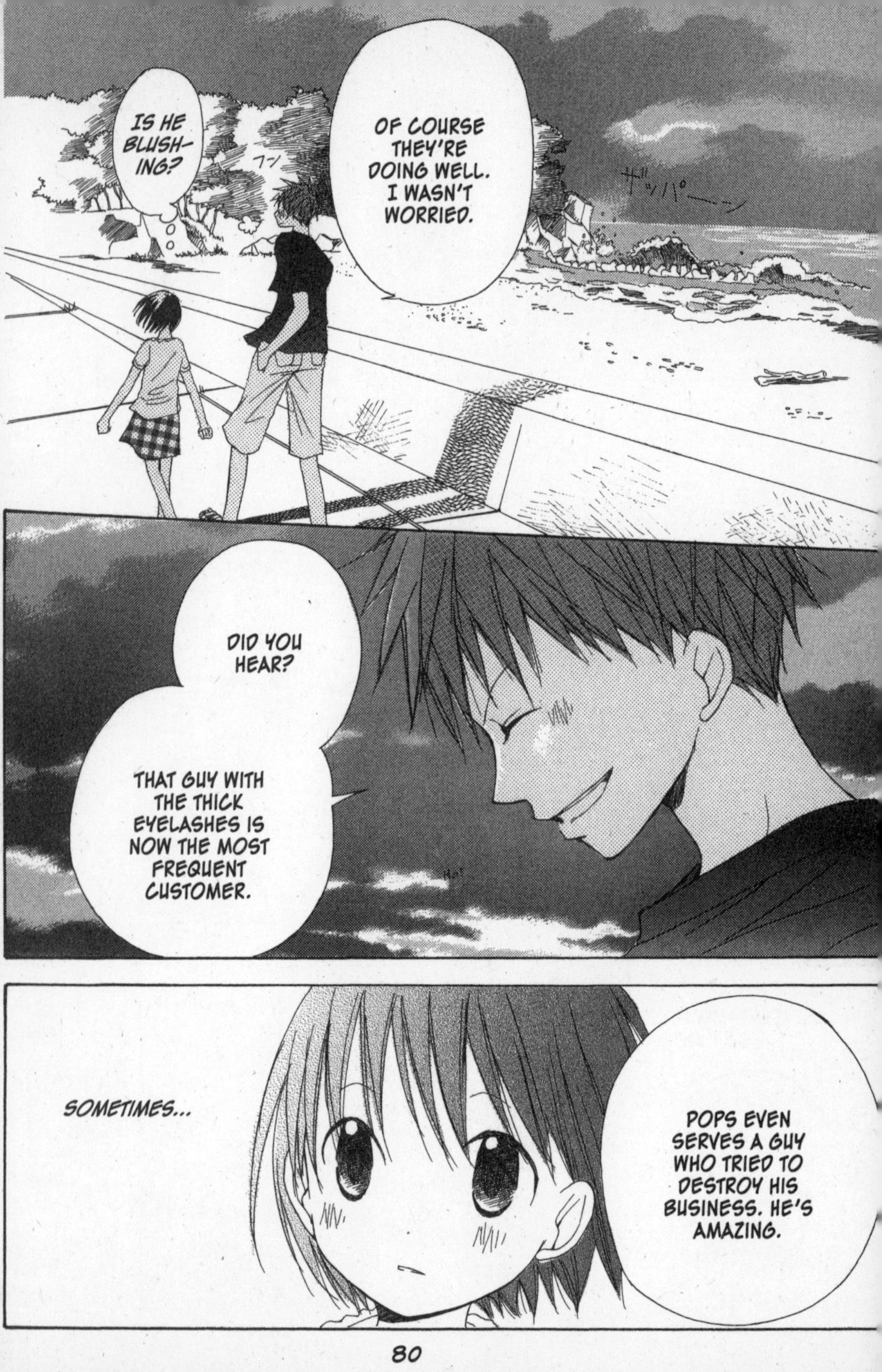
OF COURSE THEY'RE DOING WELL. I WASN'T WORRIED.
IS HE BLUSHING?
DID YOU HEAR?
THAT GUY WITH THE THICK EYELASHES IS NOW THE MOST FREQUENT CUSTOMER.
POPS EVEN SERVES A GUY WHO TRIED TO DESTROY HIS BUSINESS. HE'S AMAZING.
SOMETIMES...

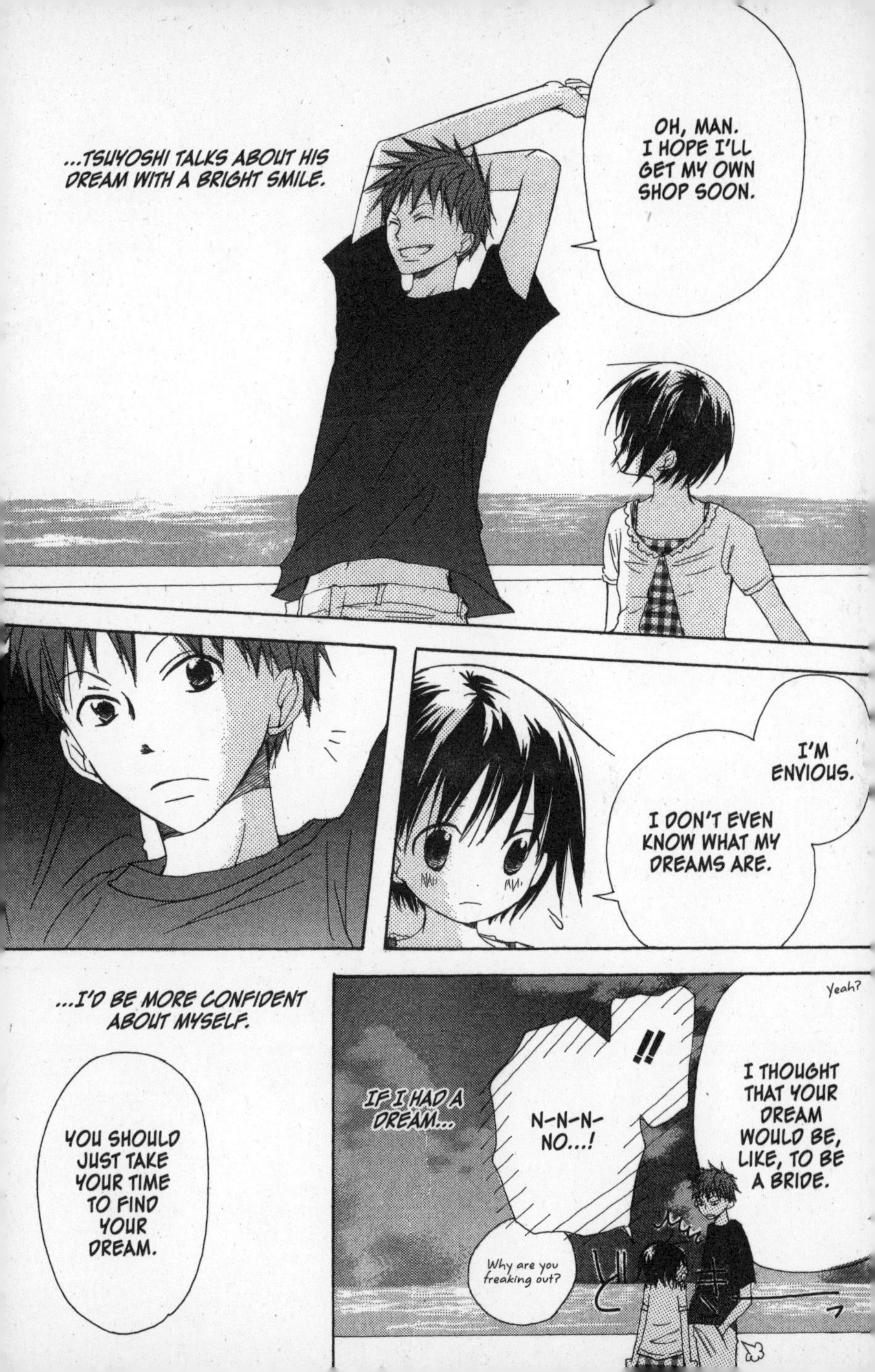
OH, MAN. I HOPE I'LL GET MY OWN SHOP SOON.
...TSUYOSHI TALKS ABOUT HIS DREAM WITH A BRIGHT SMILE.
I'M ENVIOUS.
I DON'T EVEN KNOW WHAT MY DREAMS ARE.
Yeah?
I THOUGHT THAT YOUR DREAM WOULD BE, LIKE, TO BE A BRIDE.
!!
N-N-N-NO...!
Why are you freaking out?
IF I HAD A DREAM...
...I'D BE MORE CONFIDENT ABOUT MYSELF.
YOU SHOULD JUST TAKE YOUR TIME TO FIND YOUR DREAM.

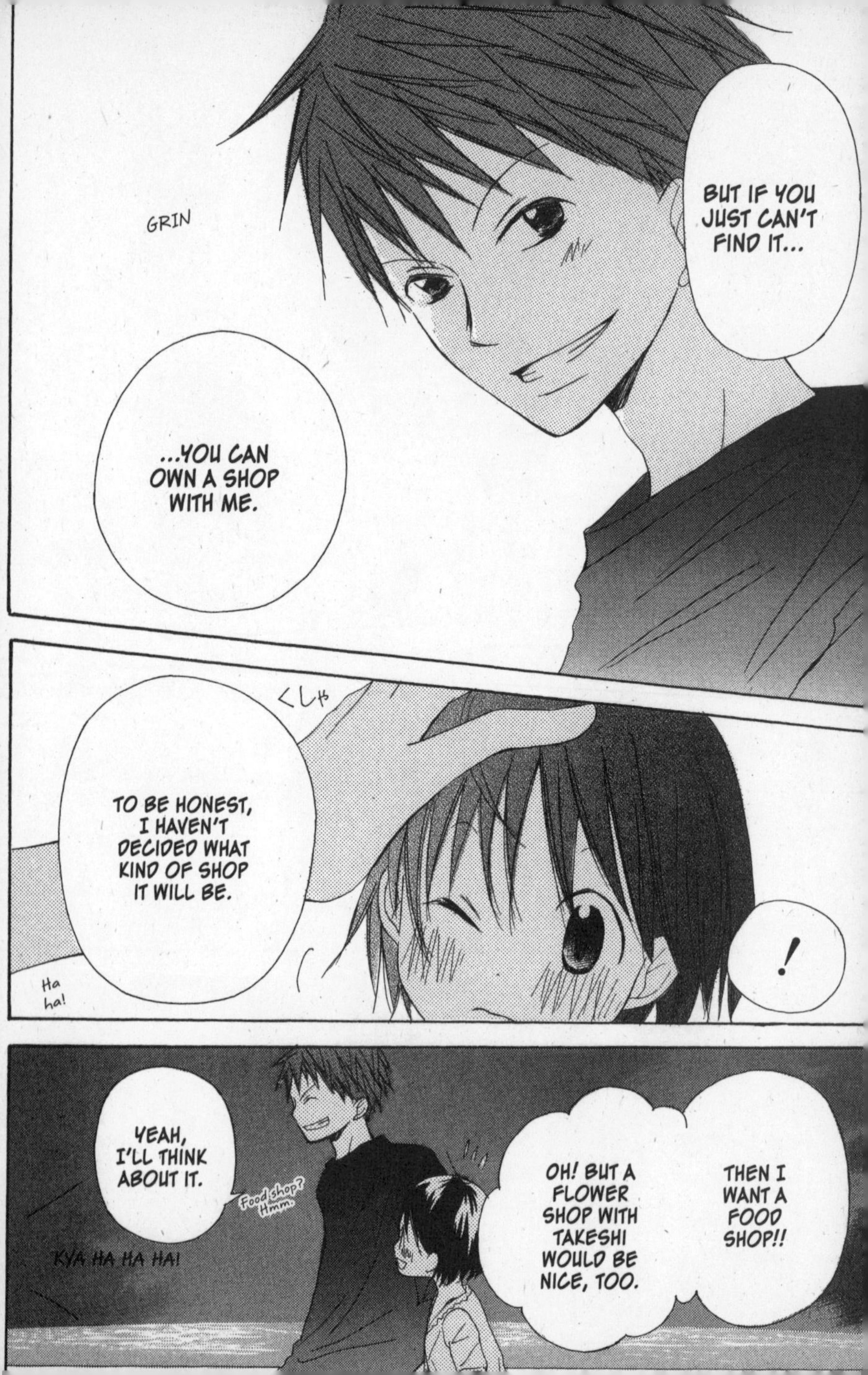
BUT IF YOU JUST CAN'T FIND IT...
GRIN
...YOU CAN OWN A SHOP WITH ME.
くしゃ
!
TO BE HONEST, I HAVEN'T DECIDED WHAT KIND OF SHOP IT WILL BE.
Ha ha!
THEN I WANT A FOOD SHOP!!
OH! BUT A FLOWER SHOP WITH TAKESHI WOULD BE NICE, TOO.
Food shop? Hmm.
YEAH, I'LL THINK ABOUT IT.
KYA HA HA HA!

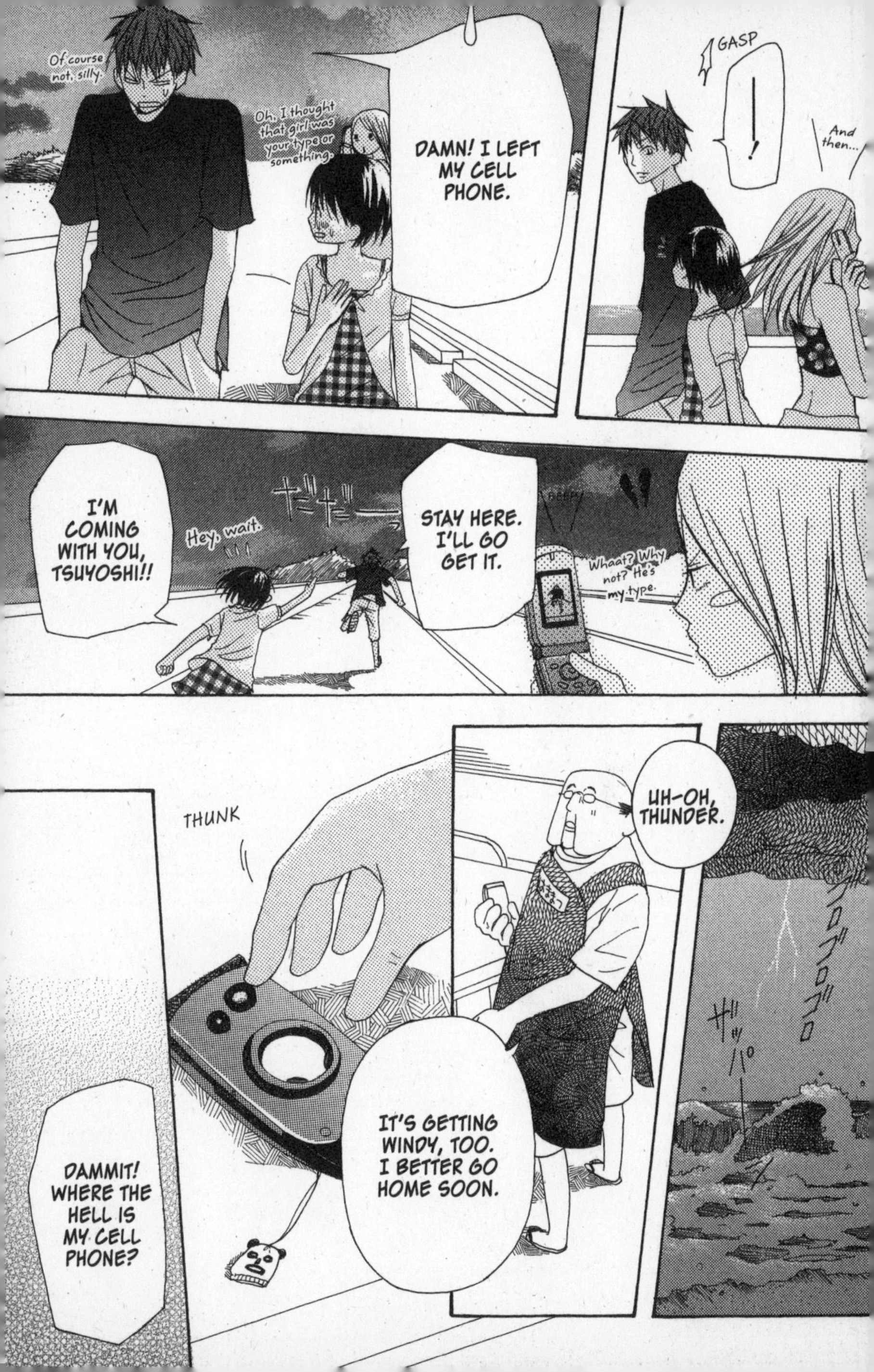
GASP
!
And then...
Oh, I thought that girl was your type or something.
Of course not, silly.
DAMN! I LEFT MY CELL PHONE.
BEEP
Whaat? Why not? He's my type.
STAY HERE. I'LL GO GET IT.
Hey, wait.
I'M COMING WITH YOU, TSUYOSHI!!
UH-OH, THUNDER.
IT'S GETTING WINDY, TOO. I BETTER GO HOME SOON.
THUNK
DAMMIT! WHERE THE HELL IS MY CELL PHONE?

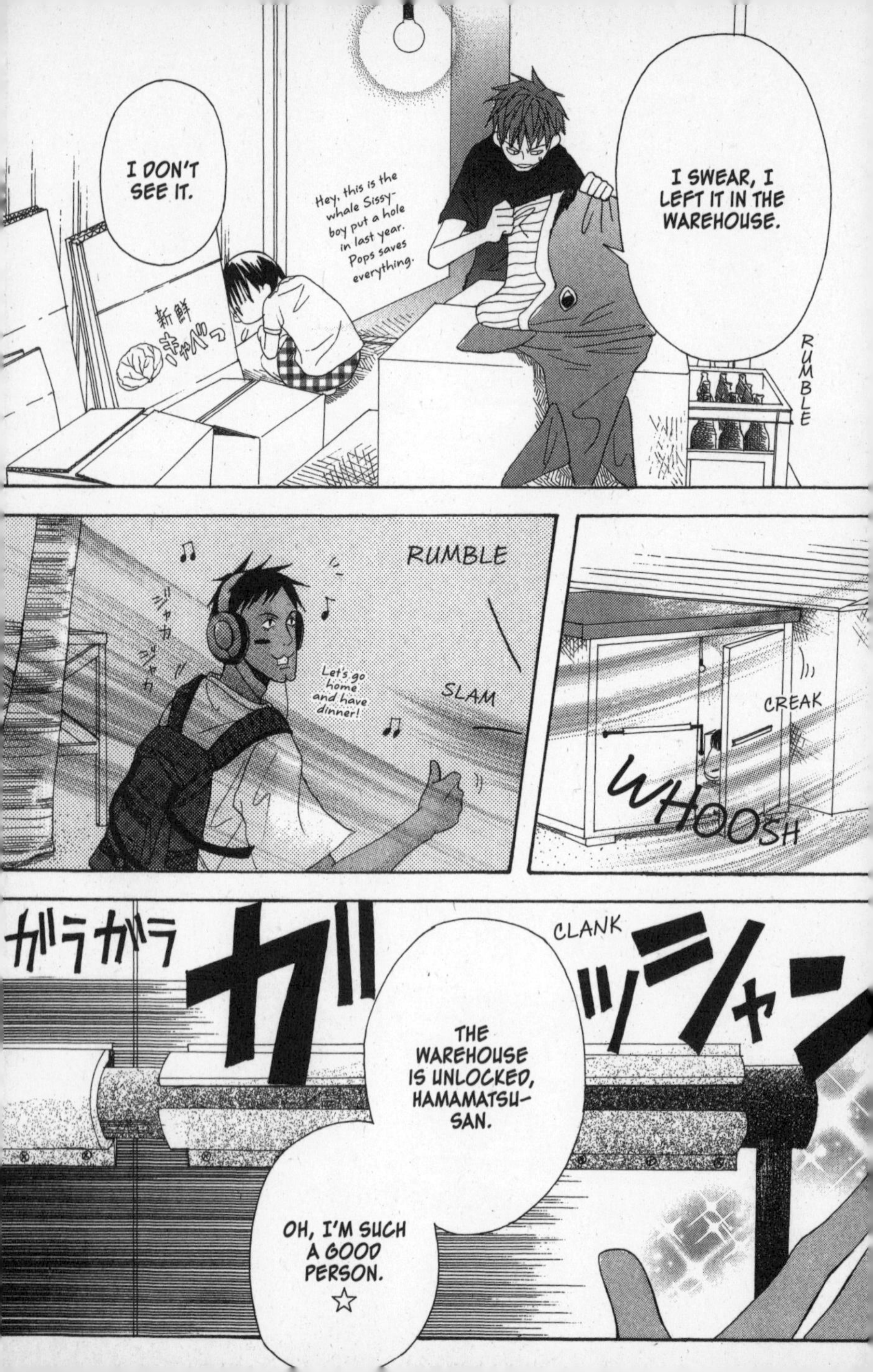
I SWEAR, I LEFT IT IN THE WAREHOUSE.
RUMBLE
Hey, this is the whale Sissy-boy put a hole in last year. Pops saves everything.
新鮮 きゃべつ
I DON'T SEE IT.
CREAK
WHOOSH
RUMBLE
SLAM
Let's go home and have dinner!
ジャカ ジャカ
ガッシャーン
CLANK
THE WAREHOUSE IS UNLOCKED, HAMAMATSU-SAN.
OH, I'M SUCH A GOOD PERSON. ☆
ガラガラ

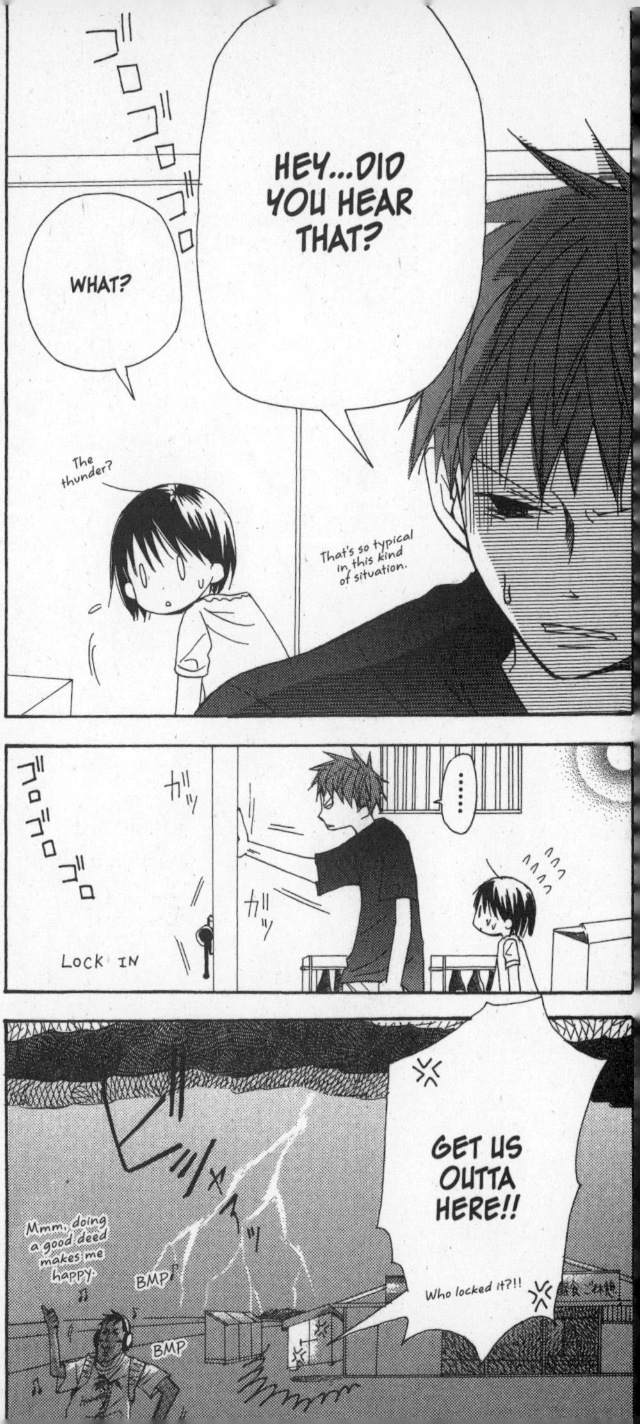
ゴロゴロゴロゴロ
HEY...DID YOU HEAR THAT?
WHAT?
The thunder?
That's so typical in this kind of situation.
......
ガッ
ガッ
ゴロゴロゴロ
LOCK IN
GET US OUTTA HERE!!
Who locked it?!!
BMP
BMP
Mmm, doing a good deed makes me happy.

3

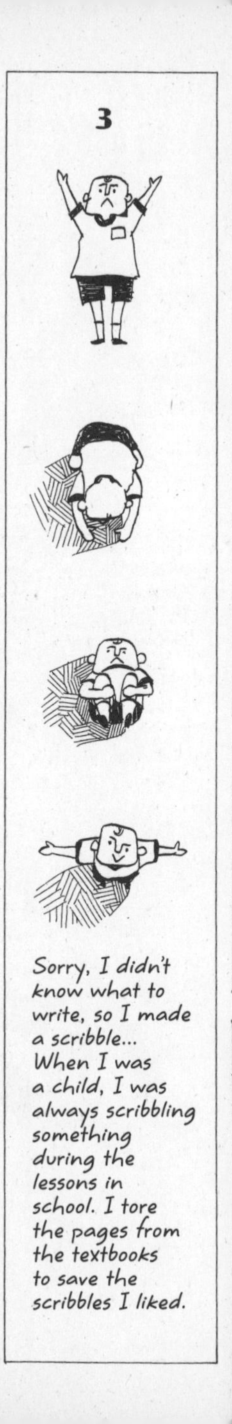

Sorry, I didn't know what to write, so I made a scribble... When I was a child, I was always scribbling something during the lessons in school. I tore the pages from the textbooks to save the scribbles I liked.

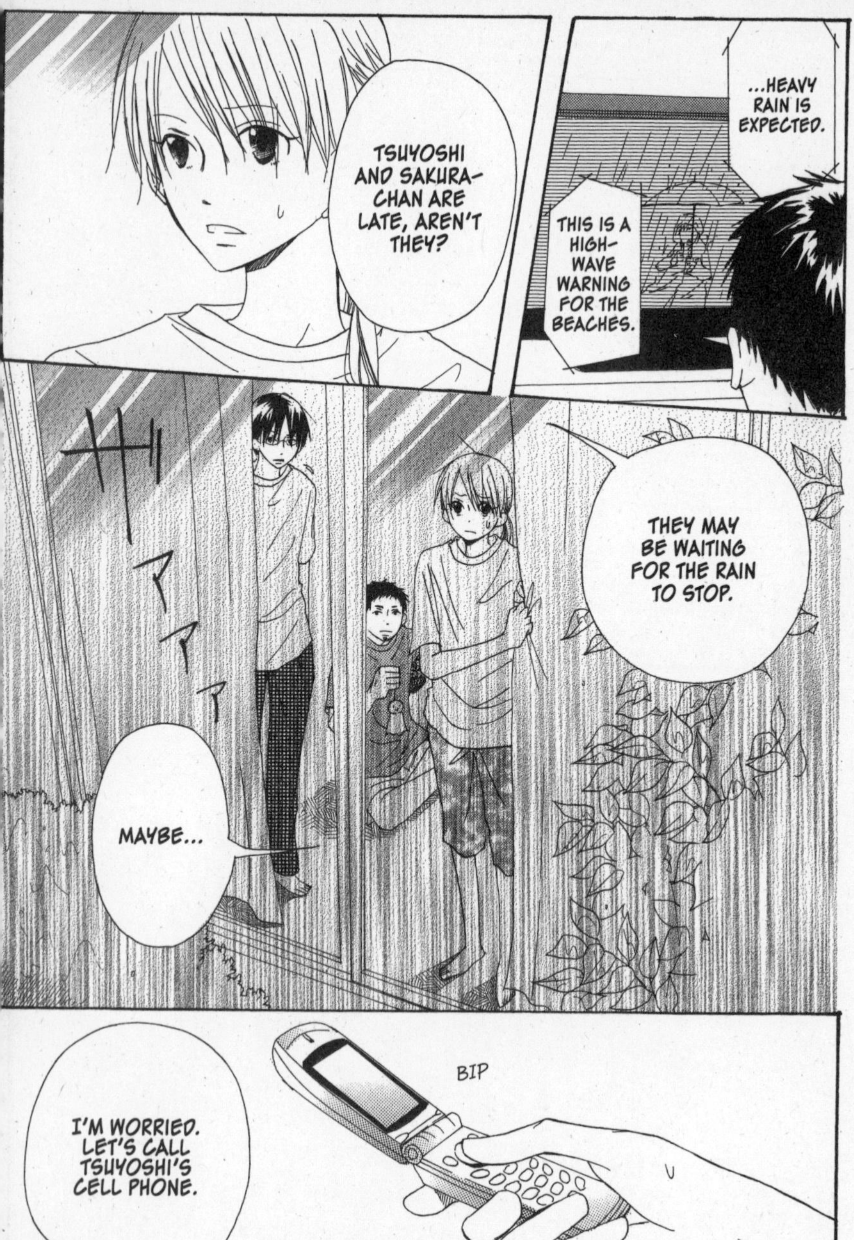
...HEAVY RAIN IS EXPECTED.
THIS IS A HIGH-WAVE WARNING FOR THE BEACHES.
TSUYOSHI AND SAKURA-CHAN ARE LATE, AREN'T THEY?
THEY MAY BE WAITING FOR THE RAIN TO STOP.
MAYBE...
BIP
I'M WORRIED. LET'S CALL TSUYOSHI'S CELL PHONE.

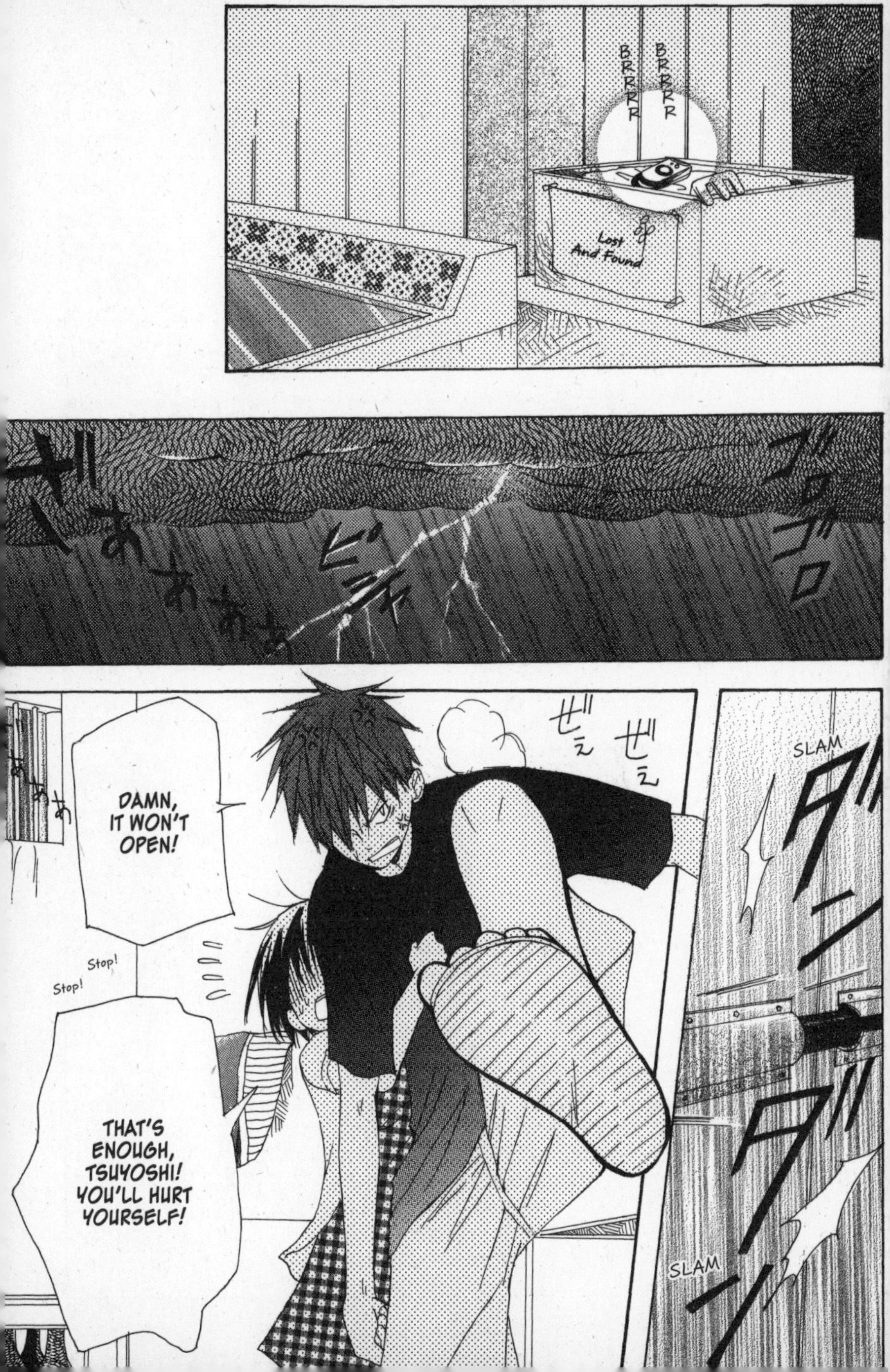
BRRRR BRRRR
Lost And Found
ゴロゴロ
ピシャ
ざあああ
SLAM
ぜぇ ぜぇ
DAMN, IT WON'T OPEN!
Stop!
Stop!
THAT'S ENOUGH, TSUYOSHI! YOU'LL HURT YOURSELF!
SLAM

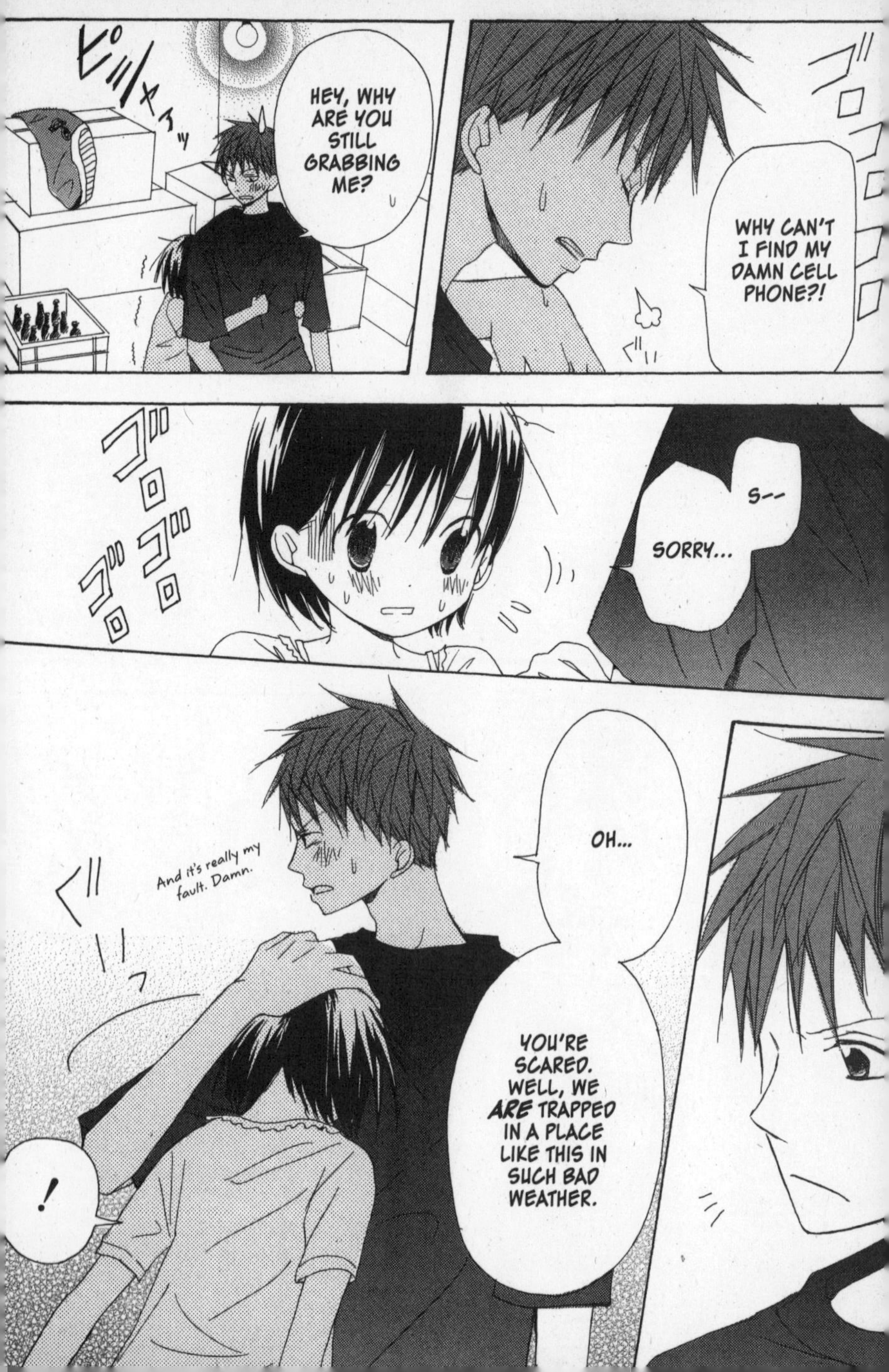
WHY CAN'T I FIND MY DAMN CELL PHONE?!
HEY, WHY ARE YOU STILL GRABBING ME?
S--
SORRY...
OH...
YOU'RE SCARED. WELL, WE **ARE** TRAPPED IN A PLACE LIKE THIS IN SUCH BAD WEATHER.
And it's really my fault. Damn.
!

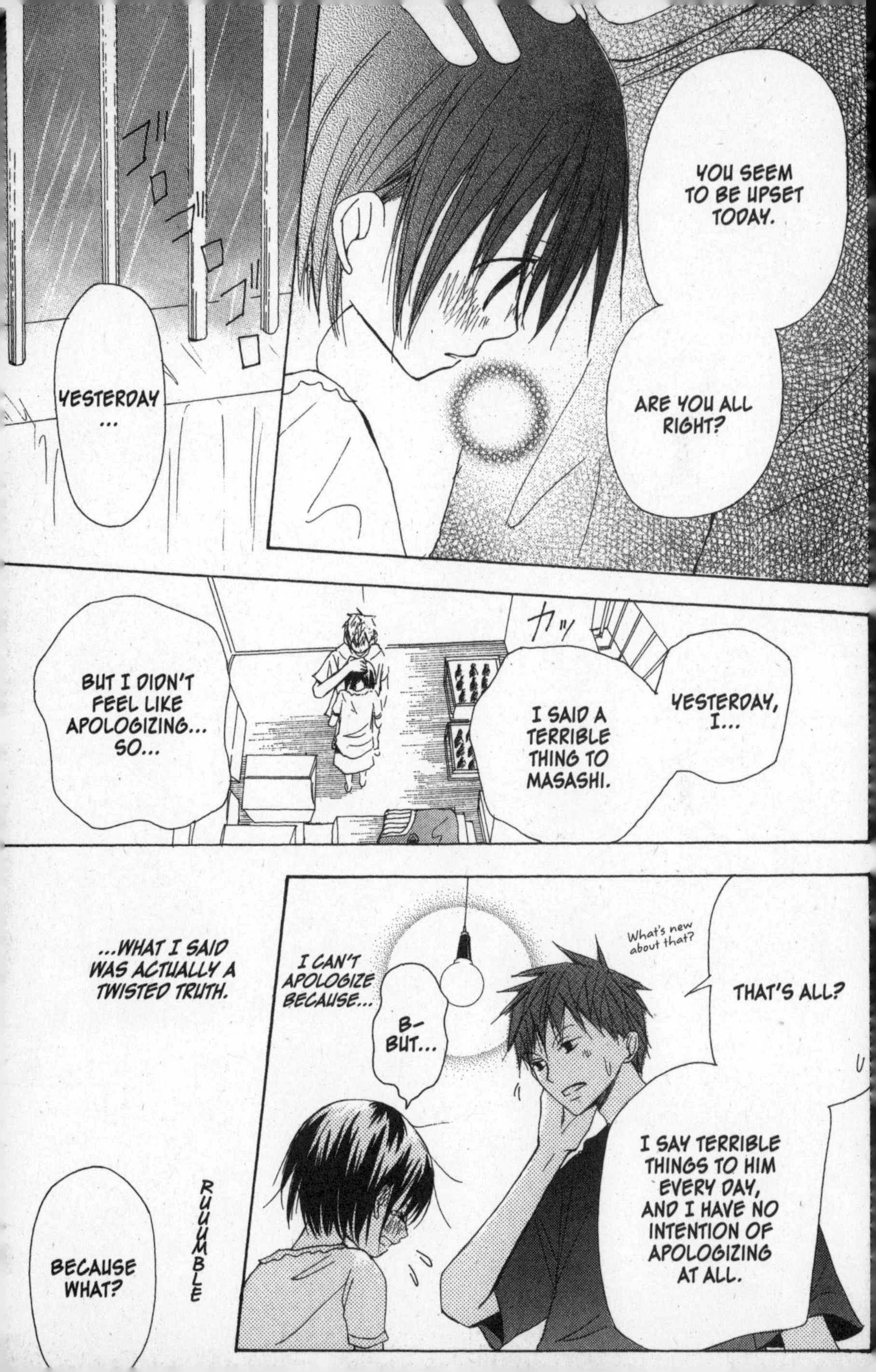
YOU SEEM TO BE UPSET TODAY.
ARE YOU ALL RIGHT?
YESTERDAY ...
YESTERDAY, I...
I SAID A TERRIBLE THING TO MASASHI.
BUT I DIDN'T FEEL LIKE APOLOGIZING... SO...
What's new about that?
THAT'S ALL?
I SAY TERRIBLE THINGS TO HIM EVERY DAY, AND I HAVE NO INTENTION OF APOLOGIZING AT ALL.
B-BUT...
I CAN'T APOLOGIZE BECAUSE...
...WHAT I SAID WAS ACTUALLY A TWISTED TRUTH.
RUUUMBLE
BECAUSE WHAT?

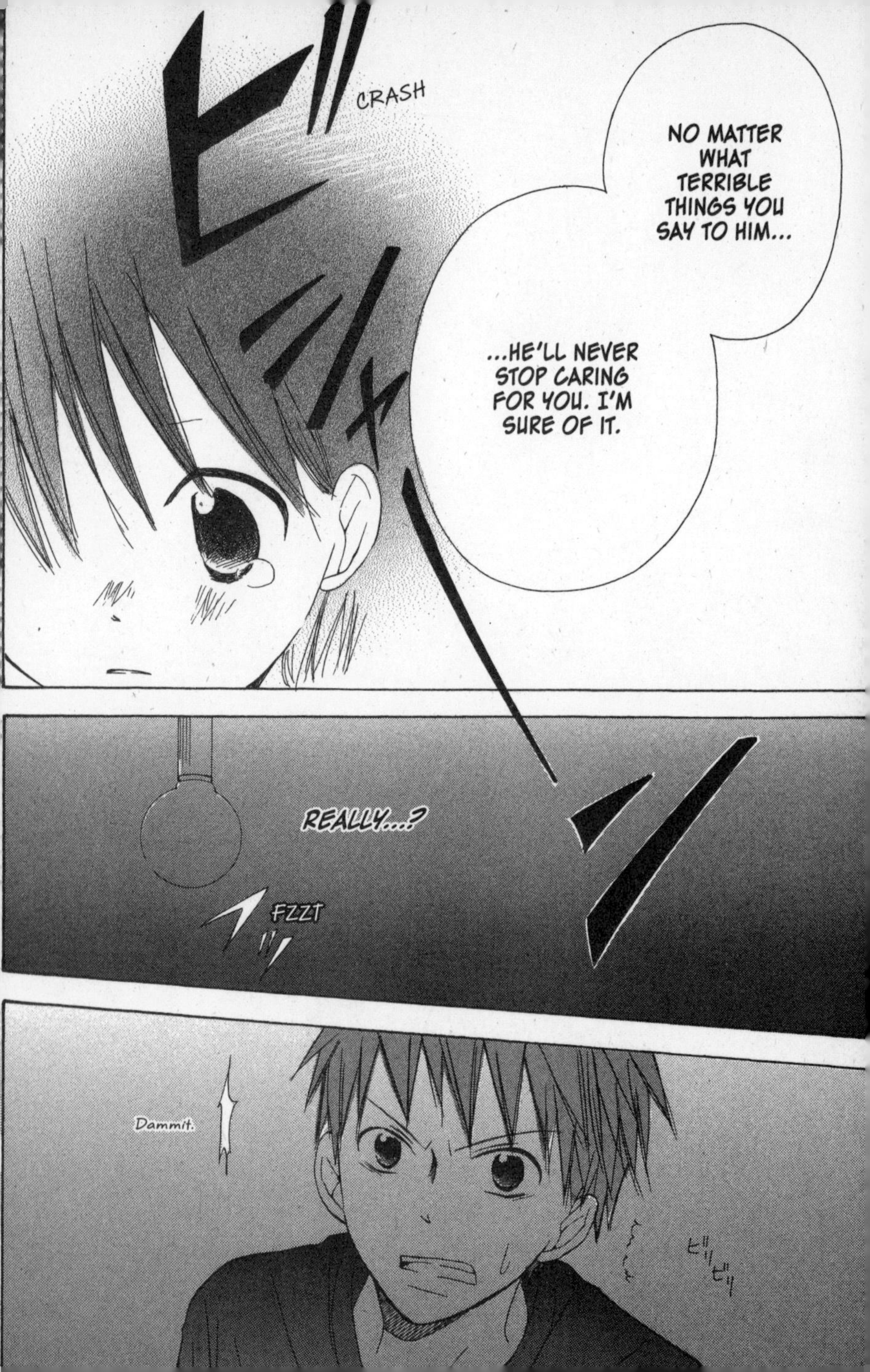
NO MATTER WHAT TERRIBLE THINGS YOU SAY TO HIM...
...HE'LL NEVER STOP CARING FOR YOU. I'M SURE OF IT.
CRASH
REALLY...?
FZZT
ビリビリ
Dammit.

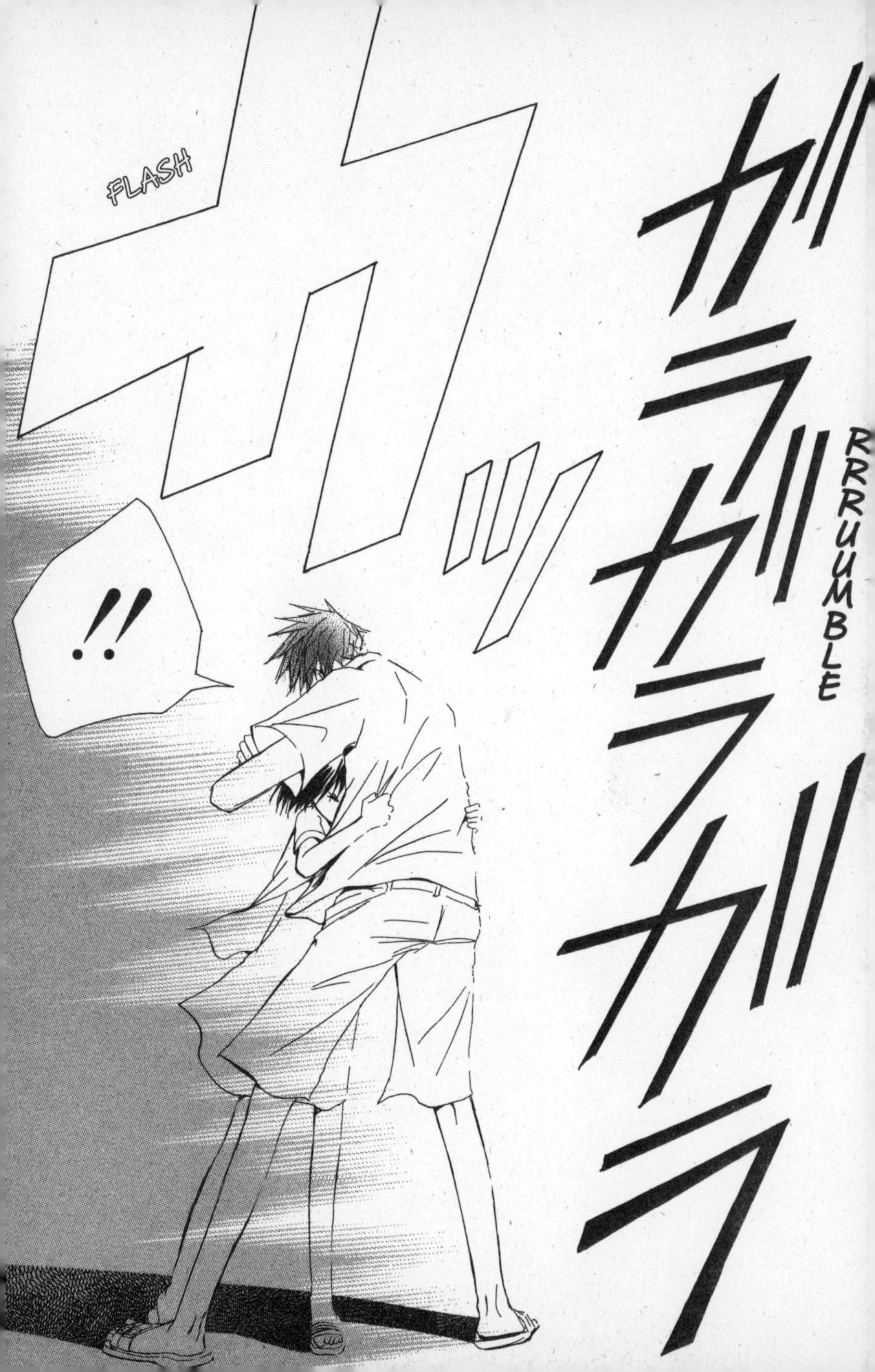
ガラガラガラ
RRRUMBLE
FLASH
!!

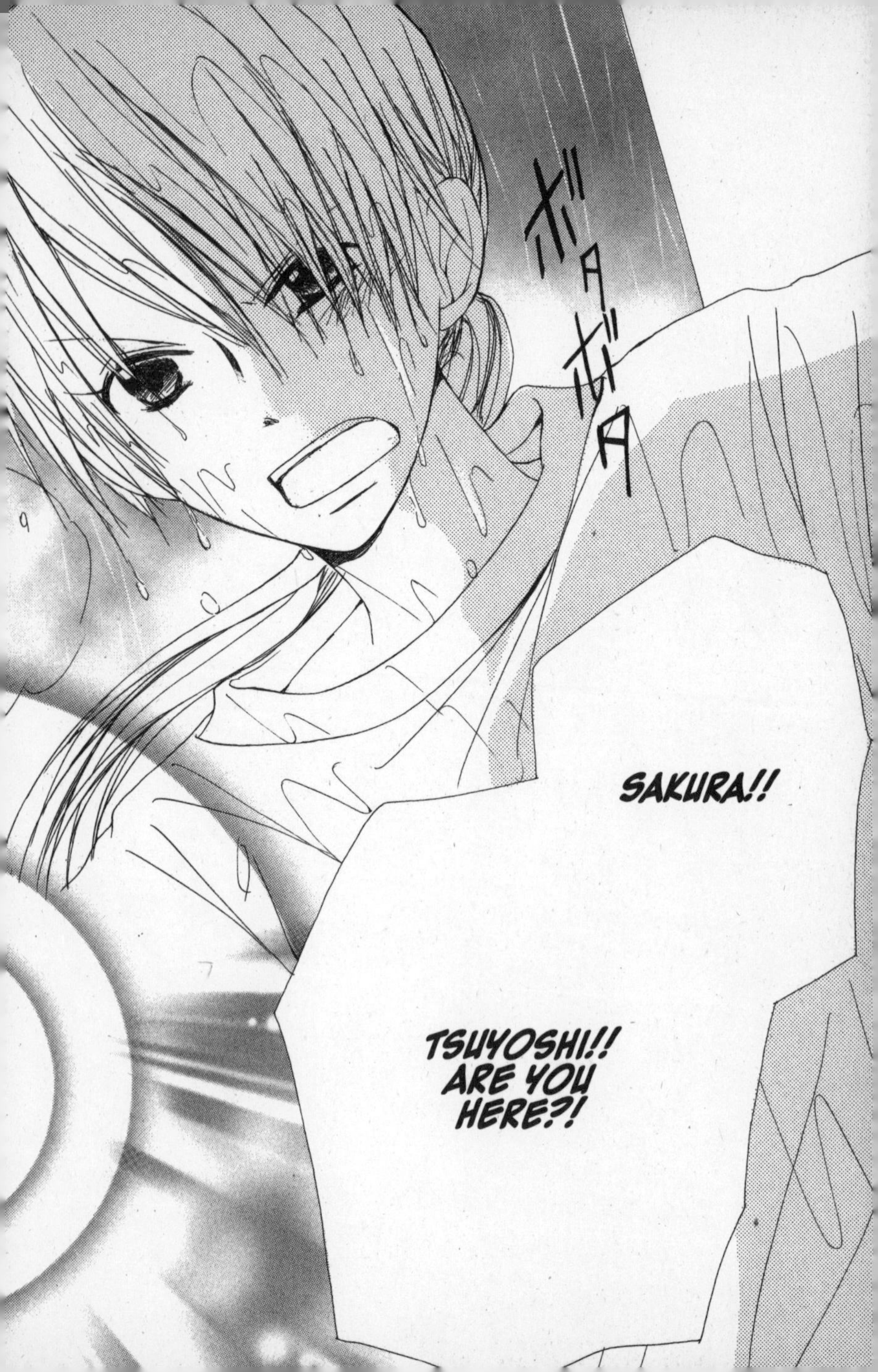
ザァザァ
SAKURA!!
TSUYOSHI!! ARE YOU HERE?!

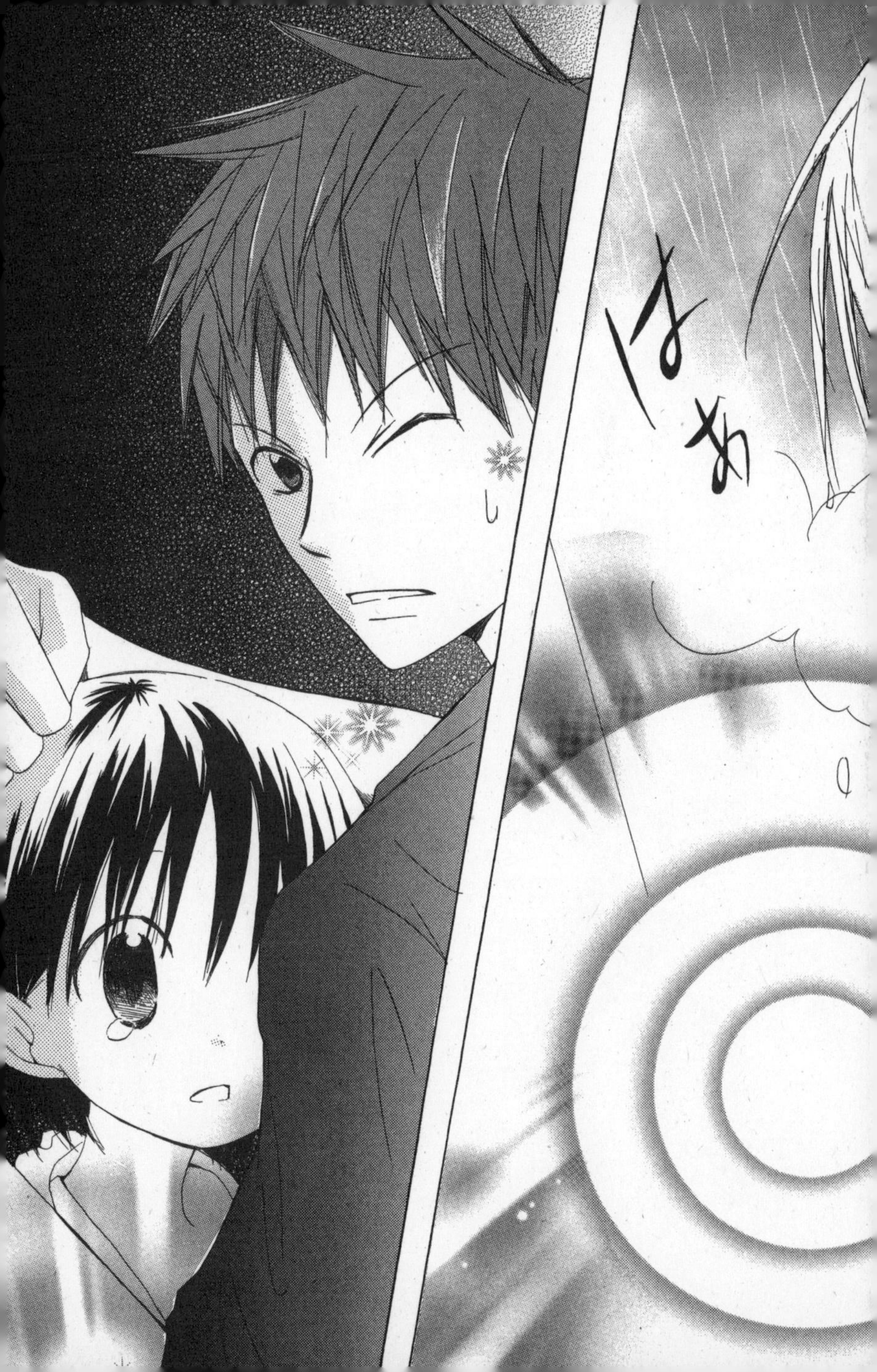
はぁ

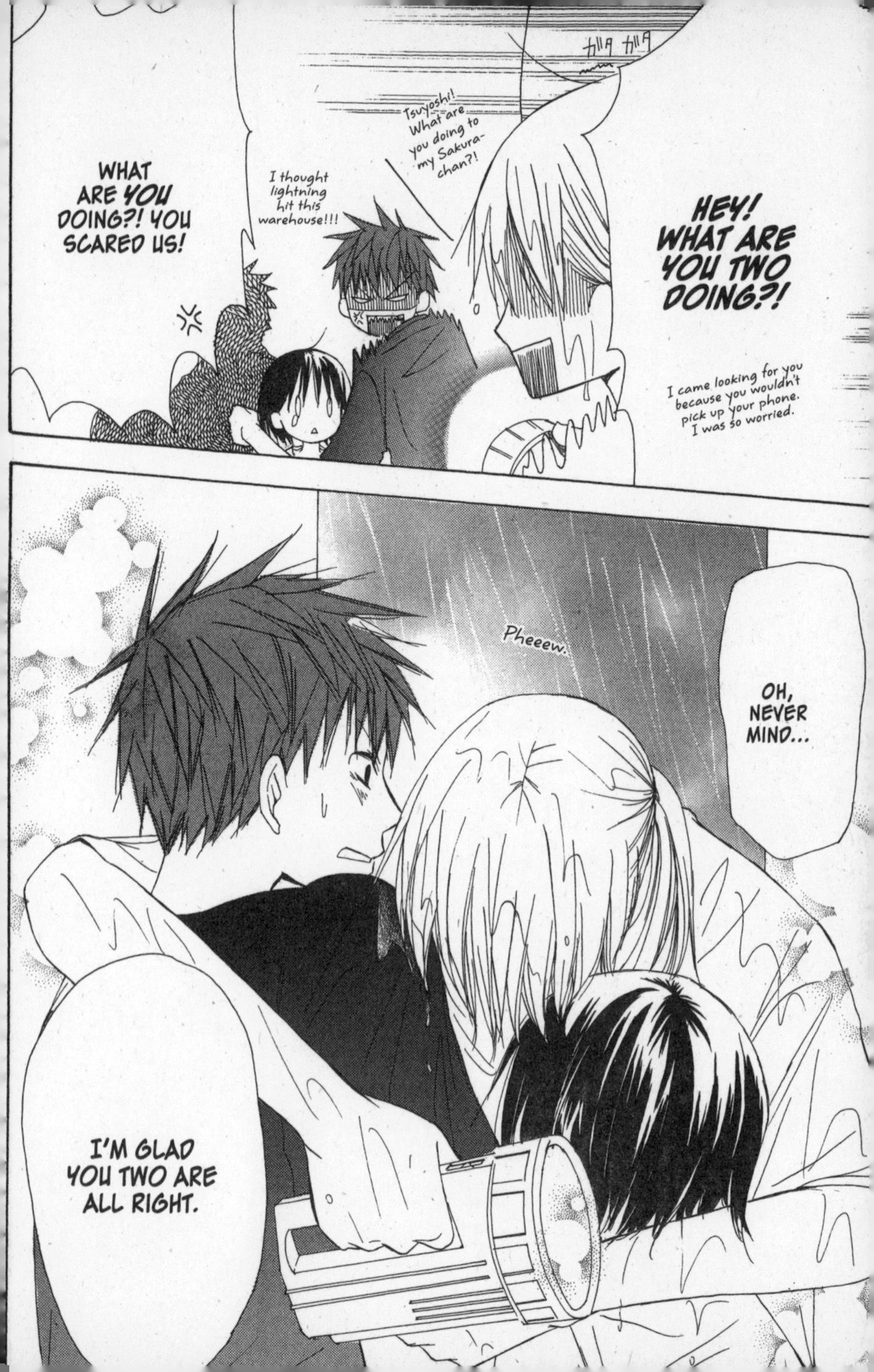
ガタ ガタ
HEY! WHAT ARE YOU TWO DOING?!
I came looking for you because you wouldn't pick up your phone. I was so worried.
Tsuyoshi! What are you doing to my Sakura-chan?!
I thought lightning hit this warehouse!!!
WHAT ARE YOU DOING?! YOU SCARED US!
OH, NEVER MIND...
Pheeew.
I'M GLAD YOU TWO ARE ALL RIGHT.

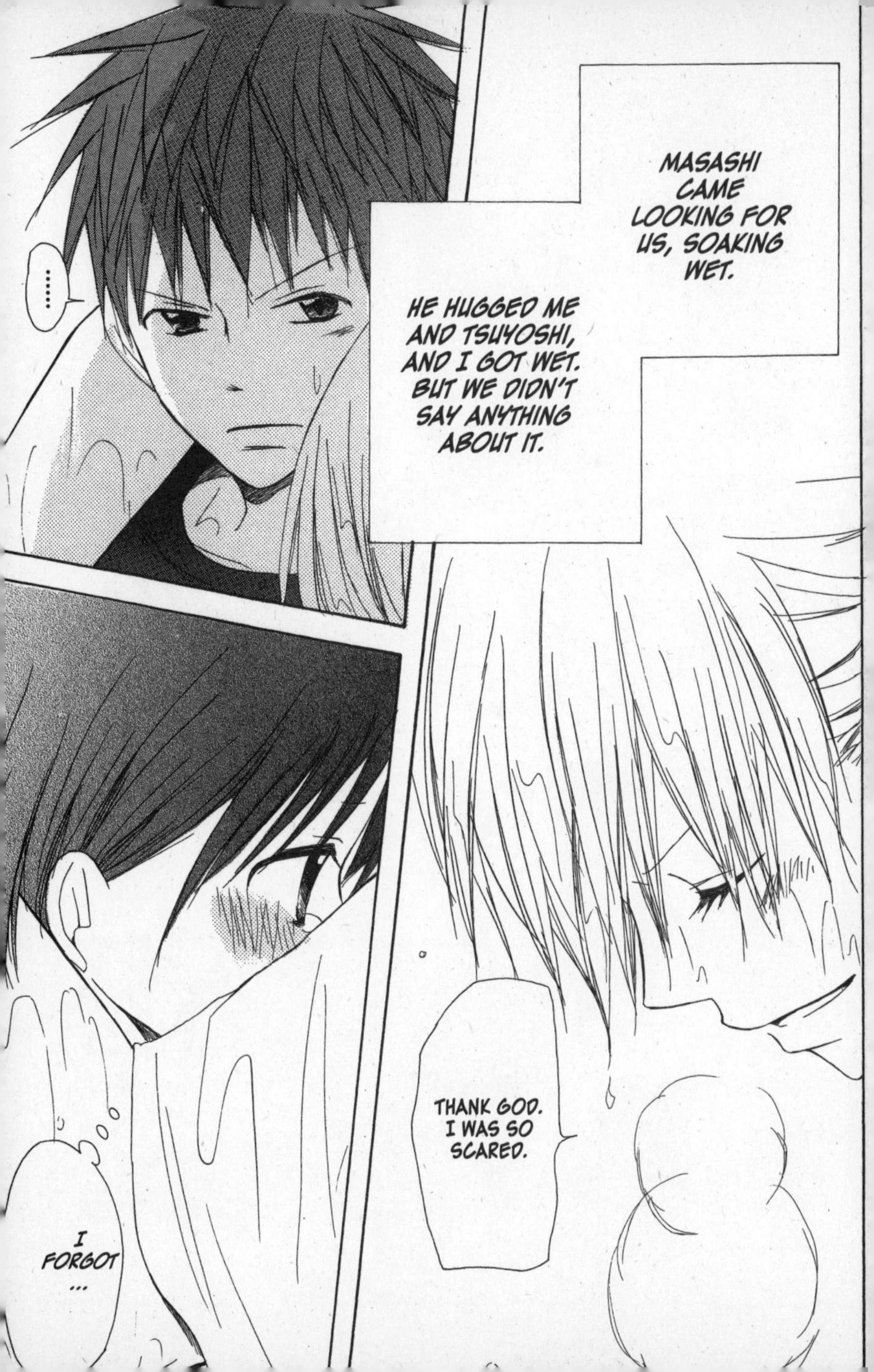
MASASHI CAME LOOKING FOR US, SOAKING WET.
HE HUGGED ME AND TSUYOSHI, AND I GOT WET. BUT WE DIDN'T SAY ANYTHING ABOUT IT.
......
THANK GOD. I WAS SO SCARED.
I FORGOT ...

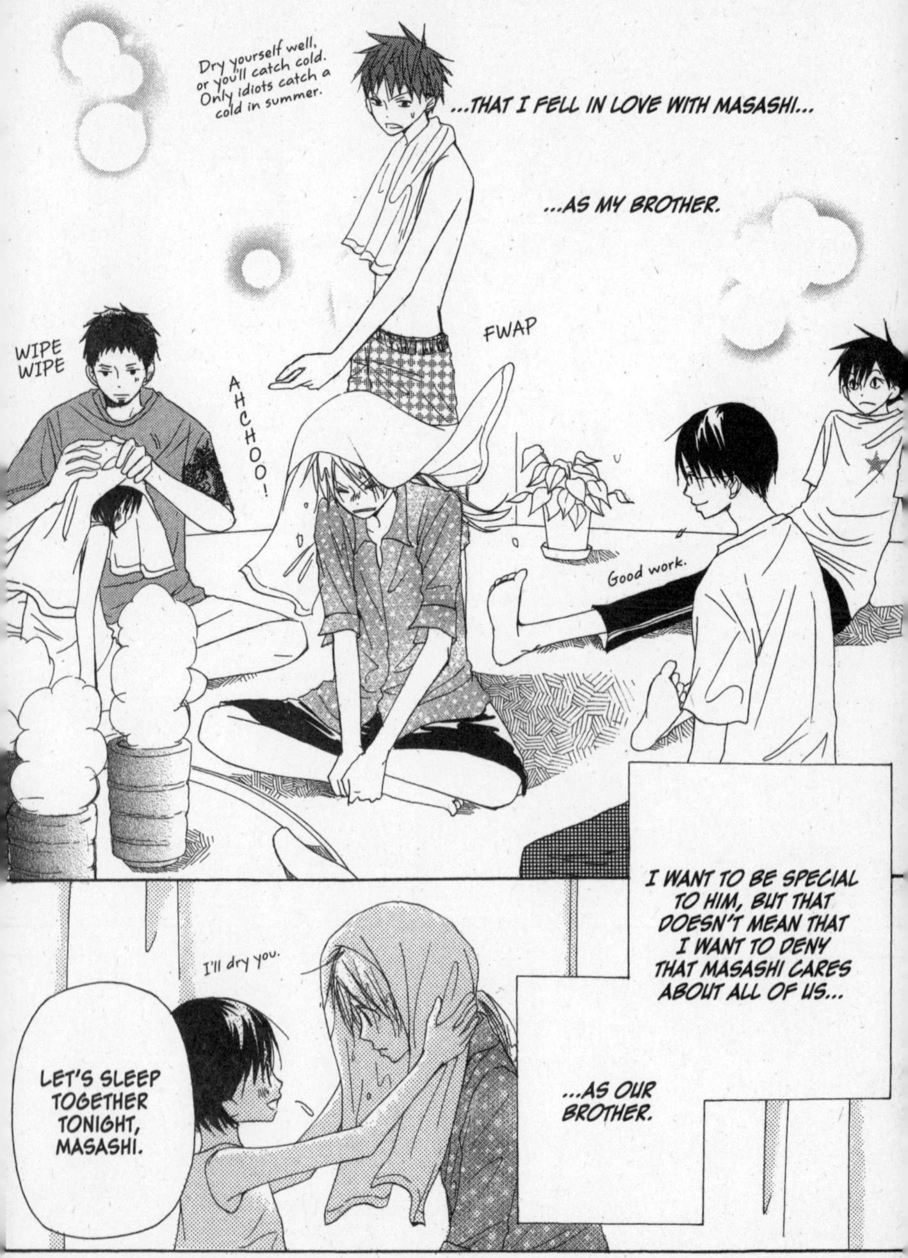
...THAT I FELL IN LOVE WITH MASASHI...
...AS MY BROTHER.
Dry yourself well, or you'll catch cold. Only idiots catch a cold in summer.
FWAP
Good work.
AHCHOO!
WIPE WIPE
I WANT TO BE SPECIAL TO HIM, BUT THAT DOESN'T MEAN THAT I WANT TO DENY THAT MASASHI CARES ABOUT ALL OF US...
...AS OUR BROTHER.
I'll dry you.
LET'S SLEEP TOGETHER TONIGHT, MASASHI.

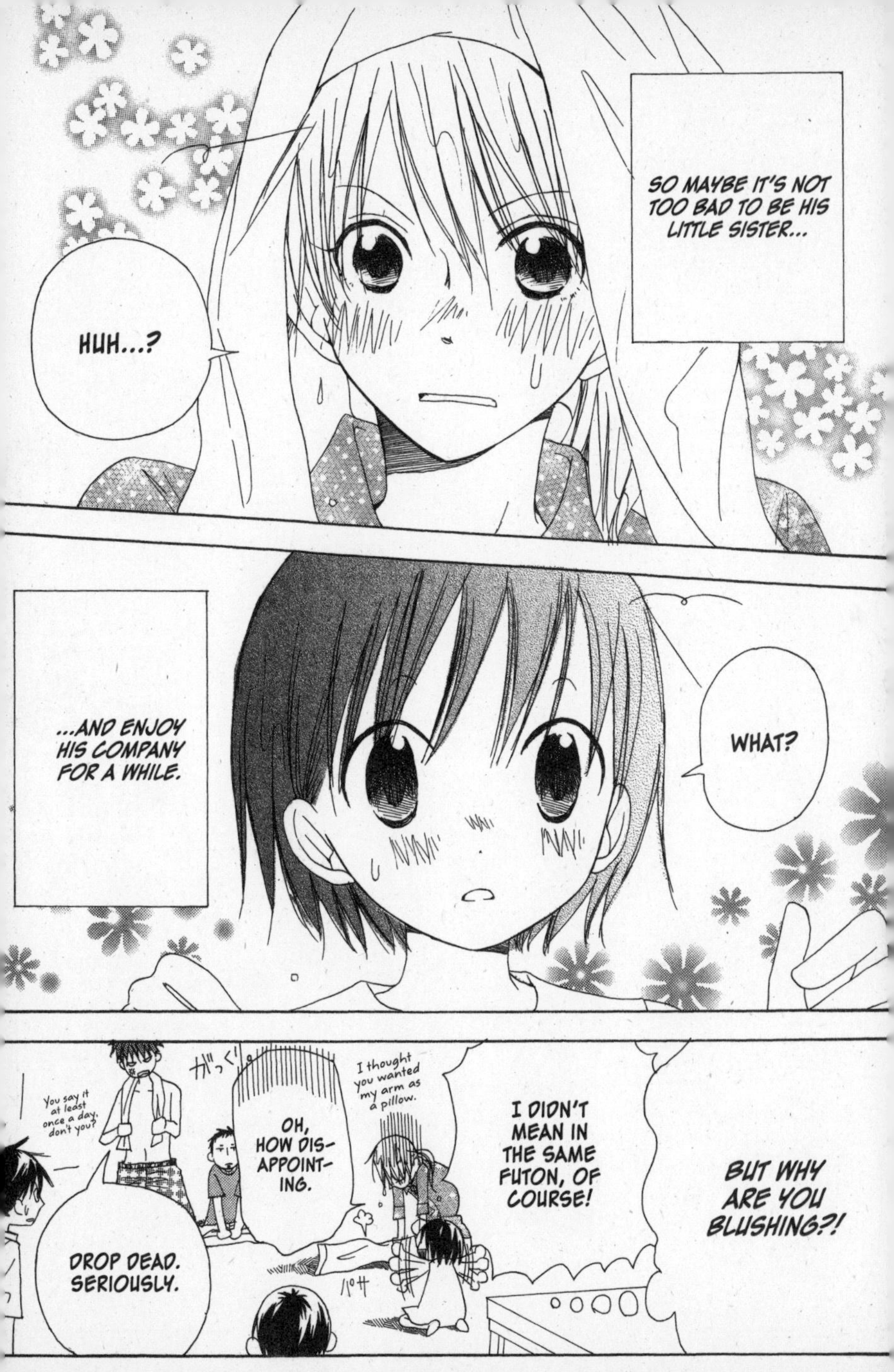
SO MAYBE IT'S NOT TOO BAD TO BE HIS LITTLE SISTER...
HUH...?
WHAT?
...AND ENJOY HIS COMPANY FOR A WHILE.
BUT WHY ARE YOU BLUSHING?!
I DIDN'T MEAN IN THE SAME FUTON, OF COURSE!
I thought you wanted my arm as a pillow.
OH, HOW DIS-APPOINT-ING.
ガっく!
You say it at least once a day, don't you?
DROP DEAD. SERIOUSLY.
パサ

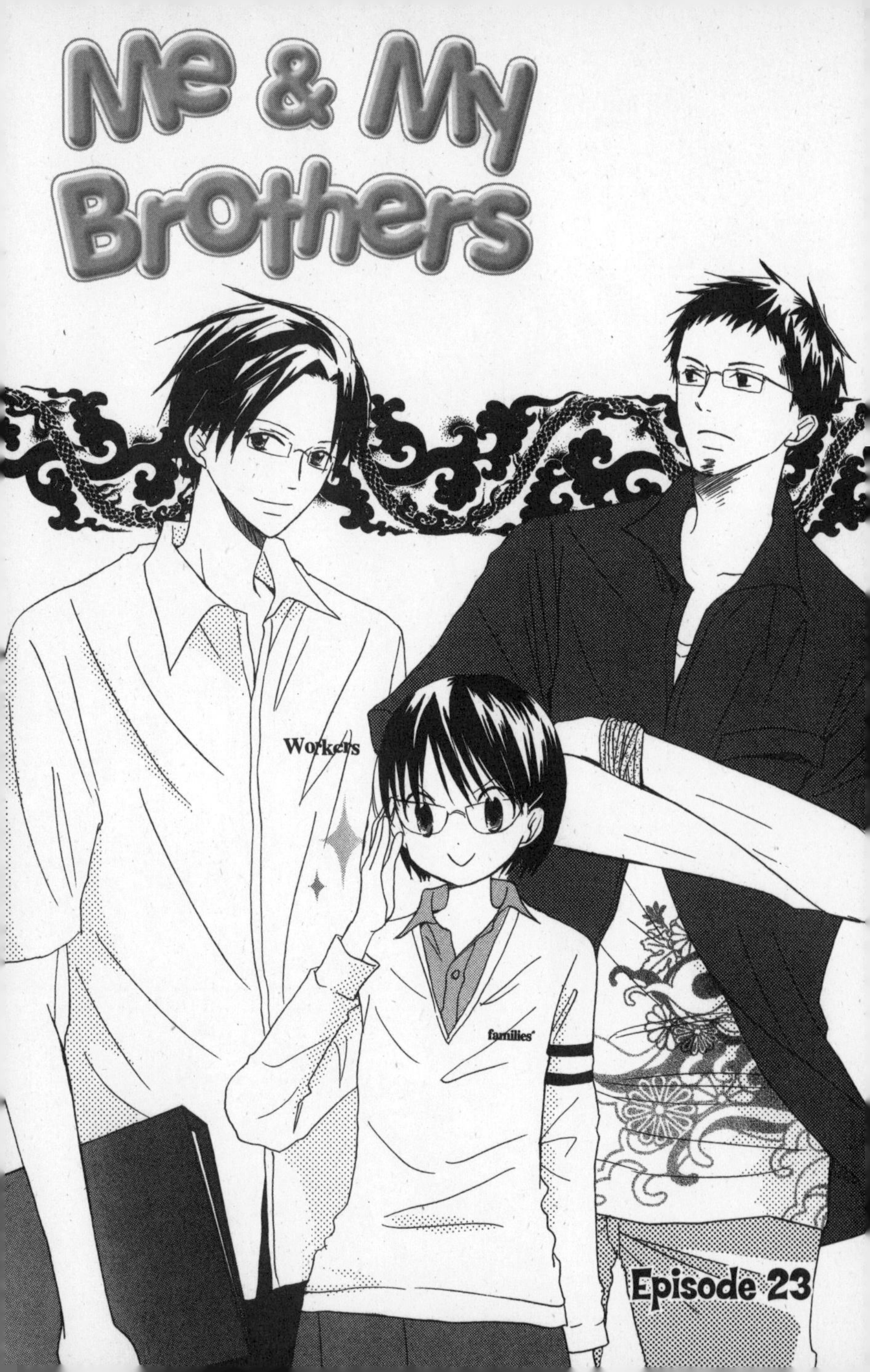
Me & My Brothers
Workers
families
Episode 23

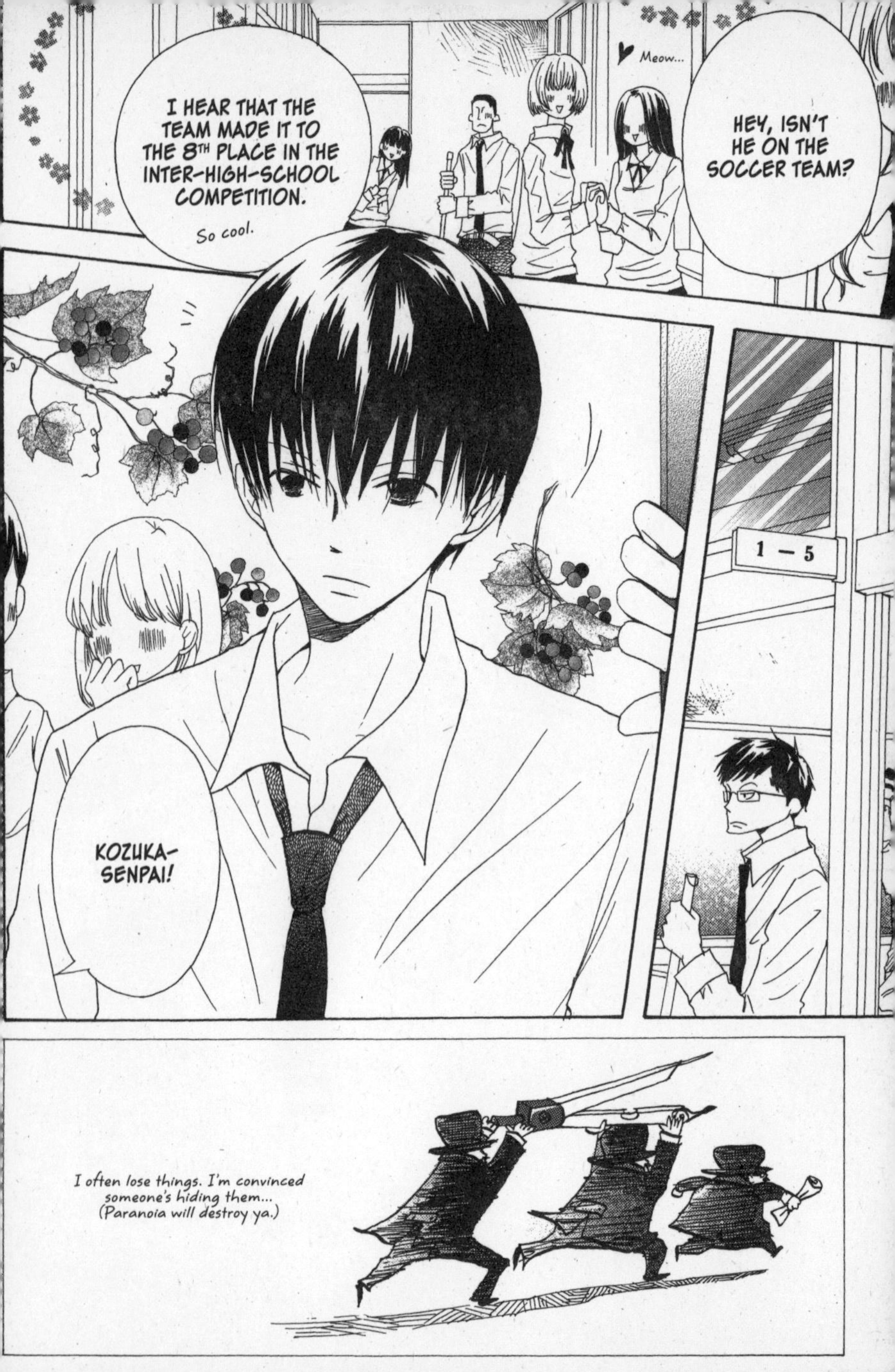
HEY, ISN'T HE ON THE SOCCER TEAM?
Meow...
I HEAR THAT THE TEAM MADE IT TO THE 8TH PLACE IN THE INTER-HIGH-SCHOOL COMPETITION.
So cool.
1 — 5
KOZUKA-SENPAI!
I often lose things. I'm convinced someone's hiding them... (Paranoia will destroy ya.)

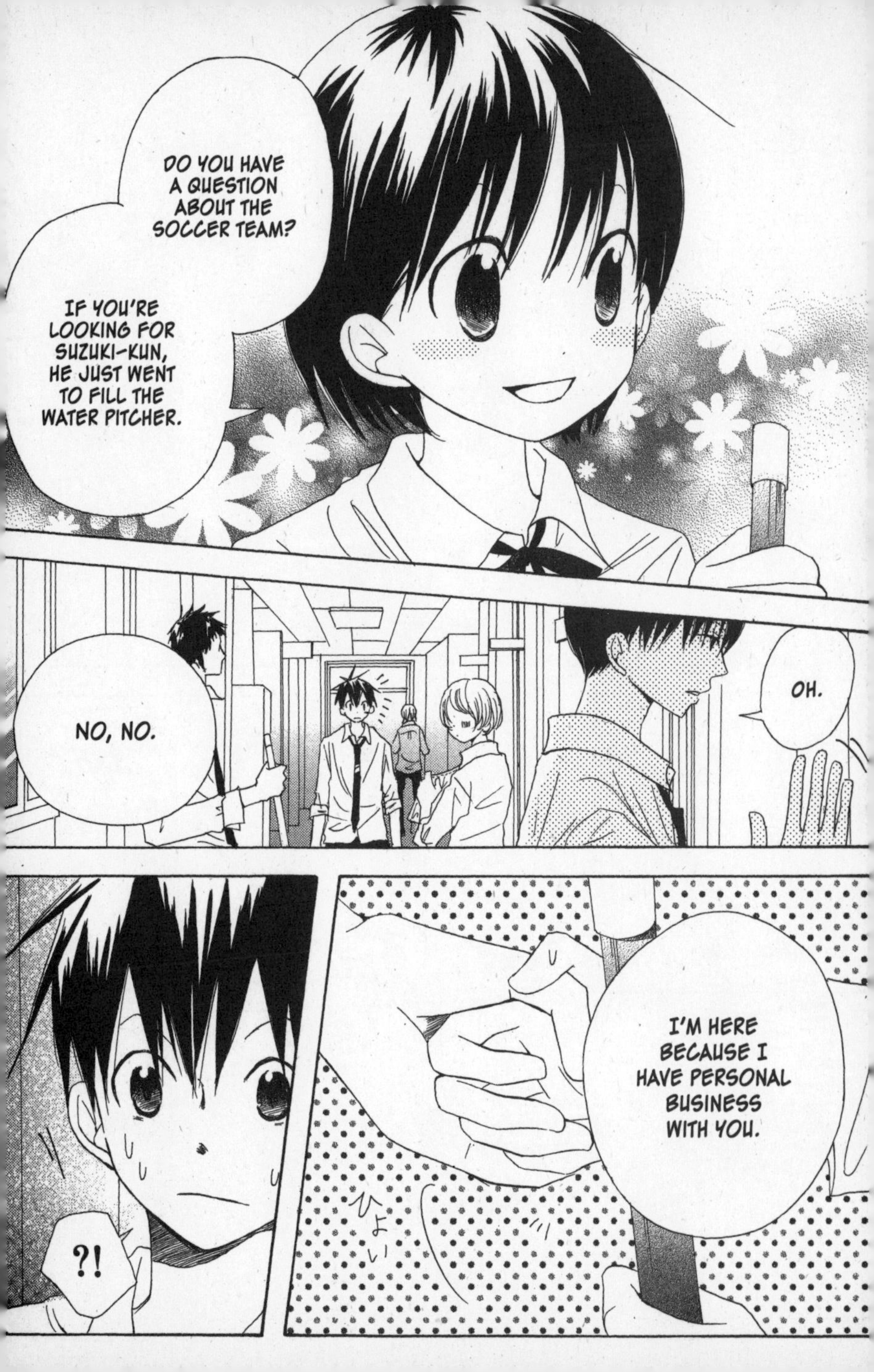
DO YOU HAVE A QUESTION ABOUT THE SOCCER TEAM?
IF YOU'RE LOOKING FOR SUZUKI-KUN, HE JUST WENT TO FILL THE WATER PITCHER.
OH.
NO, NO.
I'M HERE BECAUSE I HAVE PERSONAL BUSINESS WITH YOU.
ひょい
?!

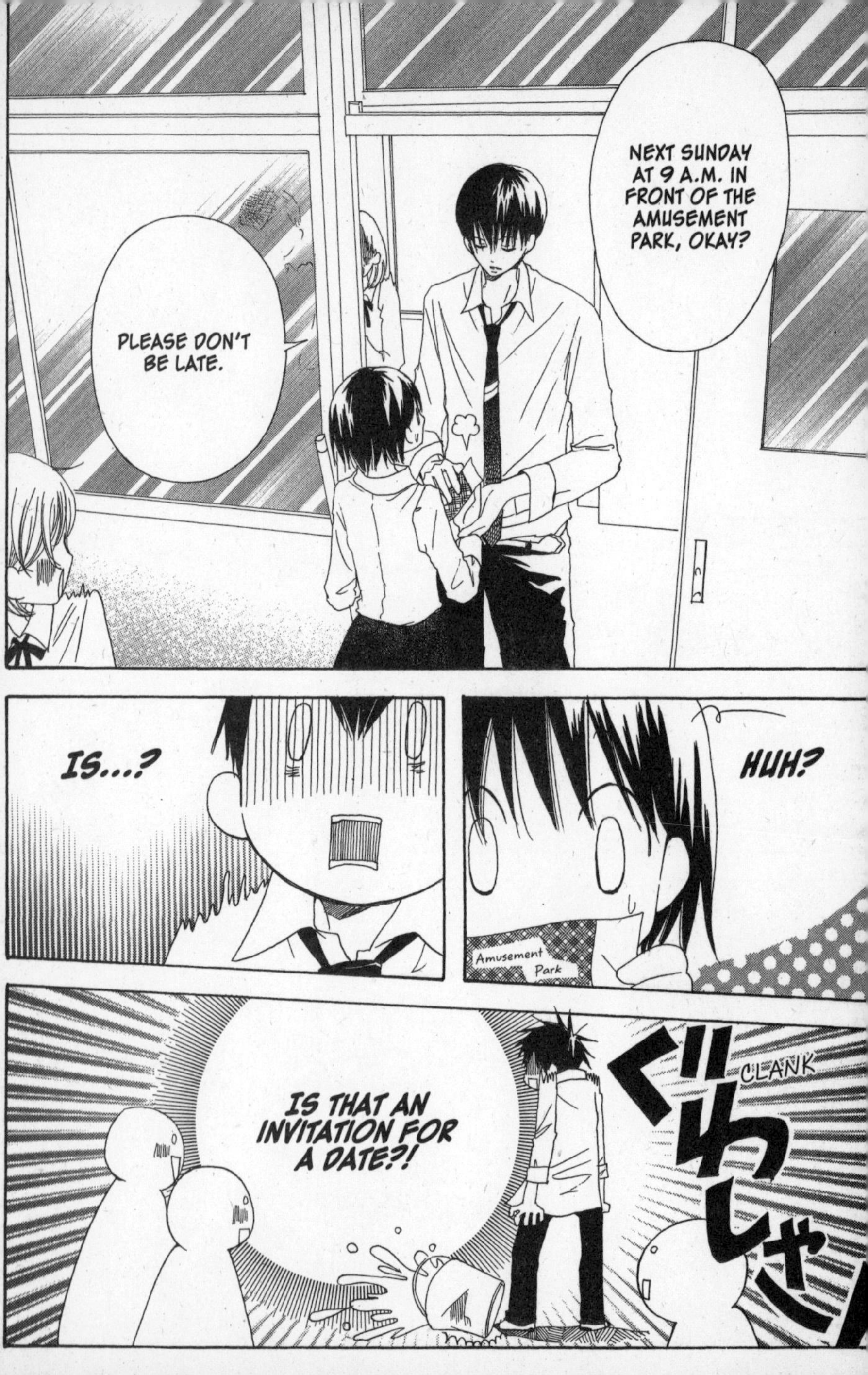
NEXT SUNDAY AT 9 A.M. IN FRONT OF THE AMUSEMENT PARK, OKAY?
PLEASE DON'T BE LATE.
HUH?
Amusement Park
IS...?
CLANK
IS THAT AN INVITATION FOR A DATE?!

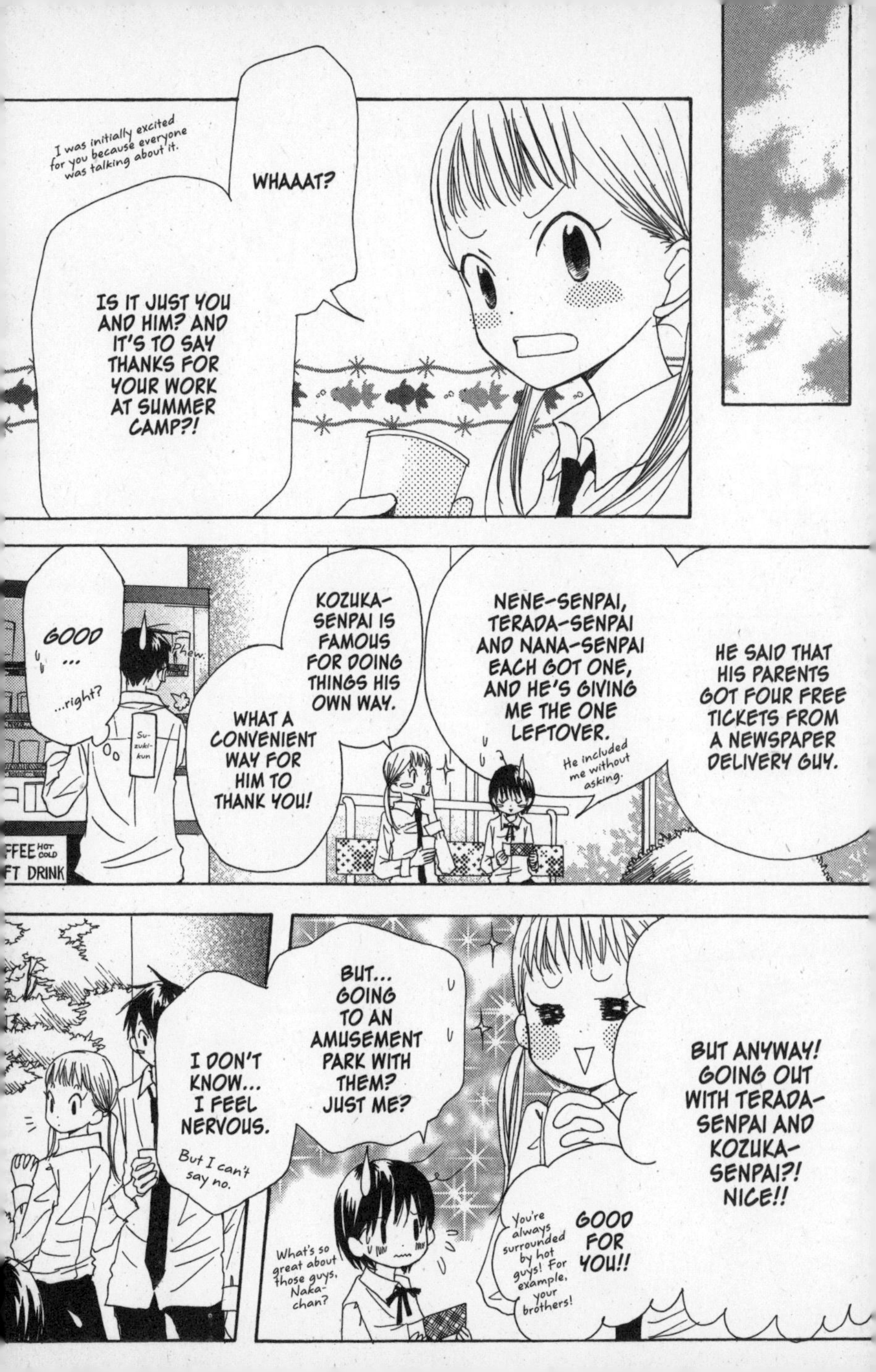
WHAAAT?
I was initially excited for you because everyone was talking about it.
IS IT JUST YOU AND HIM? AND IT'S TO SAY THANKS FOR YOUR WORK AT SUMMER CAMP?!
HE SAID THAT HIS PARENTS GOT FOUR FREE TICKETS FROM A NEWSPAPER DELIVERY GUY.
NENE-SENPAI, TERADA-SENPAI AND NANA-SENPAI EACH GOT ONE, AND HE'S GIVING ME THE ONE LEFTOVER.
He included me without asking.
KOZUKA-SENPAI IS FAMOUS FOR DOING THINGS HIS OWN WAY.
WHAT A CONVENIENT WAY FOR HIM TO THANK YOU!
Phew.
GOOD ...
...right?
Su-zuki-kun
FFEE HOT COLD
FT DRINK
BUT ANYWAY! GOING OUT WITH TERADA-SENPAI AND KOZUKA-SENPAI?! NICE!!
GOOD FOR YOU!!
You're always surrounded by hot guys! For example, your brothers!
What's so great about those guys, Naka-chan?
BUT... GOING TO AN AMUSEMENT PARK WITH THEM? JUST ME?
I DON'T KNOW... I FEEL NERVOUS.
But I can't say no.

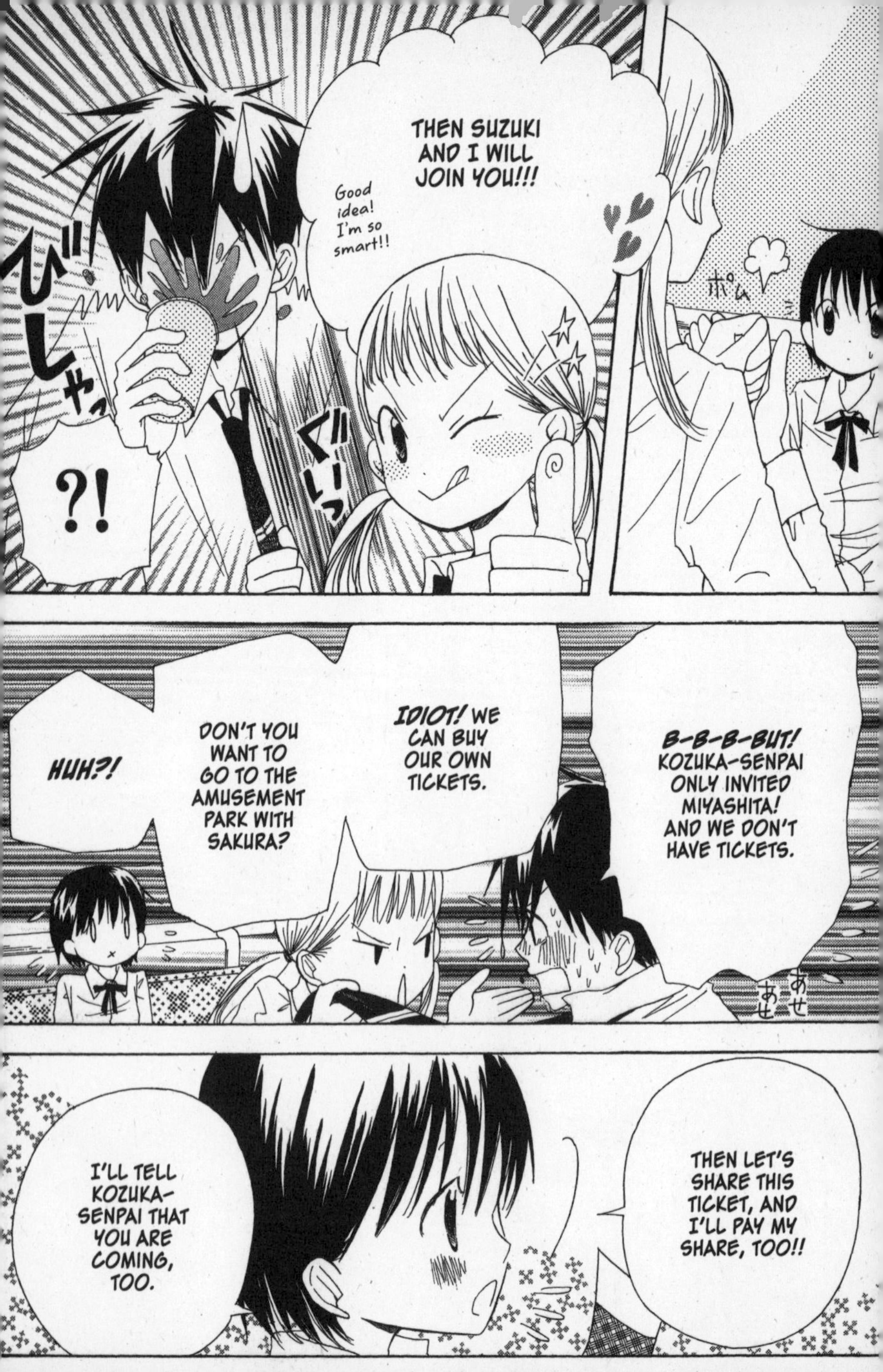
ポム
THEN SUZUKI AND I WILL JOIN YOU!!!
Good idea! I'm so smart!!
びしゃっ
?!
B-B-B-BUT! KOZUKA-SENPAI ONLY INVITED MIYASHITA! AND WE DON'T HAVE TICKETS.
IDIOT! WE CAN BUY OUR OWN TICKETS.
DON'T YOU WANT TO GO TO THE AMUSEMENT PARK WITH SAKURA?
HUH?!
あせあせ
THEN LET'S SHARE THIS TICKET, AND I'LL PAY MY SHARE, TOO!!
I'LL TELL KOZUKA-SENPAI THAT YOU ARE COMING, TOO.

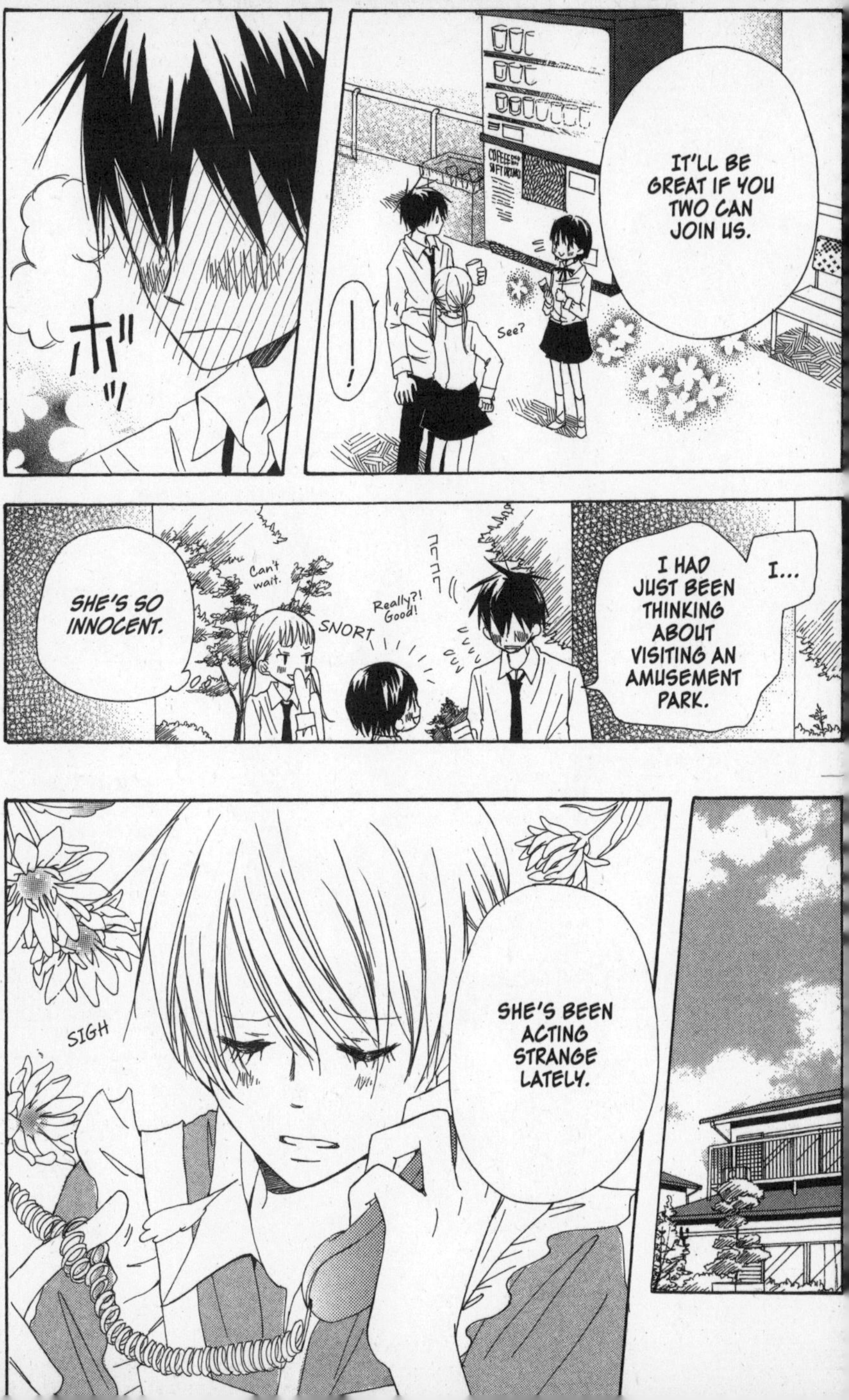
IT'LL BE GREAT IF YOU TWO CAN JOIN US.
See?
!
ボッ
I...
I HAD JUST BEEN THINKING ABOUT VISITING AN AMUSEMENT PARK.
Really?! Good!
SNORT
Can't wait.
SHE'S SO INNOCENT.
SHE'S BEEN ACTING STRANGE LATELY.
SIGH

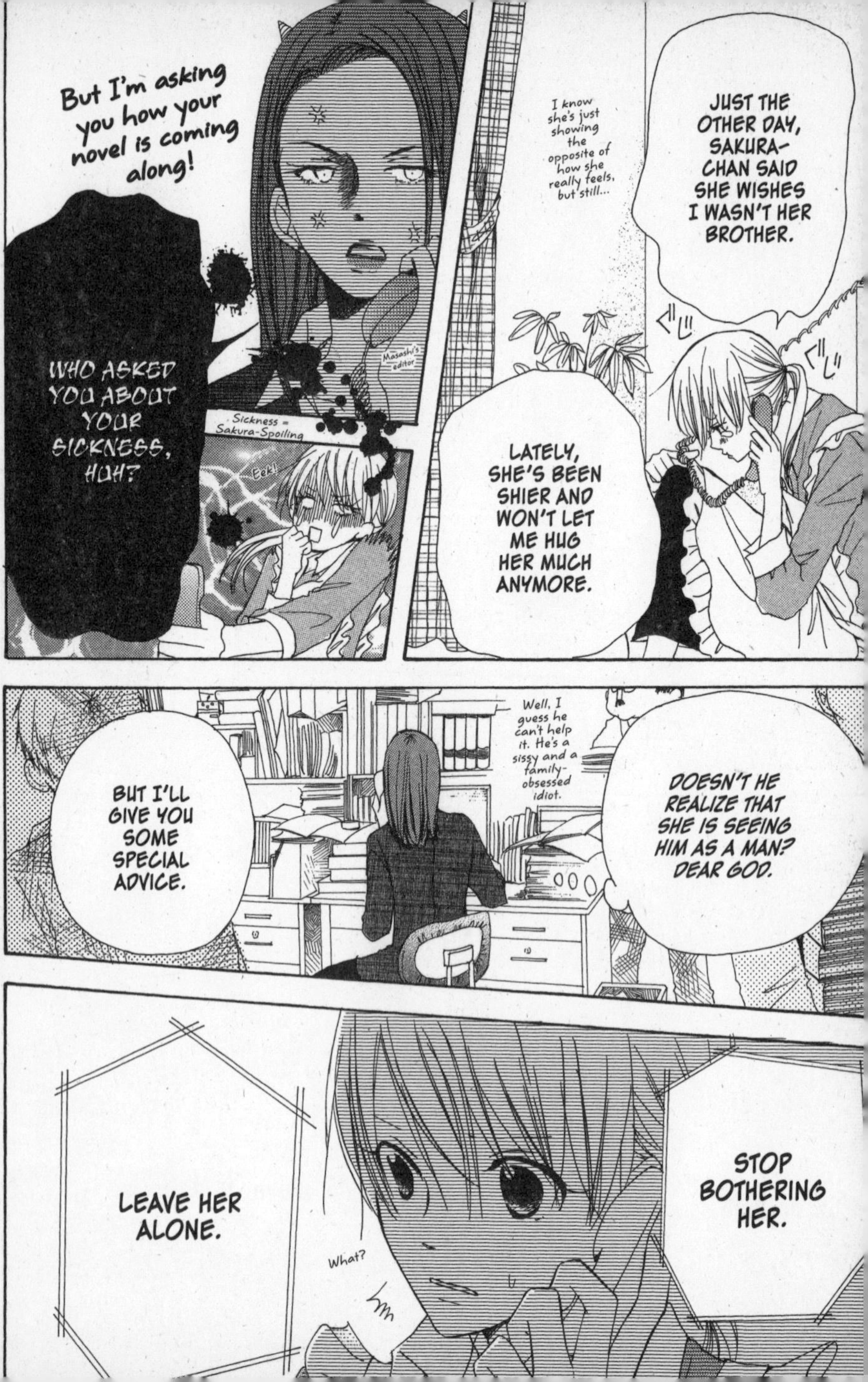
JUST THE OTHER DAY, SAKURA-CHAN SAID SHE WISHES I WASN'T HER BROTHER.
ぐじ
ぐじ
I know she's just showing the opposite of how she really feels, but still...
LATELY, SHE'S BEEN SHIER AND WON'T LET ME HUG HER MUCH ANYMORE.
But I'm asking you how your novel is coming along!
Masashi's editor
WHO ASKED YOU ABOUT YOUR SICKNESS, HUH?
Sickness = Sakura-Spoiling
Eek!
DOESN'T HE REALIZE THAT SHE IS SEEING HIM AS A MAN? DEAR GOD.
Well, I guess he can't help it. He's a sissy and a family-obsessed idiot.
BUT I'LL GIVE YOU SOME SPECIAL ADVICE.
STOP BOTHERING HER.
What?
LEAVE HER ALONE.

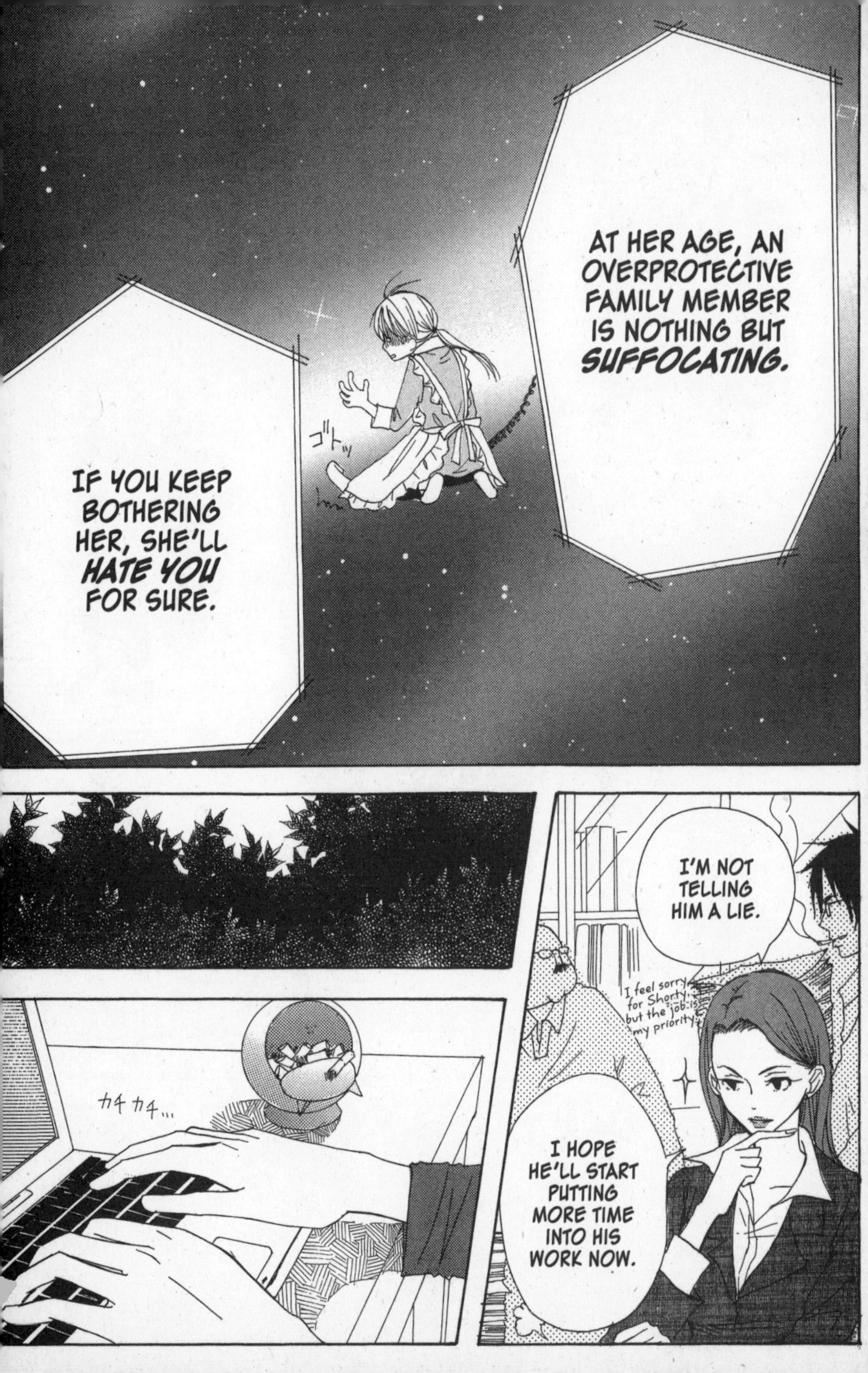
AT HER AGE, AN OVERPROTECTIVE FAMILY MEMBER IS NOTHING BUT SUFFOCATING.
ゴトッ
IF YOU KEEP BOTHERING HER, SHE'LL HATE YOU FOR SURE.
I'M NOT TELLING HIM A LIE.
I feel sorry for Shorty, but the job is my priority.
I HOPE HE'LL START PUTTING MORE TIME INTO HIS WORK NOW.
カチカチ...

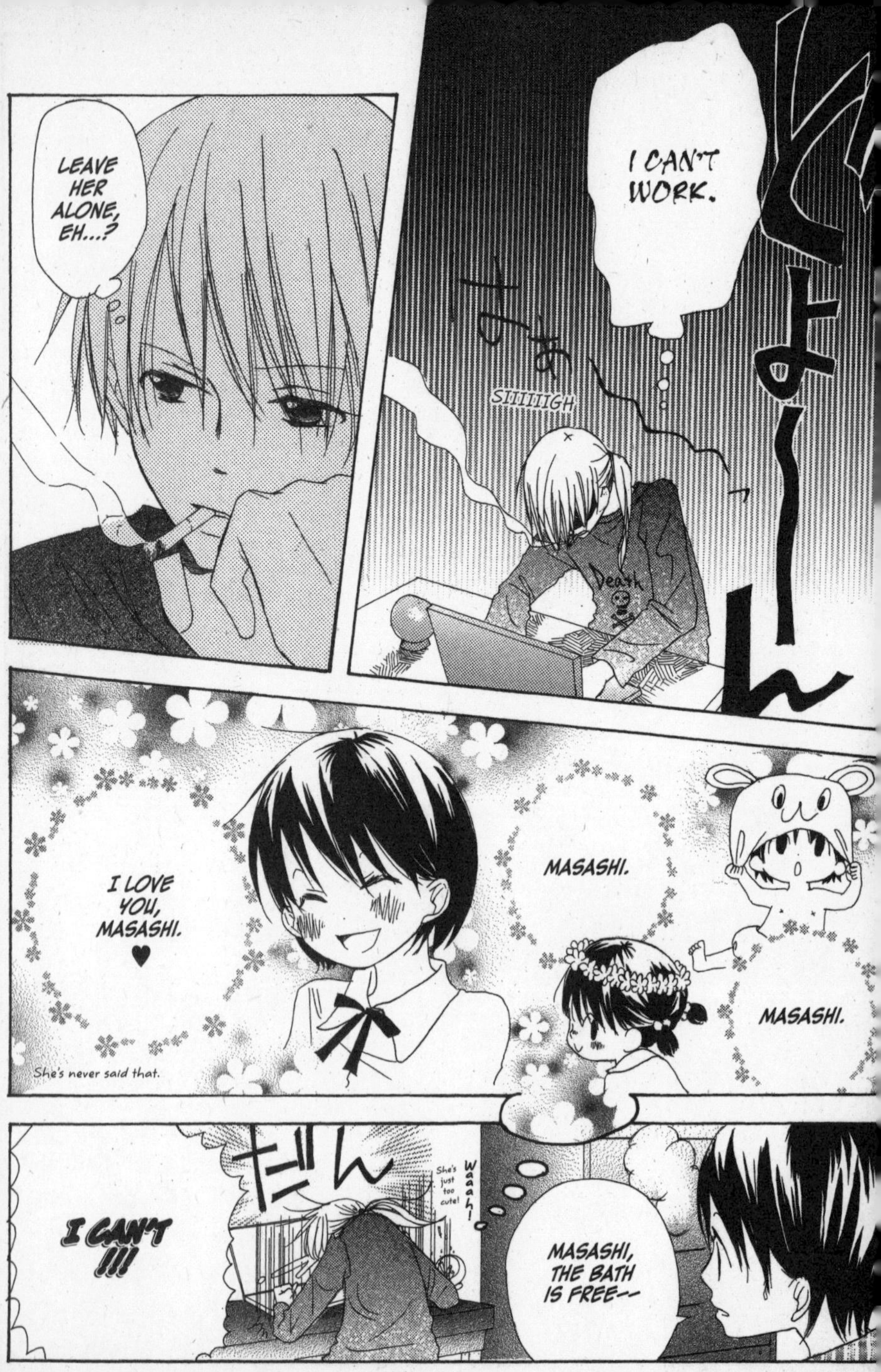
I CAN'T WORK.
どよーん
はぁ
SIIIIIIGH
Death
LEAVE HER ALONE, EH...?
MASASHI.
MASASHI.
I LOVE YOU, MASASHI. ♥
She's never said that.
MASASHI, THE BATH IS FREE--
Waaaah!
She's just too cute!
だん
I CAN'T !!!

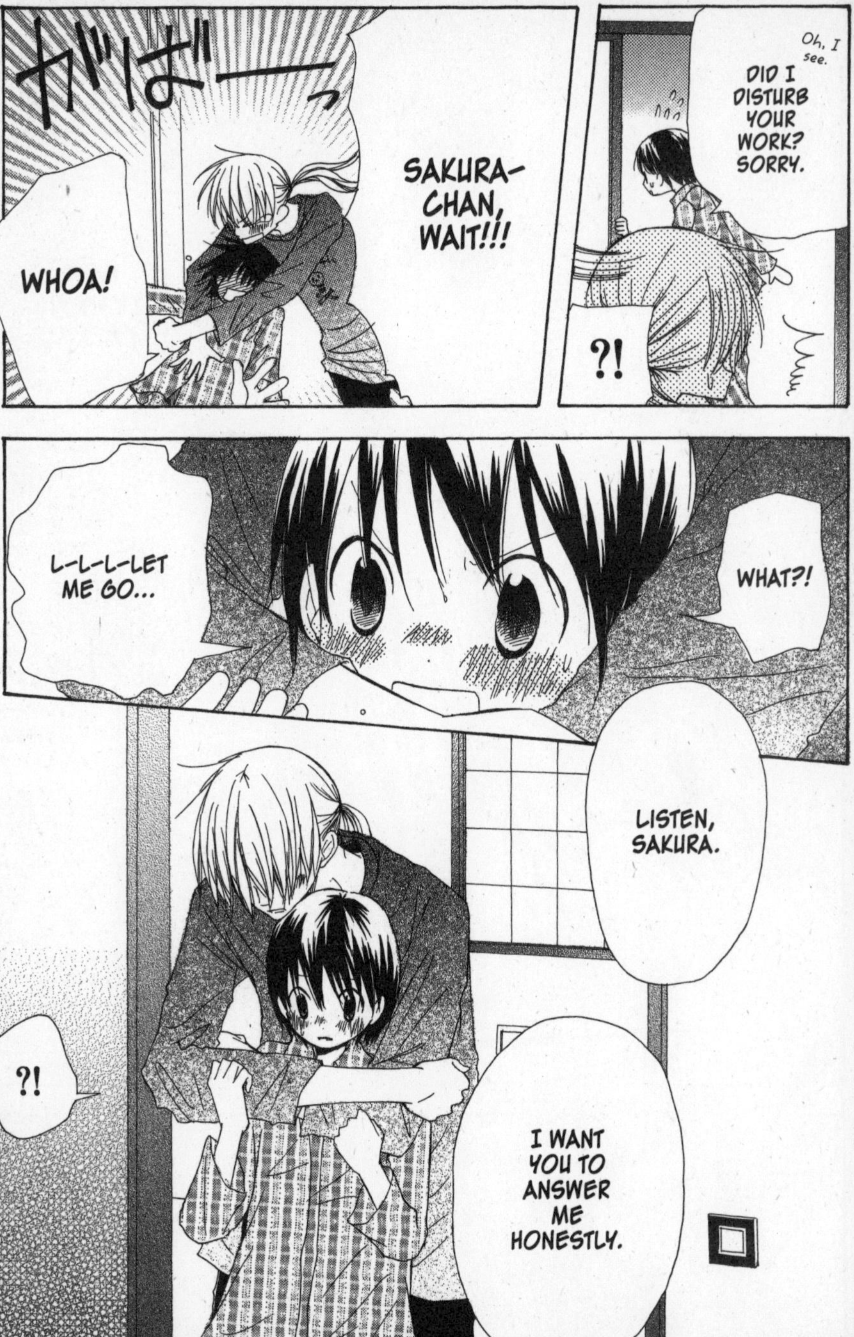
Oh, I see.
DID I DISTURB YOUR WORK? SORRY.
?!
がばーっ
SAKURA-CHAN, WAIT!!!
WHOA!
WHAT?!
L-L-L-LET ME GO...
LISTEN, SAKURA.
I WANT YOU TO ANSWER ME HONESTLY.
?!

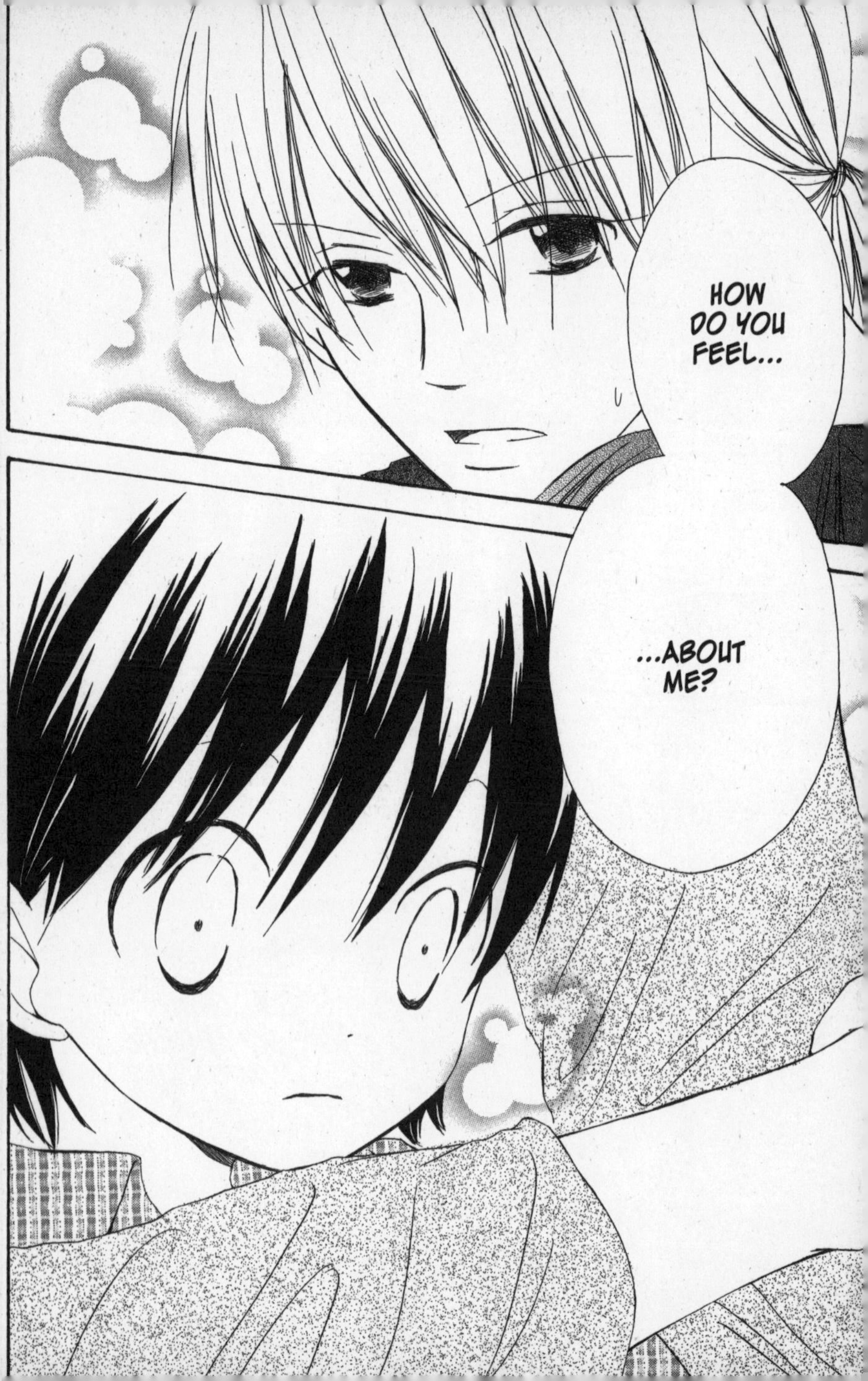
HOW DO YOU FEEL...
...ABOUT ME?

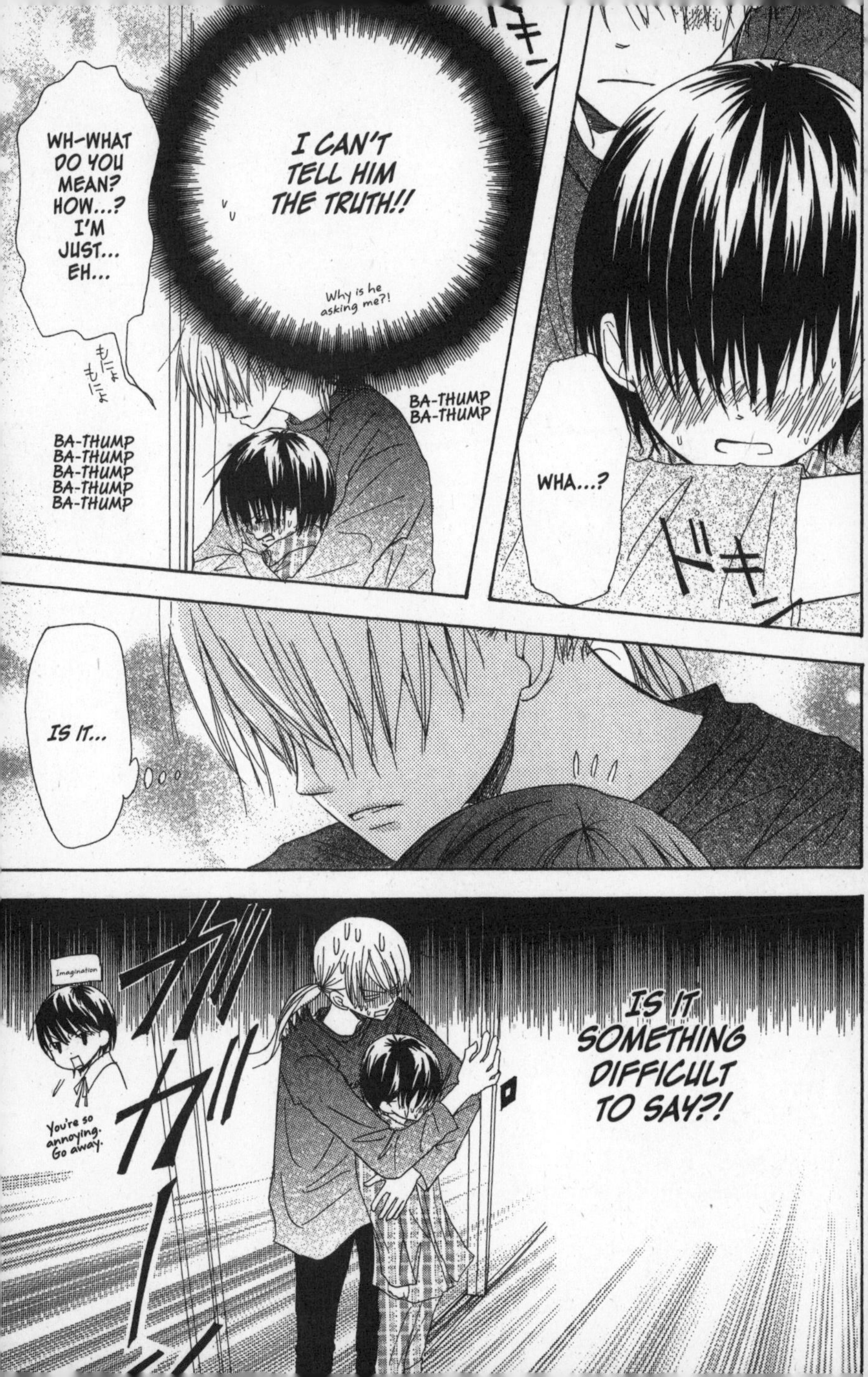
ドキン
WHA...?
ドキン
I CAN'T TELL HIM THE TRUTH!!
Why is he asking me?!
WH-WHAT DO YOU MEAN? HOW...? I'M JUST... EH...
もにょもにょ
BA-THUMP BA-THUMP
BA-THUMP BA-THUMP BA-THUMP BA-THUMP BA-THUMP
IS IT...
IS IT SOMETHING DIFFICULT TO SAY?!
Imagination
You're so annoying. Go away.

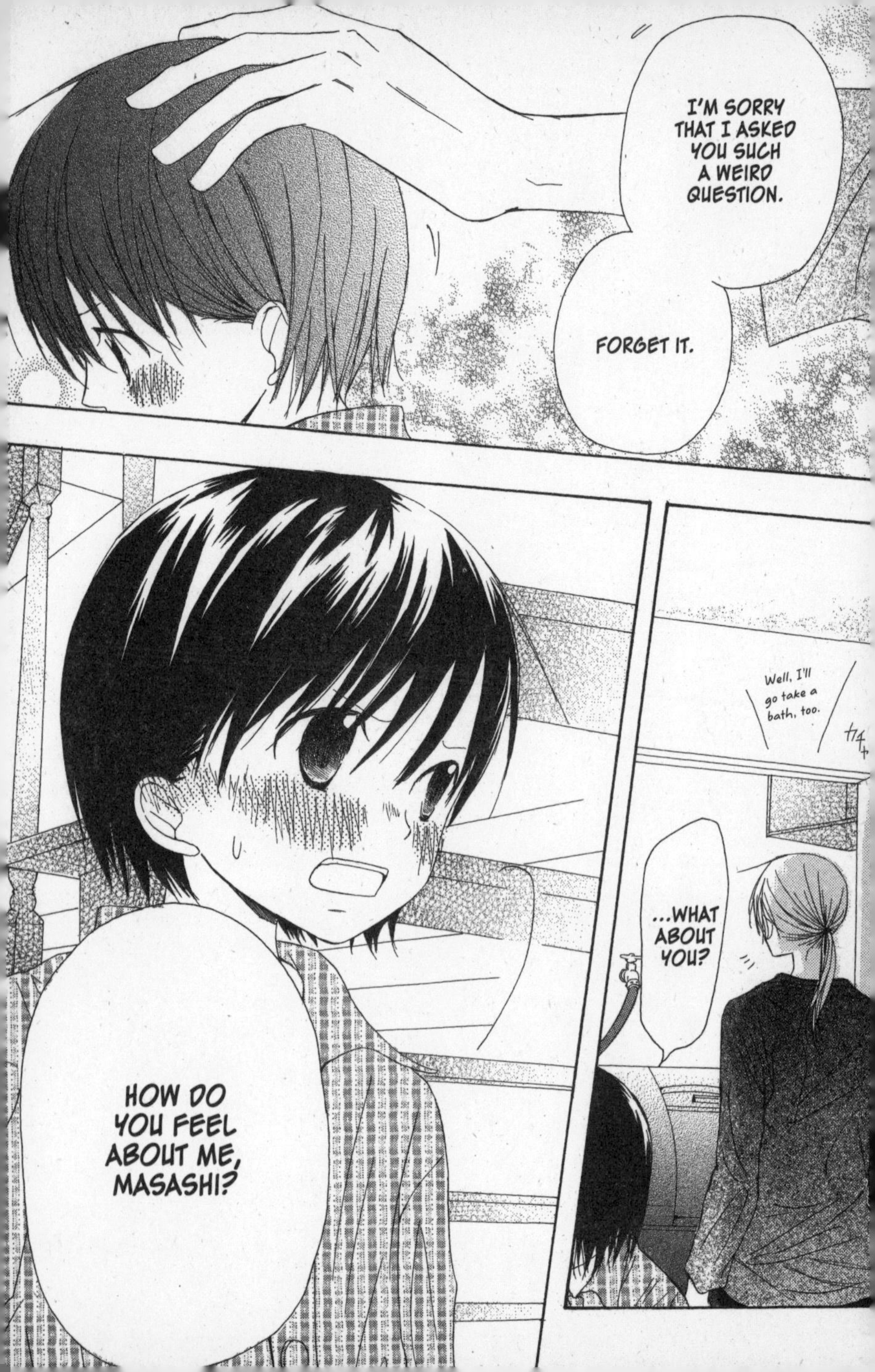
I'M SORRY THAT I ASKED YOU SUCH A WEIRD QUESTION.
FORGET IT.
Well, I'll go take a bath, too.
...WHAT ABOUT YOU?
HOW DO YOU FEEL ABOUT ME, MASASHI?

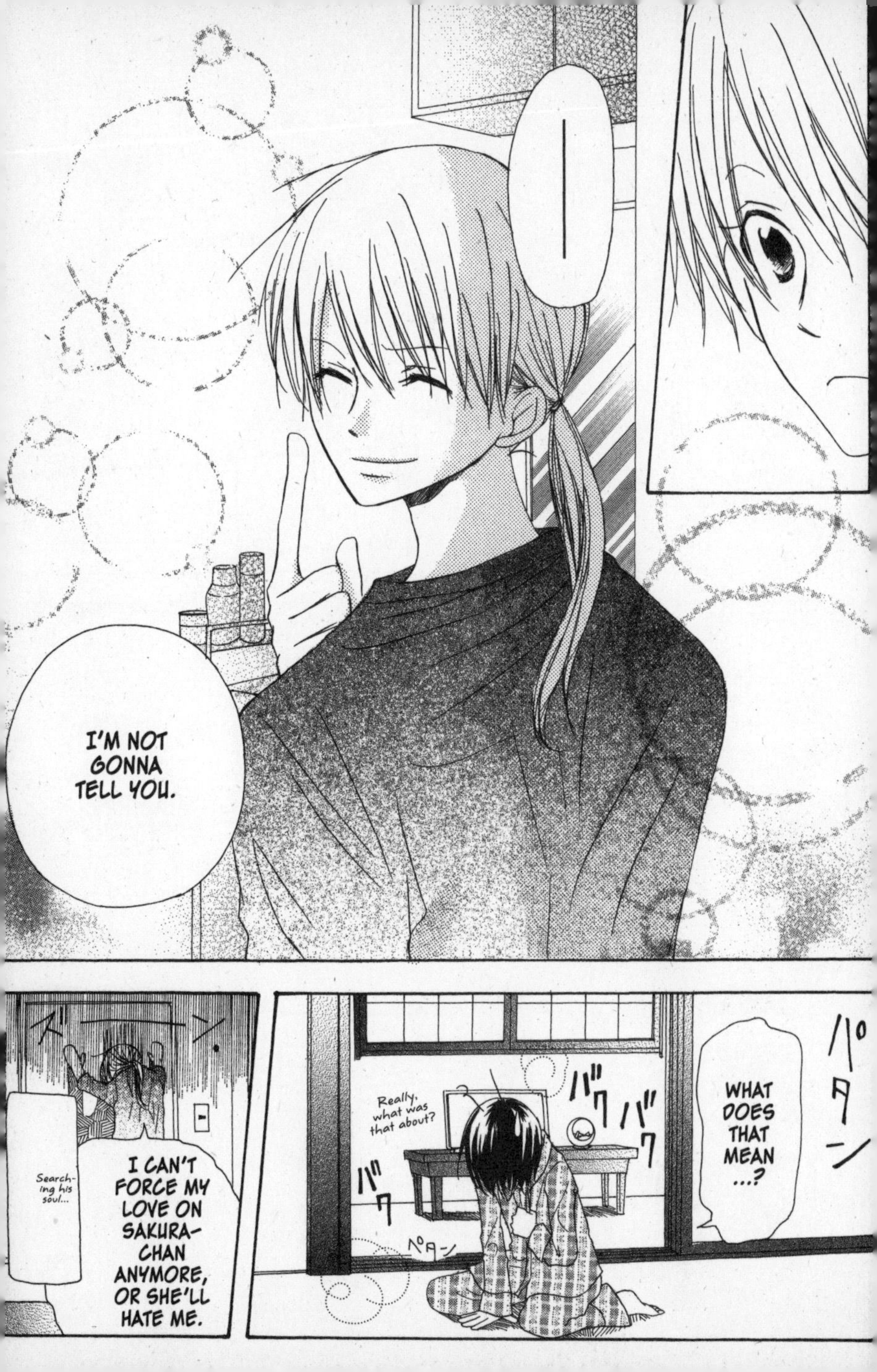
I'M NOT GONNA TELL YOU.
パタン
WHAT DOES THAT MEAN ...?
バクバク
バク
Really, what was that about?
ペターン
ズーン
I CAN'T FORCE MY LOVE ON SAKURA-CHAN ANYMORE, OR SHE'LL HATE ME.
Searching his soul...

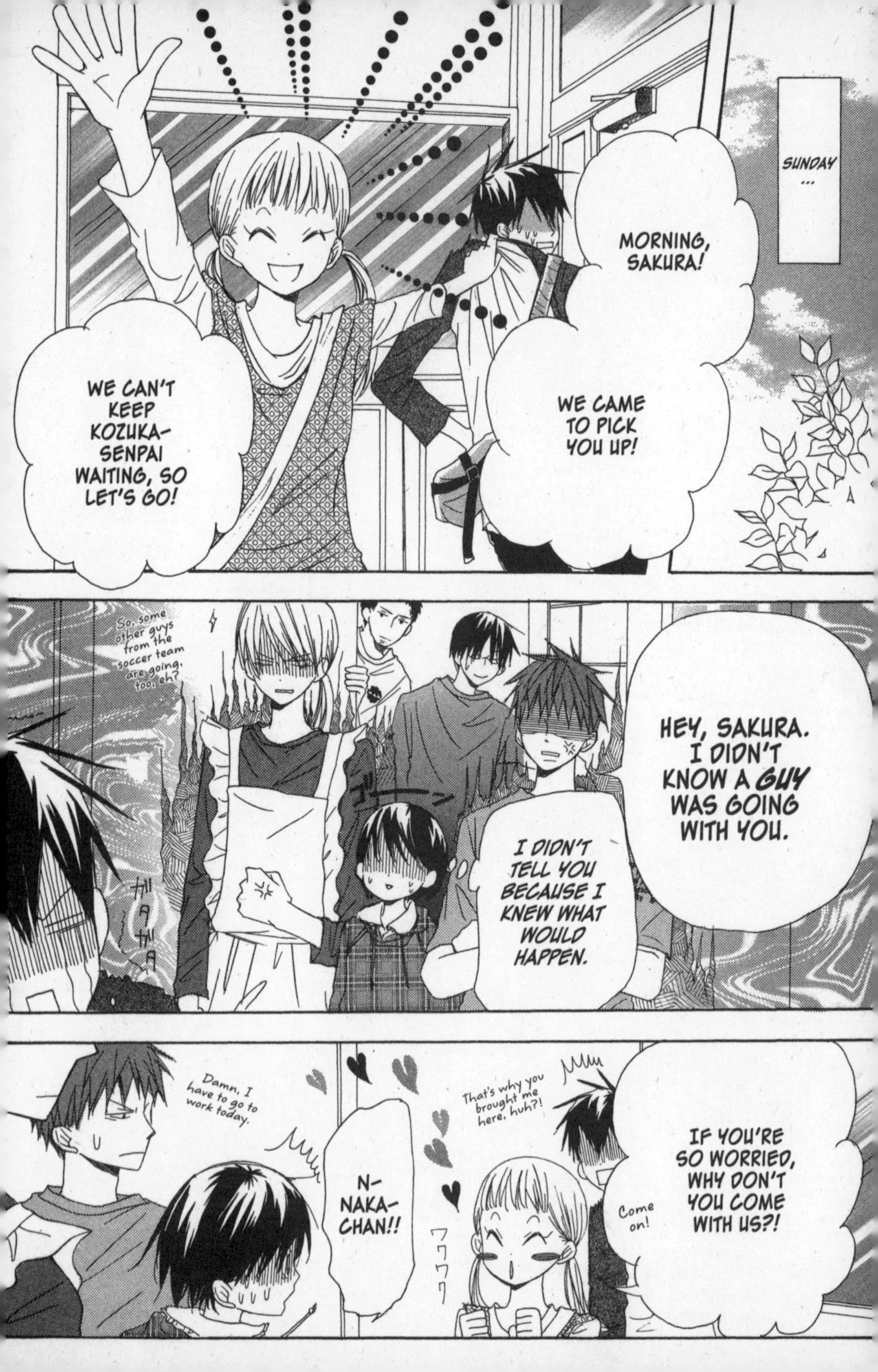
SUNDAY ...
MORNING, SAKURA!
WE CAME TO PICK YOU UP!
WE CAN'T KEEP KOZUKA-SENPAI WAITING, SO LET'S GO!
HEY, SAKURA. I DIDN'T KNOW A GUY WAS GOING WITH YOU.
I DIDN'T TELL YOU BECAUSE I KNEW WHAT WOULD HAPPEN.
So, some other guys from the soccer team are going, too, eh?
ガタガタ
IF YOU'RE SO WORRIED, WHY DON'T YOU COME WITH US?!
Come on!
That's why you brought me here, huh?!
ワクワク
N-NAKA-CHAN!!
Damn, I have to go to work today.

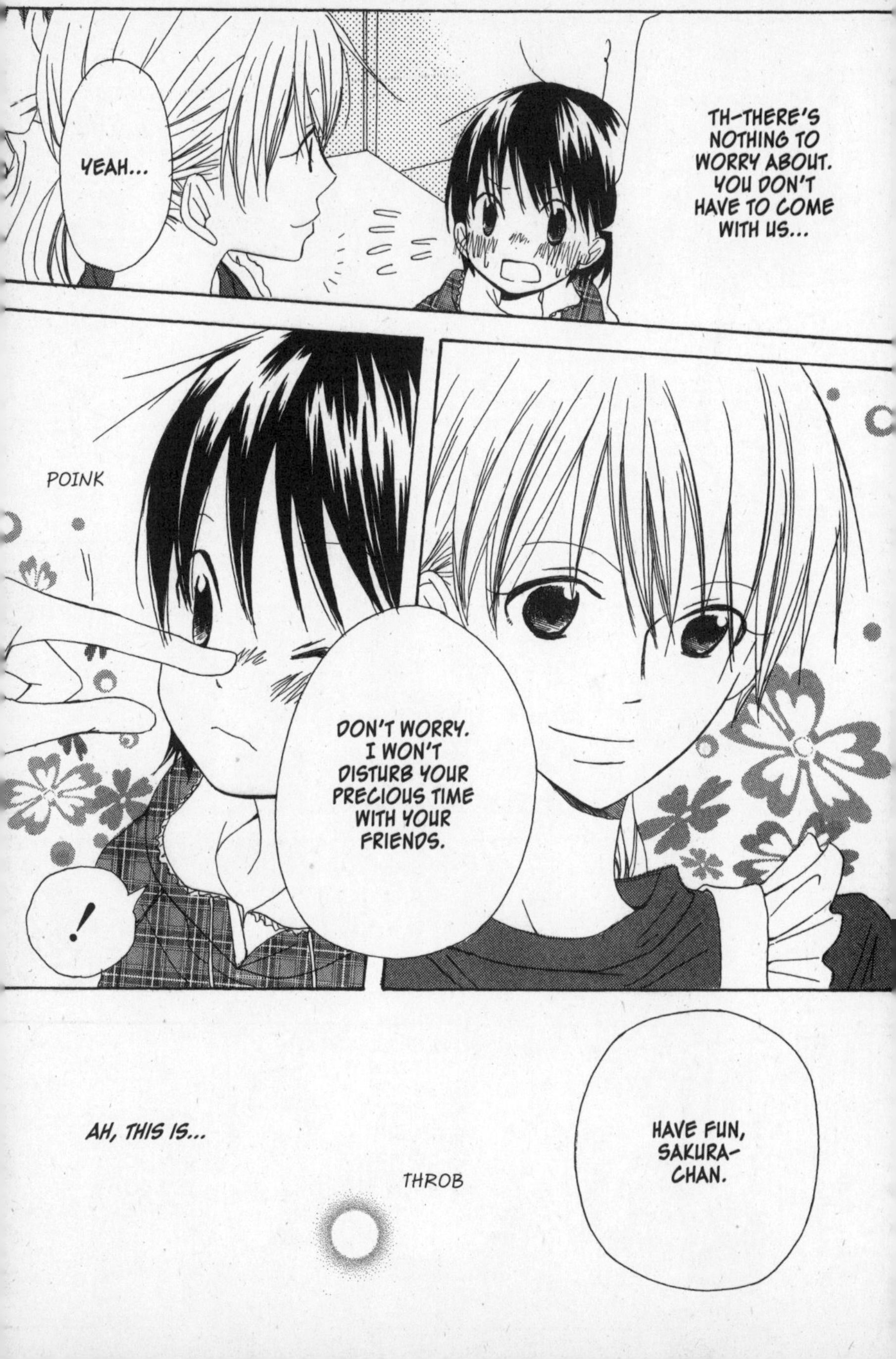
TH-THERE'S NOTHING TO WORRY ABOUT. YOU DON'T HAVE TO COME WITH US...
YEAH...
DON'T WORRY. I WON'T DISTURB YOUR PRECIOUS TIME WITH YOUR FRIENDS.
POINK
!
HAVE FUN, SAKURA-CHAN.
THROB
AH, THIS IS...

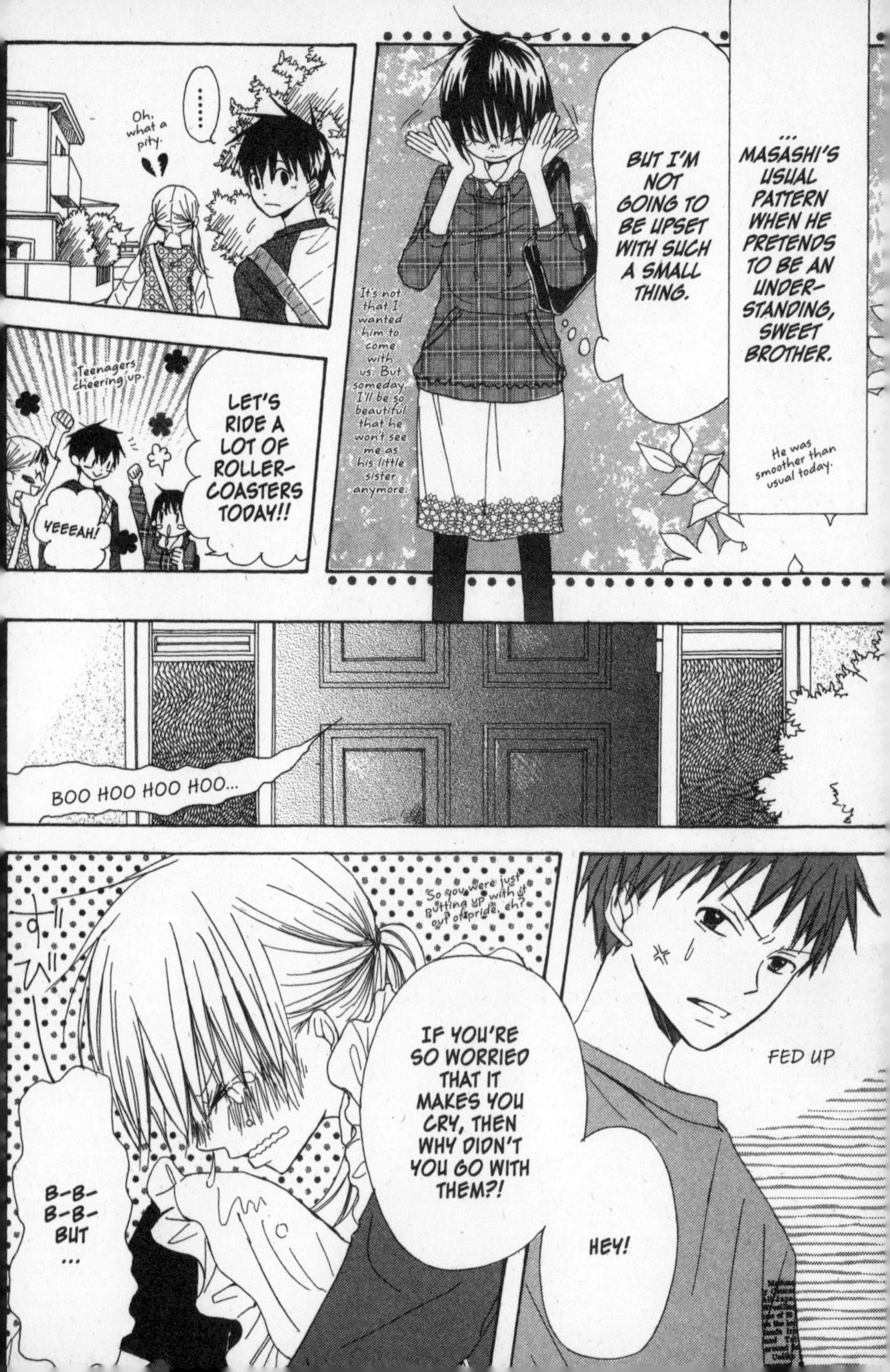
... MASASHI'S USUAL PATTERN WHEN HE PRETENDS TO BE AN UNDER-STANDING, SWEET BROTHER.
He was smoother than usual today.
BUT I'M NOT GOING TO BE UPSET WITH SUCH A SMALL THING.
It's not that I wanted him to come with us. But someday I'll be so beautiful that he won't see me as his little sister anymore.
......
Oh, what a pity.
LET'S RIDE A LOT OF ROLLER-COASTERS TODAY!!
Teenagers cheering up.
YEEEAH!
BOO HOO HOO HOO...
So you were just putting up with it out of pride, eh?
FED UP
IF YOU'RE SO WORRIED THAT IT MAKES YOU CRY, THEN WHY DIDN'T YOU GO WITH THEM?!
HEY!
B-B-B-B-BUT ...

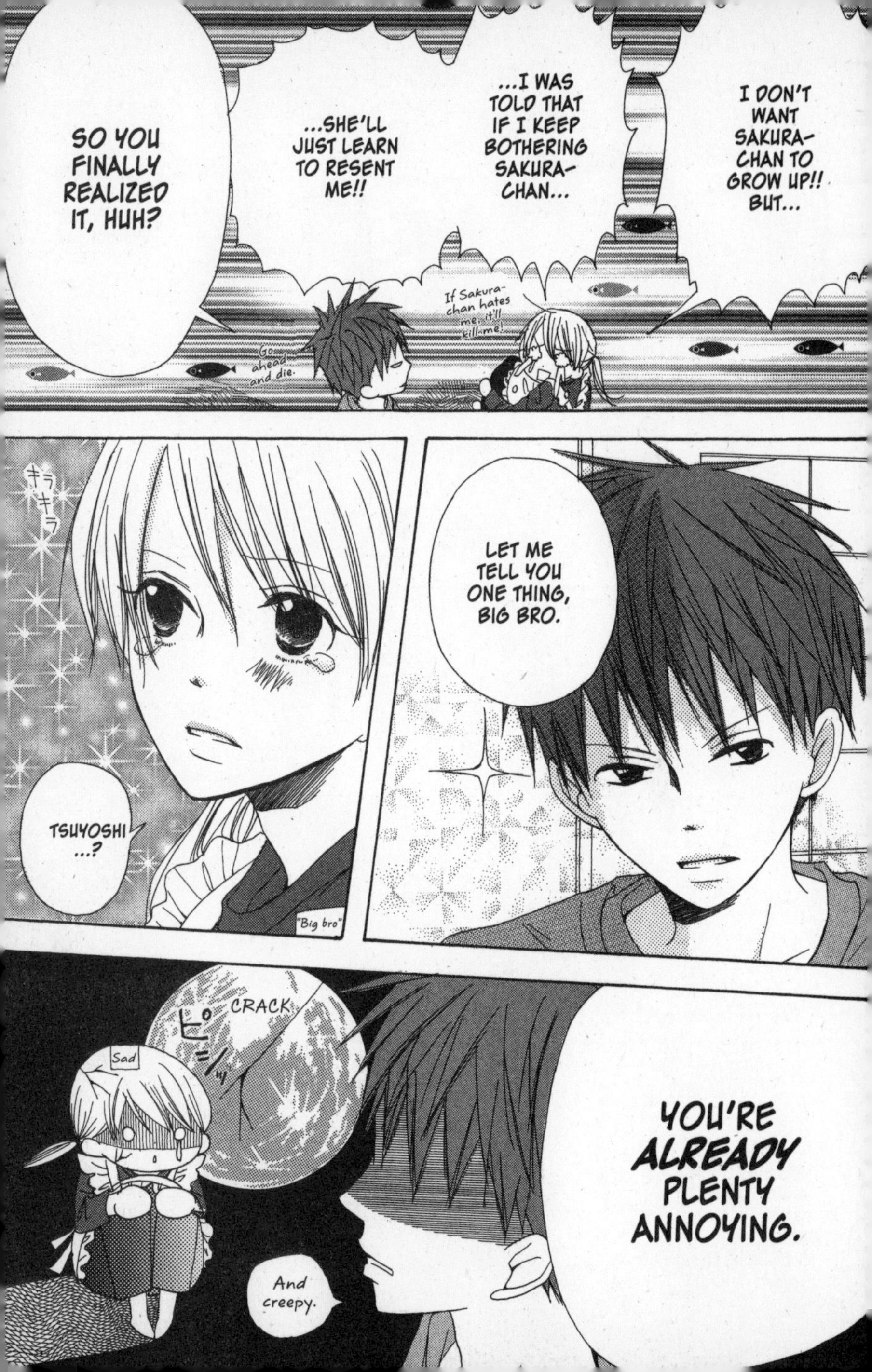
I DON'T WANT SAKURA-CHAN TO GROW UP!! BUT...
...I WAS TOLD THAT IF I KEEP BOTHERING SAKURA-CHAN...
...SHE'LL JUST LEARN TO RESENT ME!!
SO YOU FINALLY REALIZED IT, HUH?
If Sakura-chan hates me, it'll kill me!
Go ahead and die.
LET ME TELL YOU ONE THING, BIG BRO.
キラキラ
TSUYOSHI ...?
"Big bro"
YOU'RE ALREADY PLENTY ANNOYING.
CRACK
Sad
And creepy.

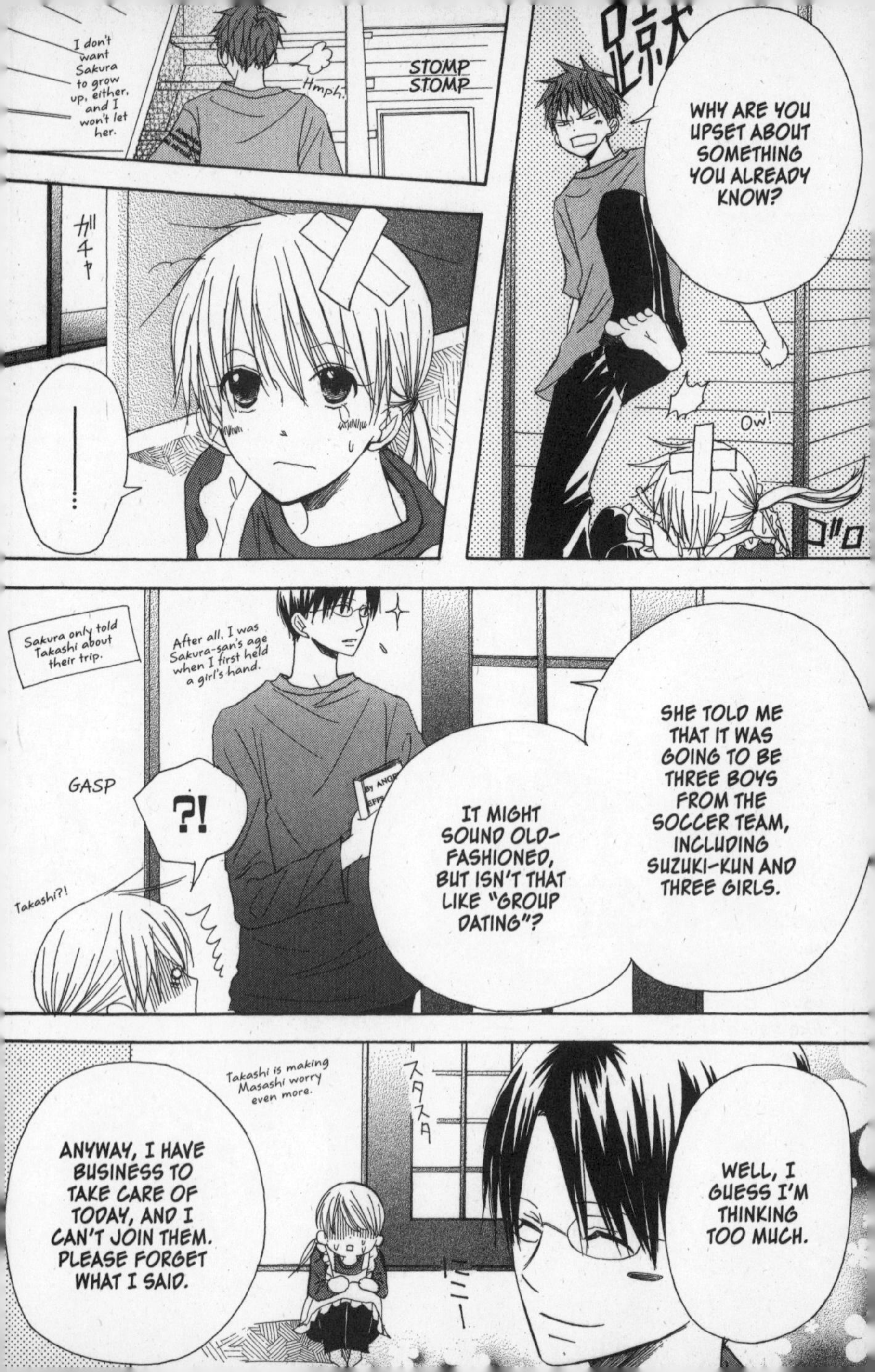
蹴
WHY ARE YOU UPSET ABOUT SOMETHING YOU ALREADY KNOW?
Ow!
ゴロ
I don't want Sakura to grow up, either, and I won't let her.
Hmph.
STOMP STOMP
ガチャ
......!
SHE TOLD ME THAT IT WAS GOING TO BE THREE BOYS FROM THE SOCCER TEAM, INCLUDING SUZUKI-KUN AND THREE GIRLS.
IT MIGHT SOUND OLD-FASHIONED, BUT ISN'T THAT LIKE "GROUP DATING"?
After all, I was Sakura-san's age when I first held a girl's hand.
Sakura only told Takashi about their trip.
GASP
?!
Takashi?!
WELL, I GUESS I'M THINKING TOO MUCH.
ニコー
スタスタ
Takashi is making Masashi worry even more.
ANYWAY, I HAVE BUSINESS TO TAKE CARE OF TODAY, AND I CAN'T JOIN THEM. PLEASE FORGET WHAT I SAID.

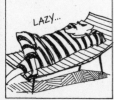

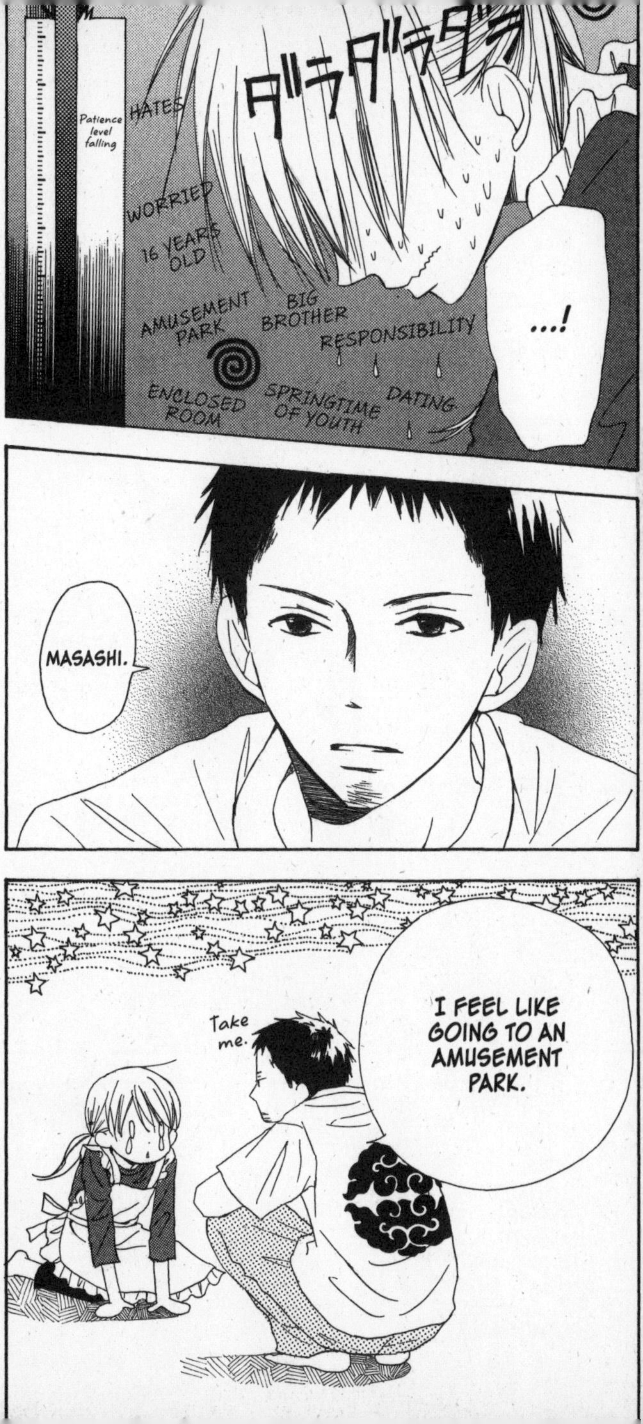
ダラダラダラ
Patience level falling
HATES
WORRIED
16 YEARS OLD
AMUSEMENT PARK
BIG BROTHER
RESPONSIBILITY
ENCLOSED ROOM
SPRINGTIME OF YOUTH
DATING
...!
MASASHI.
I FEEL LIKE GOING TO AN AMUSEMENT PARK.
Take me.

4

As I was remembering about my scribbling during lessons in school, I started to think, "How many years ago was that?" and that made me sad. All of a sudden, I'm in my 30s if I round off my age. Rounding off is a scary thing, isn't it? But if I round off the number of this book, it means that there already are 10 volumes... I think about stupid things like that. This column is starting to sound more lazy than usual. But I like being lazy. Lazy, or idle, or purposeless.

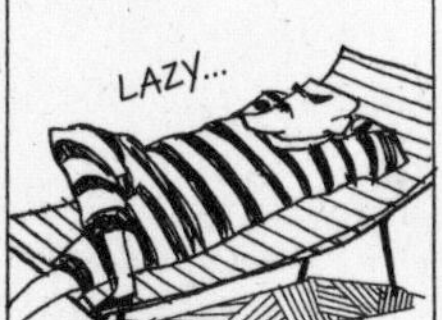
LAZY...

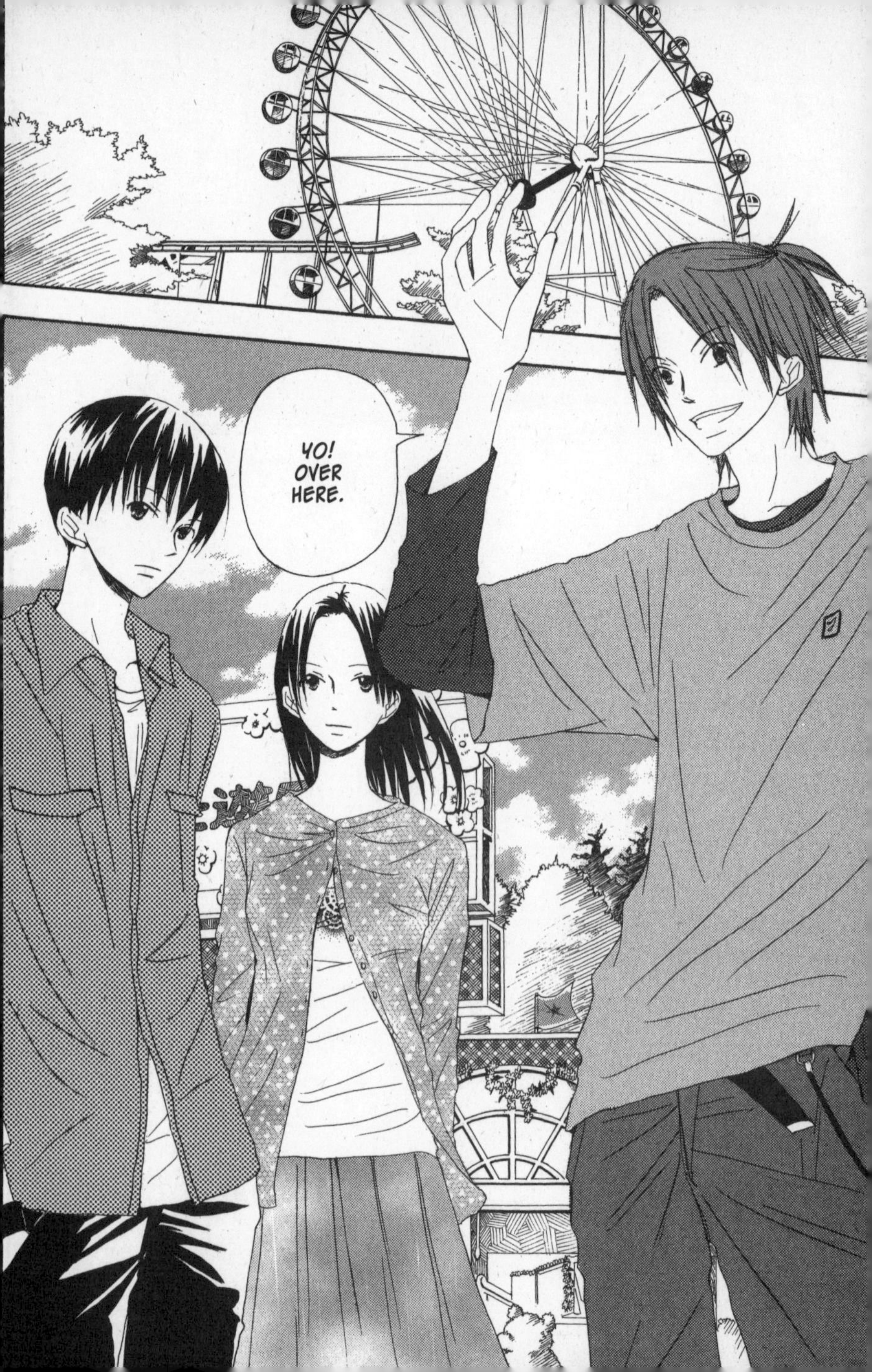
YO! OVER HERE.

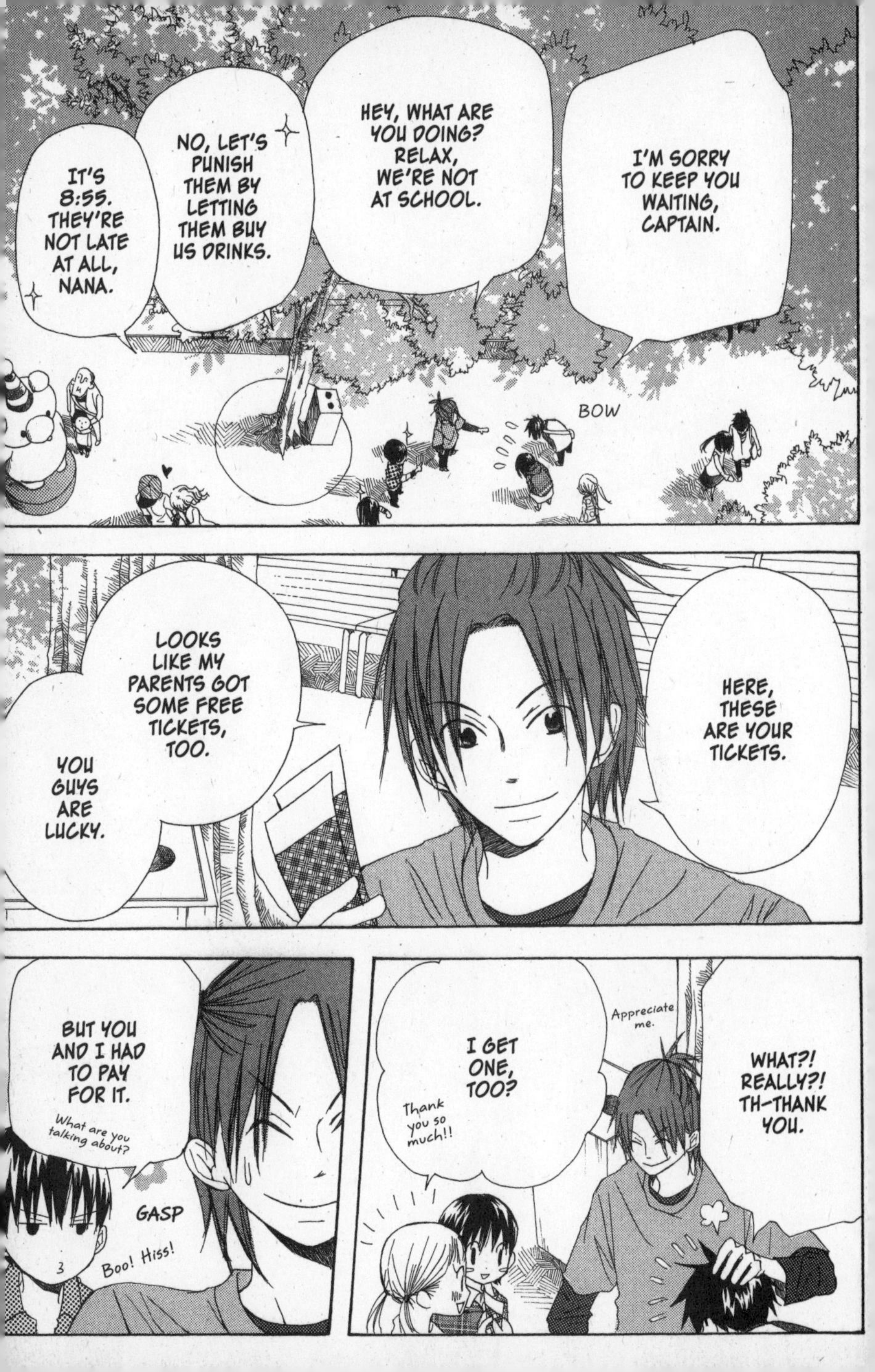

I'M SORRY TO KEEP YOU WAITING, CAPTAIN.
HEY, WHAT ARE YOU DOING? RELAX, WE'RE NOT AT SCHOOL.
NO, LET'S PUNISH THEM BY LETTING THEM BUY US DRINKS.
IT'S 8:55. THEY'RE NOT LATE AT ALL, NANA.
BOW
HERE, THESE ARE YOUR TICKETS.
LOOKS LIKE MY PARENTS GOT SOME FREE TICKETS, TOO.
YOU GUYS ARE LUCKY.
WHAT?! REALLY?! TH-THANK YOU.
Appreciate me.
I GET ONE, TOO?
Thank you so much!!
BUT YOU AND I HAD TO PAY FOR IT.
What are you talking about?
GASP
Boo! Hiss!

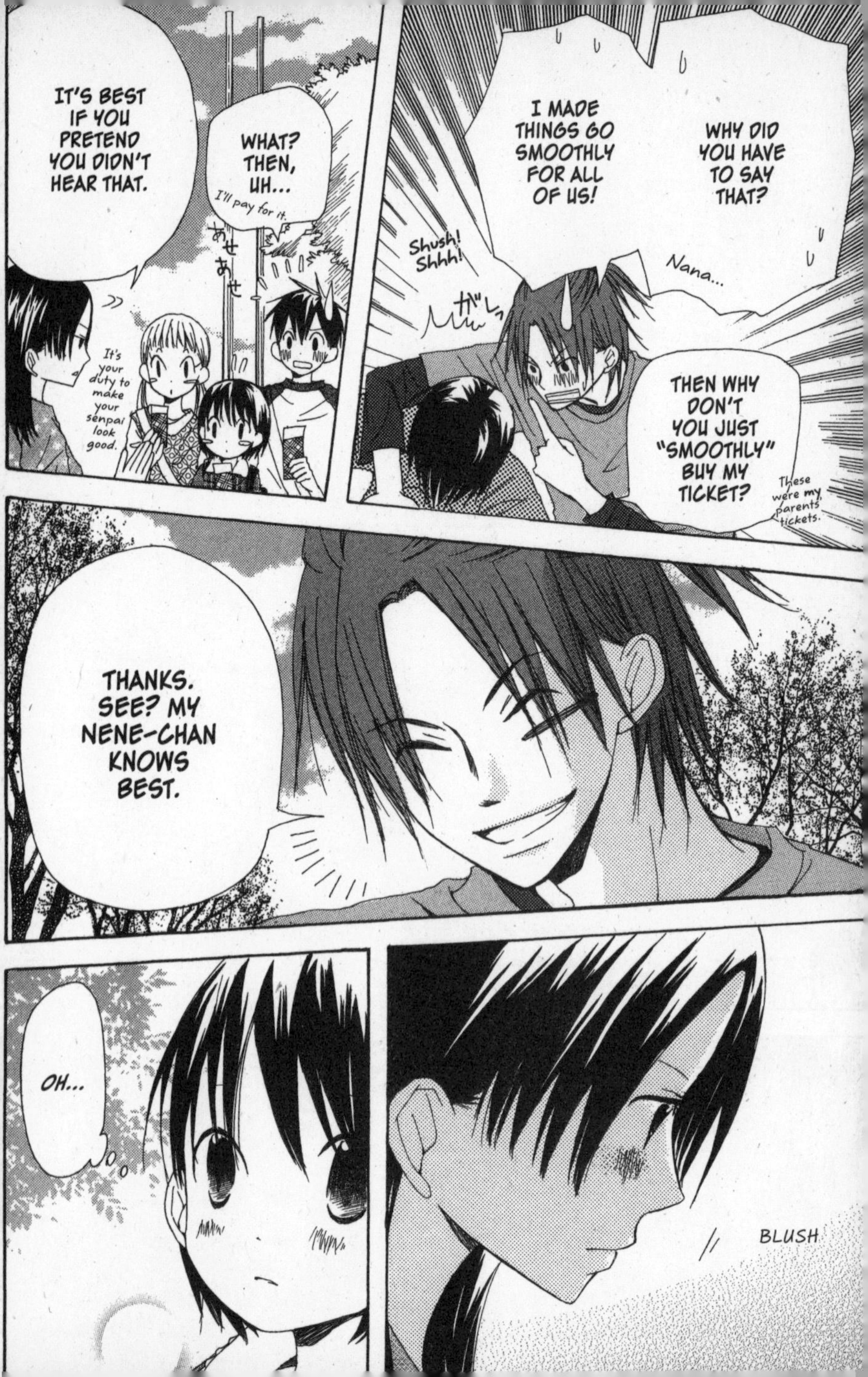
WHY DID YOU HAVE TO SAY THAT?
I MADE THINGS GO SMOOTHLY FOR ALL OF US!
Nana...
Shush! Shhh!
THEN WHY DON'T YOU JUST "SMOOTHLY" BUY MY TICKET?
These were my parents' tickets.
IT'S BEST IF YOU PRETEND YOU DIDN'T HEAR THAT.
WHAT? THEN, UH...
I'll pay for it.
あせあせ
It's your duty to make your senpai look good.
THANKS. SEE? MY NENE-CHAN KNOWS BEST.
BLUSH
OH...

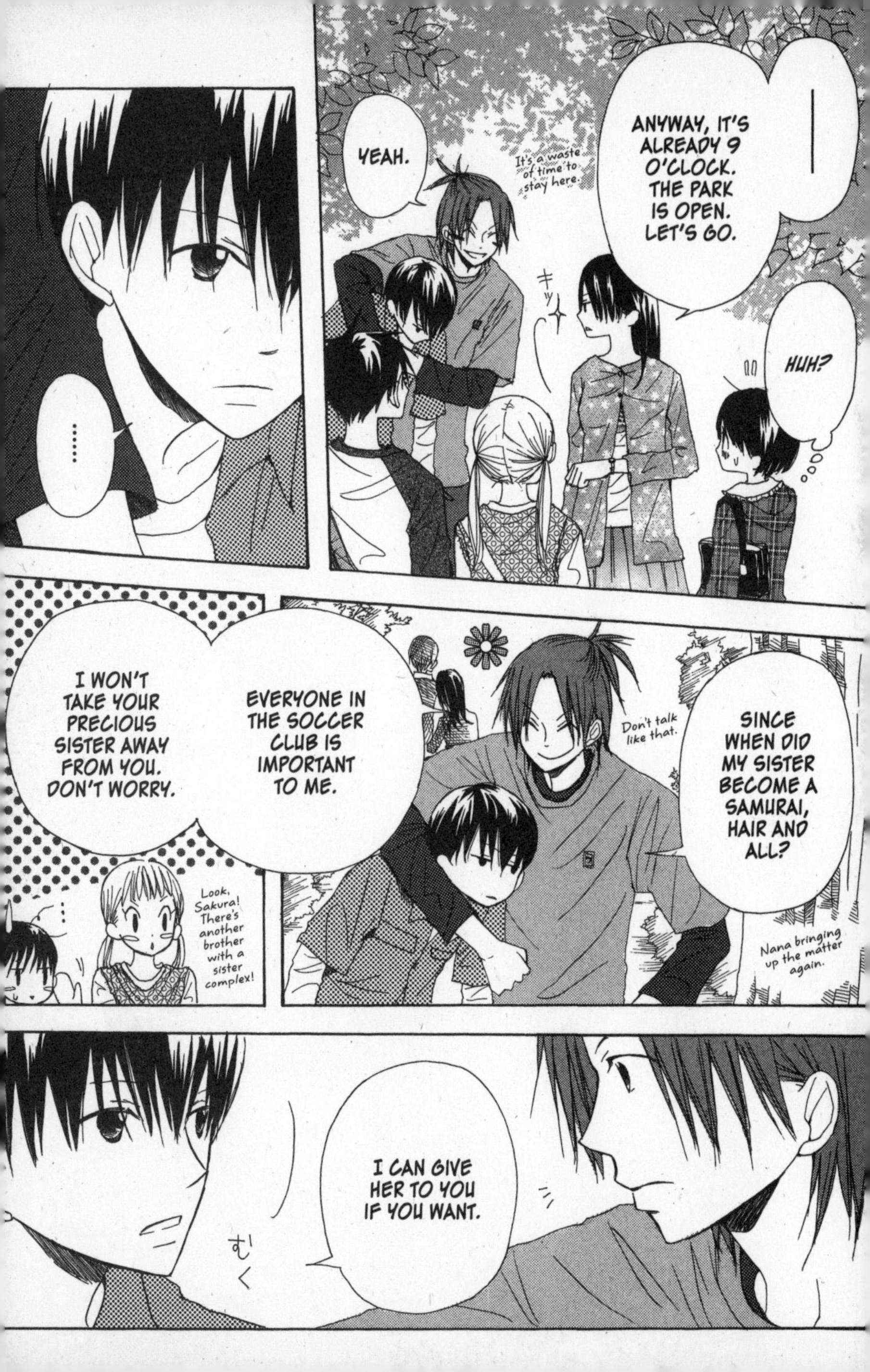

ANYWAY, IT'S ALREADY 9 O'CLOCK. THE PARK IS OPEN. LET'S GO.
HUH?
キッ
It's a waste of time to stay here.
YEAH.
......
SINCE WHEN DID MY SISTER BECOME A SAMURAI, HAIR AND ALL?
Don't talk like that.
Nana bringing up the matter again.
EVERYONE IN THE SOCCER CLUB IS IMPORTANT TO ME.
I WON'T TAKE YOUR PRECIOUS SISTER AWAY FROM YOU. DON'T WORRY.
Look, Sakura! There's another brother with a sister complex!
...
I CAN GIVE HER TO YOU IF YOU WANT.
むく

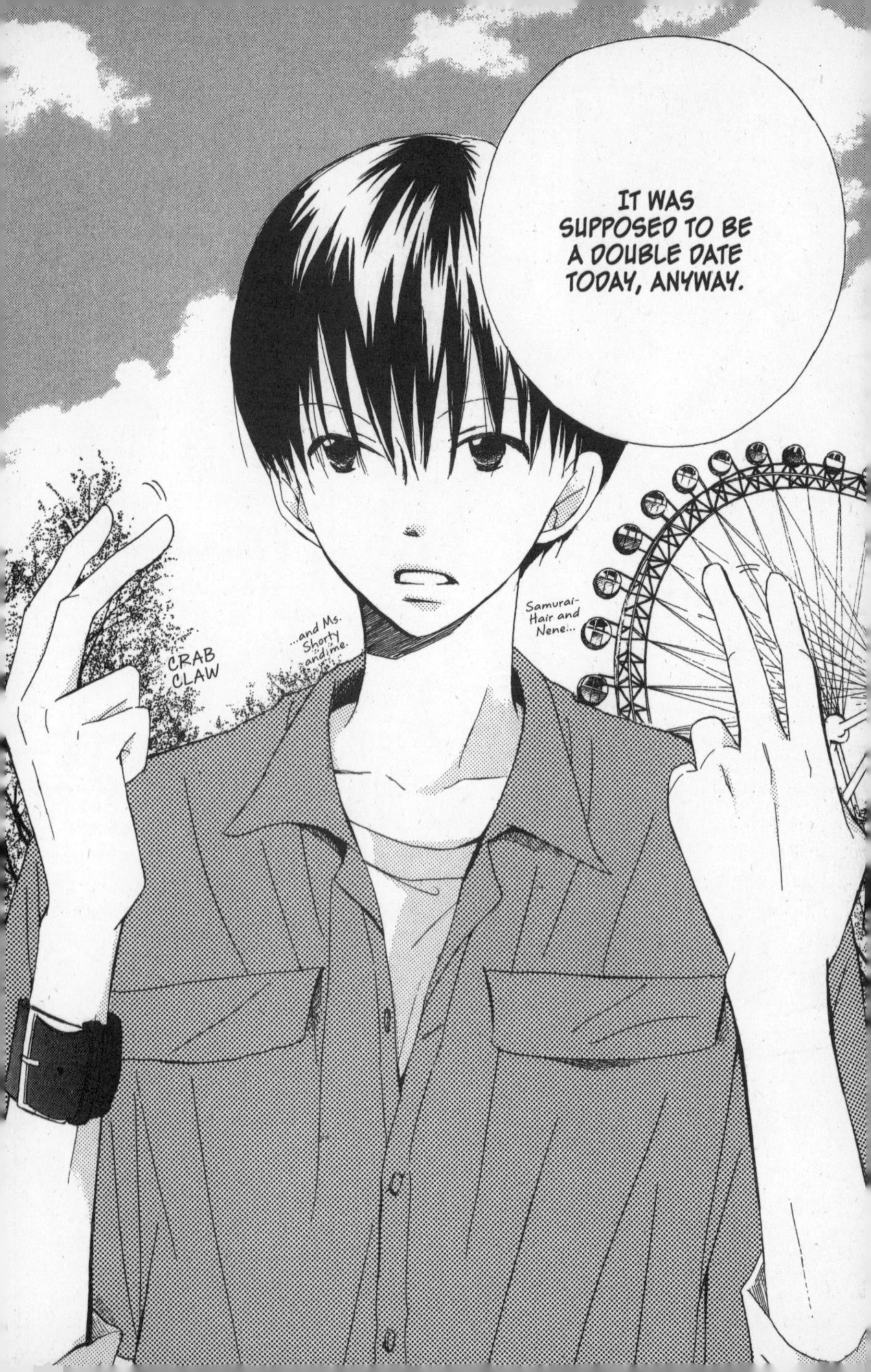
IT WAS SUPPOSED TO BE A DOUBLE DATE TODAY, ANYWAY.
Samurai-Hair and Nene...
...and Ms. Shorty and me.
CRAB CLAW

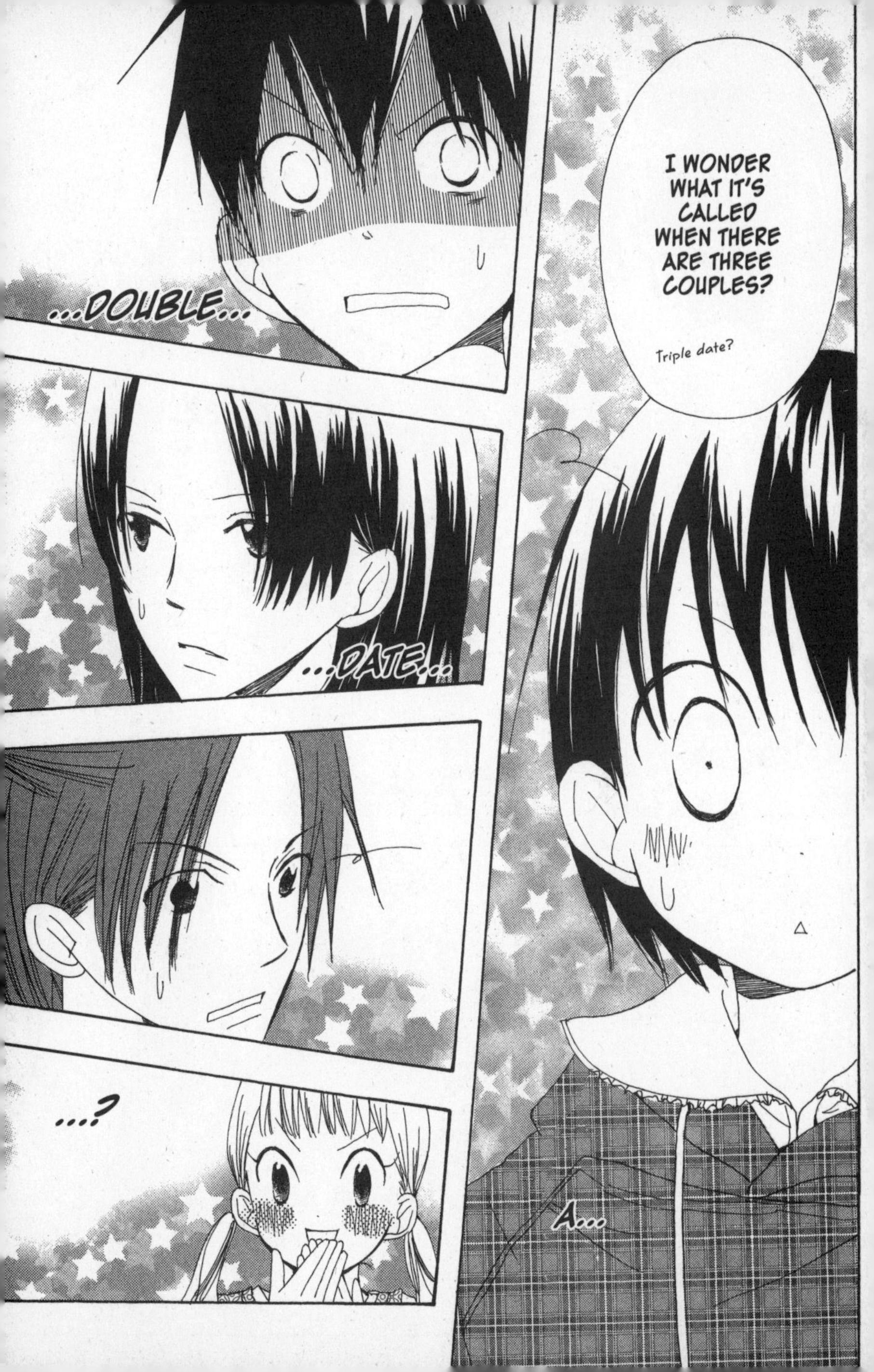
I WONDER WHAT IT'S CALLED WHEN THERE ARE THREE COUPLES?
Triple date?
A...
...DOUBLE...
...DATE...
...?

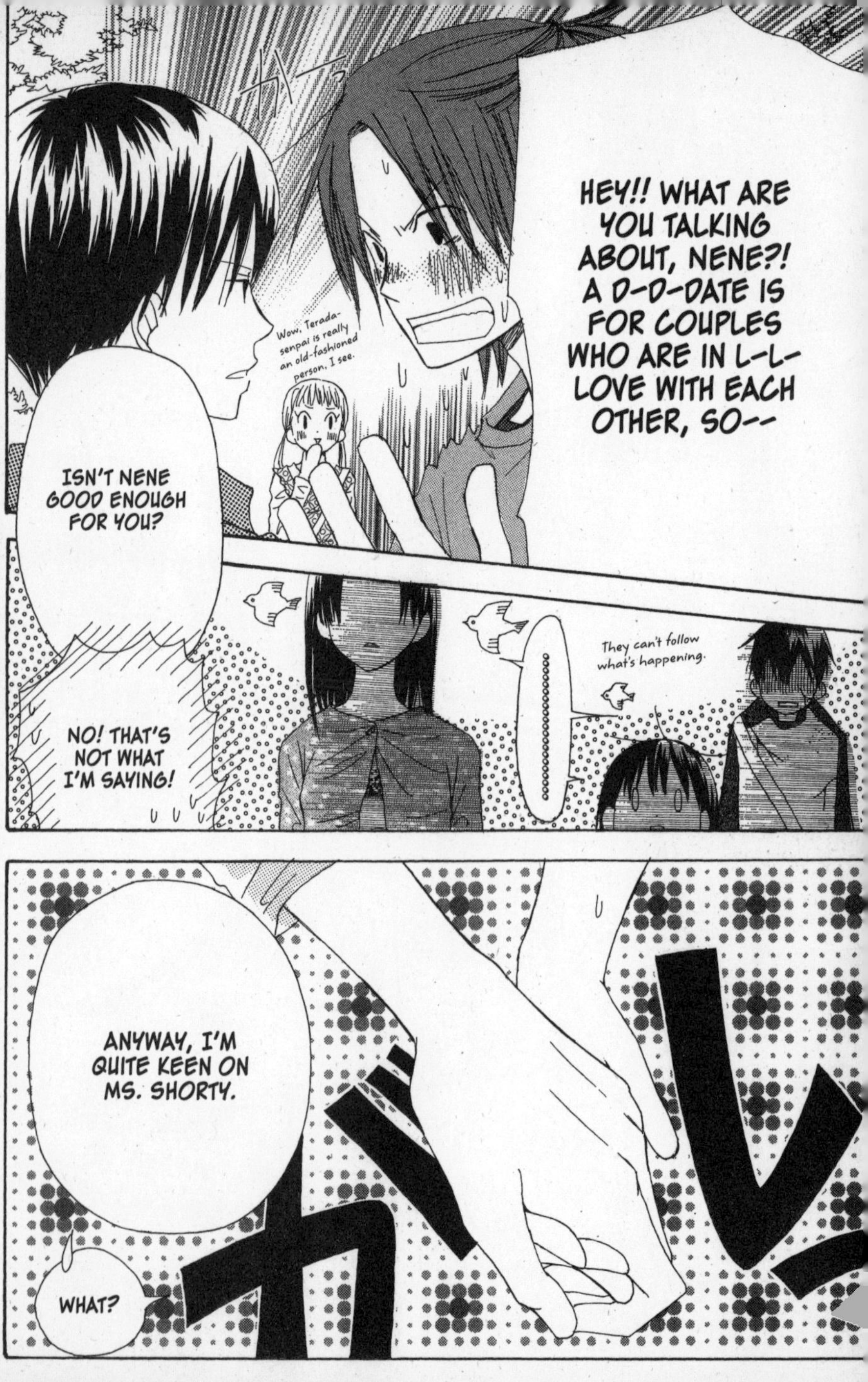
HEY!! WHAT ARE YOU TALKING ABOUT, NENE?! A D-D-DATE IS FOR COUPLES WHO ARE IN L-L-LOVE WITH EACH OTHER, SO--
Wow, Terada-senpai is really an old-fashioned person, I see.
ISN'T NENE GOOD ENOUGH FOR YOU?
They can't follow what's happening.
....
NO! THAT'S NOT WHAT I'M SAYING!
ANYWAY, I'M QUITE KEEN ON MS. SHORTY.
WHAT?

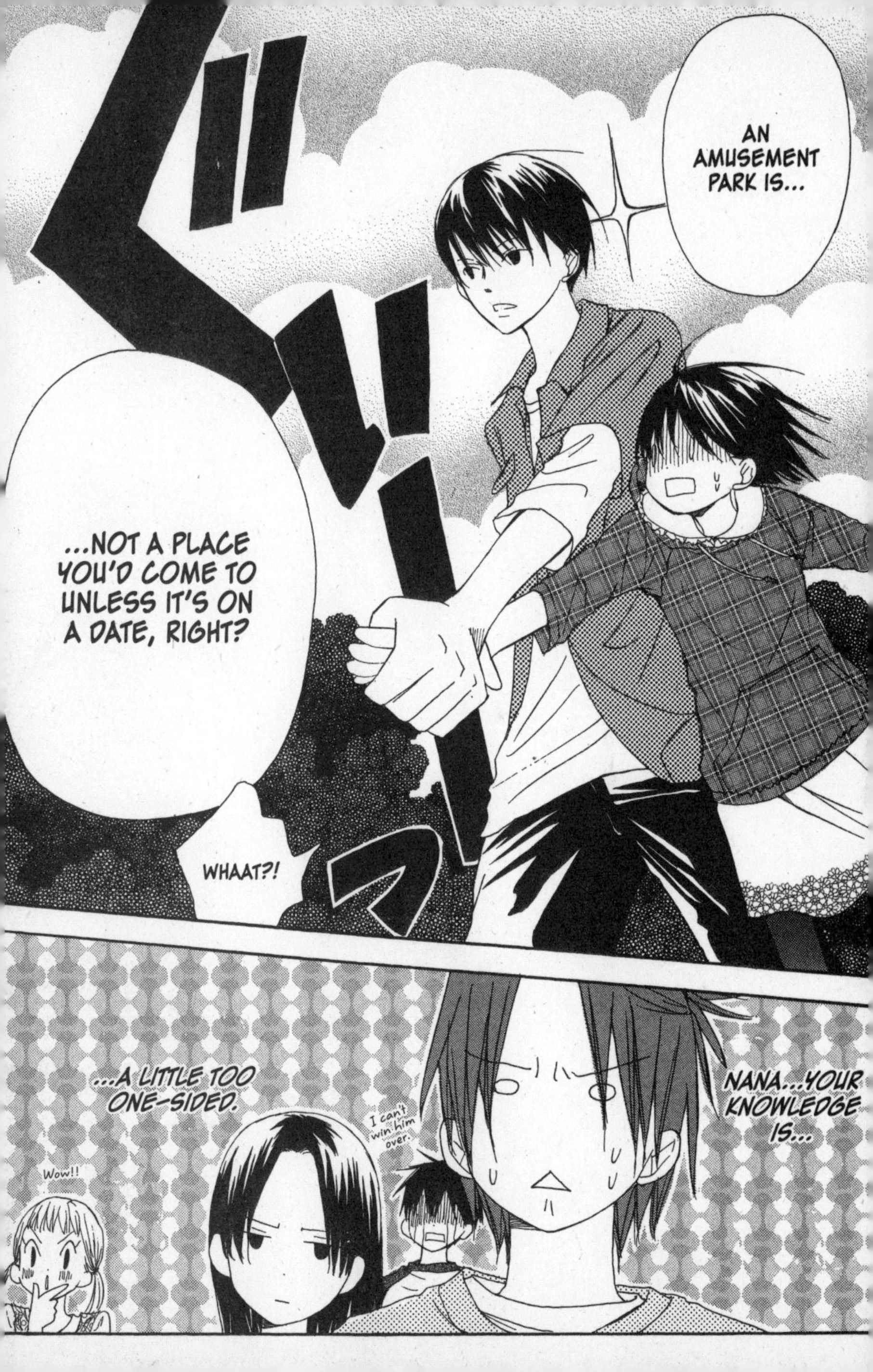

AN AMUSEMENT PARK IS...
...NOT A PLACE YOU'D COME TO UNLESS IT'S ON A DATE, RIGHT?
WHAAT?!
NANA...YOUR KNOWLEDGE IS...
...A LITTLE TOO ONE-SIDED.
I can't win him over.
Wow!!

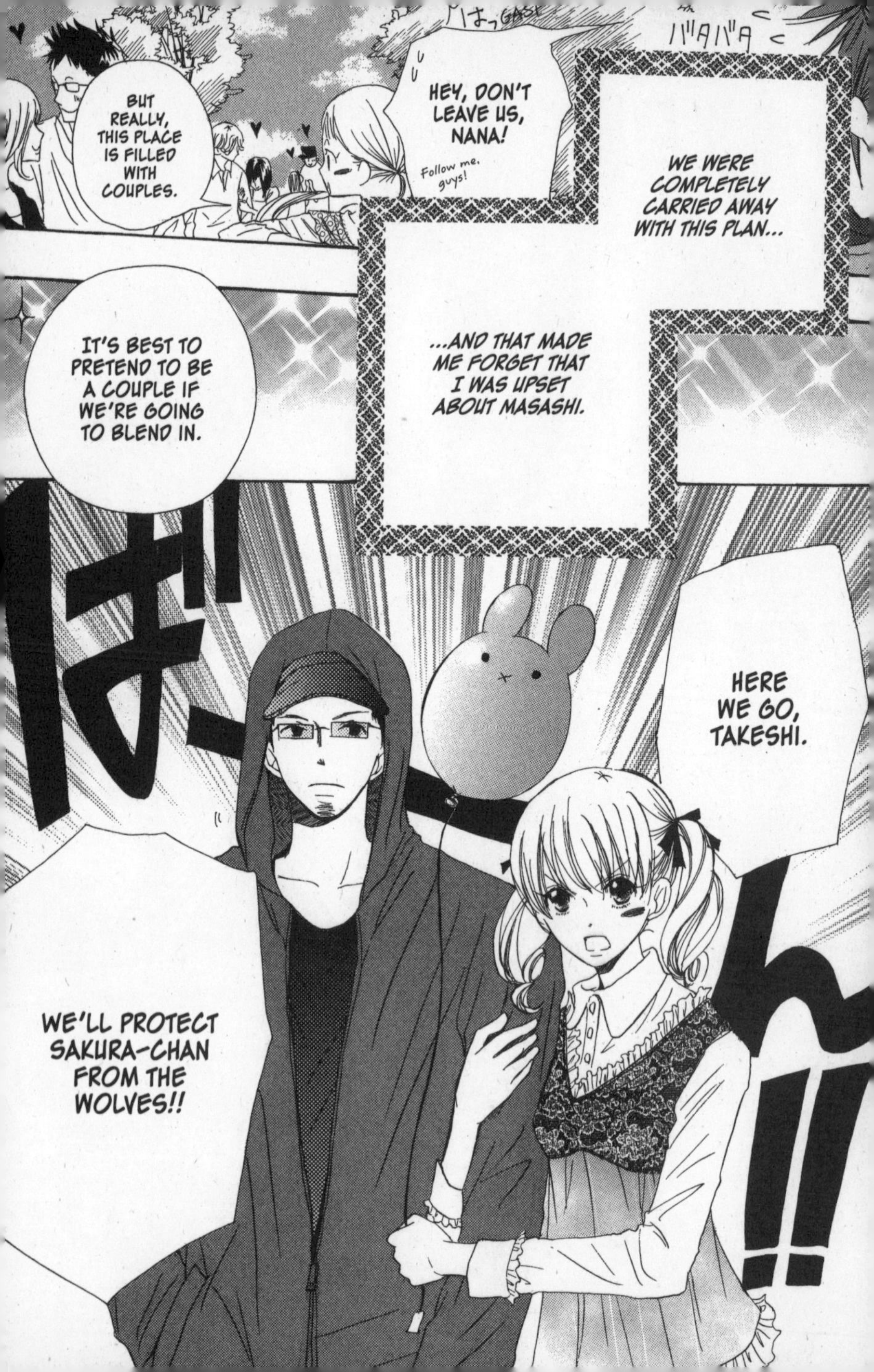
バタバタ
WE WERE COMPLETELY CARRIED AWAY WITH THIS PLAN...
HEY, DON'T LEAVE US, NANA!
Follow me, guys!
BUT REALLY, THIS PLACE IS FILLED WITH COUPLES.
...AND THAT MADE ME FORGET THAT I WAS UPSET ABOUT MASASHI.
IT'S BEST TO PRETEND TO BE A COUPLE IF WE'RE GOING TO BLEND IN.
HERE WE GO, TAKESHI.
WE'LL PROTECT SAKURA-CHAN FROM THE WOLVES!!

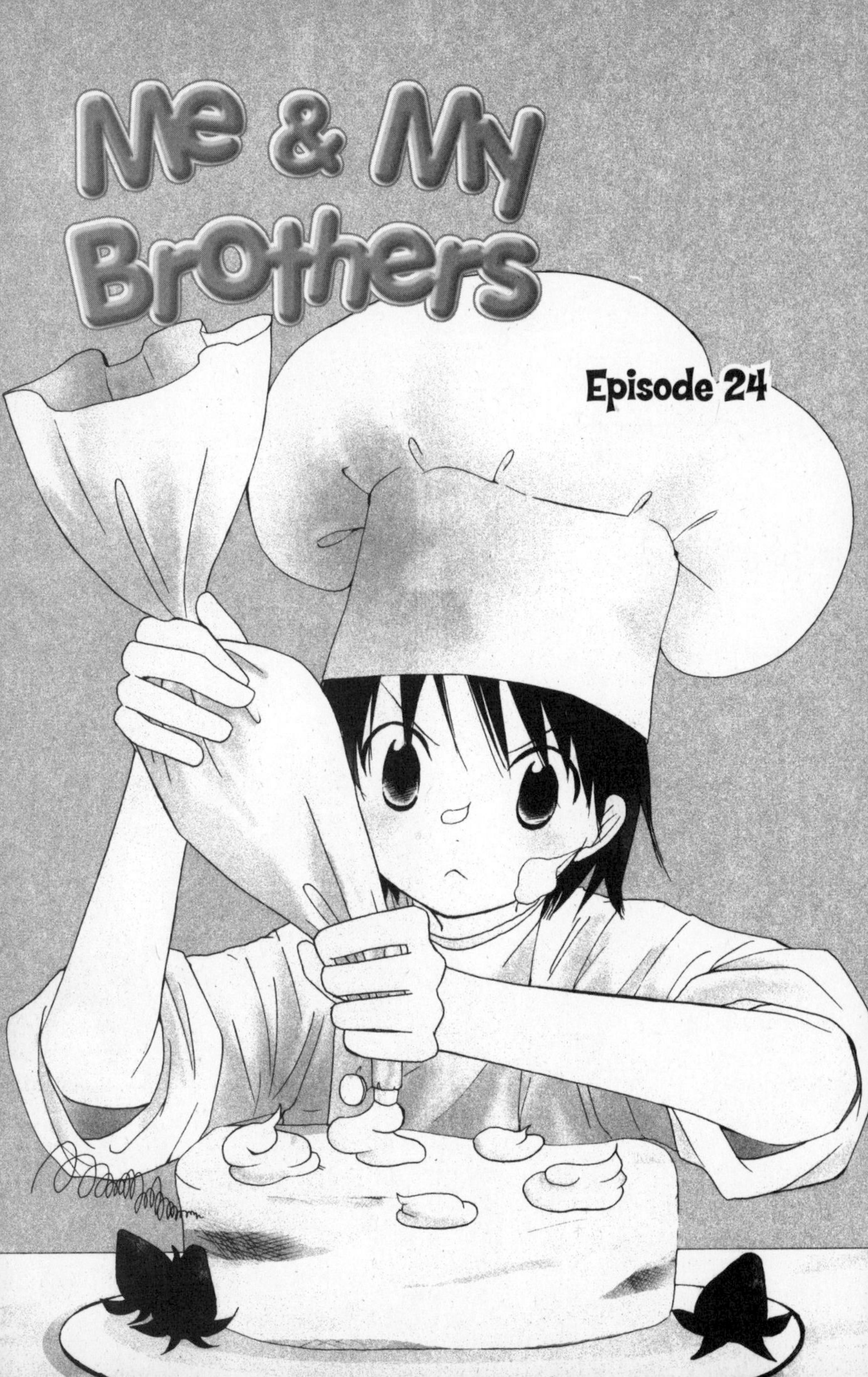
Me & My
Brothers
Episode 24

Here you are.

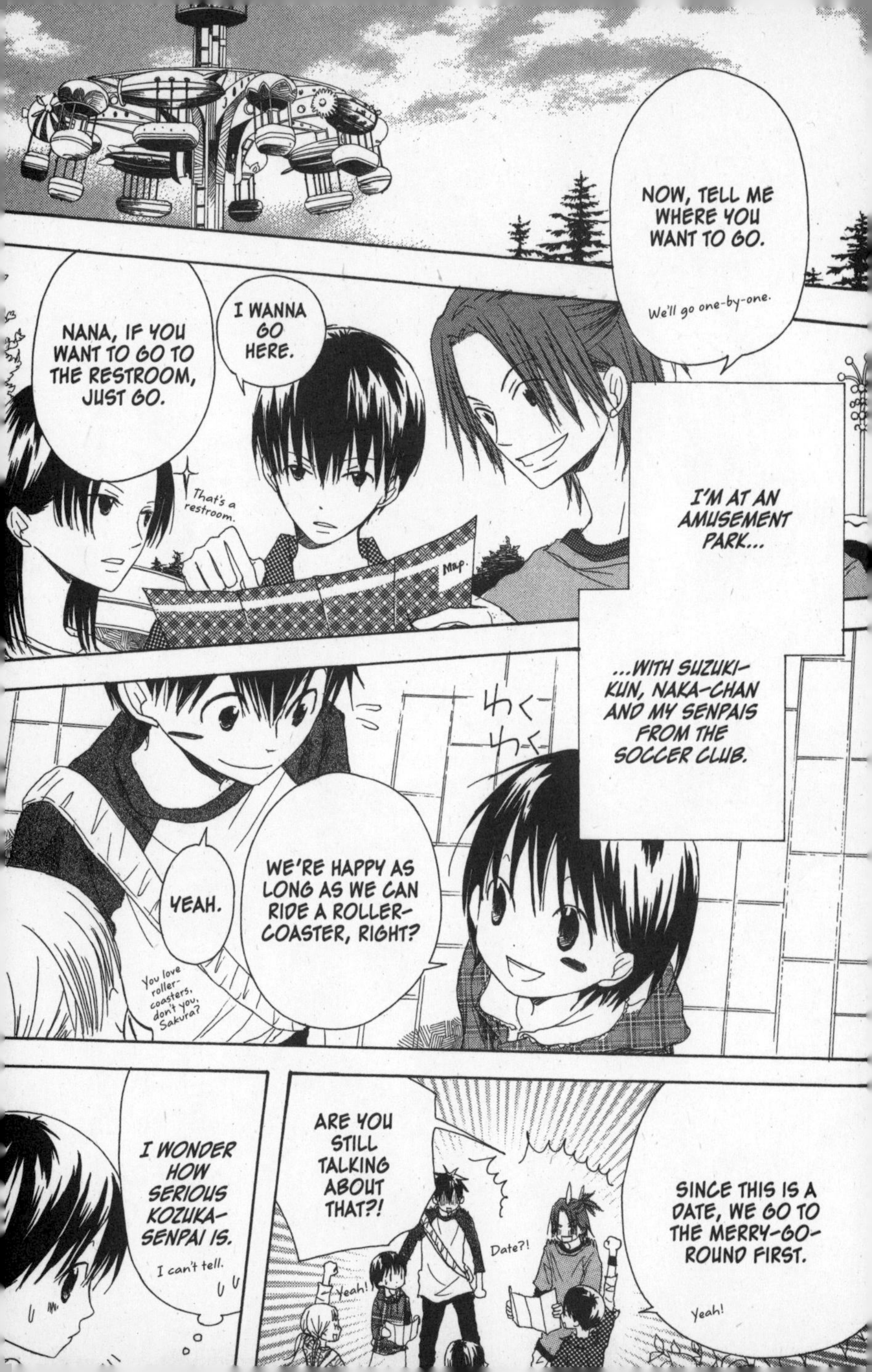
NOW, TELL ME WHERE YOU WANT TO GO.
We'll go one-by-one.
I'M AT AN AMUSEMENT PARK...
I WANNA GO HERE.
NANA, IF YOU WANT TO GO TO THE RESTROOM, JUST GO.
That's a restroom.
Map.
...WITH SUZUKI-KUN, NAKA-CHAN AND MY SENPAIS FROM THE SOCCER CLUB.
わくわく
WE'RE HAPPY AS LONG AS WE CAN RIDE A ROLLER-COASTER, RIGHT?
YEAH.
You love roller-coasters, don't you, Sakura?
SINCE THIS IS A DATE, WE GO TO THE MERRY-GO-ROUND FIRST.
Yeah!
Date?!
ARE YOU STILL TALKING ABOUT THAT?!
Yeah!
I WONDER HOW SERIOUS KOZUKA-SENPAI IS.
I can't tell.

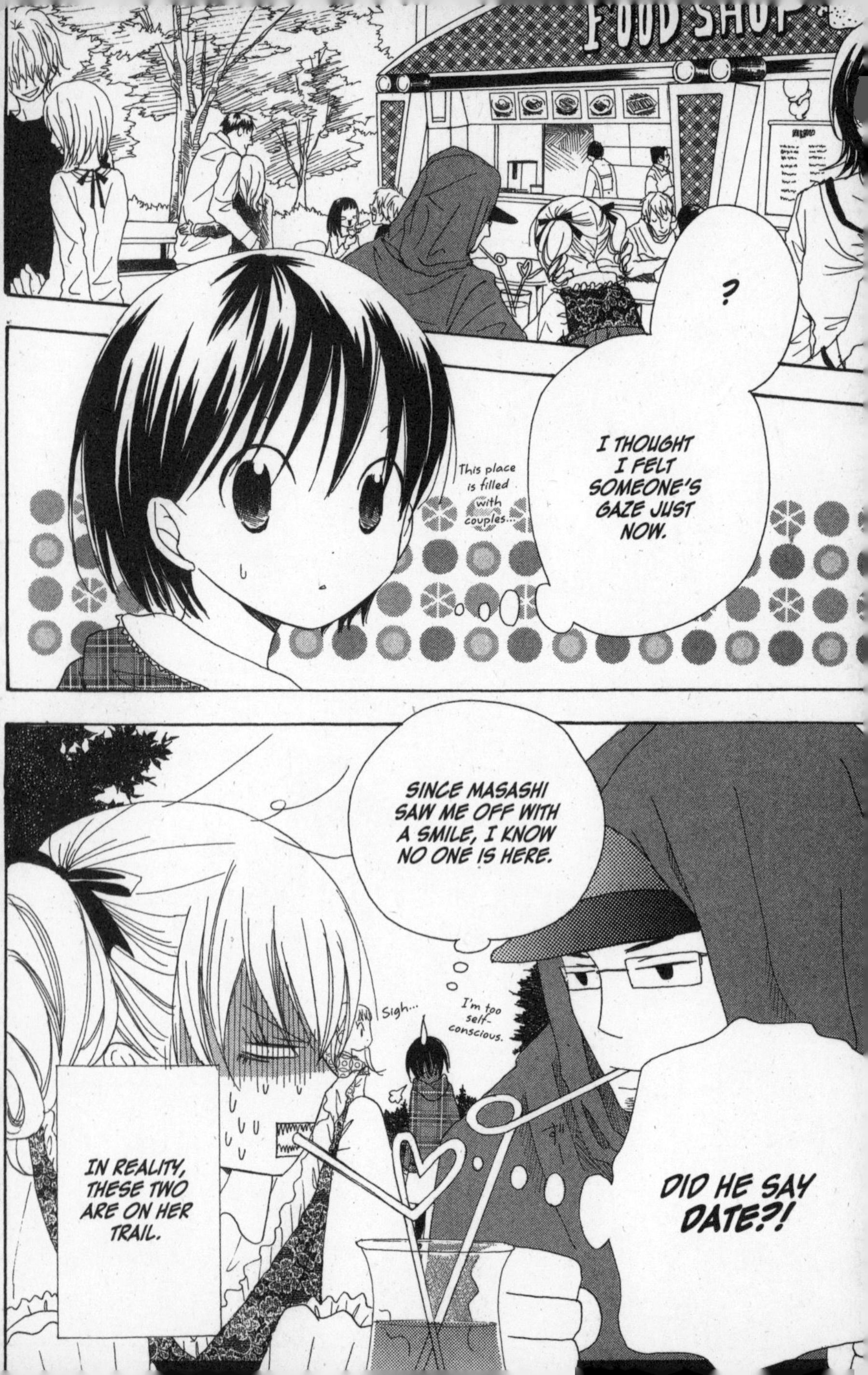
FOOD SHOP
?
I THOUGHT I FELT SOMEONE'S GAZE JUST NOW.
This place is filled with couples...
SINCE MASASHI SAW ME OFF WITH A SMILE, I KNOW NO ONE IS HERE.
I'm too self-conscious.
Sigh...
DID HE SAY DATE?!
IN REALITY, THESE TWO ARE ON HER TRAIL.

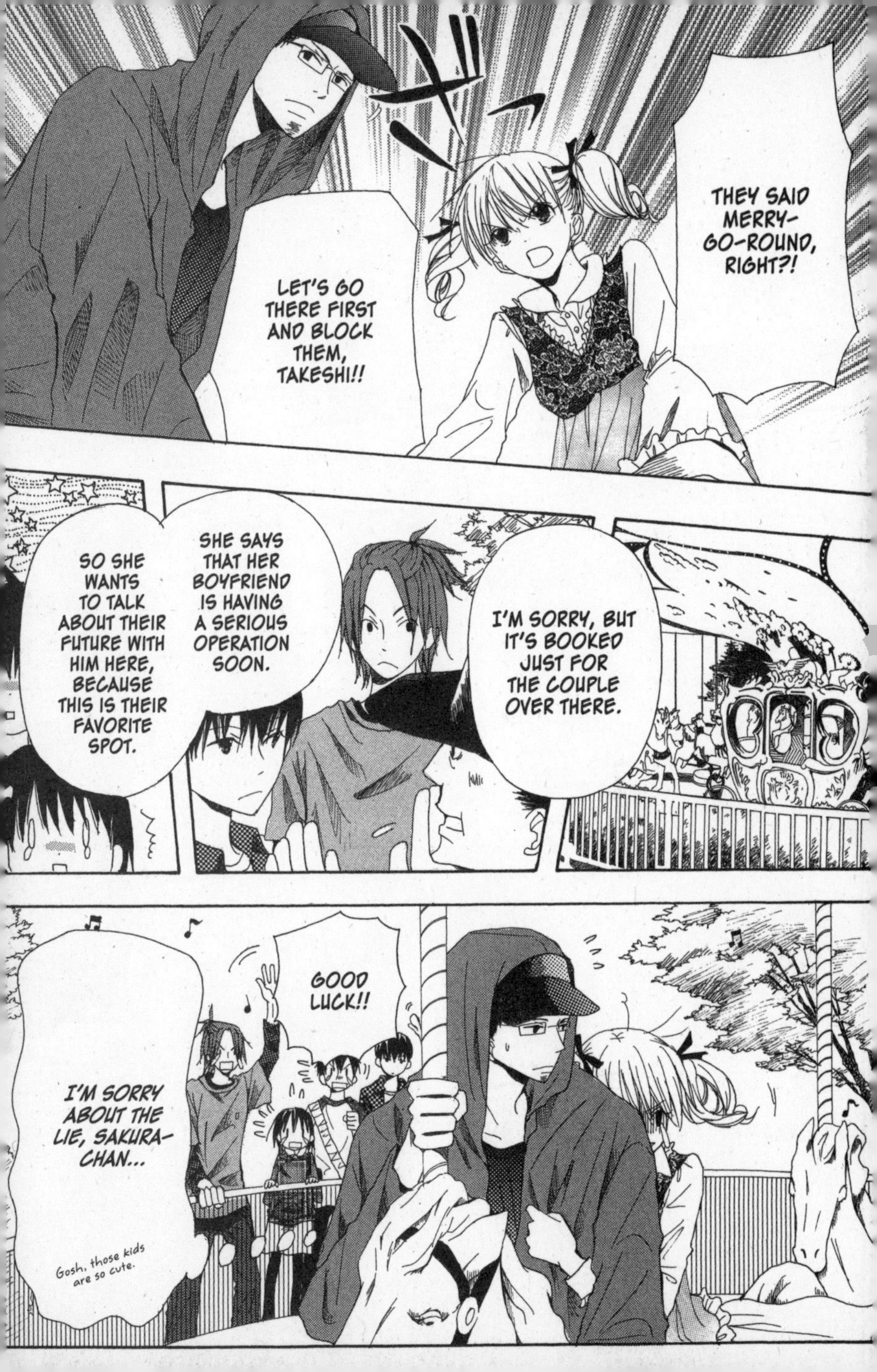
THEY SAID MERRY-GO-ROUND, RIGHT?!
LET'S GO THERE FIRST AND BLOCK THEM, TAKESHI!!
I'M SORRY, BUT IT'S BOOKED JUST FOR THE COUPLE OVER THERE.
SHE SAYS THAT HER BOYFRIEND IS HAVING A SERIOUS OPERATION SOON.
SO SHE WANTS TO TALK ABOUT THEIR FUTURE WITH HIM HERE, BECAUSE THIS IS THEIR FAVORITE SPOT.
GOOD LUCK!!
I'M SORRY ABOUT THE LIE, SAKURA-CHAN...
Gosh, those kids are so cute.

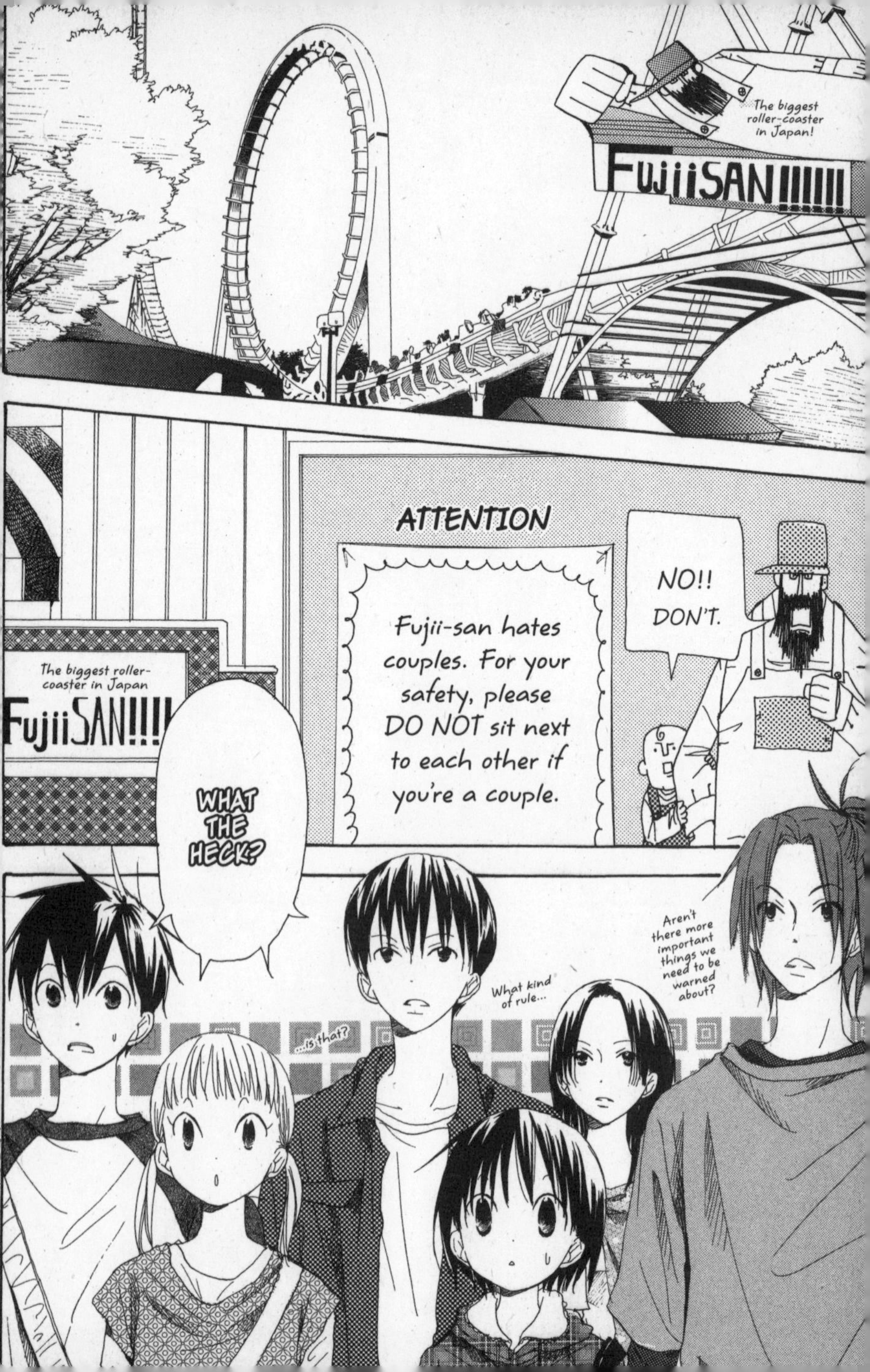
The biggest roller-coaster in Japan!
FUJIISAN!!!!!!
NO!! DON'T.
ATTENTION
Fujii-san hates couples. For your safety, please DO NOT sit next to each other if you're a couple.
The biggest roller-coaster in Japan
FujiiSAN!!!!
Aren't there more important things we need to be warned about?
What kind of rule...
...is that?
WHAT THE HECK?

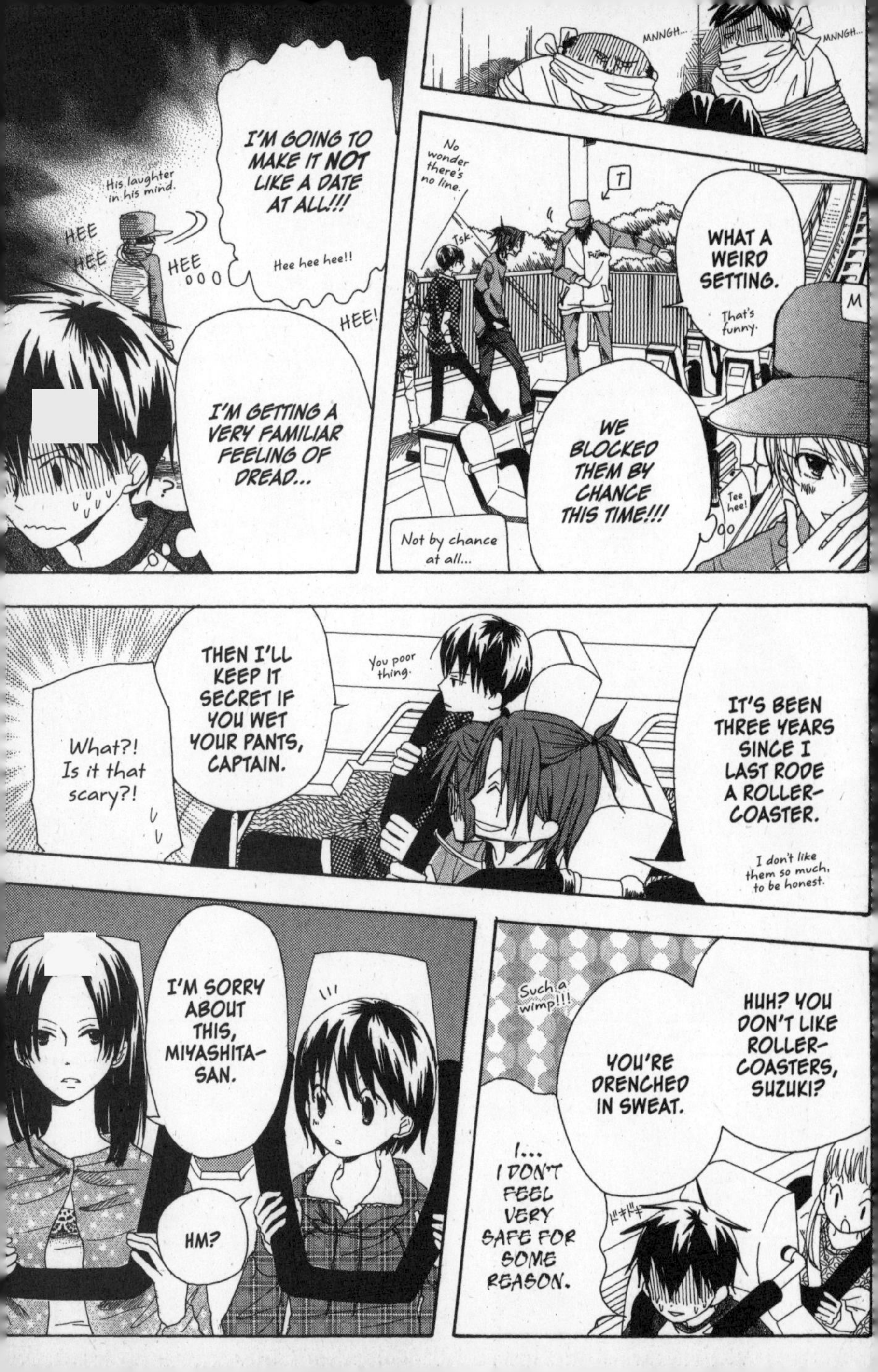
MNNGH...
MNNGH...
No wonder there's no line.
Tsk.
WHAT A WEIRD SETTING.
That's funny.
WE BLOCKED THEM BY CHANCE THIS TIME!!!
Tee hee!
Not by chance at all...
I'M GOING TO MAKE IT NOT LIKE A DATE AT ALL!!!
Hee hee hee!!
His laughter in his mind.
HEE HEE HEE HEE!
I'M GETTING A VERY FAMILIAR FEELING OF DREAD...
IT'S BEEN THREE YEARS SINCE I LAST RODE A ROLLER-COASTER.
I don't like them so much, to be honest.
You poor thing.
THEN I'LL KEEP IT SECRET IF YOU WET YOUR PANTS, CAPTAIN.
What?! Is it that scary?!
HUH? YOU DON'T LIKE ROLLER-COASTERS, SUZUKI?
YOU'RE DRENCHED IN SWEAT.
Such a wimp!!!
I... I DON'T FEEL VERY SAFE FOR SOME REASON.
I'M SORRY ABOUT THIS, MIYASHITA-SAN.
HM?

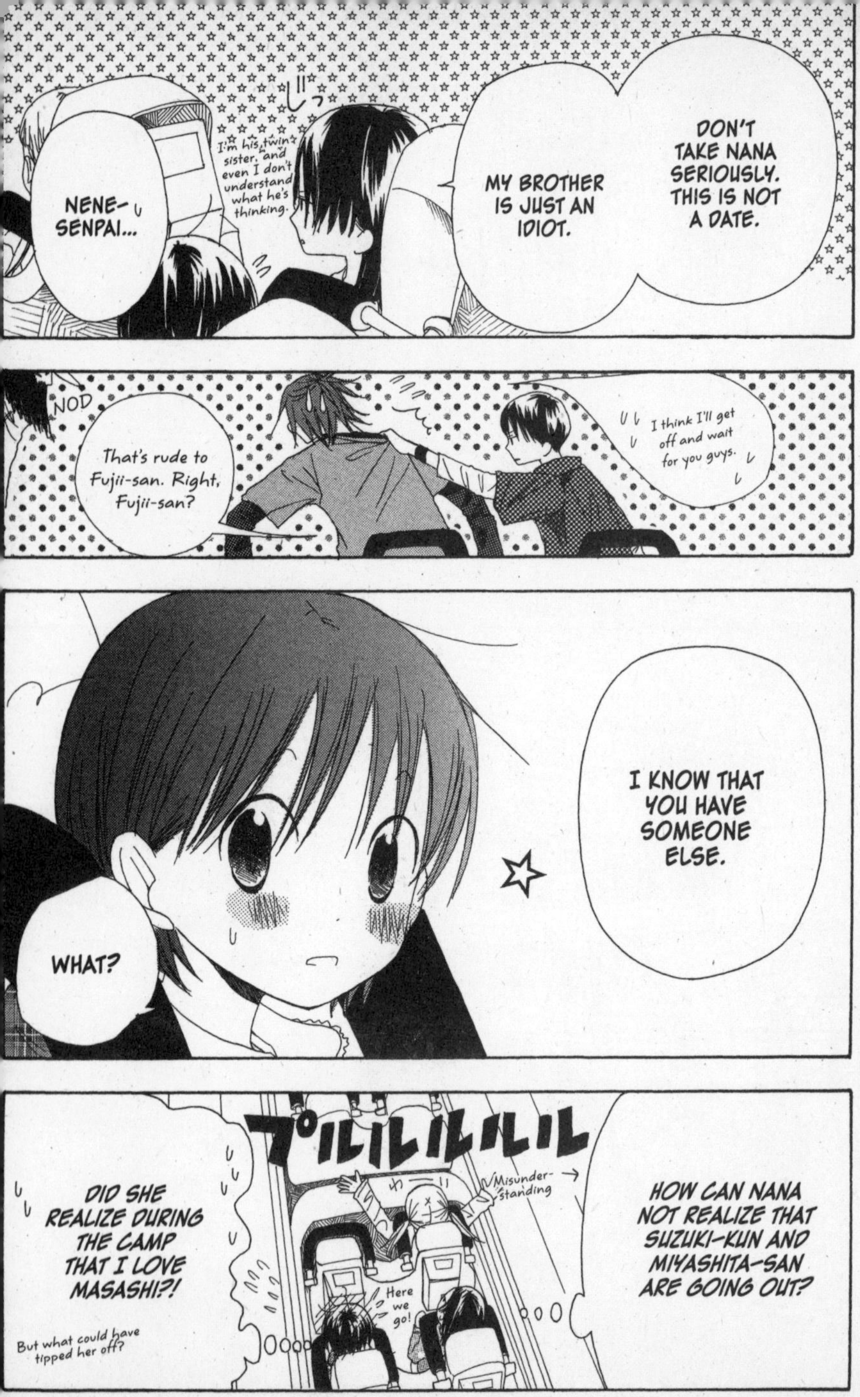
DON'T TAKE NANA SERIOUSLY. THIS IS NOT A DATE.
MY BROTHER IS JUST AN IDIOT.
I'm his twin sister, and even I don't understand what he's thinking.
NENE-SENPAI...
I think I'll get off and wait for you guys.
That's rude to Fujii-san. Right, Fujii-san?
NOD
I KNOW THAT YOU HAVE SOMEONE ELSE.
WHAT?
HOW CAN NANA NOT REALIZE THAT SUZUKI-KUN AND MIYASHITA-SAN ARE GOING OUT?
Misunder-standing
Here we go!
DID SHE REALIZE DURING THE CAMP THAT I LOVE MASASHI?!
But what could have tipped her off?

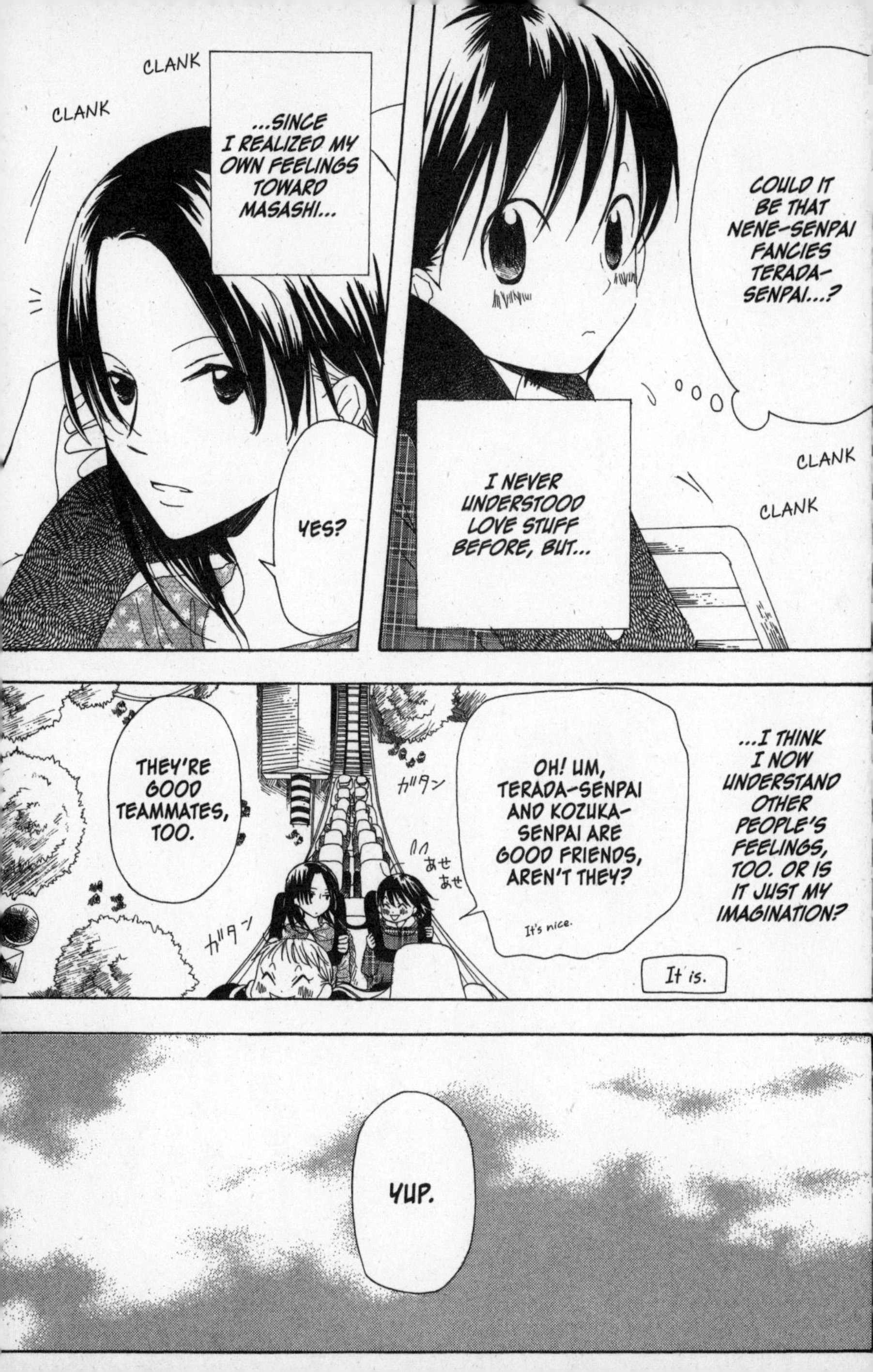
COULD IT BE THAT NENE-SENPAI FANCIES TERADA-SENPAI...?
I NEVER UNDERSTOOD LOVE STUFF BEFORE, BUT...
CLANK
CLANK
...SINCE I REALIZED MY OWN FEELINGS TOWARD MASASHI...
CLANK
CLANK
YES?
...I THINK I NOW UNDERSTAND OTHER PEOPLE'S FEELINGS, TOO. OR IS IT JUST MY IMAGINATION?
OH! UM, TERADA-SENPAI AND KOZUKA-SENPAI ARE GOOD FRIENDS, AREN'T THEY?
It's nice.
It is.
ガタン
あせ あせ
THEY'RE GOOD TEAMMATES, TOO.
ガタン
YUP.

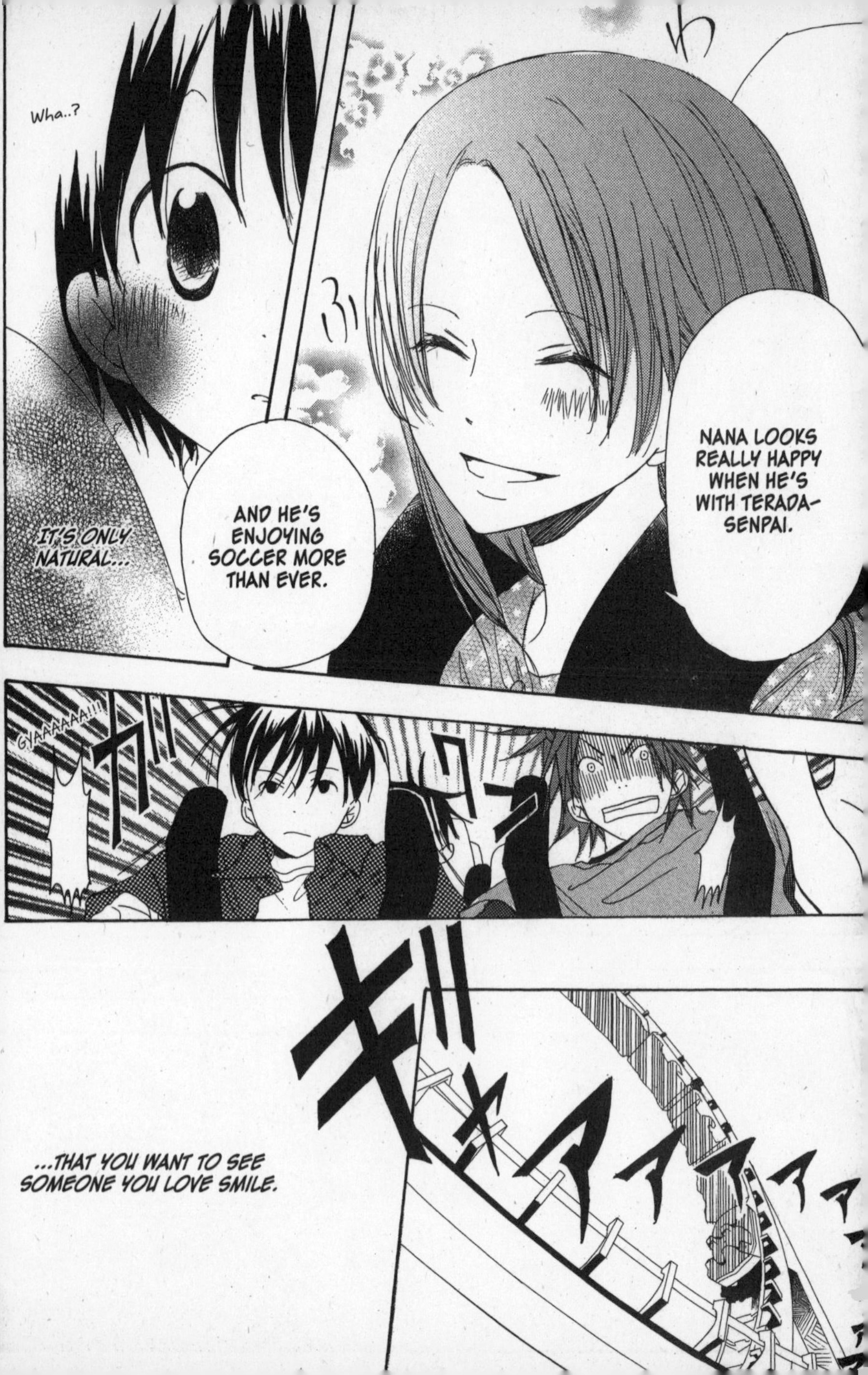
NANA LOOKS REALLY HAPPY WHEN HE'S WITH TERADA-SENPAI.
AND HE'S ENJOYING SOCCER MORE THAN EVER.
Wha..?
IT'S ONLY NATURAL...
GYAAAAAA!!!
...THAT YOU WANT TO SEE SOMEONE YOU LOVE SMILE.

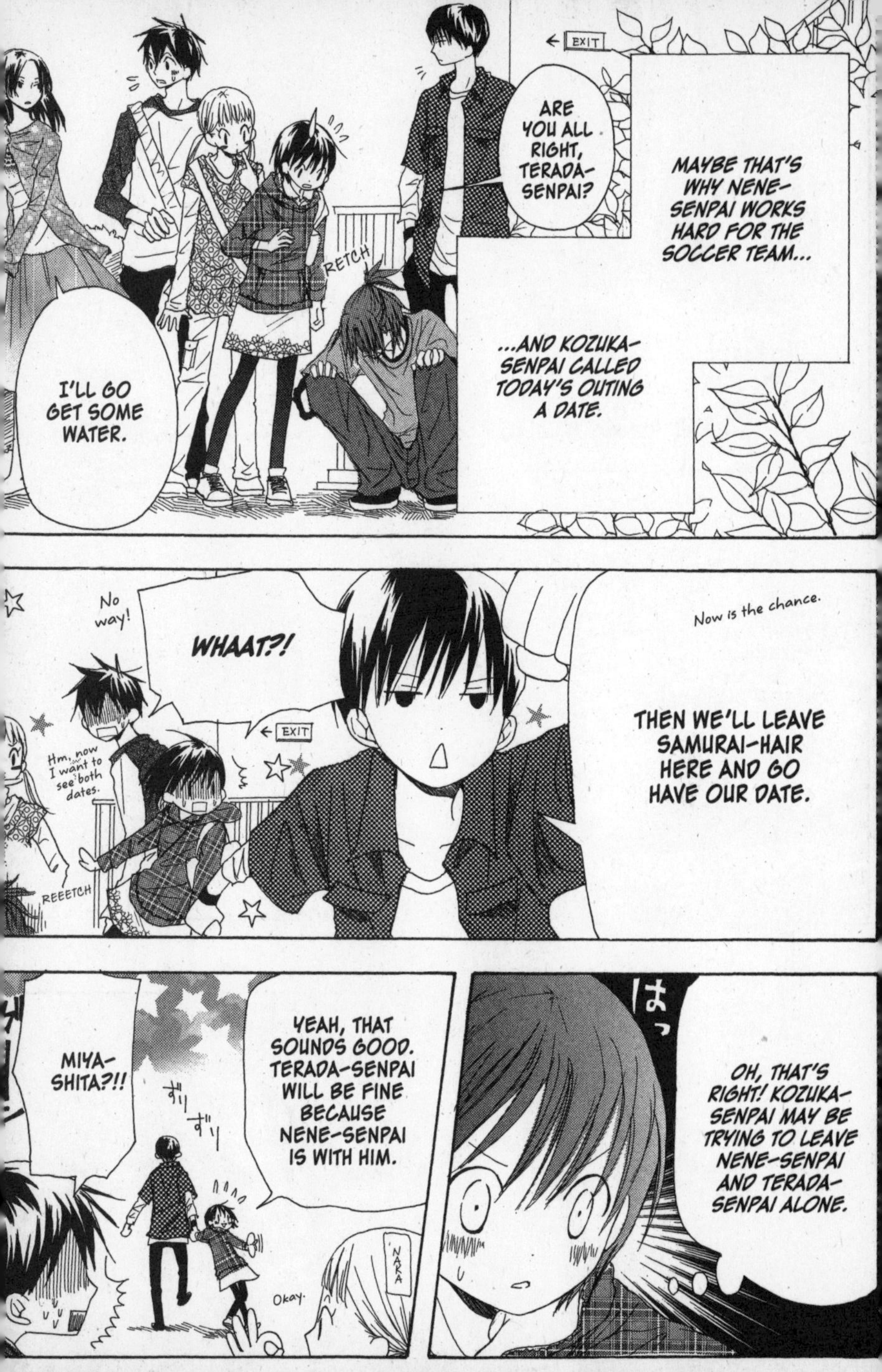
MAYBE THAT'S WHY NENE-SENPAI WORKS HARD FOR THE SOCCER TEAM...
...AND KOZUKA-SENPAI CALLED TODAY'S OUTING A DATE.
ARE YOU ALL RIGHT, TERADA-SENPAI?
EXIT
RETCH
I'LL GO GET SOME WATER.
Now is the chance.
THEN WE'LL LEAVE SAMURAI-HAIR HERE AND GO HAVE OUR DATE.
WHAAT?!
No way!
EXIT
Hm, now I want to see both dates.
REEETCH
はっ
OH, THAT'S RIGHT! KOZUKA-SENPAI MAY BE TRYING TO LEAVE NENE-SENPAI AND TERADA-SENPAI ALONE.
YEAH, THAT SOUNDS GOOD. TERADA-SENPAI WILL BE FINE BECAUSE NENE-SENPAI IS WITH HIM.
MIYA-SHITA?!!
ずり ずり
NAKA
Okay.

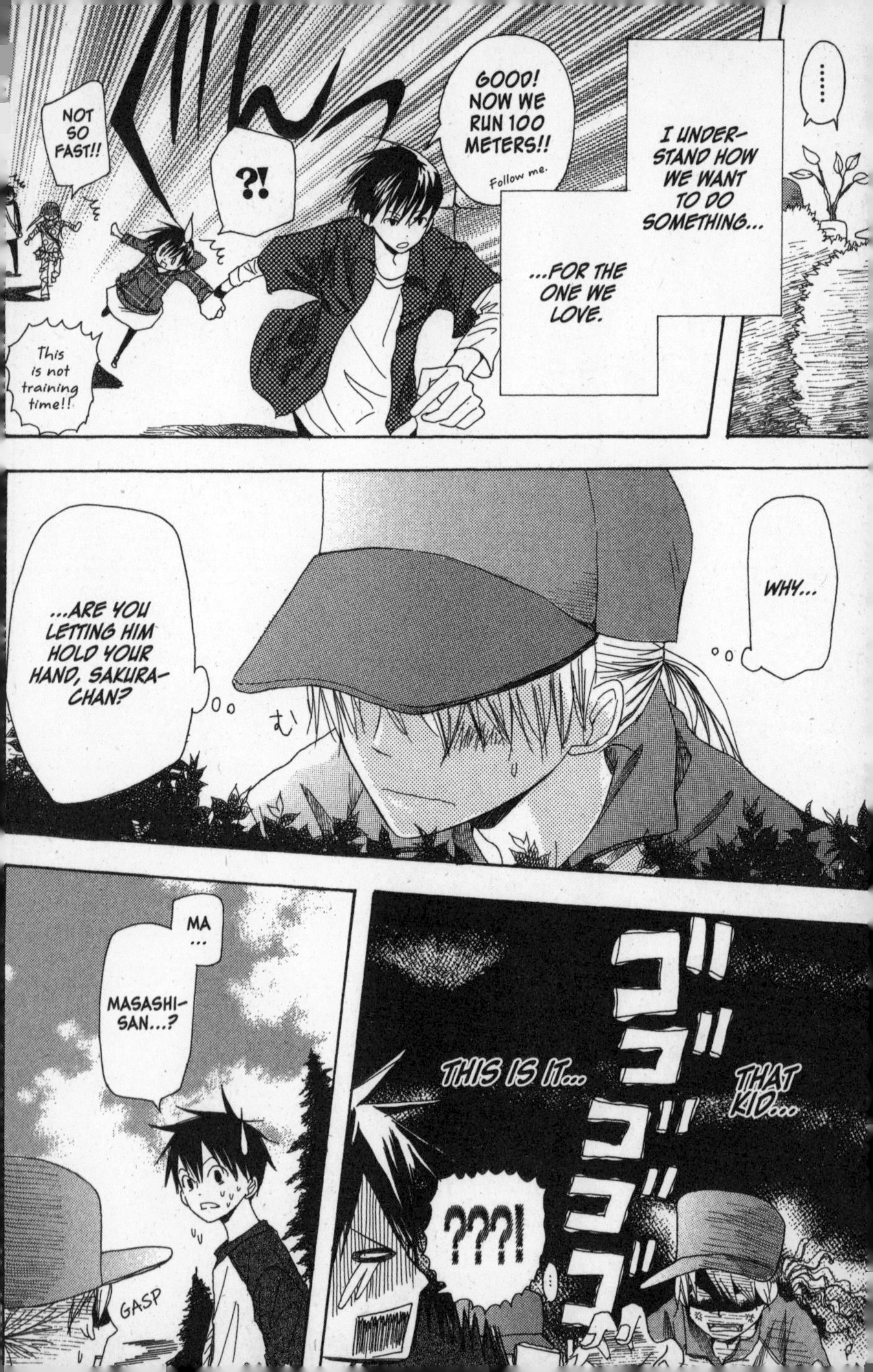
......
I UNDERSTAND HOW WE WANT TO DO SOMETHING...
...FOR THE ONE WE LOVE.
GOOD! NOW WE RUN 100 METERS!!
Follow me.
?!
NOT SO FAST!!
This is not training time!!
WHY...
...ARE YOU LETTING HIM HOLD YOUR HAND, SAKURA-CHAN?
THAT KID...
THIS IS IT...
???!
MA...
MASASHI-SAN...?
GASP

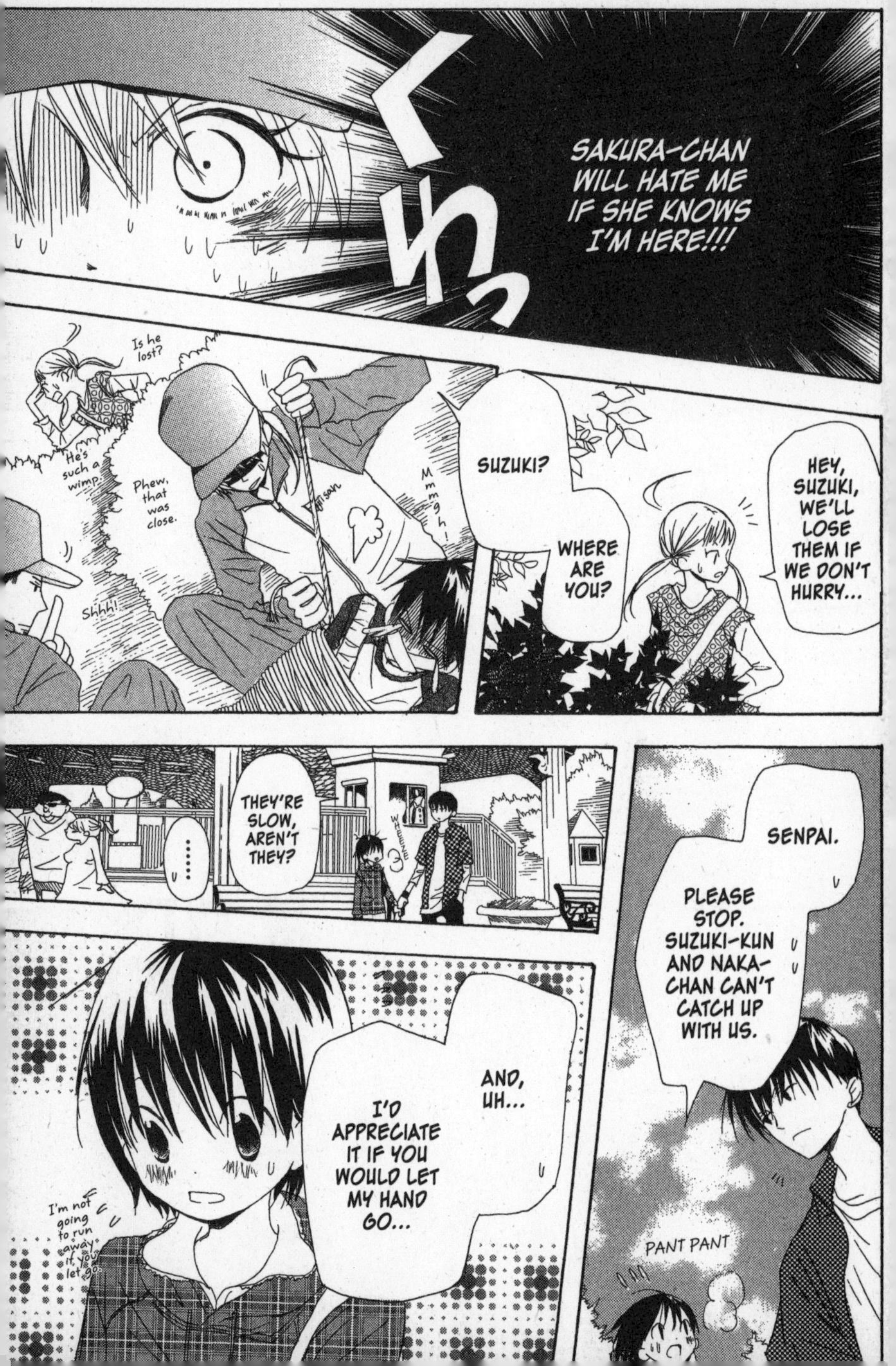
くわっ
SAKURA-CHAN WILL HATE ME IF SHE KNOWS I'M HERE!!!
HEY, SUZUKI, WE'LL LOSE THEM IF WE DON'T HURRY...
SUZUKI?
WHERE ARE YOU?
Mmmgh!
Phew, that was close.
He's such a wimp.
Is he lost?
Shhh!
SENPAI.
PLEASE STOP. SUZUKI-KUN AND NAKA-CHAN CAN'T CATCH UP WITH US.
PANT PANT
THEY'RE SLOW, AREN'T THEY?
......
WHEEZE
AND, UH...
I'D APPRECIATE IT IF YOU WOULD LET MY HAND GO...
I'm not going to run away if you let go.

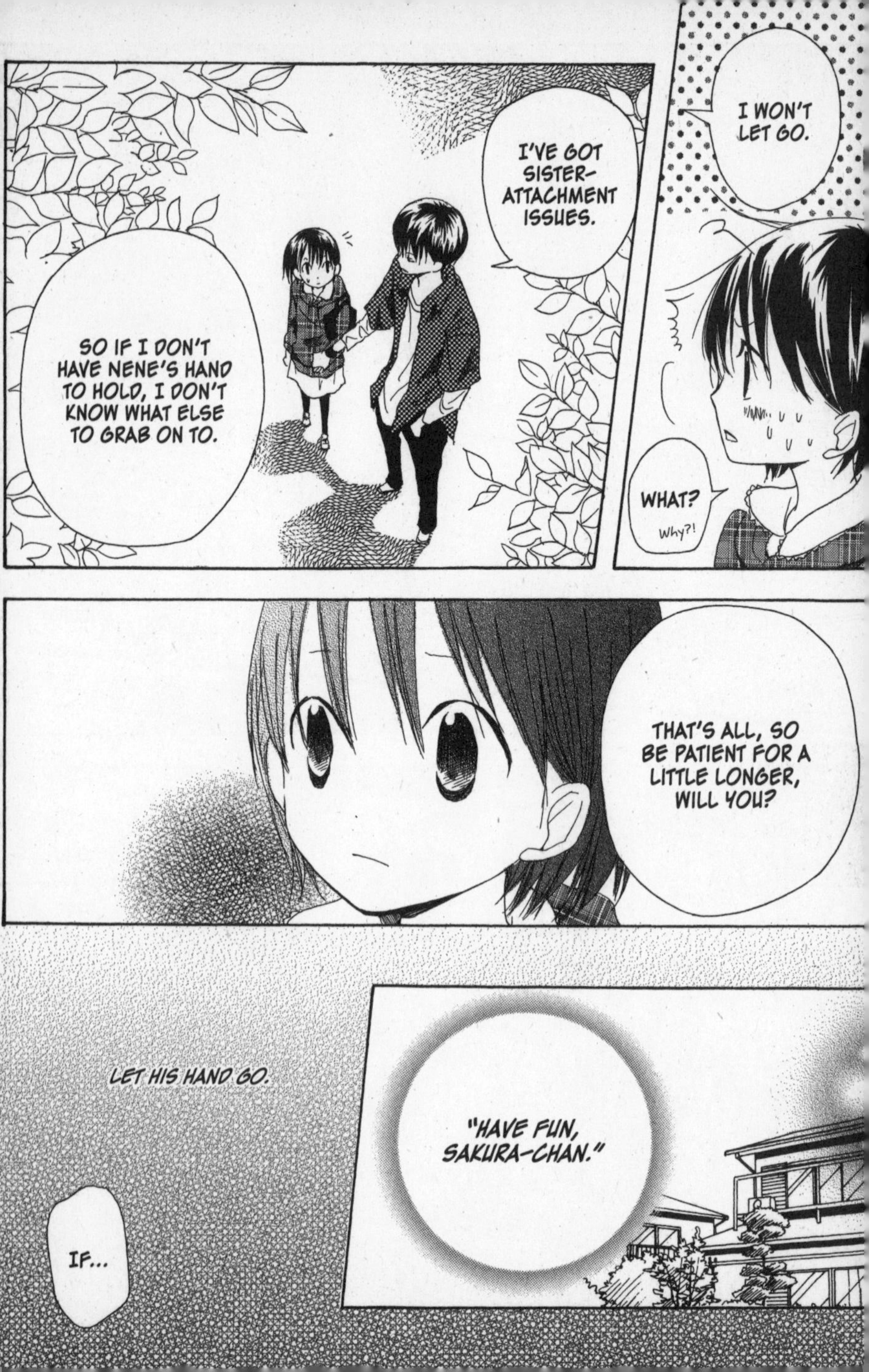
I WON'T LET GO.
WHAT?
Why?!
I'VE GOT SISTER-ATTACHMENT ISSUES.
SO IF I DON'T HAVE NENE'S HAND TO HOLD, I DON'T KNOW WHAT ELSE TO GRAB ON TO.
THAT'S ALL, SO BE PATIENT FOR A LITTLE LONGER, WILL YOU?
"HAVE FUN, SAKURA-CHAN."
LET HIS HAND GO.
IF...

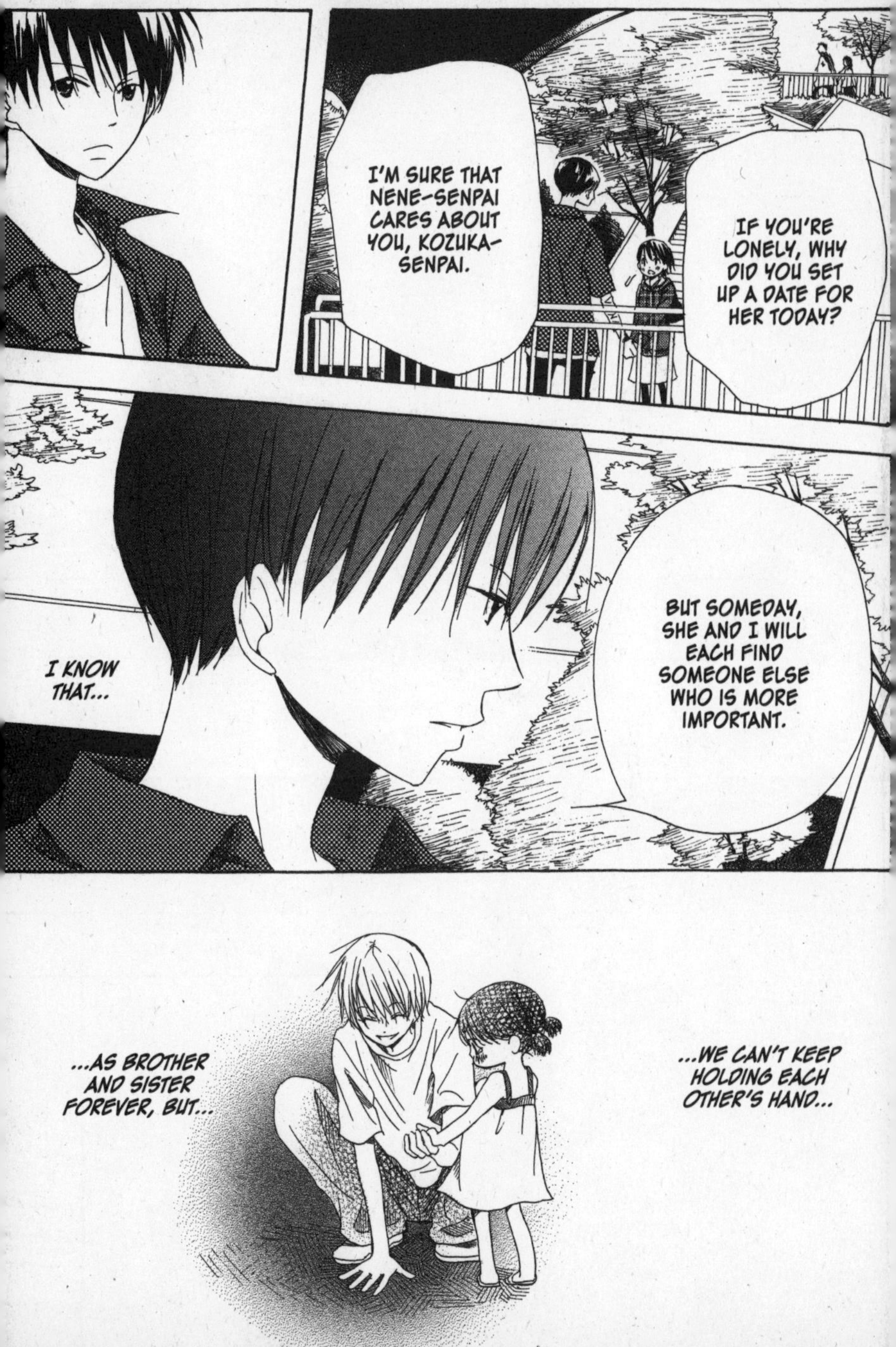
I'M SURE THAT NENE-SENPAI CARES ABOUT YOU, KOZUKA-SENPAI.
IF YOU'RE LONELY, WHY DID YOU SET UP A DATE FOR HER TODAY?
BUT SOMEDAY, SHE AND I WILL EACH FIND SOMEONE ELSE WHO IS MORE IMPORTANT.
I KNOW THAT...
...WE CAN'T KEEP HOLDING EACH OTHER'S HAND...
...AS BROTHER AND SISTER FOREVER, BUT...

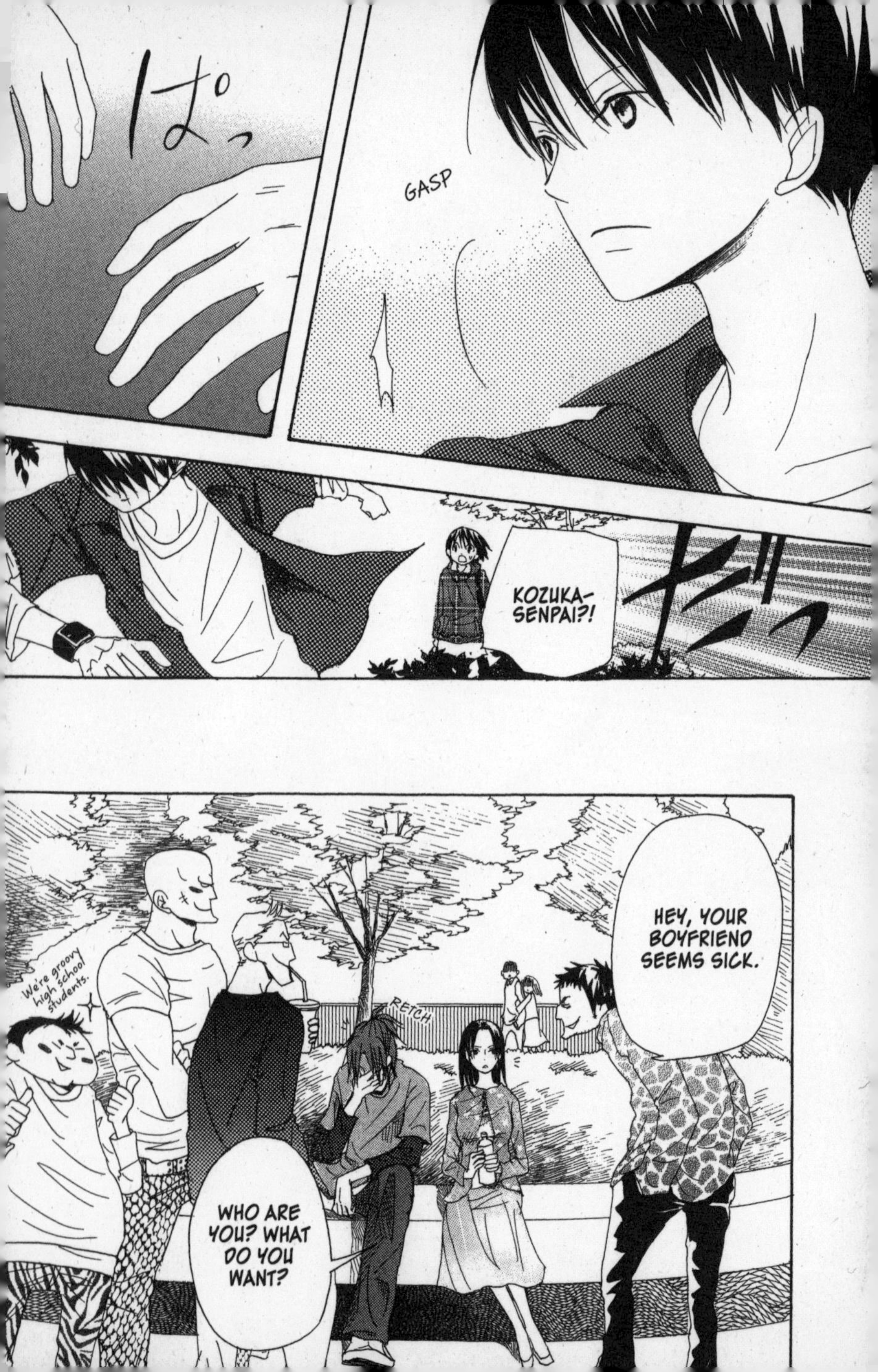
GASP
ぱっ
KOZUKA-SENPAI?!
HEY, YOUR BOYFRIEND SEEMS SICK.
RETCH
We're groovy high school students.
WHO ARE YOU? WHAT DO YOU WANT?

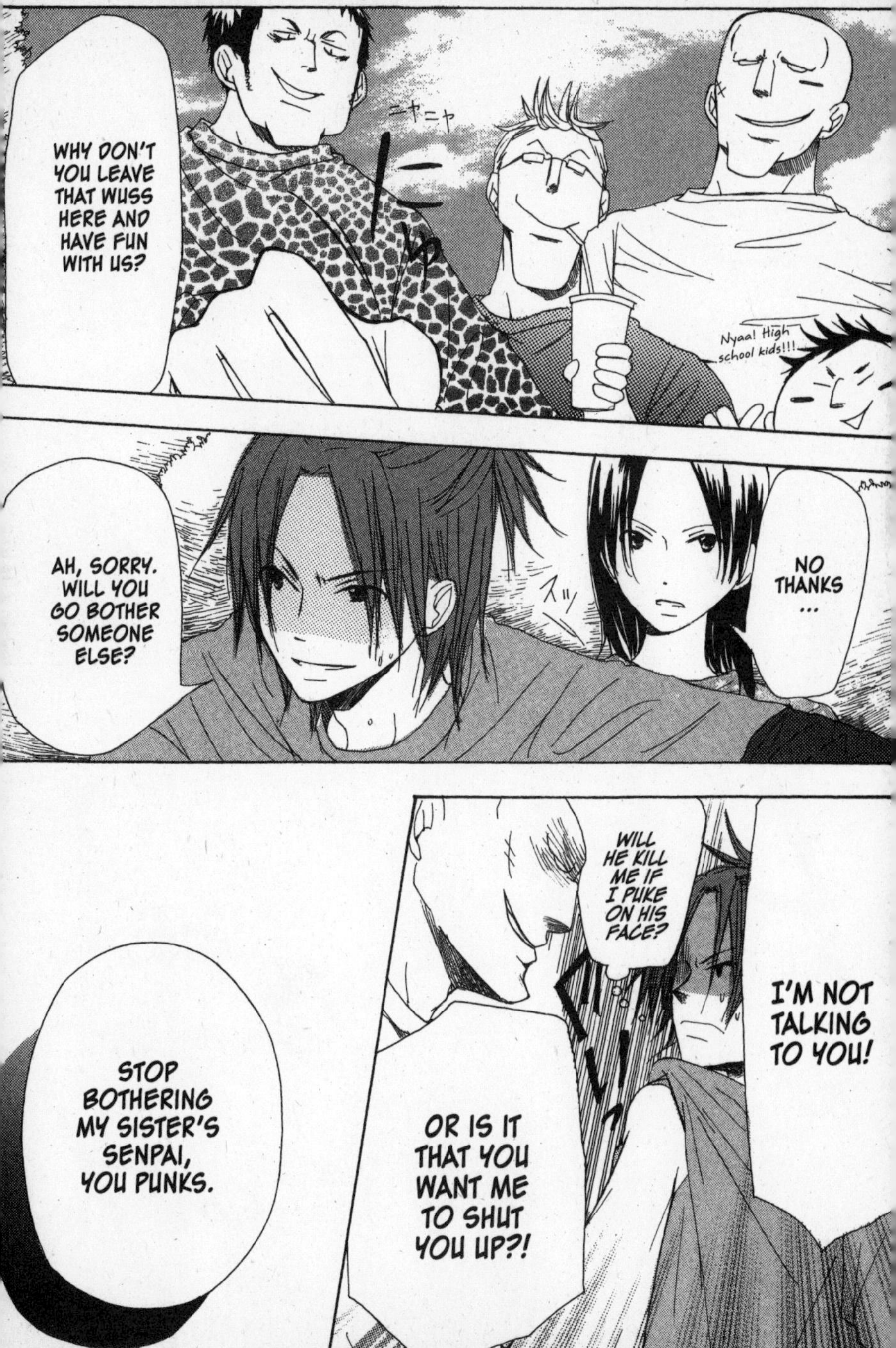
ニヤニヤ
WHY DON'T YOU LEAVE THAT WUSS HERE AND HAVE FUN WITH US?
Nyaa! High school kids!!!
NO THANKS ...
ズッ
AH, SORRY. WILL YOU GO BOTHER SOMEONE ELSE?
I'M NOT TALKING TO YOU!
WILL HE KILL ME IF I PUKE ON HIS FACE?
STOP BOTHERING MY SISTER'S SENPAI, YOU PUNKS.
OR IS IT THAT YOU WANT ME TO SHUT YOU UP?!

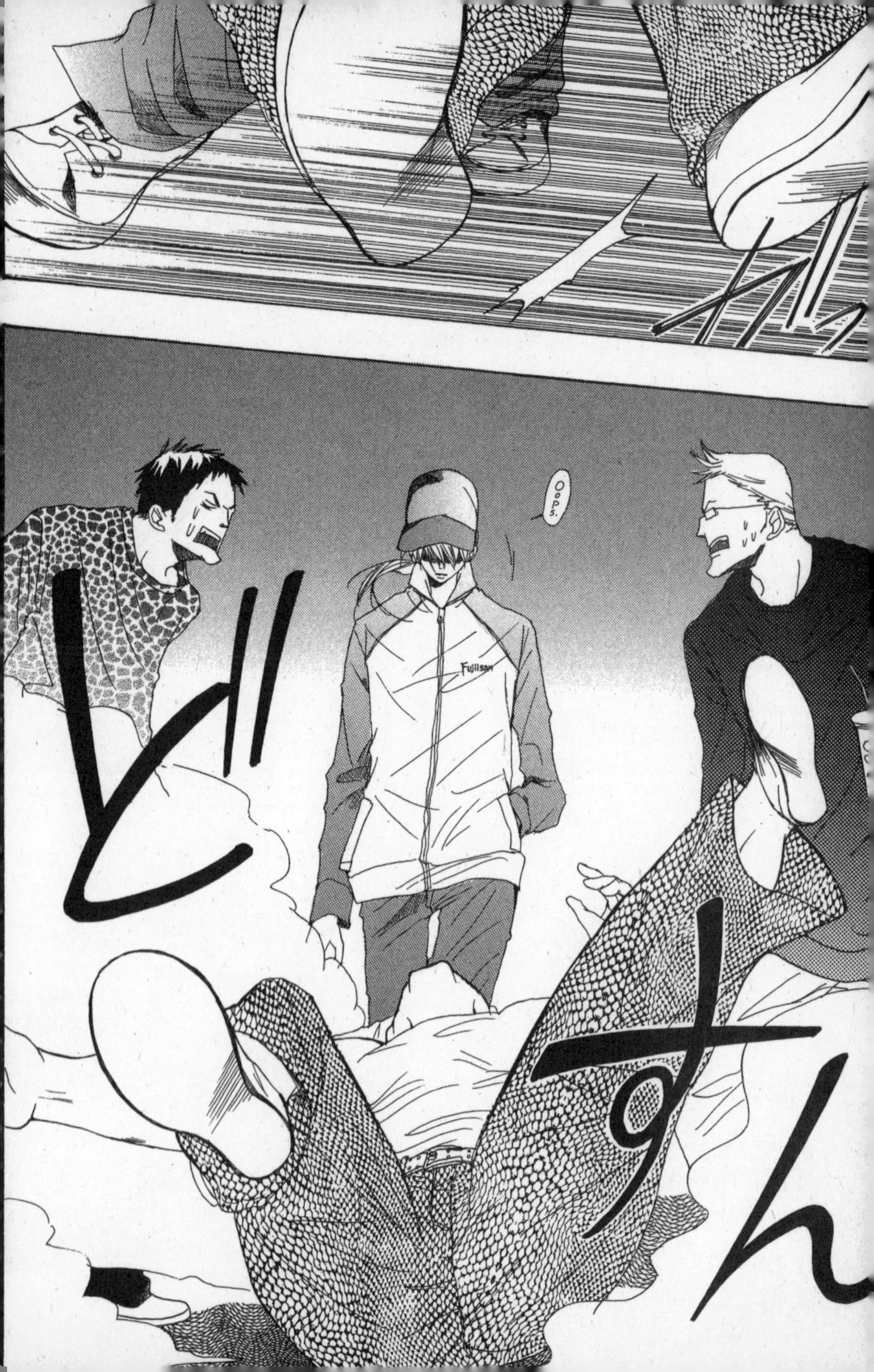
Oops.
Fujisan
どすん

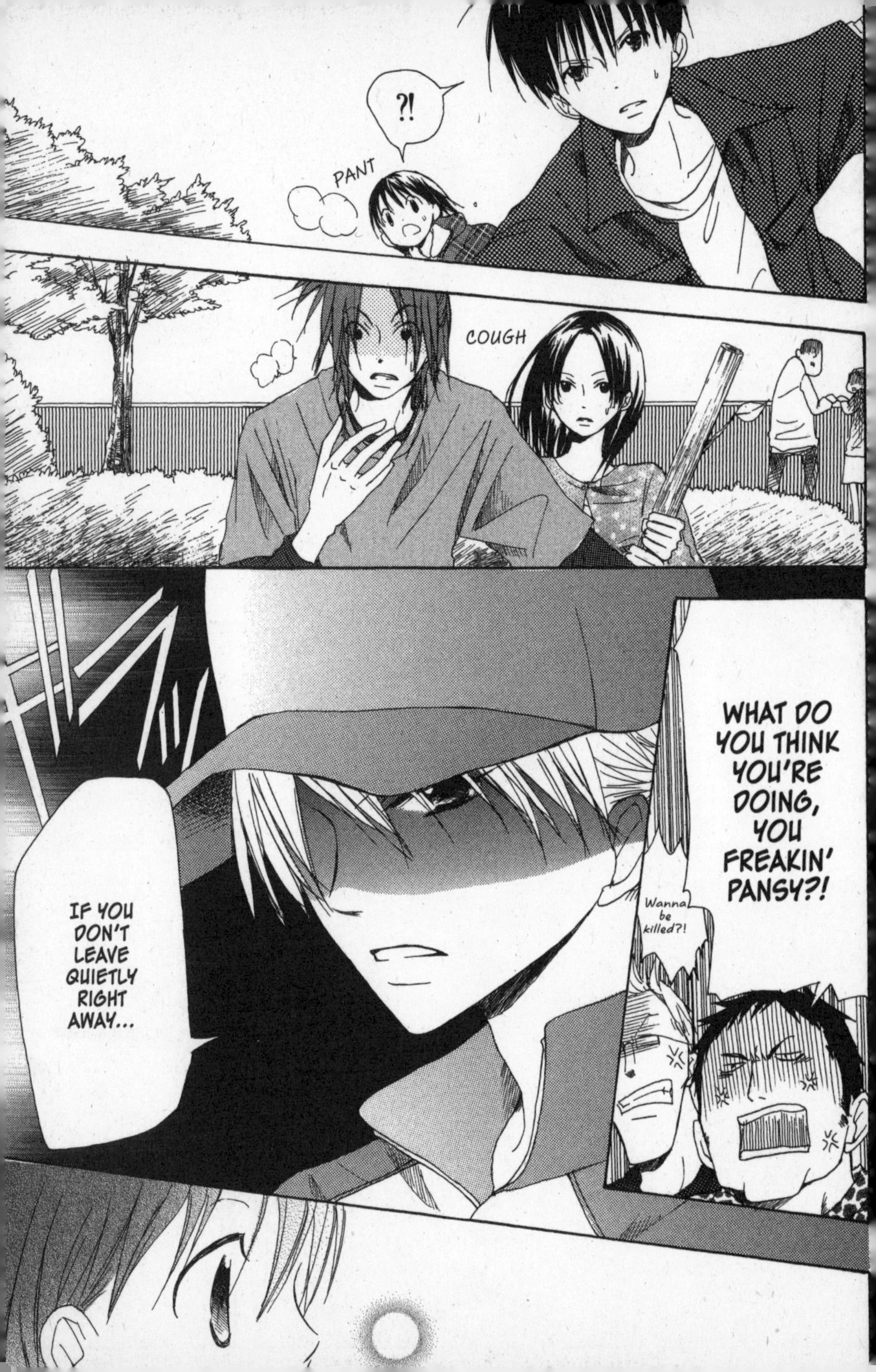
?!
PANT
COUGH
WHAT DO YOU THINK YOU'RE DOING, YOU FREAKIN' PANSY?!
Wanna be killed?!
IF YOU DON'T LEAVE QUIETLY RIGHT AWAY...

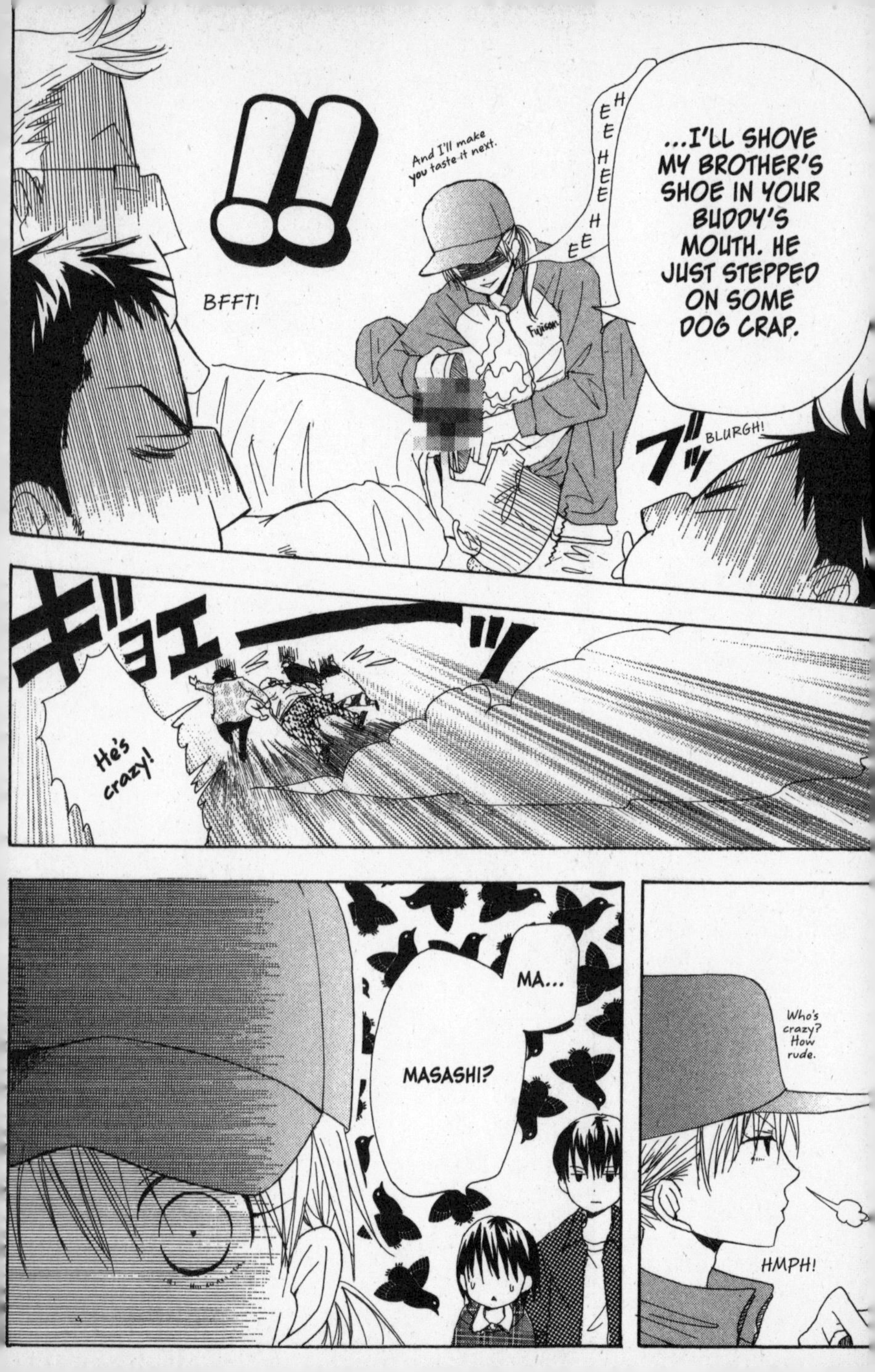
...I'LL SHOVE MY BROTHER'S SHOE IN YOUR BUDDY'S MOUTH. HE JUST STEPPED ON SOME DOG CRAP.
HEE HEE HEE HEE
And I'll make you taste it next.
!!
ブッ
BLURGH!
BFFT!
ギョエーーッ
He's crazy!
Who's crazy? How rude.
HMPH!
MA...
MASASHI?

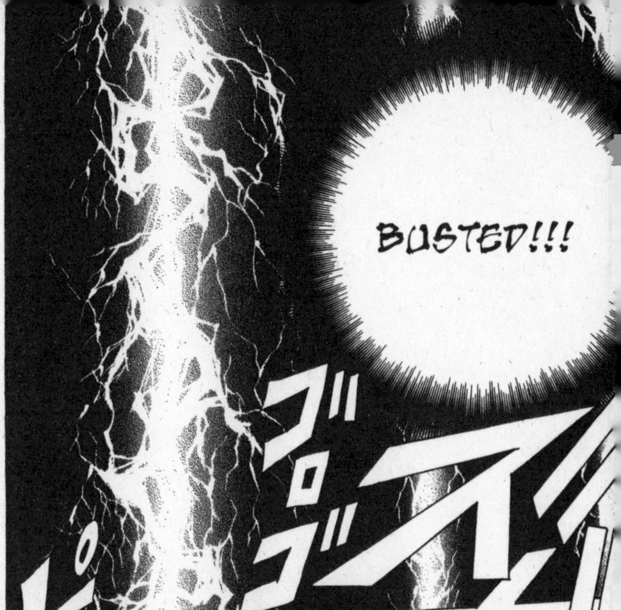
BUSTED!!!
ズガーン
ゴロゴロゴロ
ピシャア
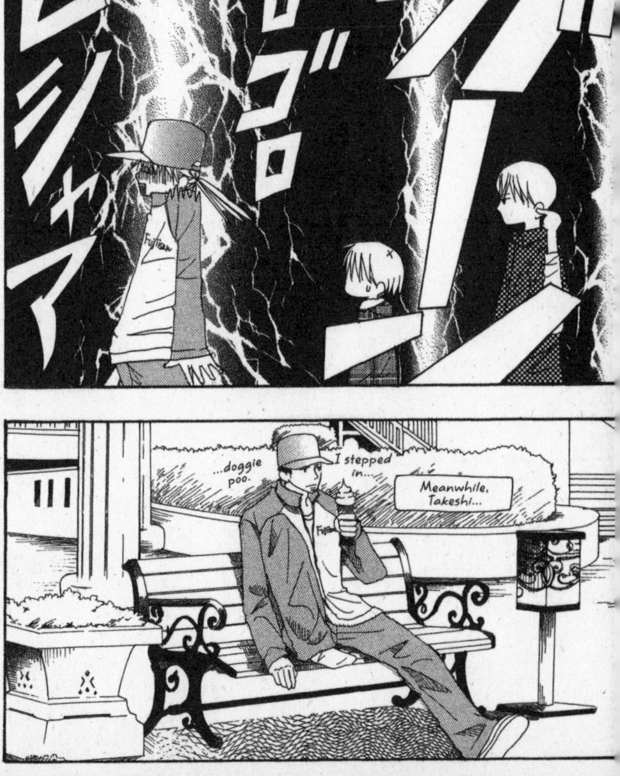
Meanwhile, Takeshi...
I stepped in...
...doggie poo.

5

In column 4, I sounded like a loser, so I'd like to change my image here. I'll show you my hard-working side.

FLIP FLIP FLIP

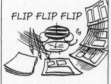

I work hard and make manga.

Did that work? Oh well.

On a completely different subject, when I was a high school kid, I once forgot to say good-bye to my friend. I was on a train, and when I got to my stop, I totally forgot that I was with my friend and got off the train without saying anything. The next day, my friend laughed and forgave me. I'm that kind of person...

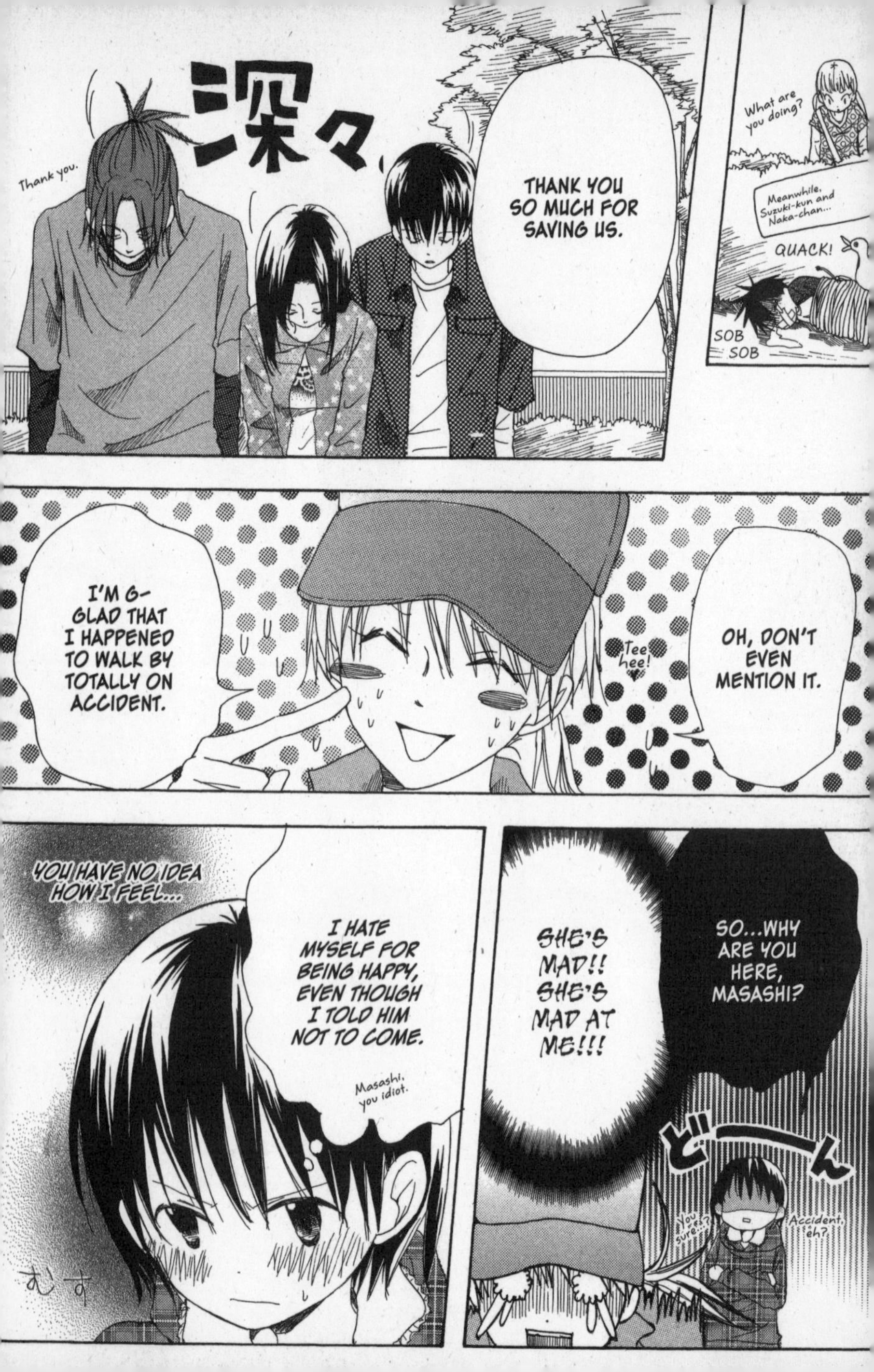
What are you doing?
Meanwhile, Suzuki-kun and Naka-chan...
QUACK!
SOB SOB
THANK YOU SO MUCH FOR SAVING US.
深々
Thank you.
OH, DON'T EVEN MENTION IT.
Tee hee!
I'M G-GLAD THAT I HAPPENED TO WALK BY TOTALLY ON ACCIDENT.
SO...WHY ARE YOU HERE, MASASHI?
SHE'S MAD!! SHE'S MAD AT ME!!!
どーん
Accident, eh?
You sure...?
I HATE MYSELF FOR BEING HAPPY, EVEN THOUGH I TOLD HIM NOT TO COME.
YOU HAVE NO IDEA HOW I FEEL...
Masashi, you idiot.
むす

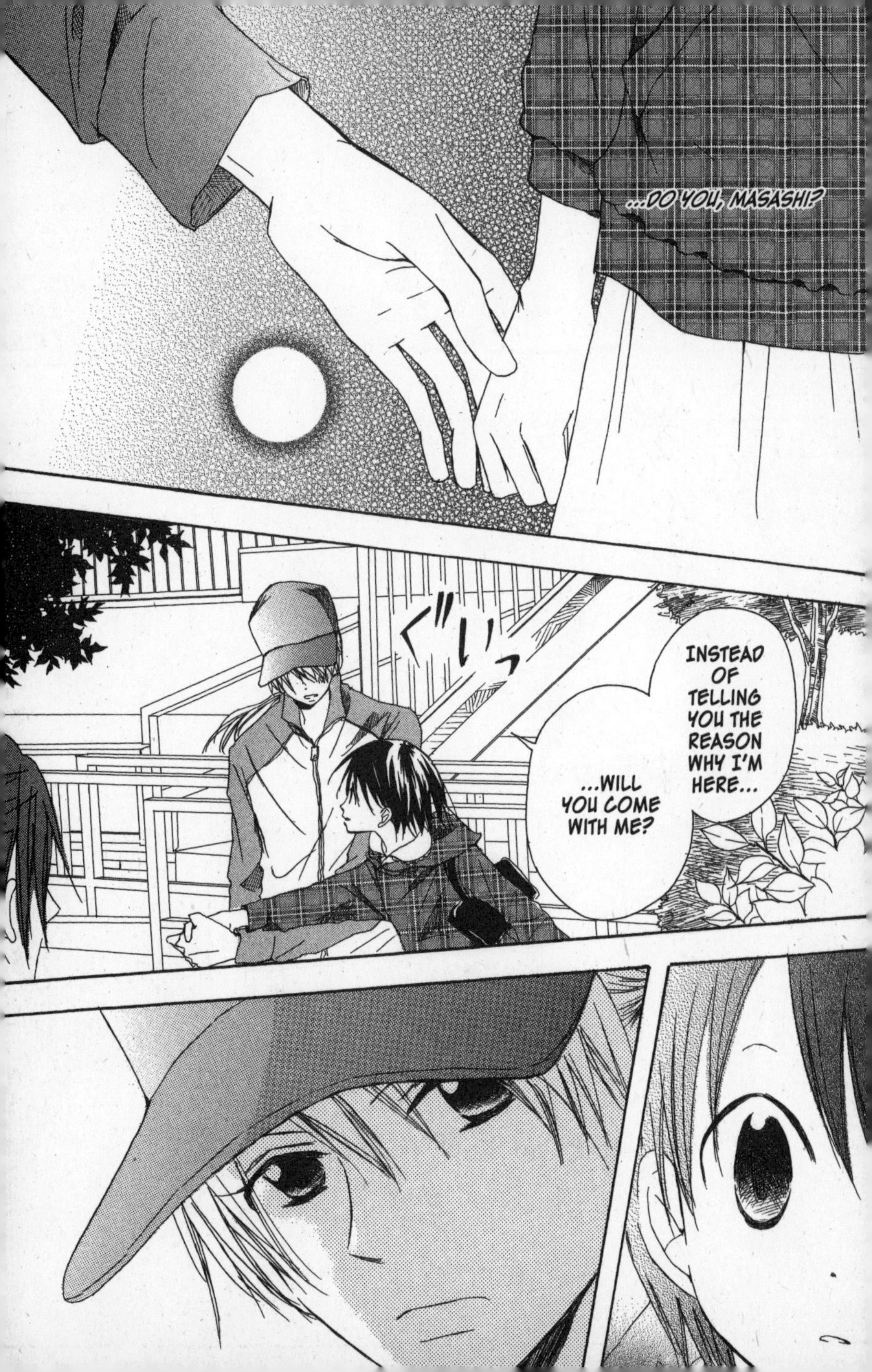
...DO YOU, MASASHI?
INSTEAD OF TELLING YOU THE REASON WHY I'M HERE...
...WILL YOU COME WITH ME?
ぐいっ

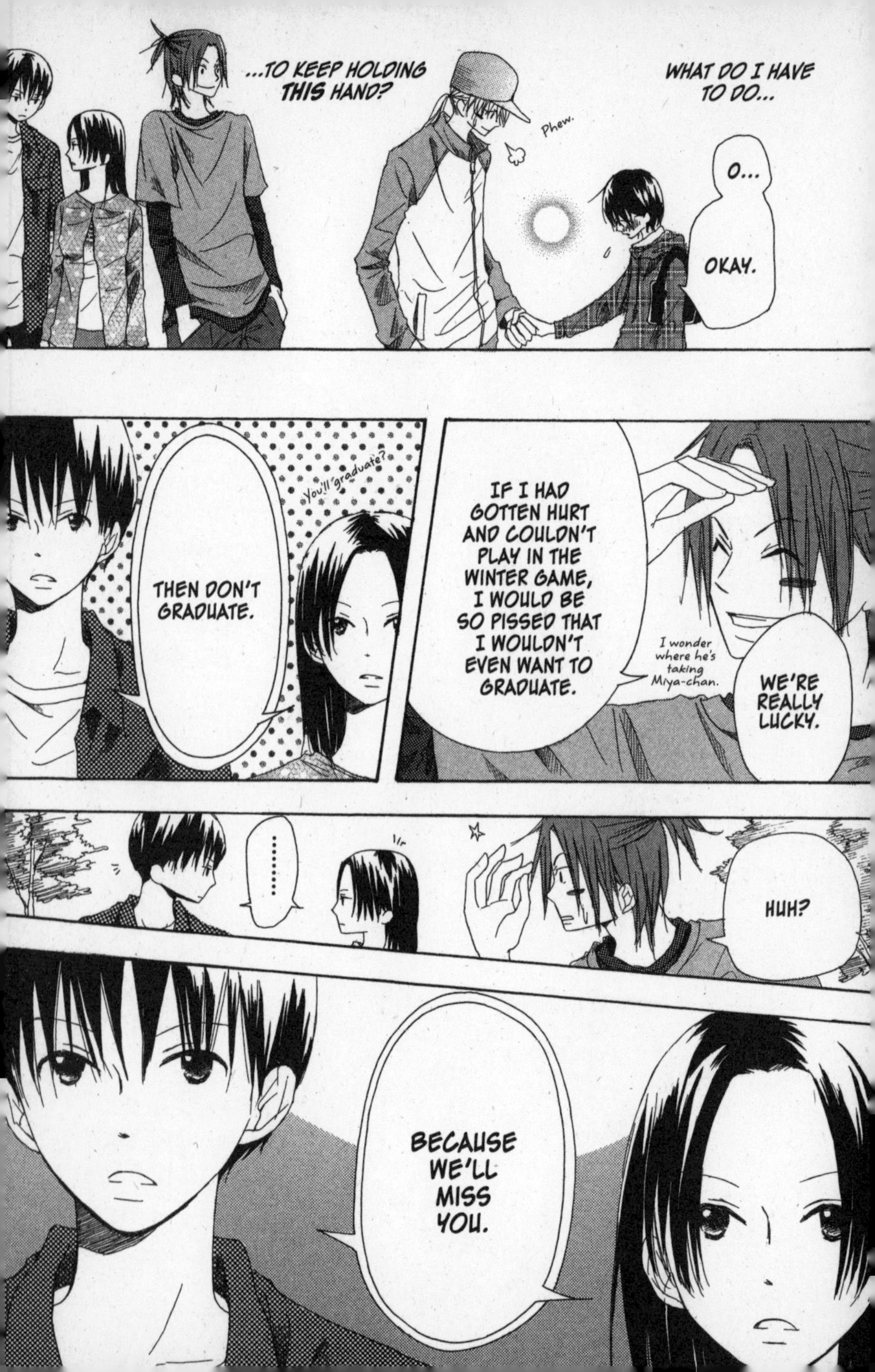
WHAT DO I HAVE TO DO...
O...
OKAY.
Phew.
...TO KEEP HOLDING THIS HAND?
WE'RE REALLY LUCKY.
IF I HAD GOTTEN HURT AND COULDN'T PLAY IN THE WINTER GAME, I WOULD BE SO PISSED THAT I WOULDN'T EVEN WANT TO GRADUATE.
I wonder where he's taking Miya-chan.
You'll graduate?
THEN DON'T GRADUATE.
HUH?
....
BECAUSE WE'LL MISS YOU.

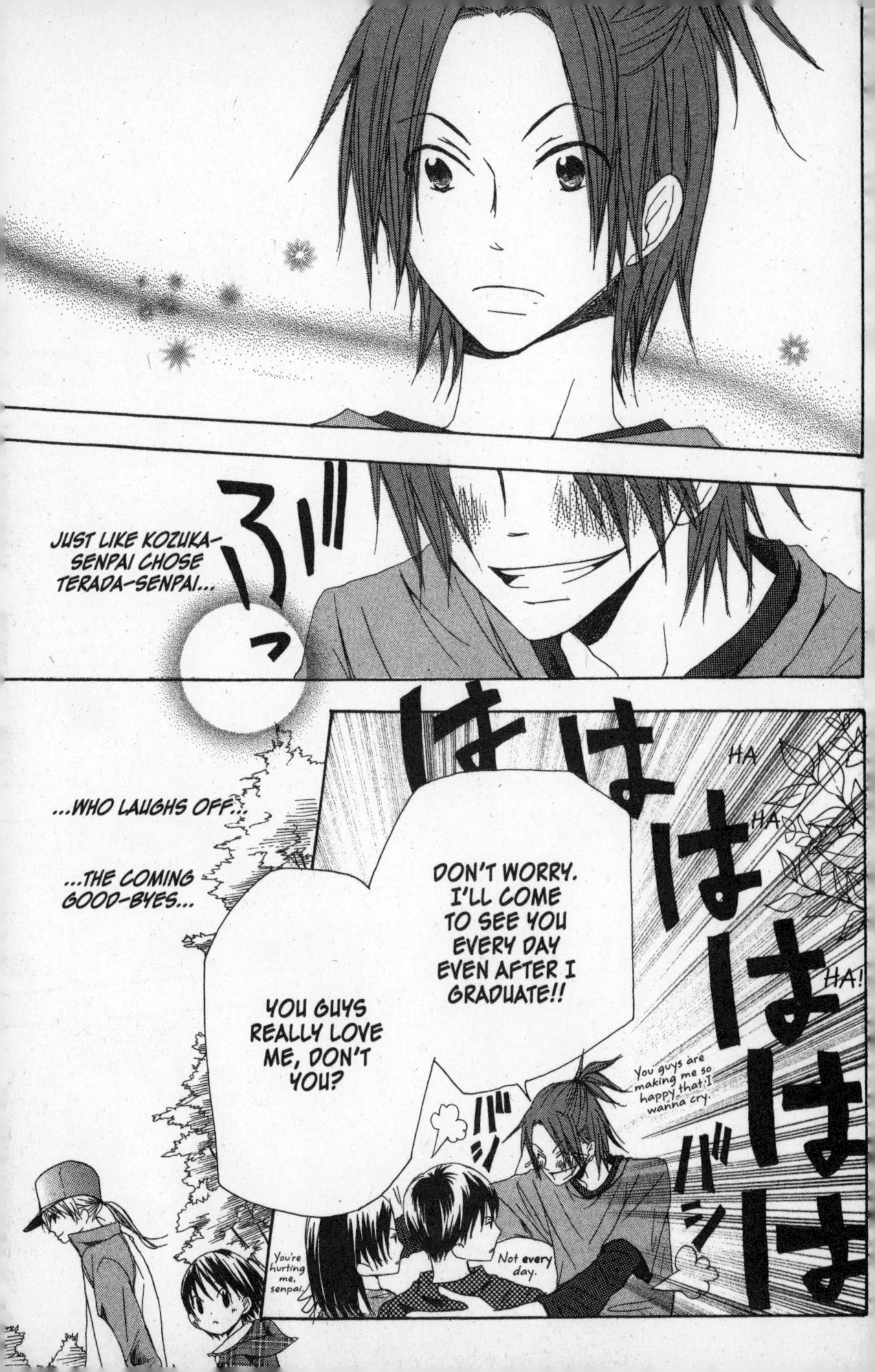
JUST LIKE KOZUKA-SENPAI CHOSE TERADA-SENPAI...
ぶっ
はははは
HA
HA
HA!
DON'T WORRY. I'LL COME TO SEE YOU EVERY DAY EVEN AFTER I GRADUATE!!
You guys are making me so happy that I wanna cry.
YOU GUYS REALLY LOVE ME, DON'T YOU?
バシ
バシ
Not every day.
You're hurting me, senpai.
...WHO LAUGHS OFF...
...THE COMING GOOD-BYES...

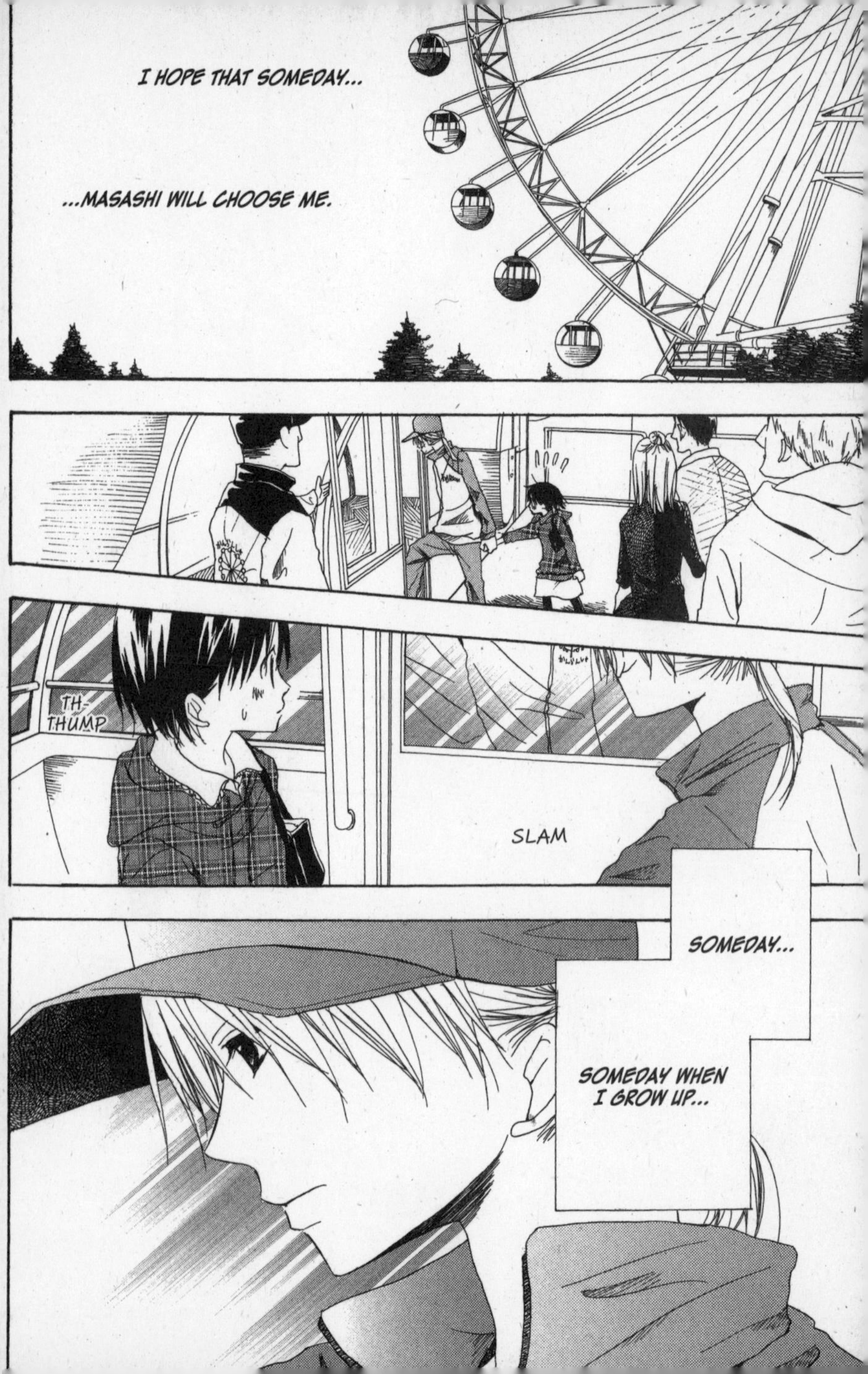
I HOPE THAT SOMEDAY...
...MASASHI WILL CHOOSE ME.
SLAM
TH-THUMP
SOMEDAY...
SOMEDAY WHEN I GROW UP...

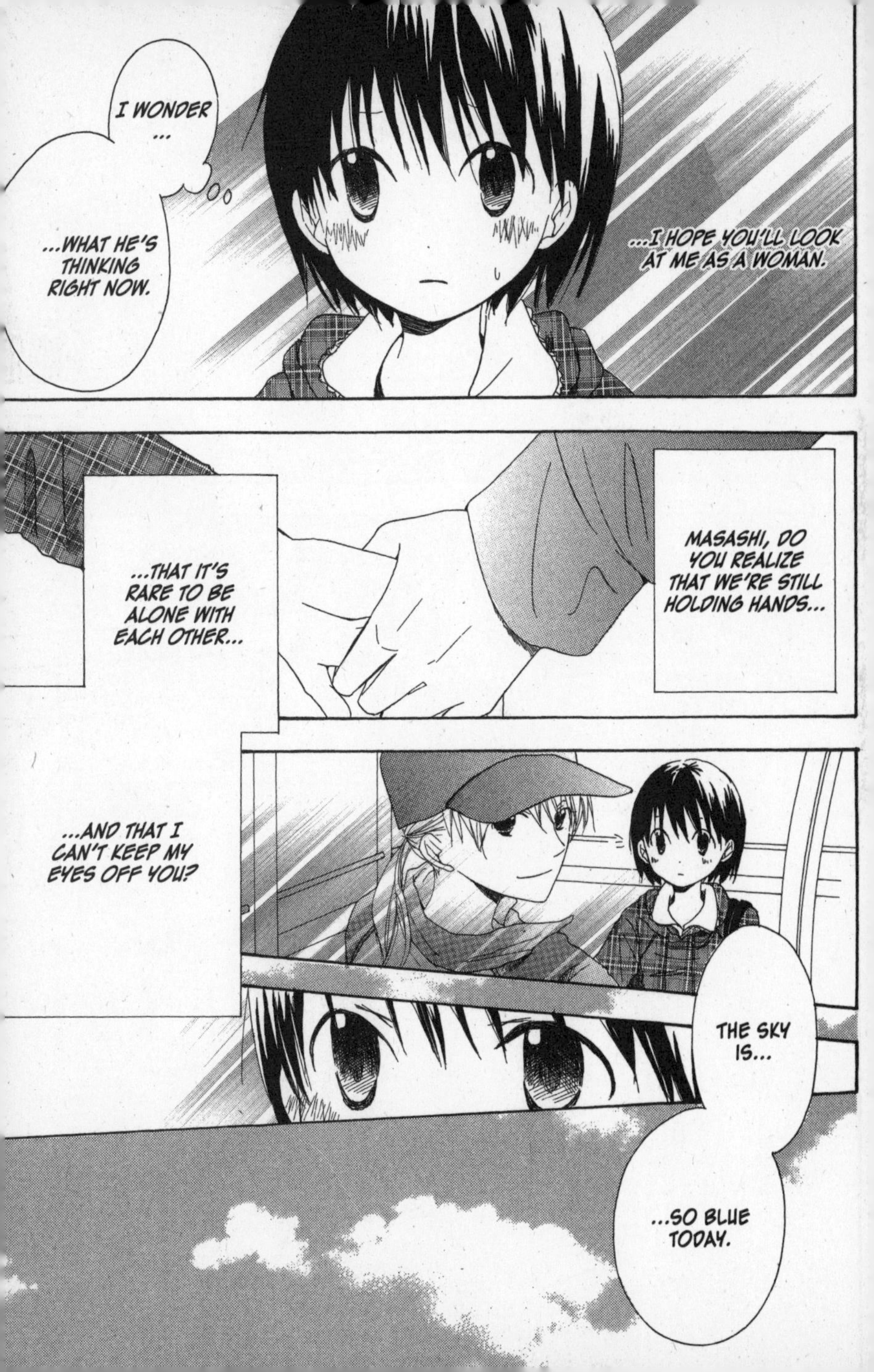
...I HOPE YOU'LL LOOK AT ME AS A WOMAN.
I WONDER ...
...WHAT HE'S THINKING RIGHT NOW.
MASASHI, DO YOU REALIZE THAT WE'RE STILL HOLDING HANDS...
...THAT IT'S RARE TO BE ALONE WITH EACH OTHER...
...AND THAT I CAN'T KEEP MY EYES OFF YOU?
THE SKY IS...
...SO BLUE TODAY.

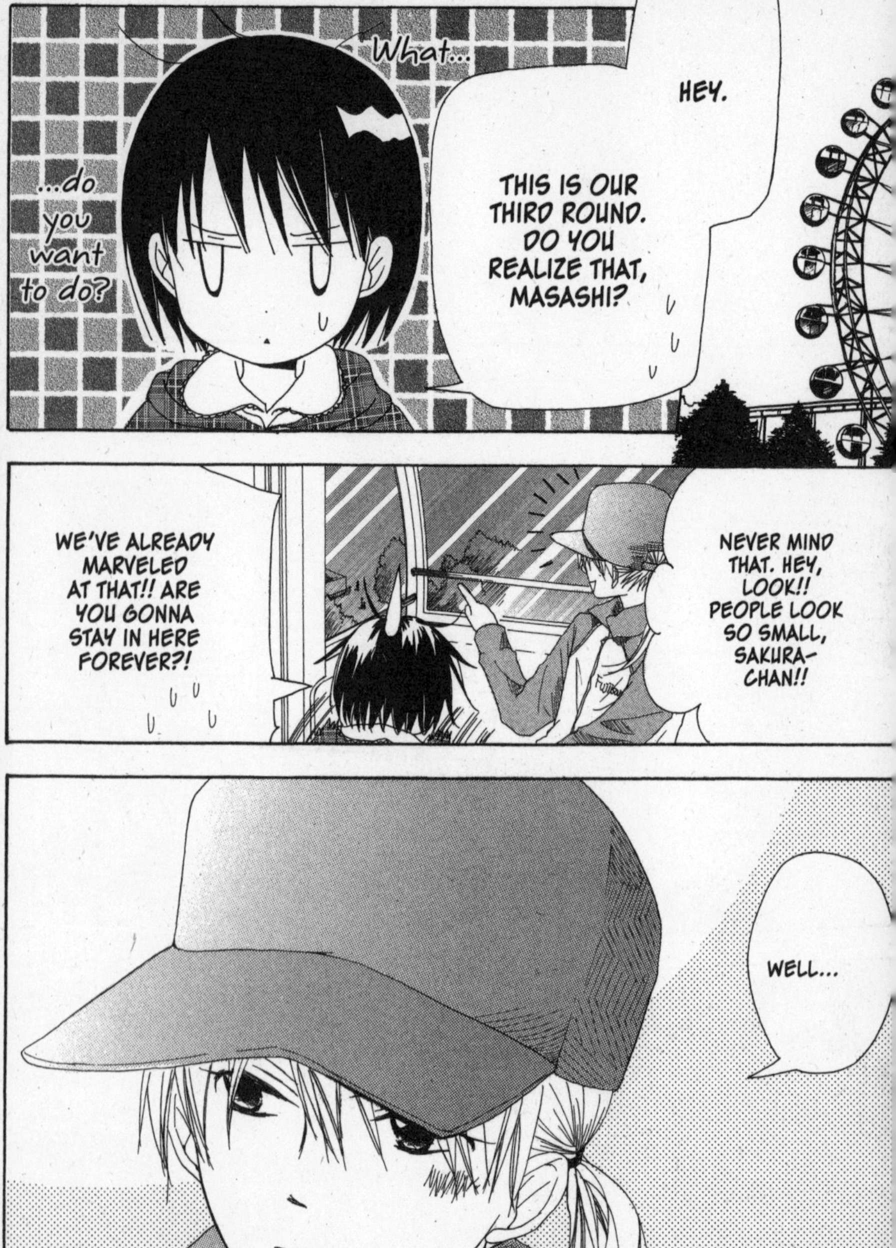
HEY.
THIS IS OUR THIRD ROUND. DO YOU REALIZE THAT, MASASHI?
What...
...do you want to do?
NEVER MIND THAT. HEY, LOOK!! PEOPLE LOOK SO SMALL, SAKURA-CHAN!!
WE'VE ALREADY MARVELED AT THAT!! ARE YOU GONNA STAY IN HERE FOREVER?!
WELL...

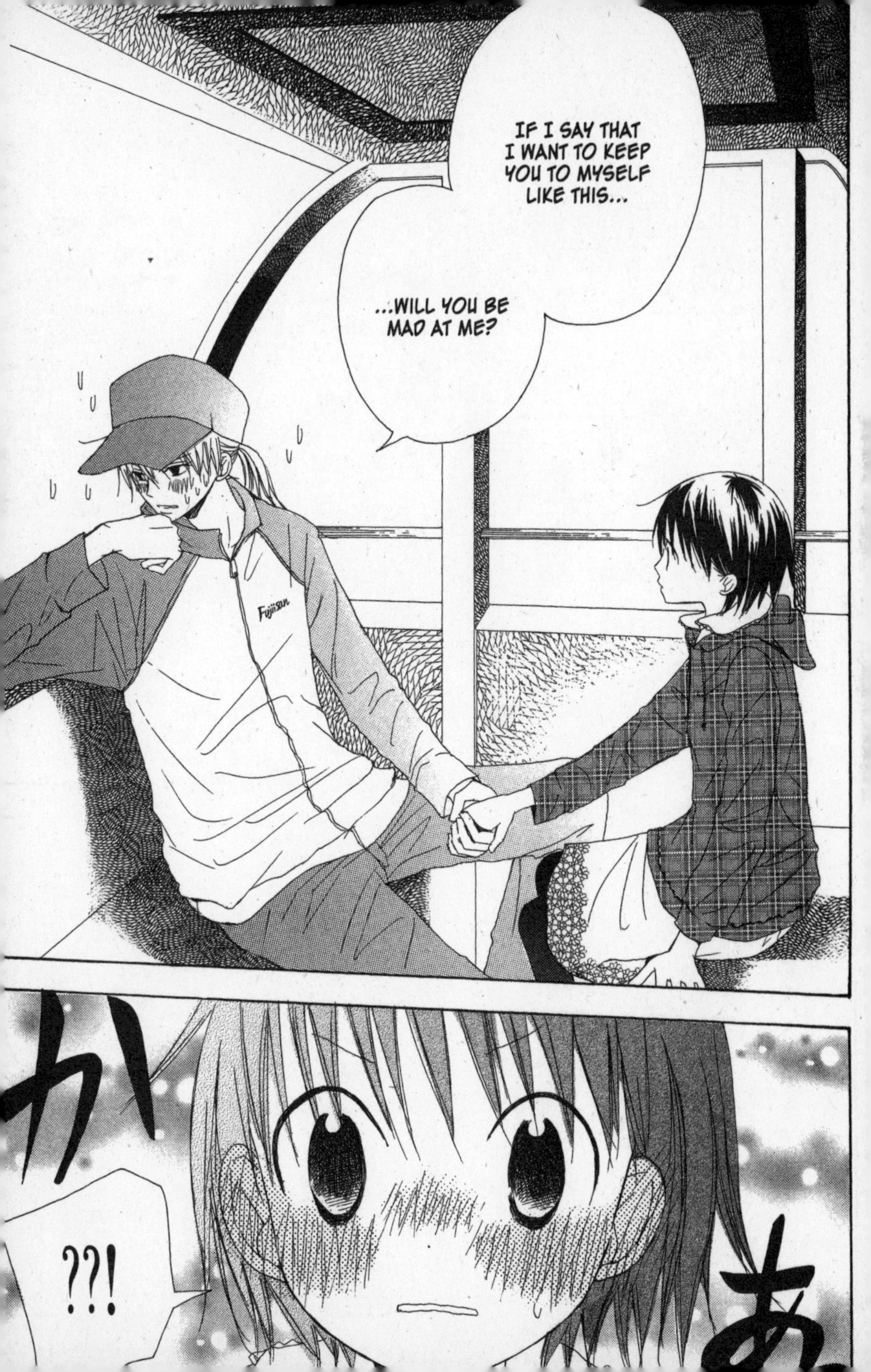
IF I SAY THAT I WANT TO KEEP YOU TO MYSELF LIKE THIS...
...WILL YOU BE MAD AT ME?
Fujisan
かあ
??!

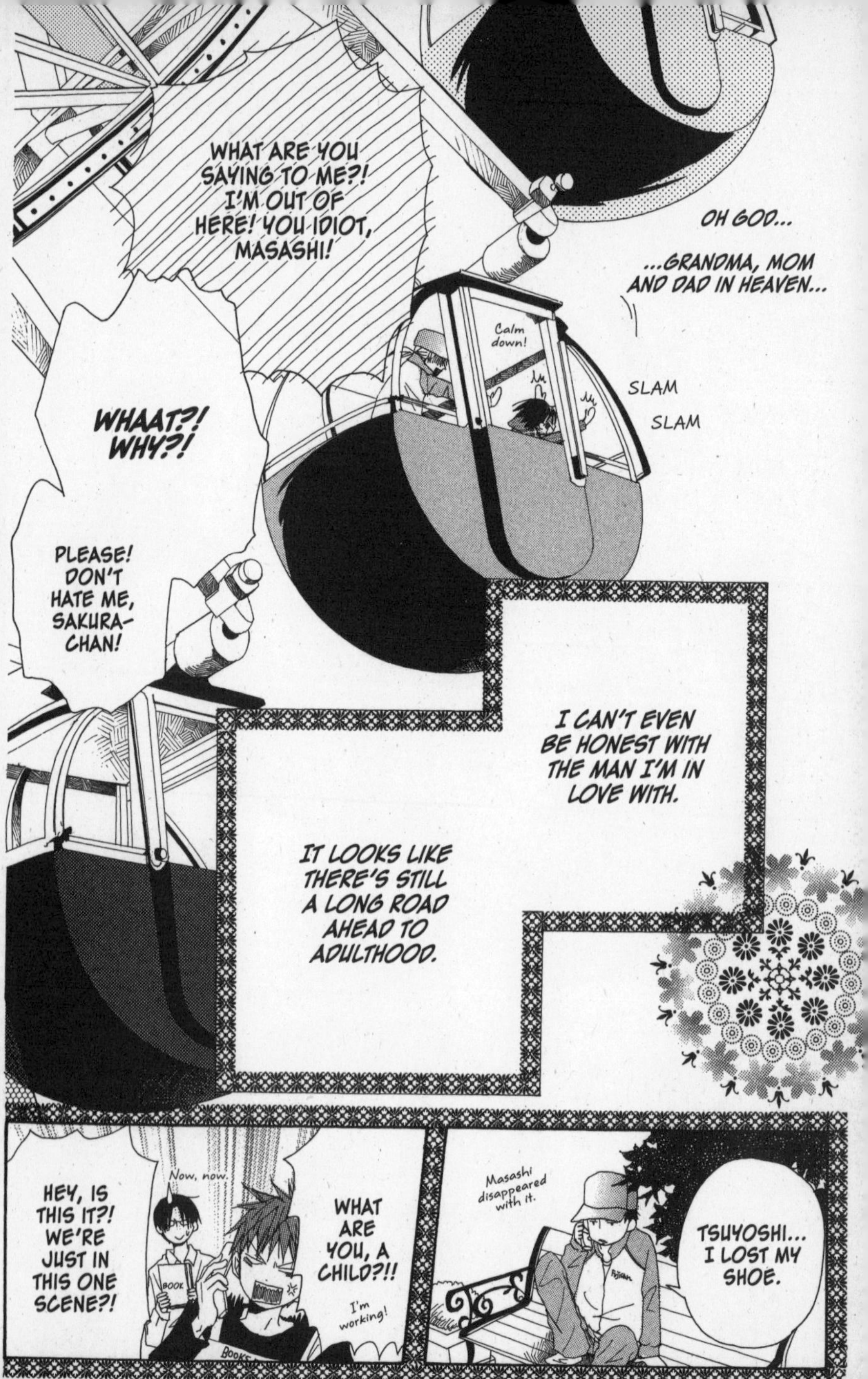
OH GOD...
...GRANDMA, MOM AND DAD IN HEAVEN...
WHAT ARE YOU SAYING TO ME?! I'M OUT OF HERE! YOU IDIOT, MASASHI!
Calm down!
SLAM
SLAM
WHAAT?! WHY?!
PLEASE! DON'T HATE ME, SAKURA-CHAN!
I CAN'T EVEN BE HONEST WITH THE MAN I'M IN LOVE WITH.
IT LOOKS LIKE THERE'S STILL A LONG ROAD AHEAD TO ADULTHOOD.
Masashi disappeared with it.
TSUYOSHI... I LOST MY SHOE.
WHAT ARE YOU, A CHILD?!!
I'm working!
Now, now.
HEY, IS THIS IT?! WE'RE JUST IN THIS ONE SCENE?!
BOOK

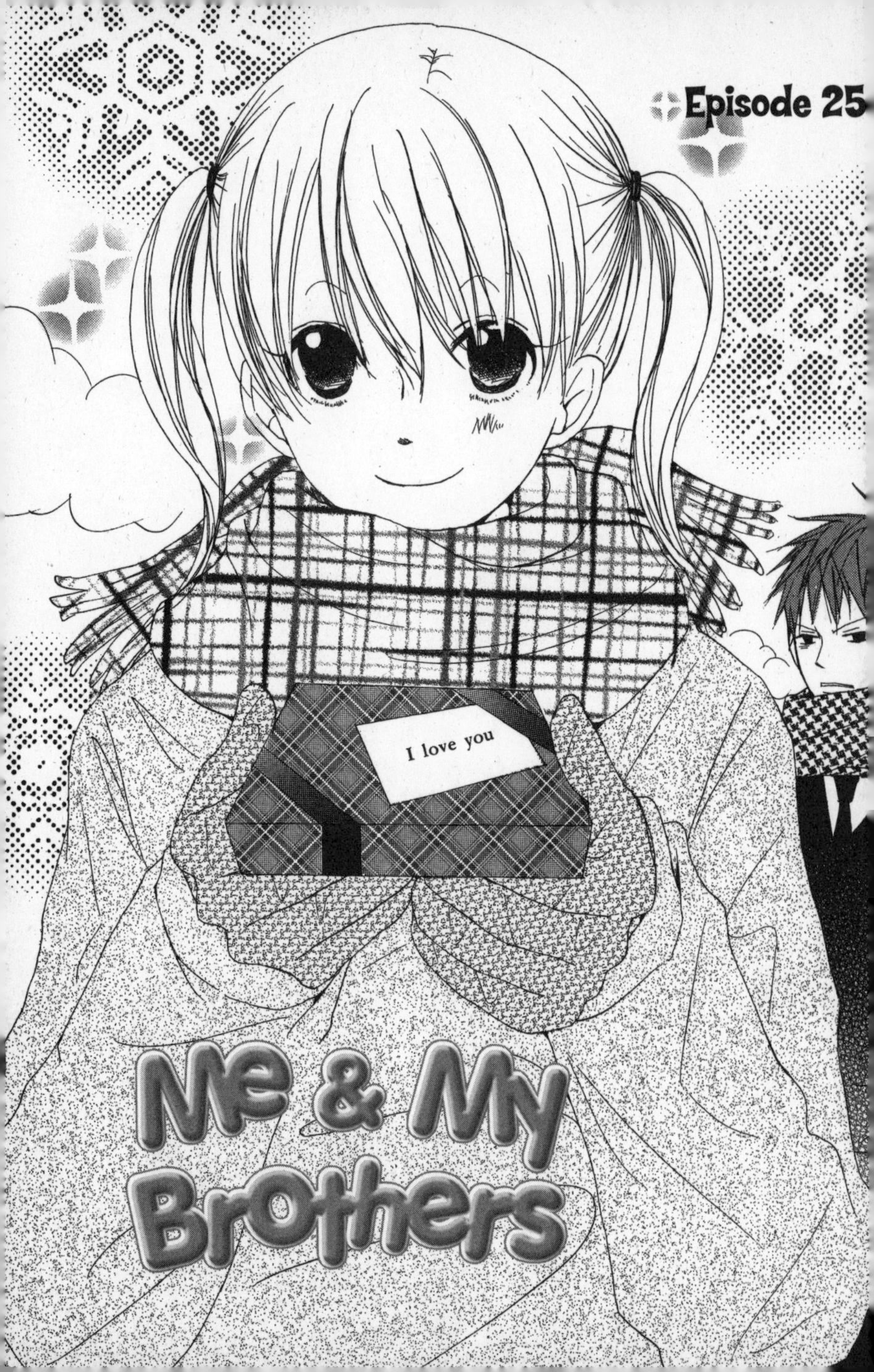
Episode 25
I love you
Me & My Brothers

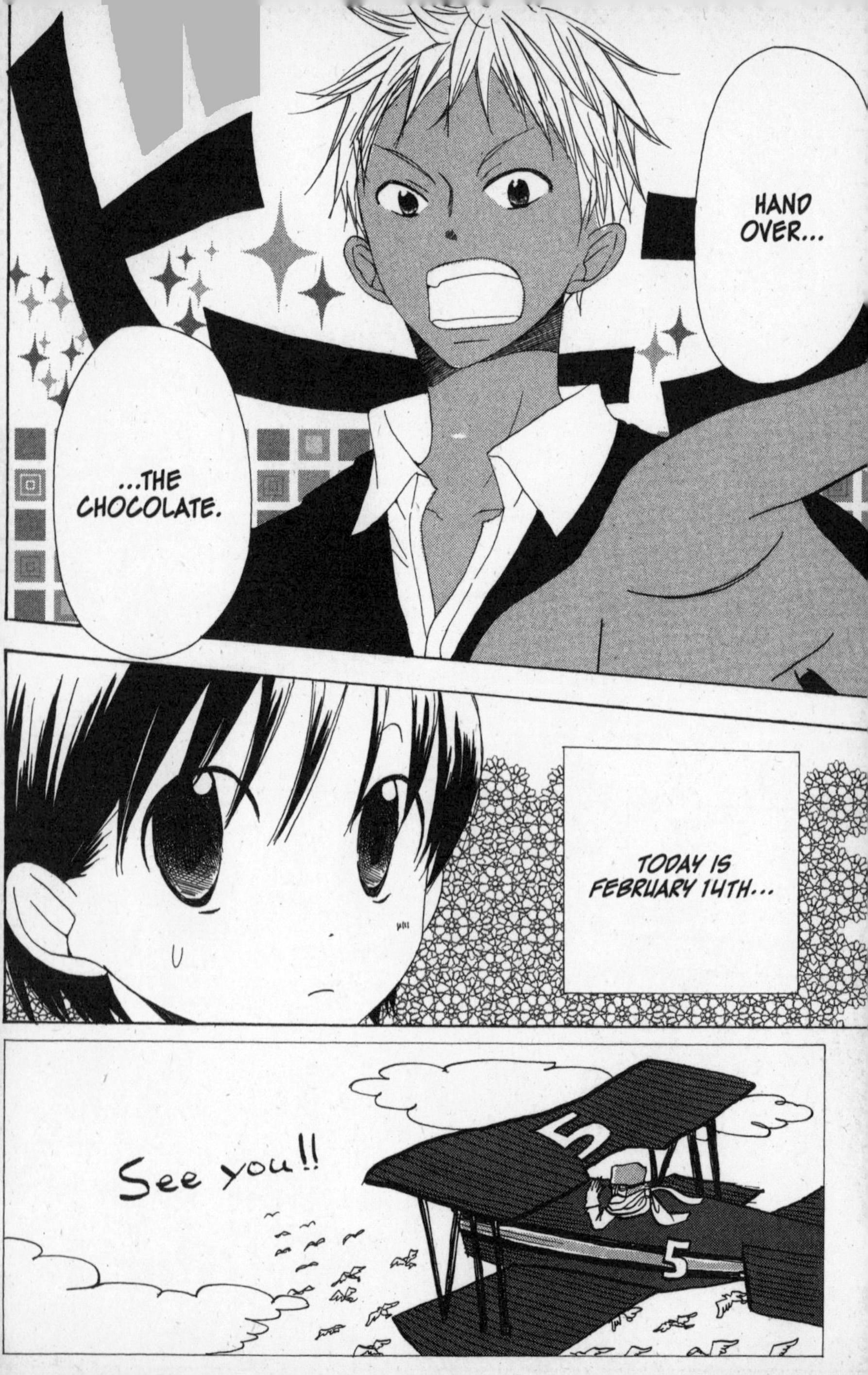
HAND OVER...
...THE CHOCOLATE.
TODAY IS FEBRUARY 14TH...
See you!!

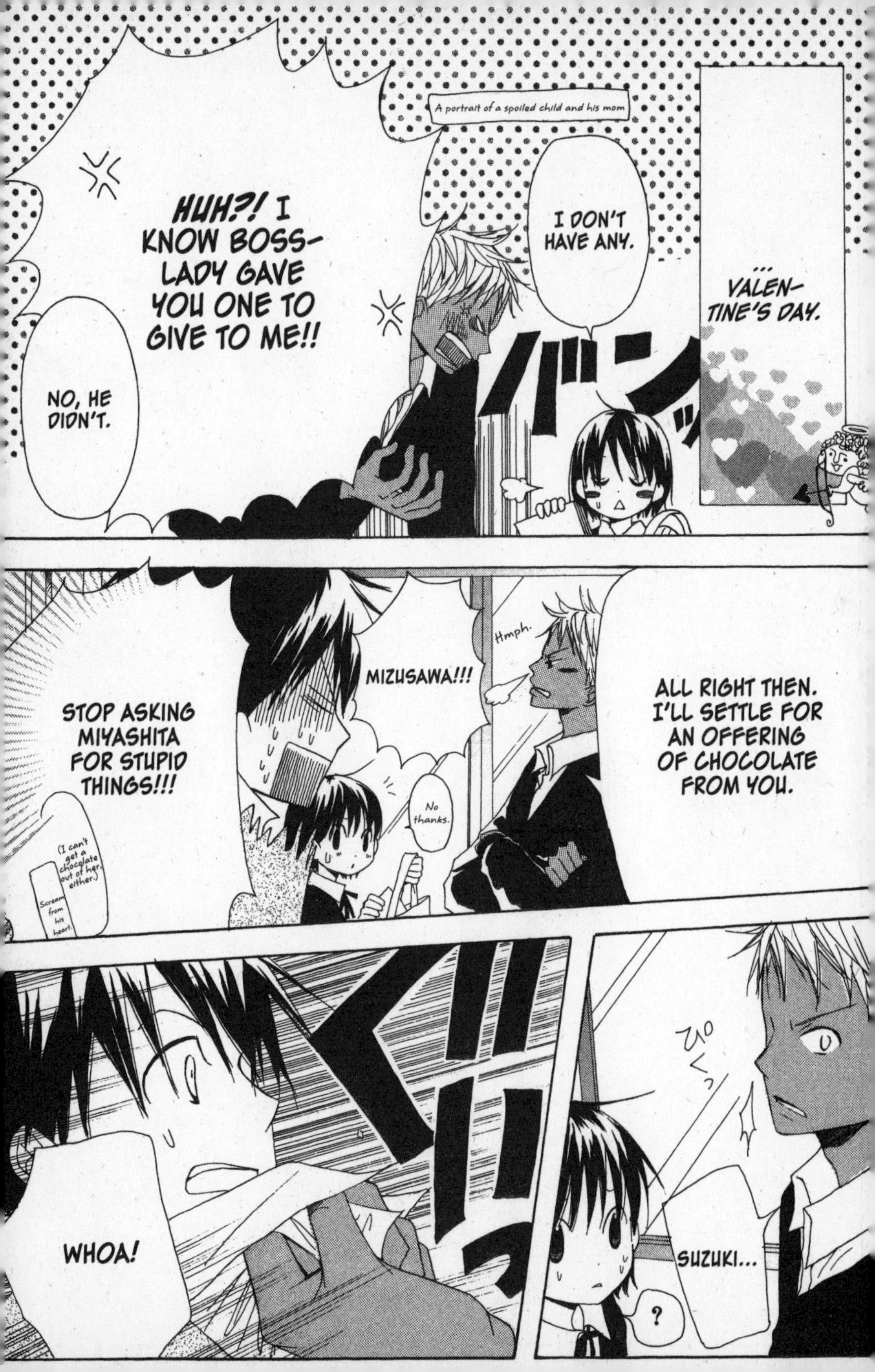
...VALEN-TINE'S DAY.
A portrait of a spoiled child and his mom
I DON'T HAVE ANY.
HUH?! I KNOW BOSS-LADY GAVE YOU ONE TO GIVE TO ME!!
NO, HE DIDN'T.
ALL RIGHT THEN. I'LL SETTLE FOR AN OFFERING OF CHOCOLATE FROM YOU.
Hmph.
MIZUSAWA!!!
No thanks.
STOP ASKING MIYASHITA FOR STUPID THINGS!!!
(I can't get a chocolate out of her, either.)
Scream from his heart.
SUZUKI...
?
WHOA!

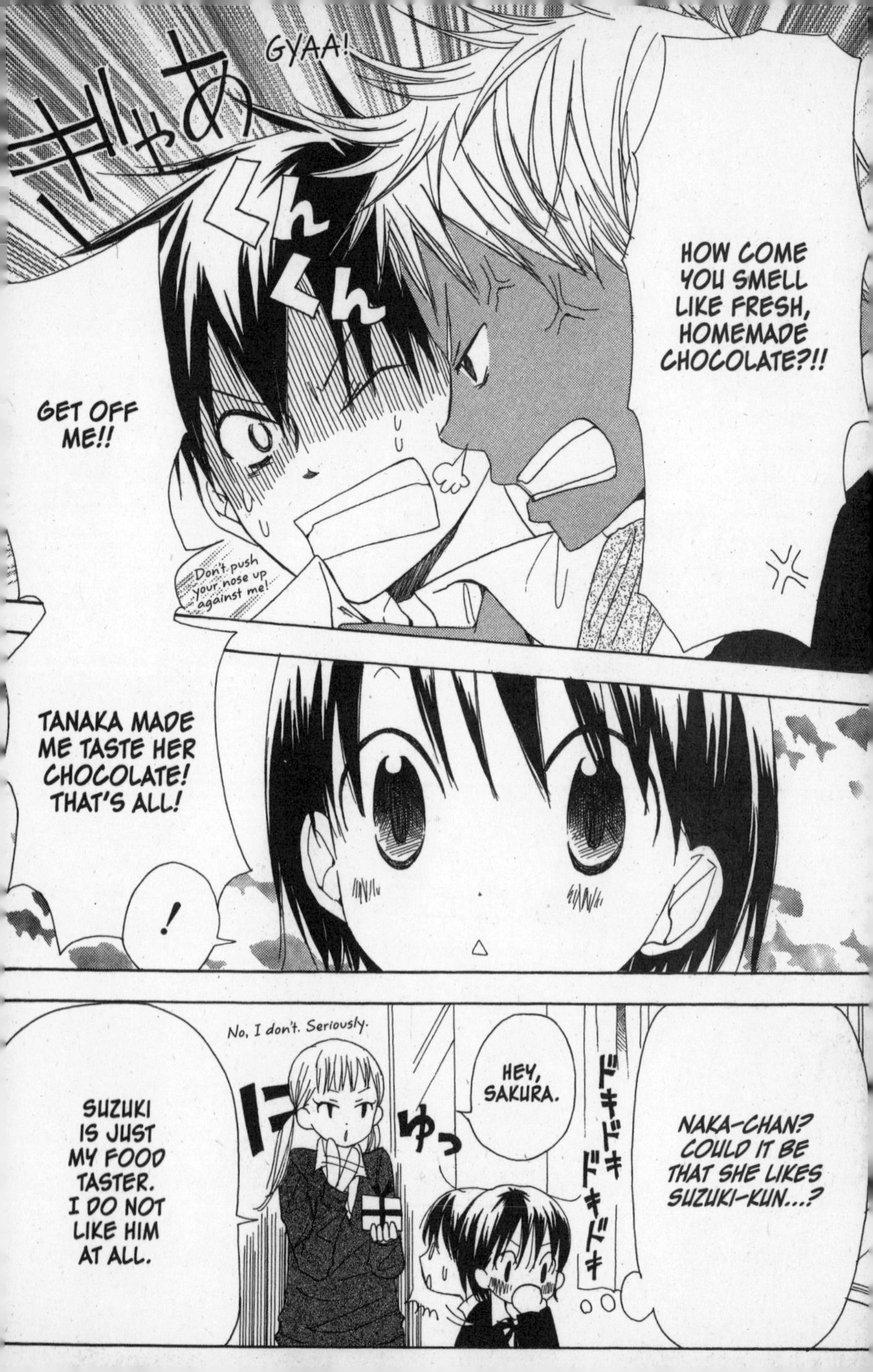
ぎゃあ
GYAA!
くんくん
HOW COME YOU SMELL LIKE FRESH, HOMEMADE CHOCOLATE?!!
GET OFF ME!!
Don't push your nose up against me!
TANAKA MADE ME TASTE HER CHOCOLATE! THAT'S ALL!
!
NAKA-CHAN? COULD IT BE THAT SHE LIKES SUZUKI-KUN...?
ドキドキ
ドキドキ
HEY, SAKURA.
ゆっ
に
SUZUKI IS JUST MY FOOD TASTER. I DO NOT LIKE HIM AT ALL.
No, I don't. Seriously.

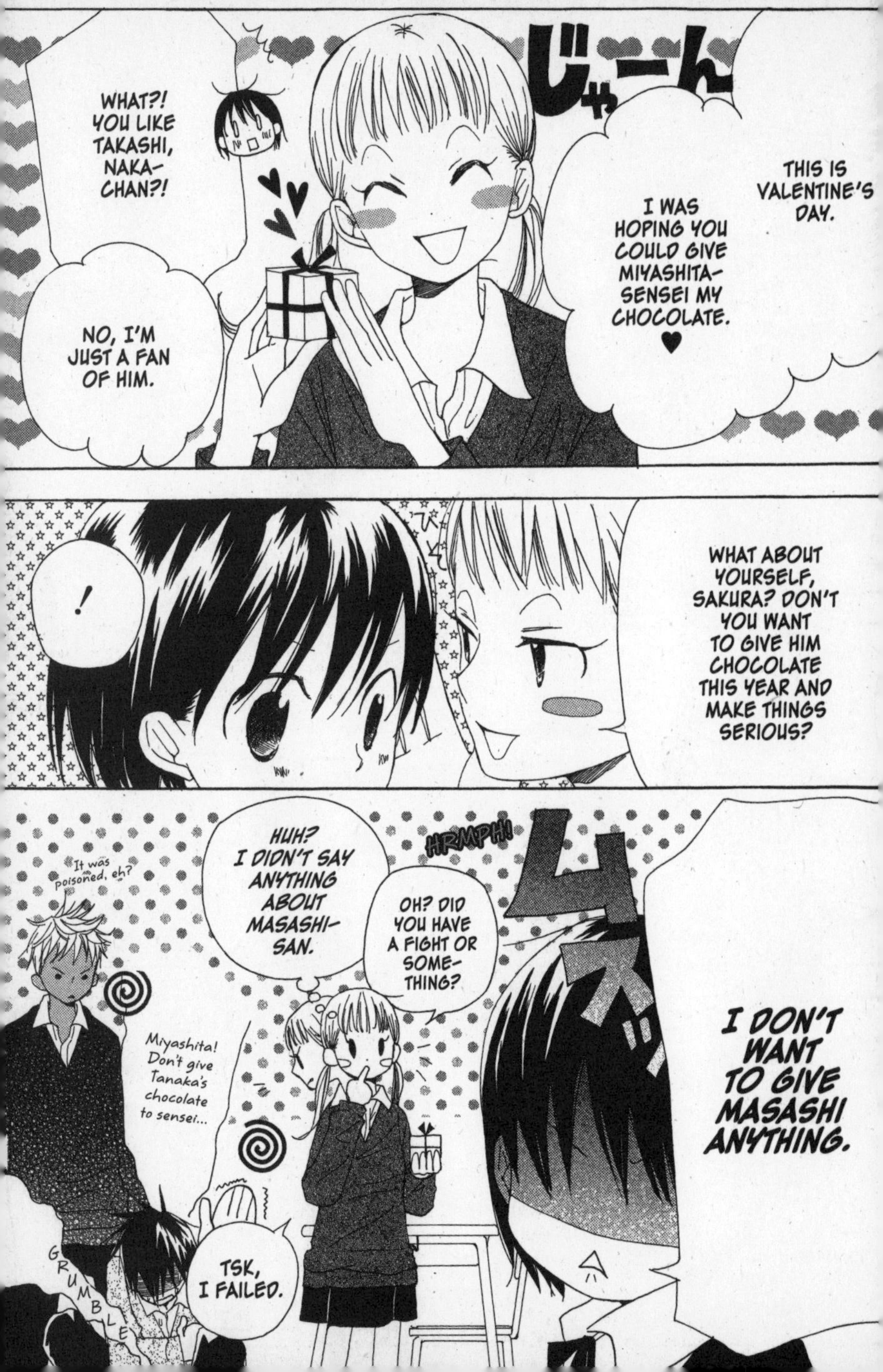
じゃーん
THIS IS VALENTINE'S DAY.
I WAS HOPING YOU COULD GIVE MIYASHITA-SENSEI MY CHOCOLATE. ♥
WHAT?! YOU LIKE TAKASHI, NAKA-CHAN?!
NO, I'M JUST A FAN OF HIM.
WHAT ABOUT YOURSELF, SAKURA? DON'T YOU WANT TO GIVE HIM CHOCOLATE THIS YEAR AND MAKE THINGS SERIOUS?
!
I DON'T WANT TO GIVE MASASHI ANYTHING.
ムス
HRMPH!
OH? DID YOU HAVE A FIGHT OR SOMETHING?
HUH? I DIDN'T SAY ANYTHING ABOUT MASASHI-SAN.
It was poisoned, eh?
Miyashita! Don't give Tanaka's chocolate to sensei...
TSK, I FAILED.
GRUMBLE

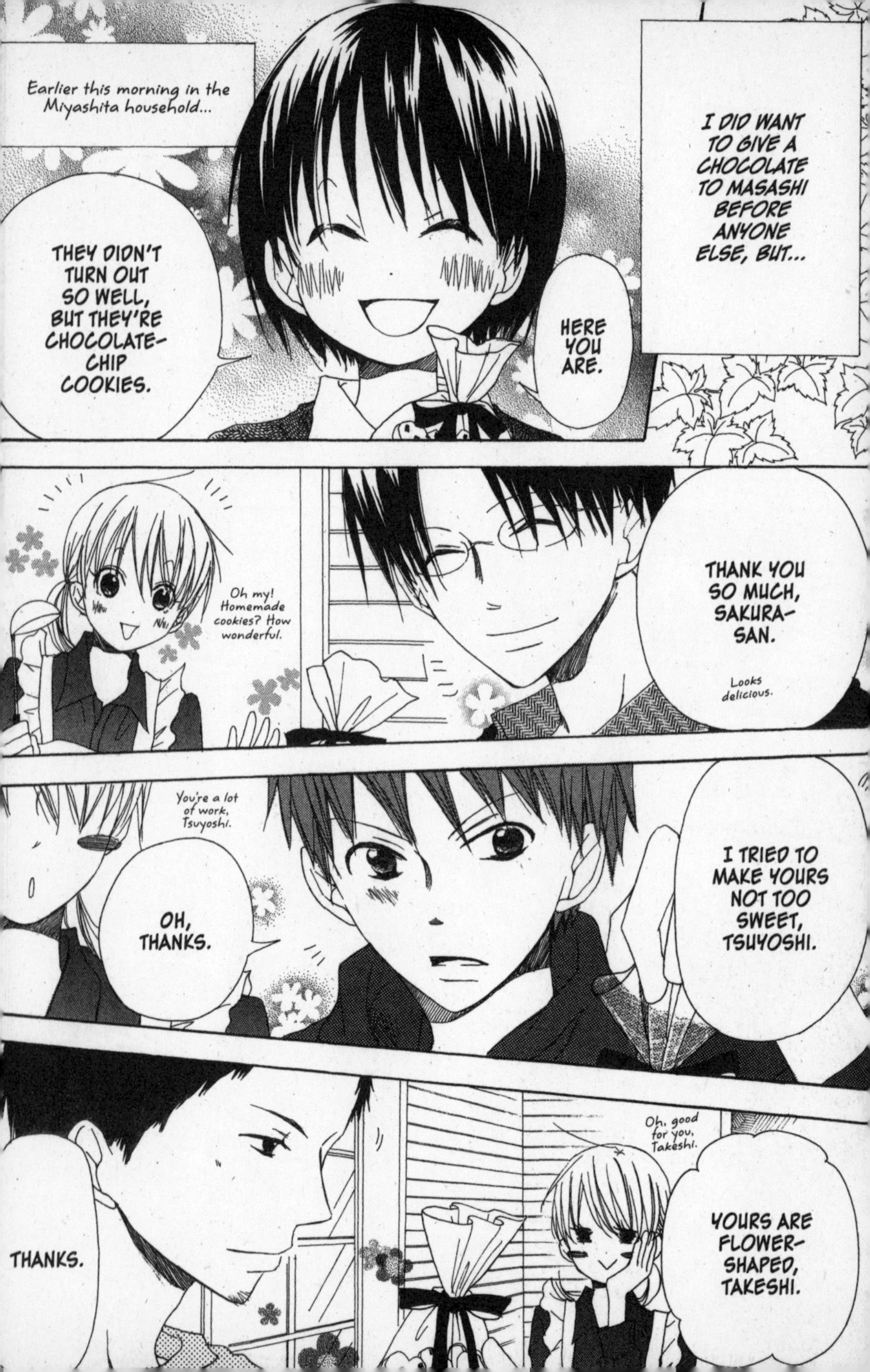
I DID WANT TO GIVE A CHOCOLATE TO MASASHI BEFORE ANYONE ELSE, BUT...
HERE YOU ARE.
Earlier this morning in the Miyashita household...
THEY DIDN'T TURN OUT SO WELL, BUT THEY'RE CHOCOLATE-CHIP COOKIES.
THANK YOU SO MUCH, SAKURA-SAN.
Looks delicious.
Oh my! Homemade cookies? How wonderful.
I TRIED TO MAKE YOURS NOT TOO SWEET, TSUYOSHI.
OH, THANKS.
You're a lot of work, Tsuyoshi.
YOURS ARE FLOWER-SHAPED, TAKESHI.
Oh, good for you, Takeshi.
THANKS.

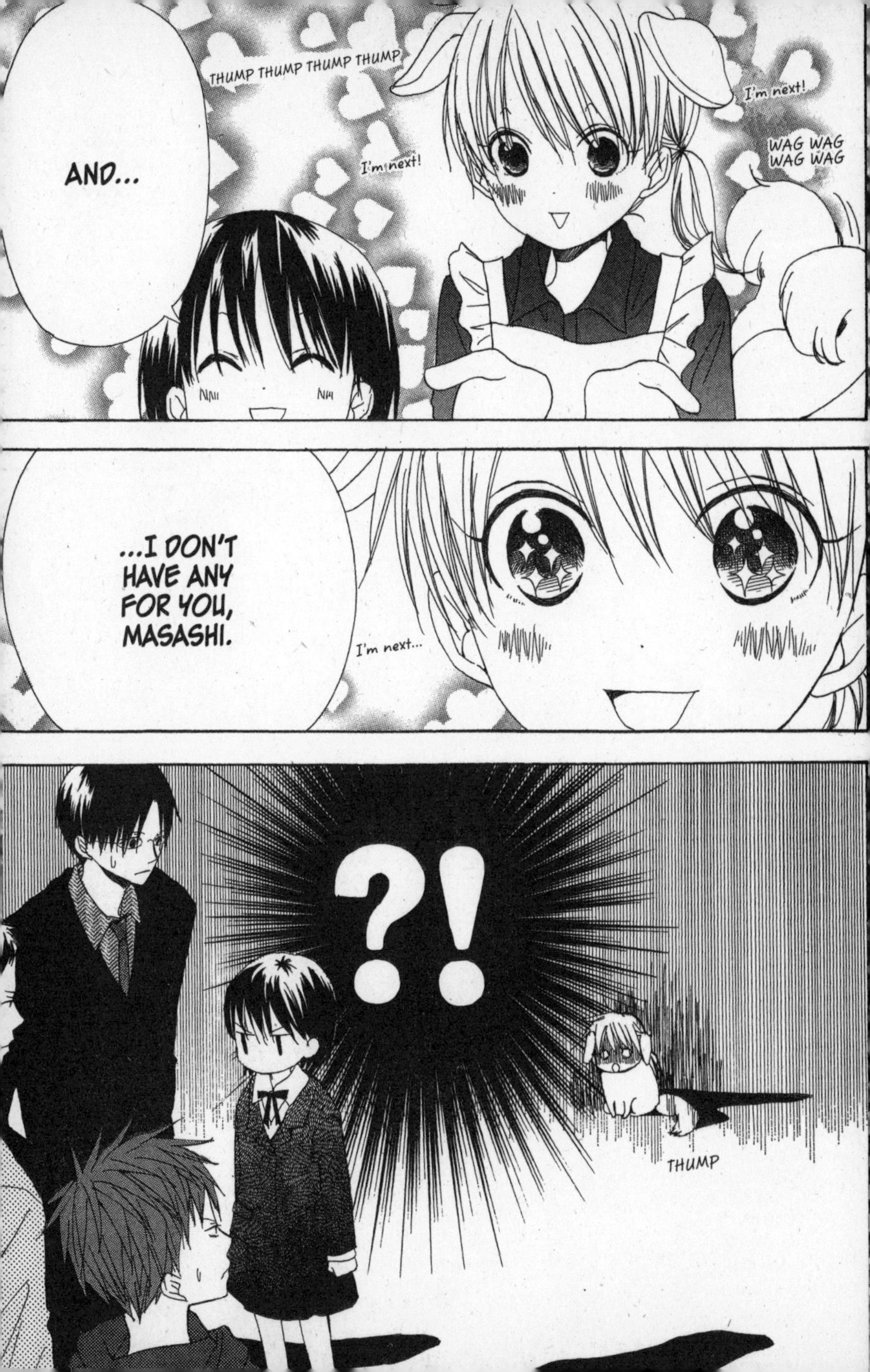
I'm next!
WAG WAG WAG WAG
THUMP THUMP THUMP THUMP
I'm next!
AND...
I'm next...
...I DON'T HAVE ANY FOR YOU, MASASHI.
THUMP
?!

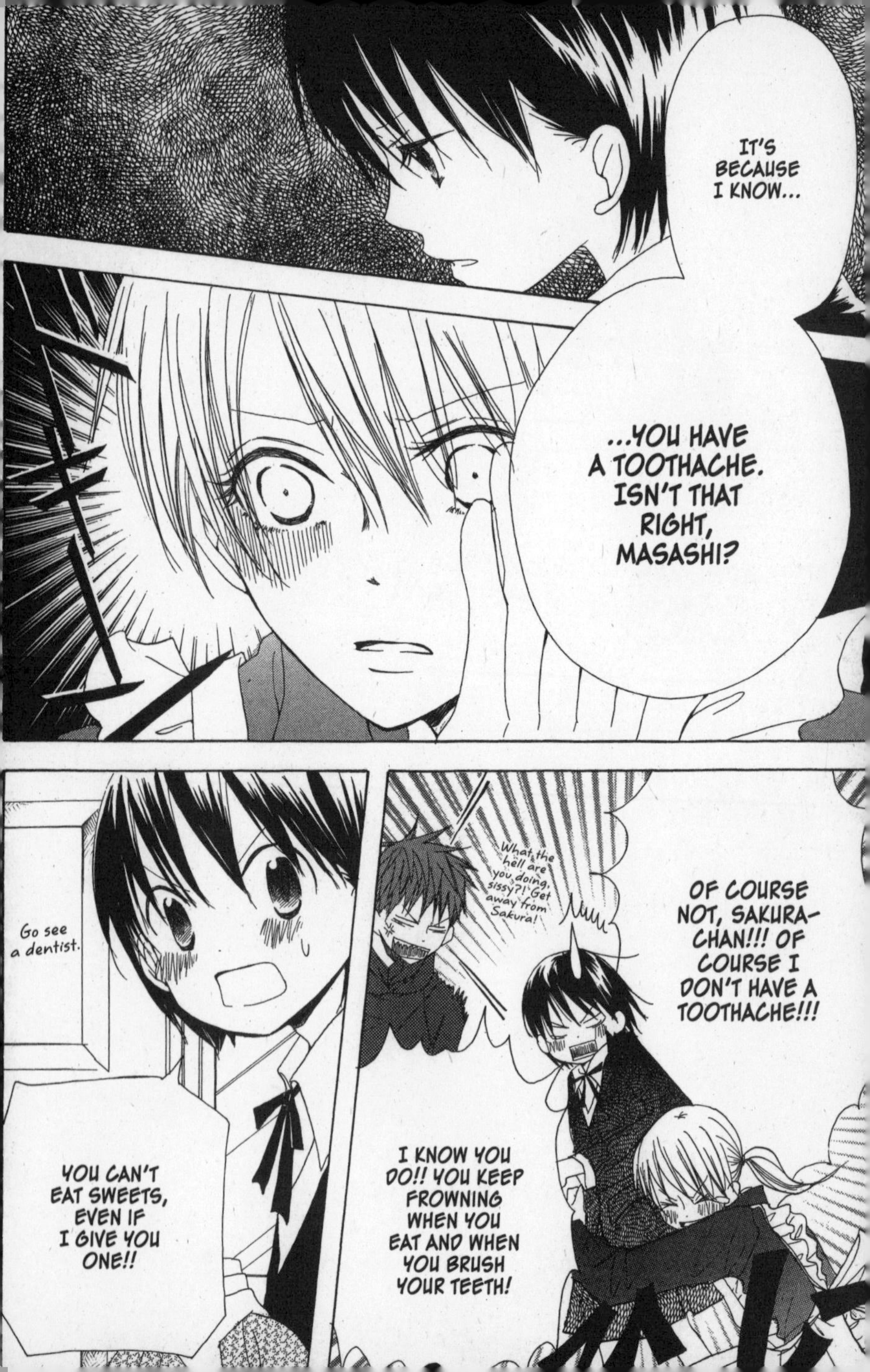
IT'S BECAUSE I KNOW...
...YOU HAVE A TOOTHACHE. ISN'T THAT RIGHT, MASASHI?
OF COURSE NOT, SAKURA-CHAN!!! OF COURSE I DON'T HAVE A TOOTHACHE!!!
What the hell are you doing, sissy?! Get away from Sakura!
I KNOW YOU DO!! YOU KEEP FROWNING WHEN YOU EAT AND WHEN YOU BRUSH YOUR TEETH!
YOU CAN'T EAT SWEETS, EVEN IF I GIVE YOU ONE!!
Go see a dentist.

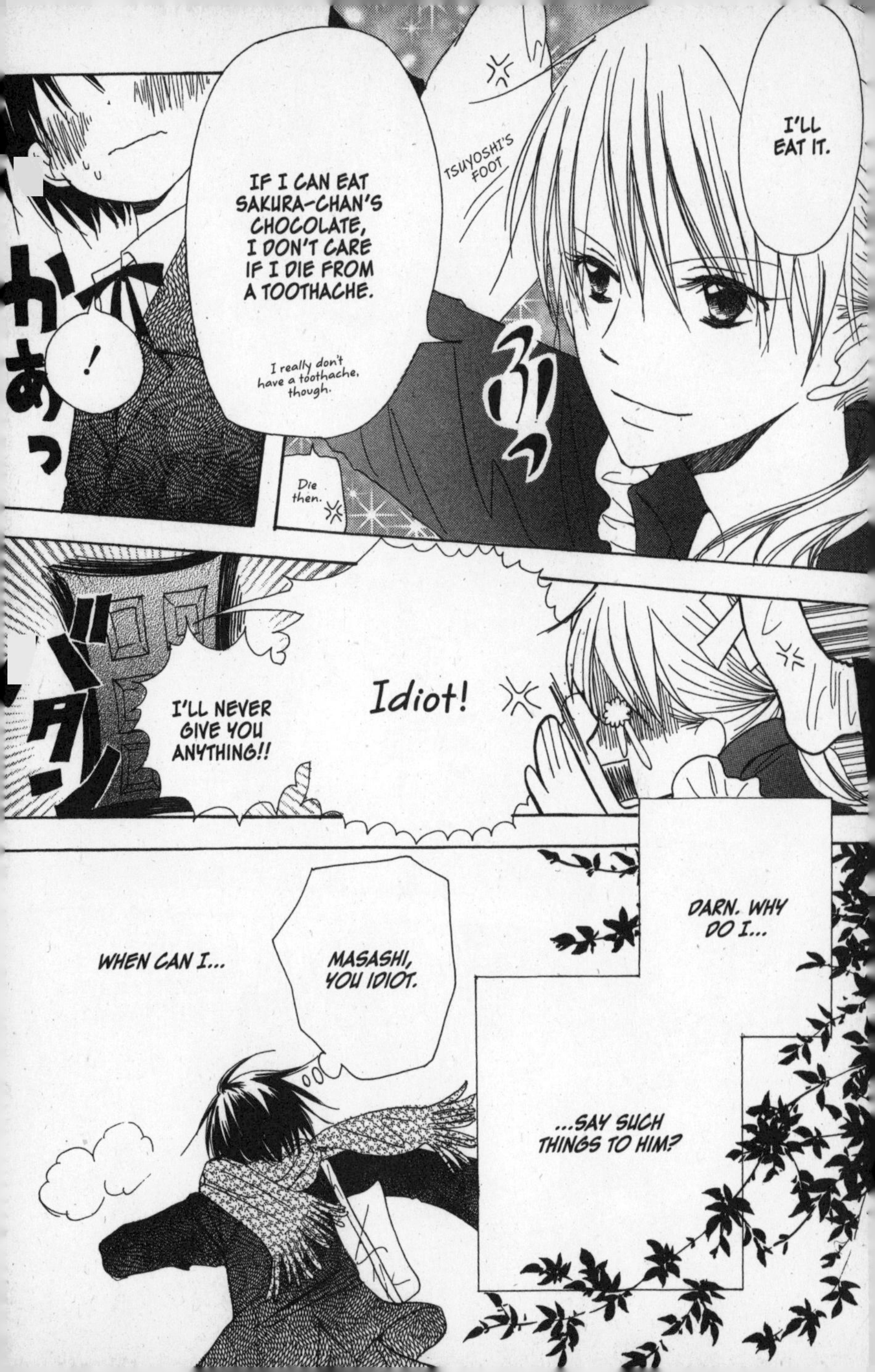
I'LL EAT IT.
TSUYOSHI'S FOOT
ふっ
IF I CAN EAT SAKURA-CHAN'S CHOCOLATE, I DON'T CARE IF I DIE FROM A TOOTHACHE.
I really don't have a toothache, though.
Die then.
かあっ
!
Idiot!
I'LL NEVER GIVE YOU ANYTHING!!
バタン
DARN. WHY DO I...
...SAY SUCH THINGS TO HIM?
MASASHI, YOU IDIOT.
WHEN CAN I...

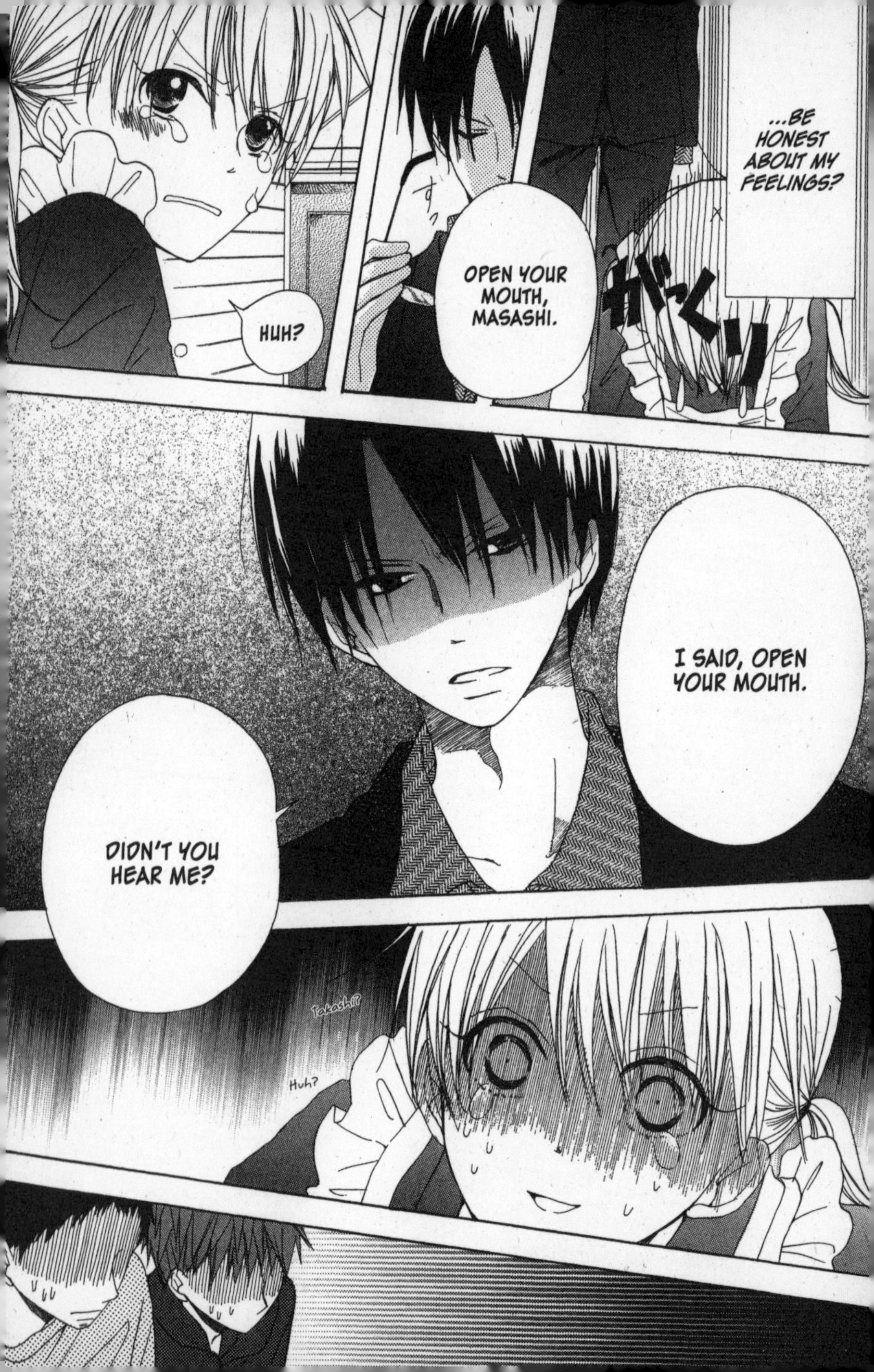
...BE HONEST ABOUT MY FEELINGS?
OPEN YOUR MOUTH, MASASHI.
HUH?
I SAID, OPEN YOUR MOUTH.
DIDN'T YOU HEAR ME?
Takashi?
Huh?

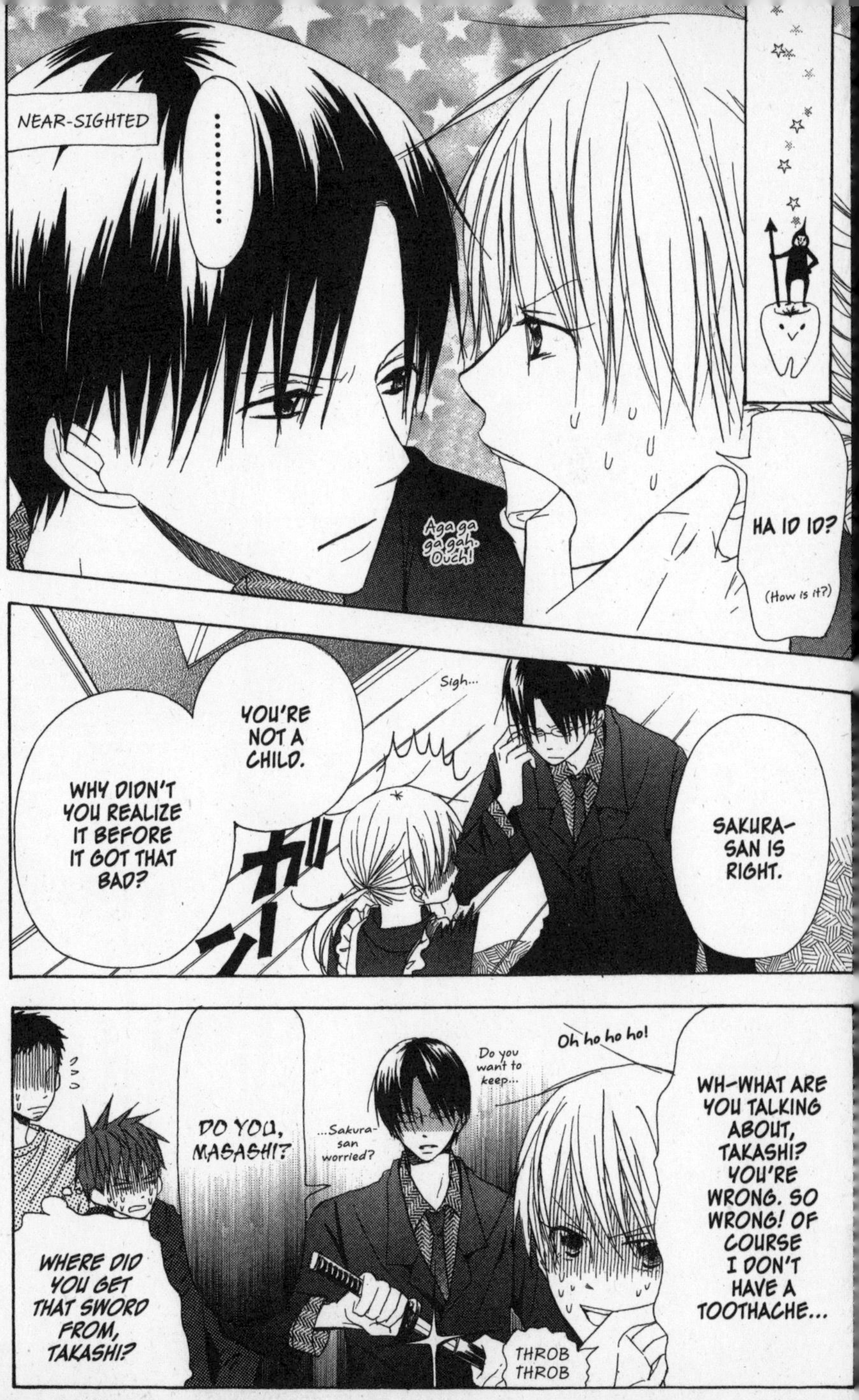
HA ID ID?
(How is it?)
Aga ga ga gah. Ouch!
......
NEAR-SIGHTED
SAKURA-SAN IS RIGHT.
Sigh...
YOU'RE NOT A CHILD.
WHY DIDN'T YOU REALIZE IT BEFORE IT GOT THAT BAD?
ガーン
WH-WHAT ARE YOU TALKING ABOUT, TAKASHI? YOU'RE WRONG. SO WRONG! OF COURSE I DON'T HAVE A TOOTHACHE...
Oh ho ho ho!
THROB THROB
Do you want to keep...
...Sakura-san worried?
DO YOU, MASASHI?
WHERE DID YOU GET THAT SWORD FROM, TAKASHI?

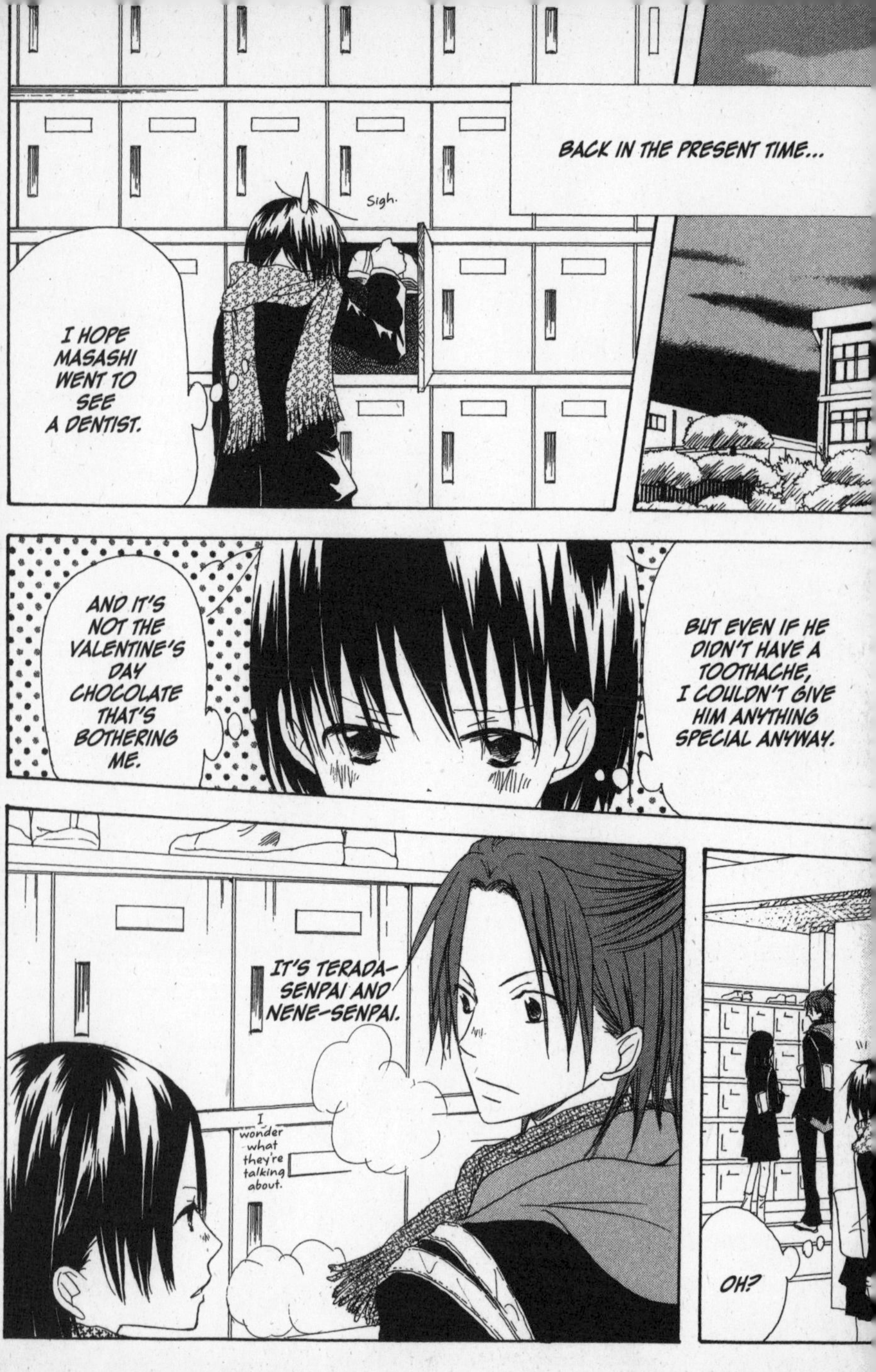
BACK IN THE PRESENT TIME...
Sigh.
I HOPE MASASHI WENT TO SEE A DENTIST.
BUT EVEN IF HE DIDN'T HAVE A TOOTHACHE, I COULDN'T GIVE HIM ANYTHING SPECIAL ANYWAY.
AND IT'S NOT THE VALENTINE'S DAY CHOCOLATE THAT'S BOTHERING ME.
OH?
IT'S TERADA-SENPAI AND NENE-SENPAI.
I wonder what they're talking about.

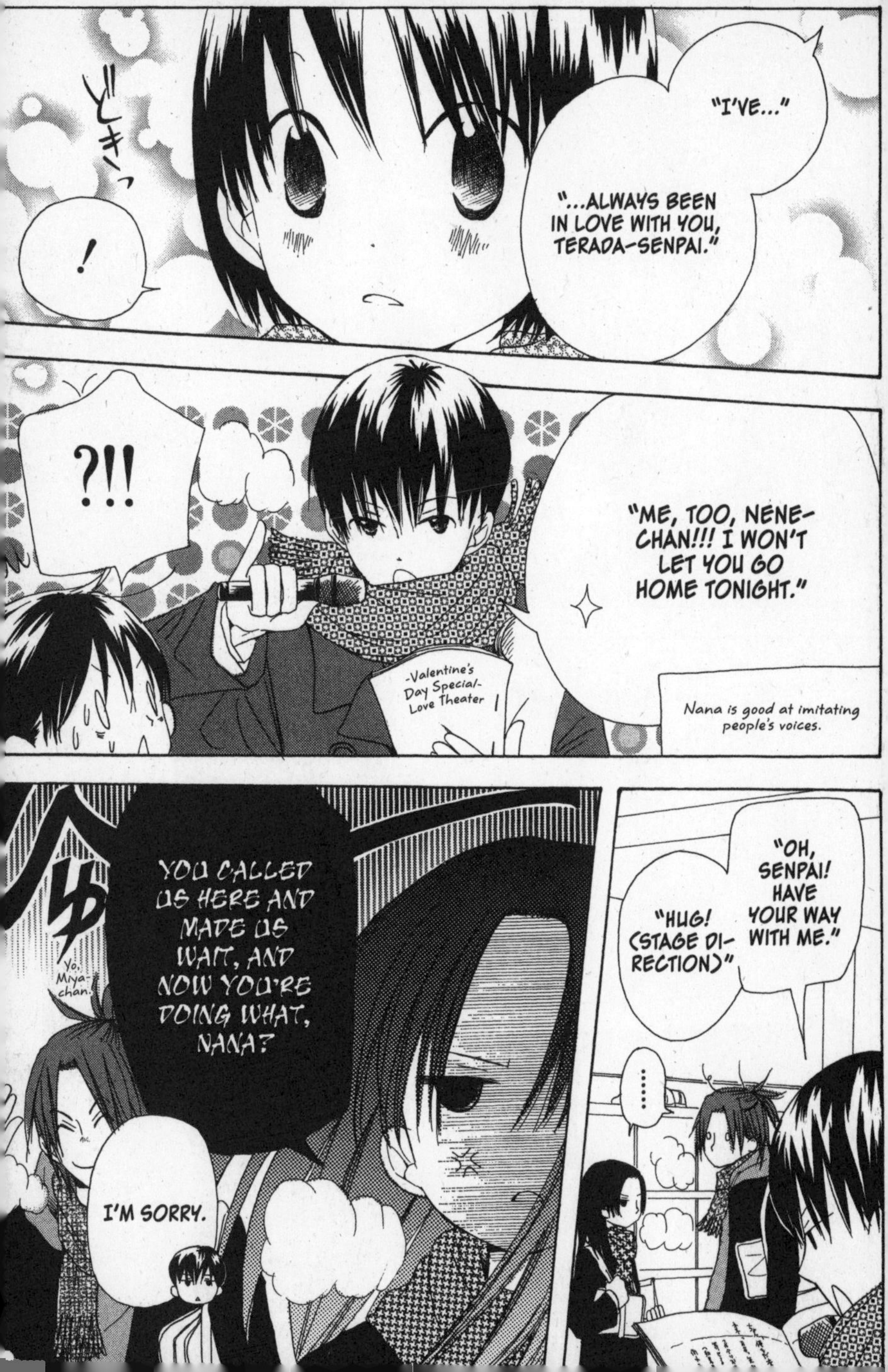
"I'VE..."
"...ALWAYS BEEN IN LOVE WITH YOU, TERADA-SENPAI."
どきっ
!
"ME, TOO, NENE-CHAN!!! I WON'T LET YOU GO HOME TONIGHT."
?!!
-Valentine's Day Special- Love Theater
Nana is good at imitating people's voices.
"OH, SENPAI! HAVE YOUR WAY WITH ME."
"HUG! (STAGE DI-RECTION)"
......
YOU CALLED US HERE AND MADE US WAIT, AND NOW YOU'RE DOING WHAT, NANA?
Yo, Miya-chan.
I'M SORRY.

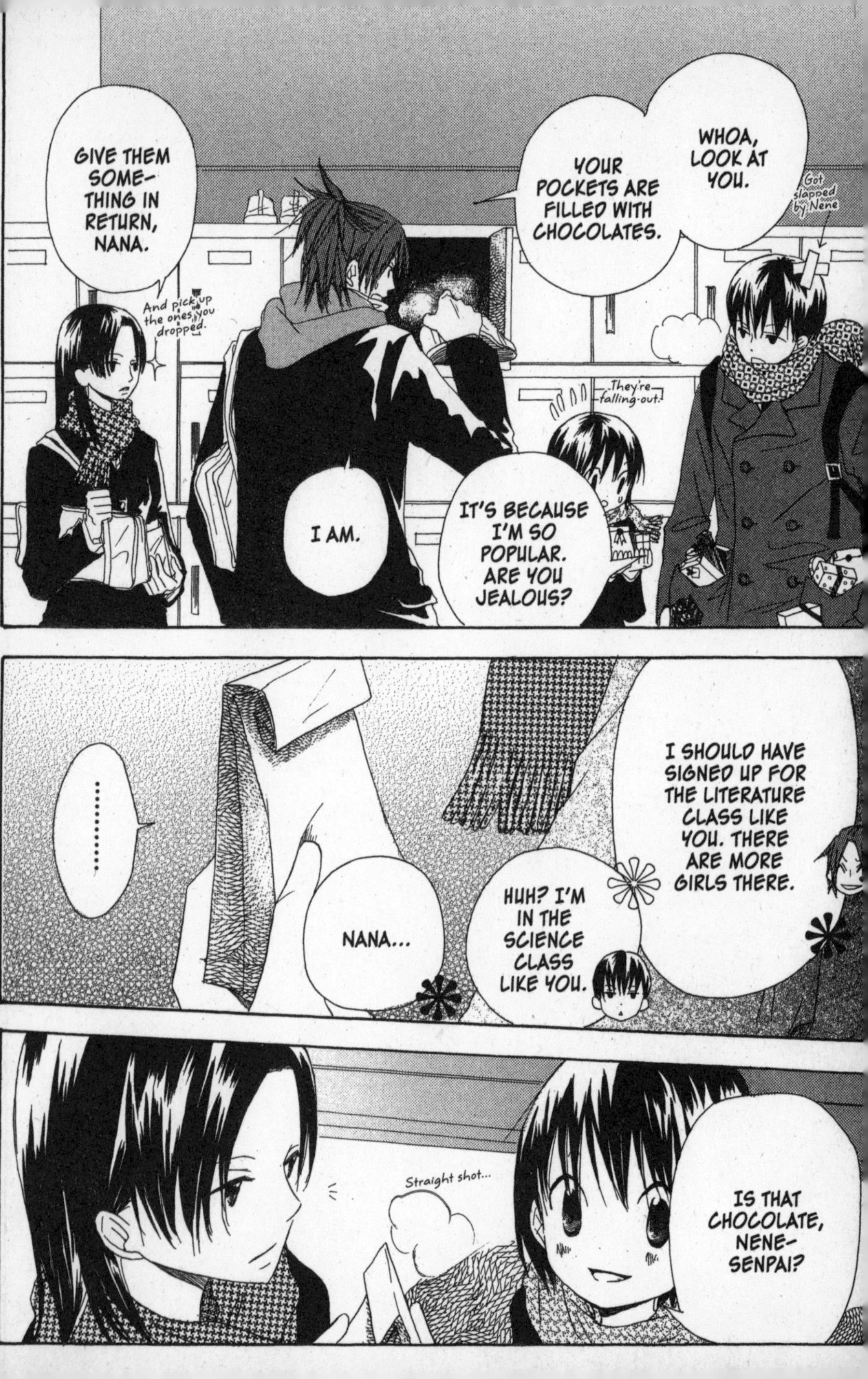
WHOA, LOOK AT YOU.
YOUR POCKETS ARE FILLED WITH CHOCOLATES.
Got slapped by Nene
They're falling out.
IT'S BECAUSE I'M SO POPULAR. ARE YOU JEALOUS?
I AM.
GIVE THEM SOME-THING IN RETURN, NANA.
And pick up the ones you dropped.
I SHOULD HAVE SIGNED UP FOR THE LITERATURE CLASS LIKE YOU. THERE ARE MORE GIRLS THERE.
HUH? I'M IN THE SCIENCE CLASS LIKE YOU.
NANA...
....
IS THAT CHOCOLATE, NENE-SENPAI?
Straight shot...

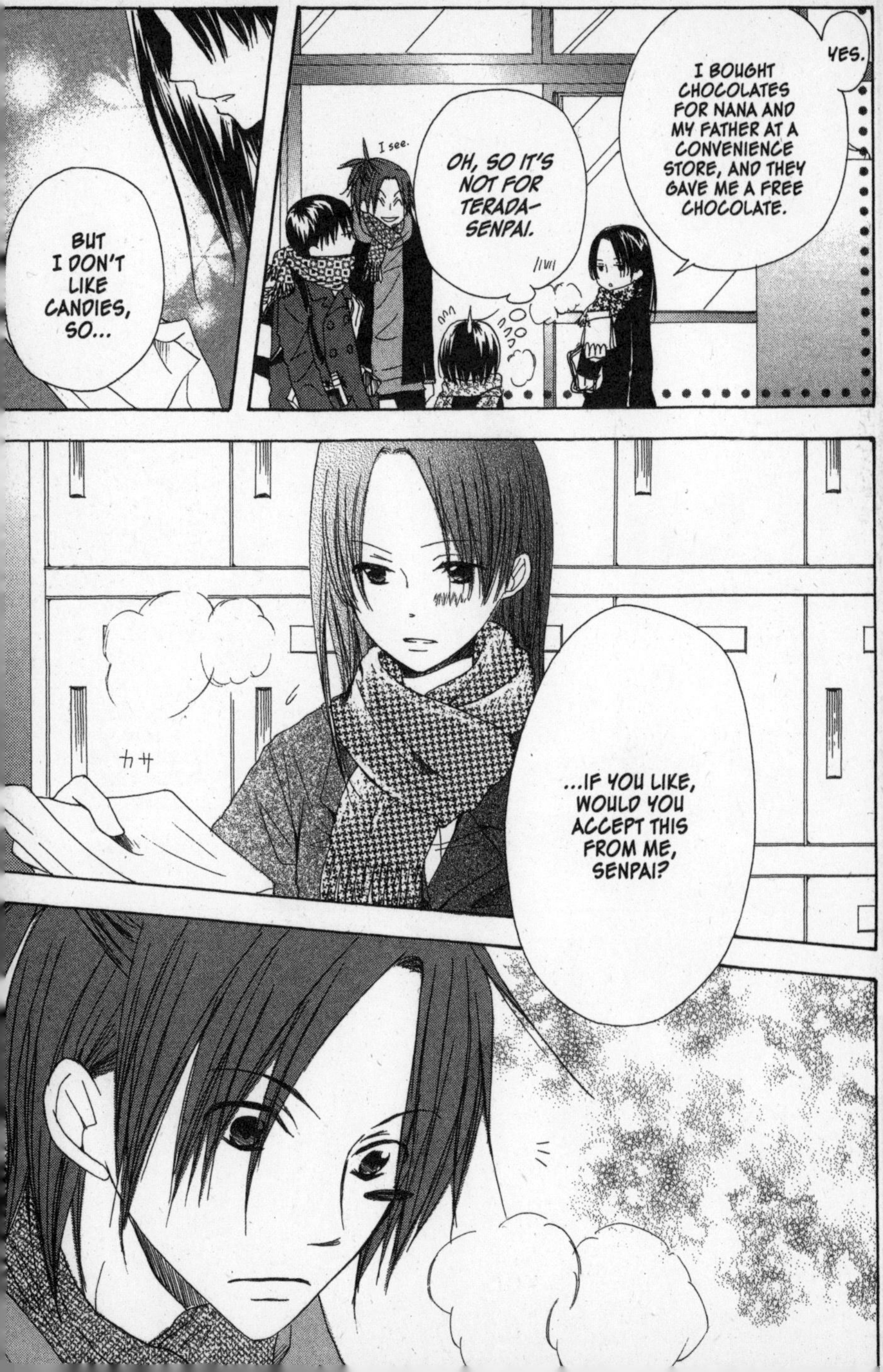
YES.
I BOUGHT CHOCOLATES FOR NANA AND MY FATHER AT A CONVENIENCE STORE, AND THEY GAVE ME A FREE CHOCOLATE.
OH, SO IT'S NOT FOR TERADA-SENPAI.
I see.
BUT I DON'T LIKE CANDIES, SO...
...IF YOU LIKE, WOULD YOU ACCEPT THIS FROM ME, SENPAI?
カサ

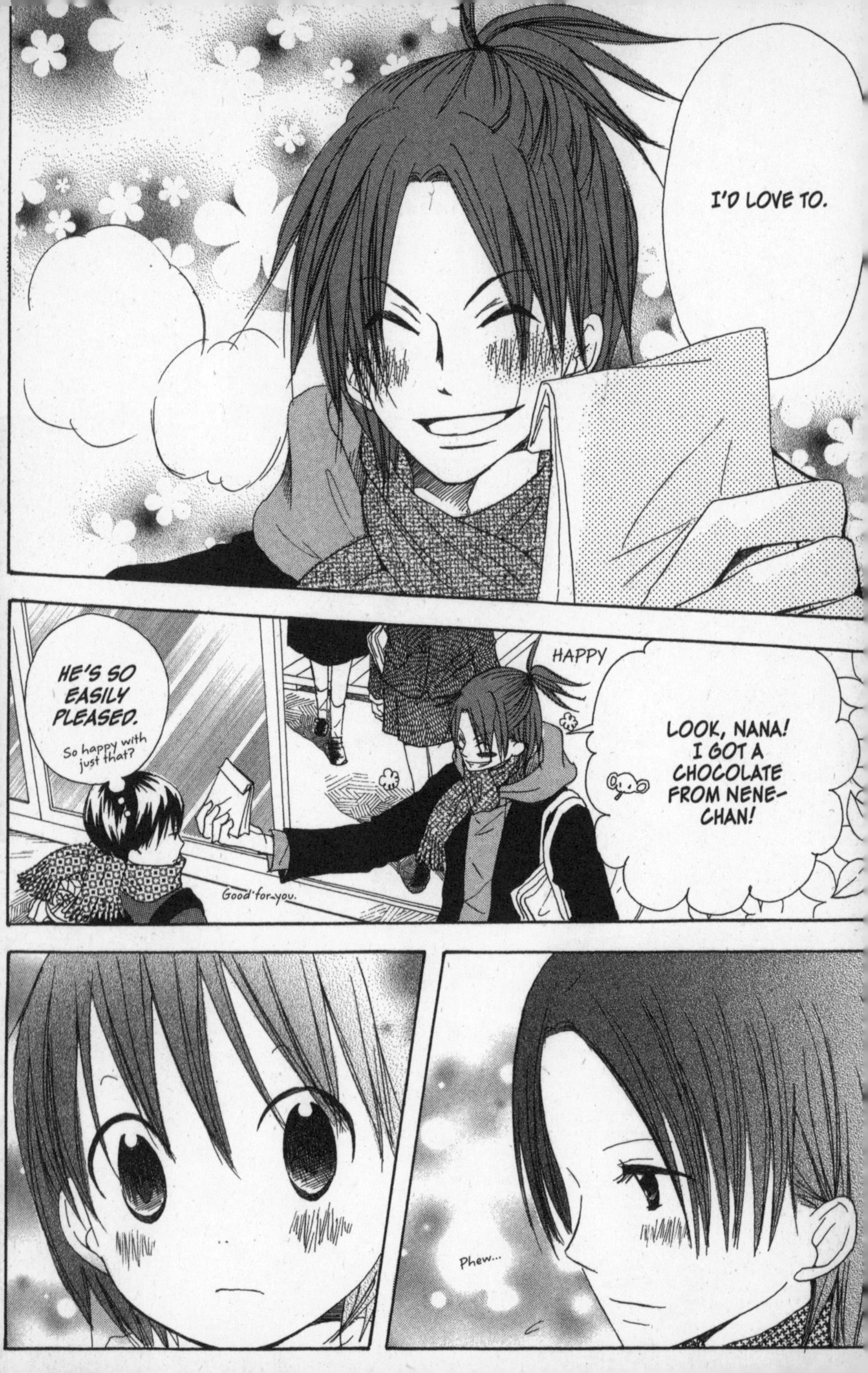
I'D LOVE TO.
HAPPY
LOOK, NANA! I GOT A CHOCOLATE FROM NENE-CHAN!
HE'S SO EASILY PLEASED.
So happy with just that?
Good for you.
Phew...

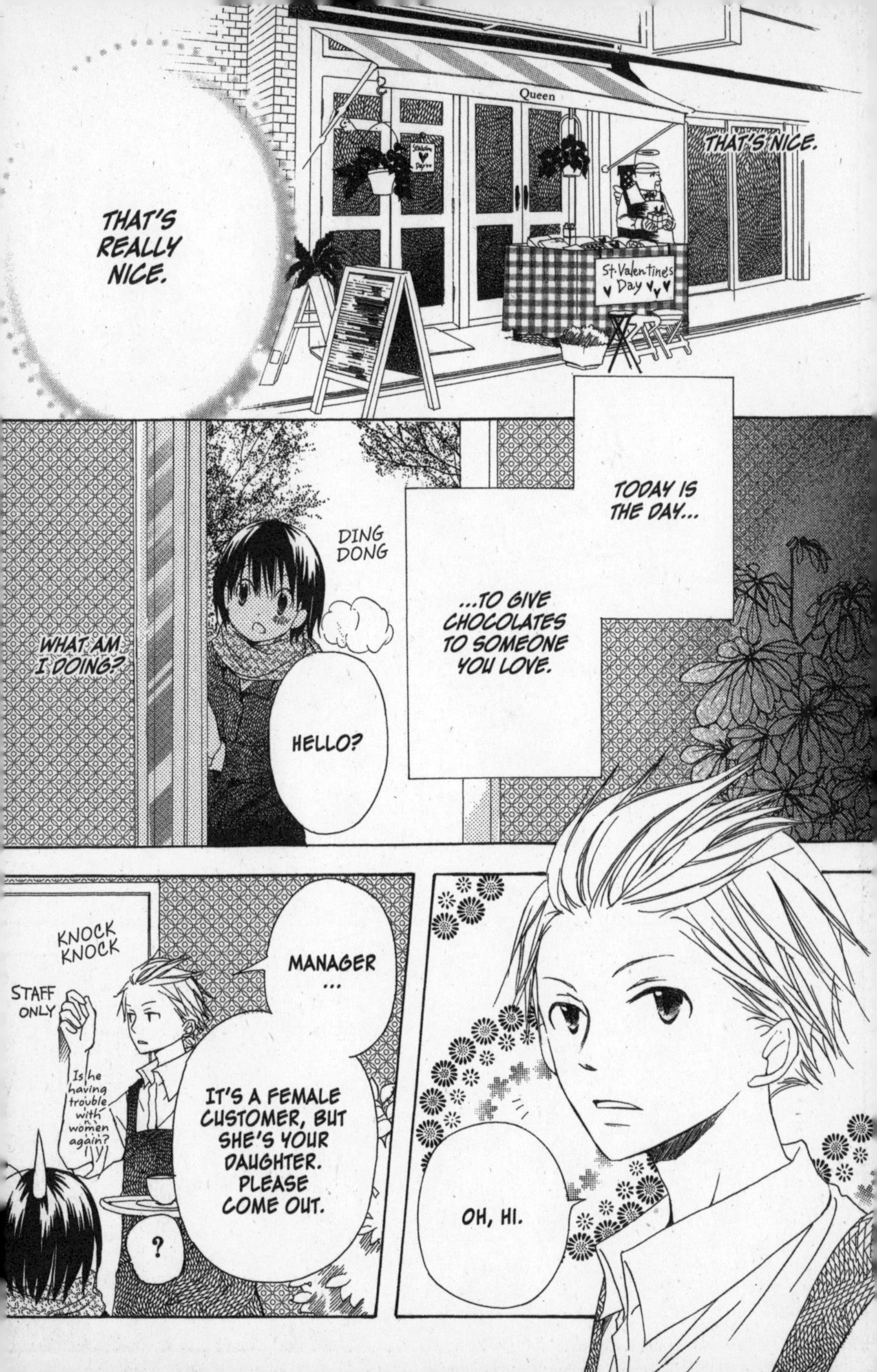
THAT'S NICE.
Queen
St. Valentine's Day
THAT'S REALLY NICE.
TODAY IS THE DAY...
...TO GIVE CHOCOLATES TO SOMEONE YOU LOVE.
DING DONG
HELLO?
WHAT AM I DOING?
OH, HI.
MANAGER ...
IT'S A FEMALE CUSTOMER, BUT SHE'S YOUR DAUGHTER. PLEASE COME OUT.
KNOCK KNOCK
STAFF ONLY
Is he having trouble with women again?
?

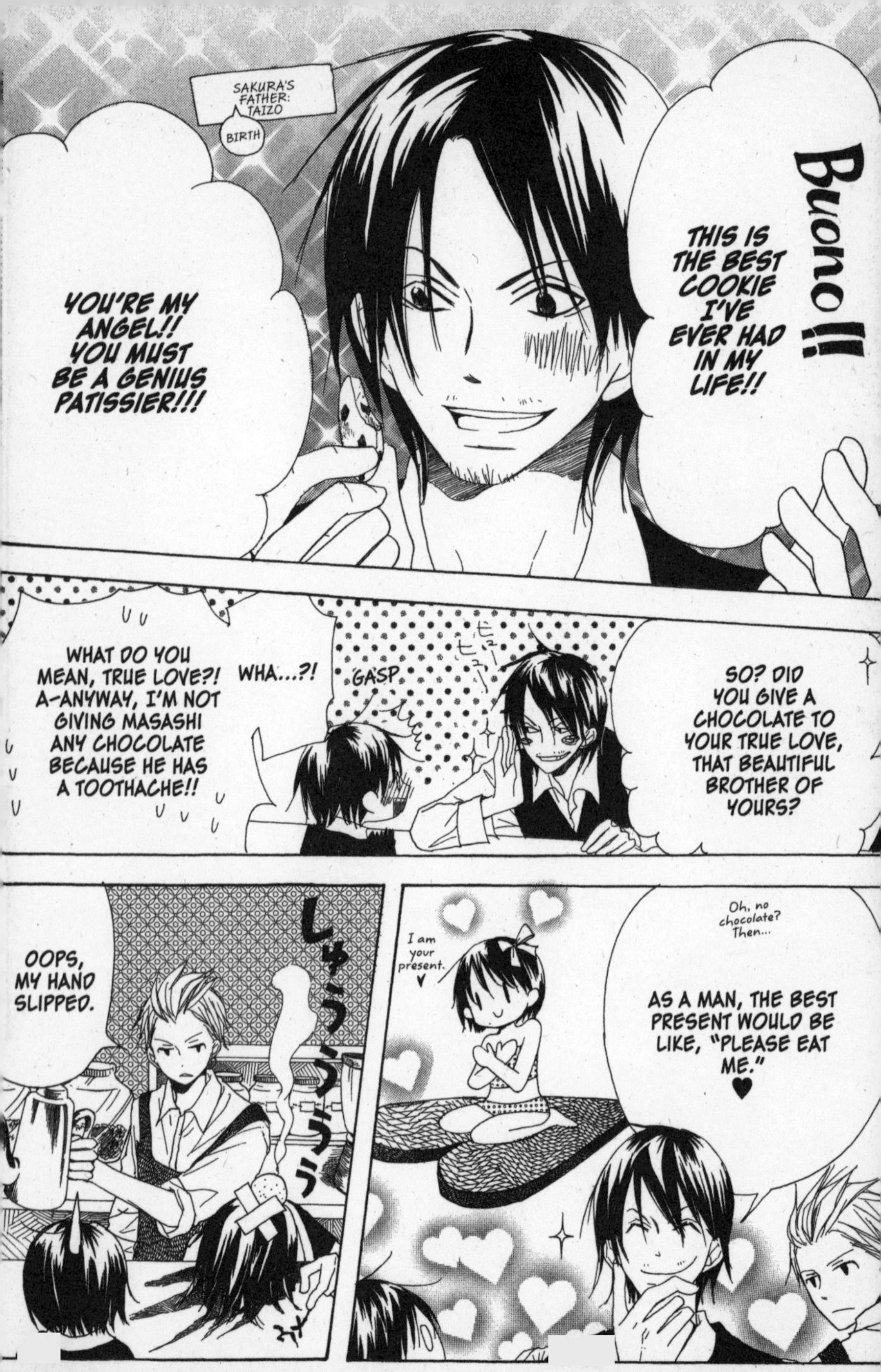
Buono!!
THIS IS THE BEST COOKIE I'VE EVER HAD IN MY LIFE!!
SAKURA'S FATHER: TAIZO
BIRTH
YOU'RE MY ANGEL!! YOU MUST BE A GENIUS PATISSIER!!!
SO? DID YOU GIVE A CHOCOLATE TO YOUR TRUE LOVE, THAT BEAUTIFUL BROTHER OF YOURS?
GASP
WHA...?!
WHAT DO YOU MEAN, TRUE LOVE?! A-ANYWAY, I'M NOT GIVING MASASHI ANY CHOCOLATE BECAUSE HE HAS A TOOTHACHE!!
Oh, no chocolate? Then...
AS A MAN, THE BEST PRESENT WOULD BE LIKE, "PLEASE EAT ME." ♥
I am your present. ♥
OOPS, MY HAND SLIPPED.

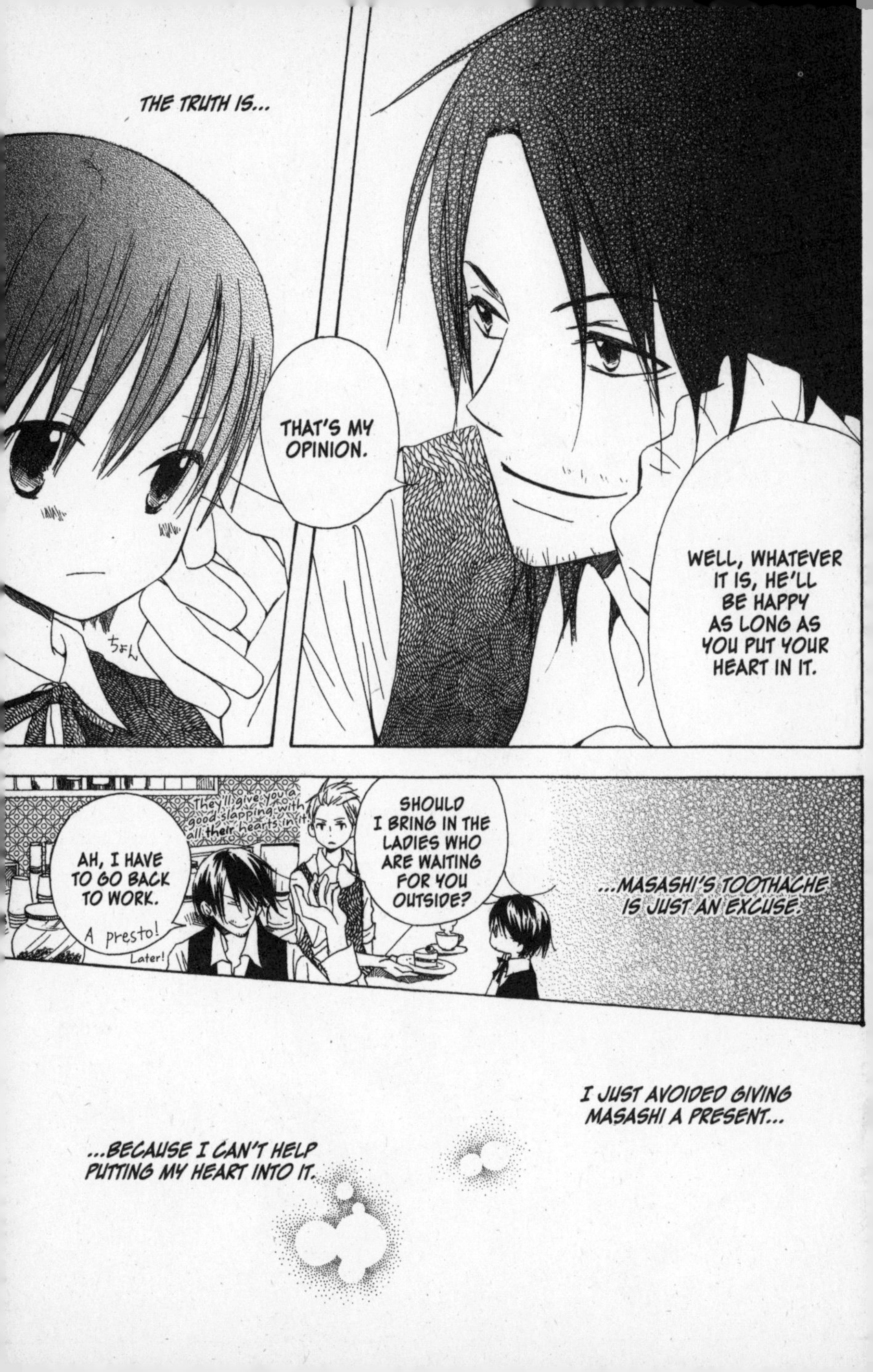
WELL, WHATEVER IT IS, HE'LL BE HAPPY AS LONG AS YOU PUT YOUR HEART IN IT.
THAT'S MY OPINION.
THE TRUTH IS...
ちょん
...MASASHI'S TOOTHACHE IS JUST AN EXCUSE.
SHOULD I BRING IN THE LADIES WHO ARE WAITING FOR YOU OUTSIDE?
They'll give you a good slapping with all their hearts in it.
AH, I HAVE TO GO BACK TO WORK.
A presto!
Later!
I JUST AVOIDED GIVING MASASHI A PRESENT...
...BECAUSE I CAN'T HELP PUTTING MY HEART INTO IT.

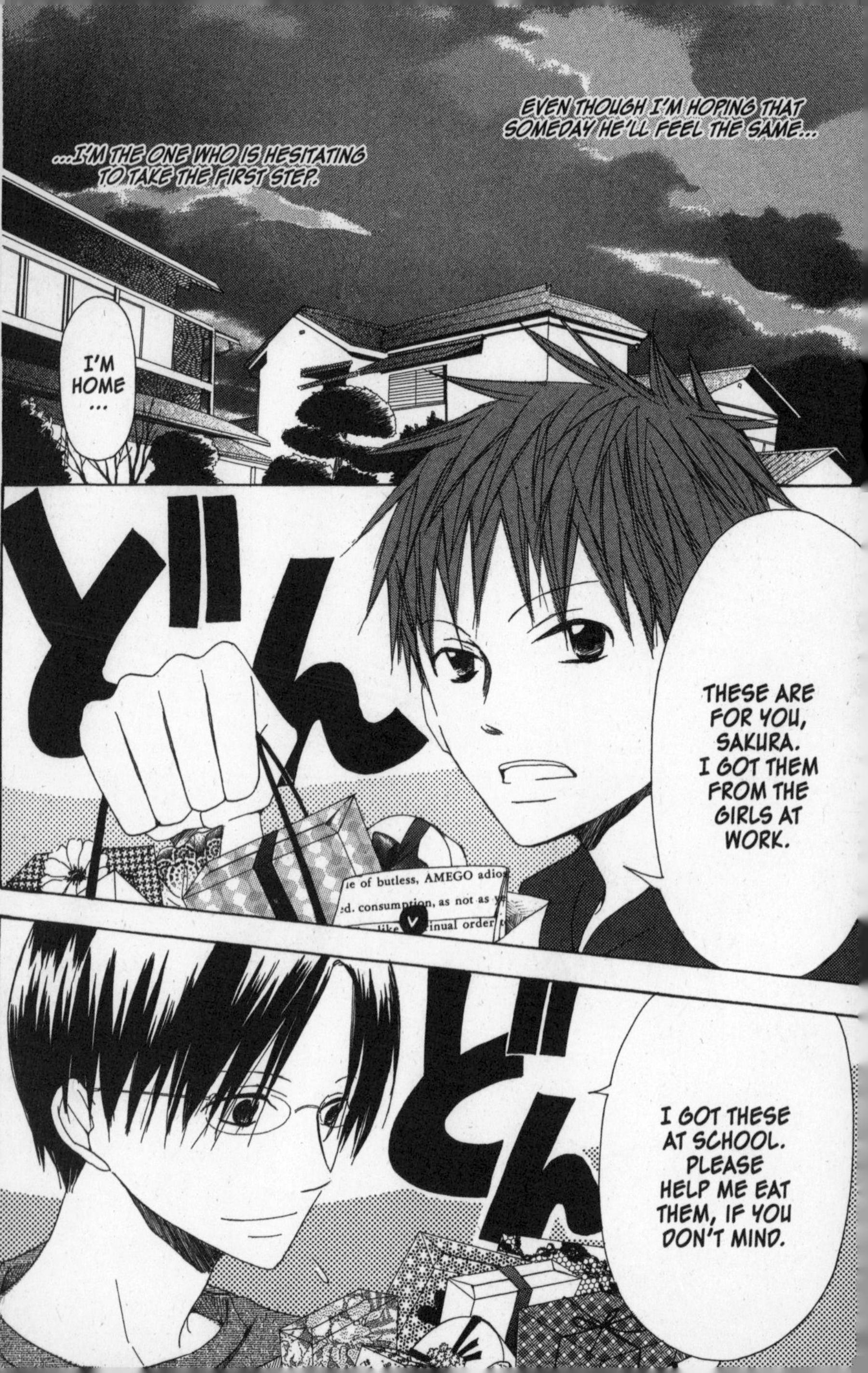
EVEN THOUGH I'M HOPING THAT SOMEDAY HE'LL FEEL THE SAME...
...I'M THE ONE WHO IS HESITATING TO TAKE THE FIRST STEP.
I'M HOME...
THESE ARE FOR YOU, SAKURA. I GOT THEM FROM THE GIRLS AT WORK.
I GOT THESE AT SCHOOL. PLEASE HELP ME EAT THEM, IF YOU DON'T MIND.

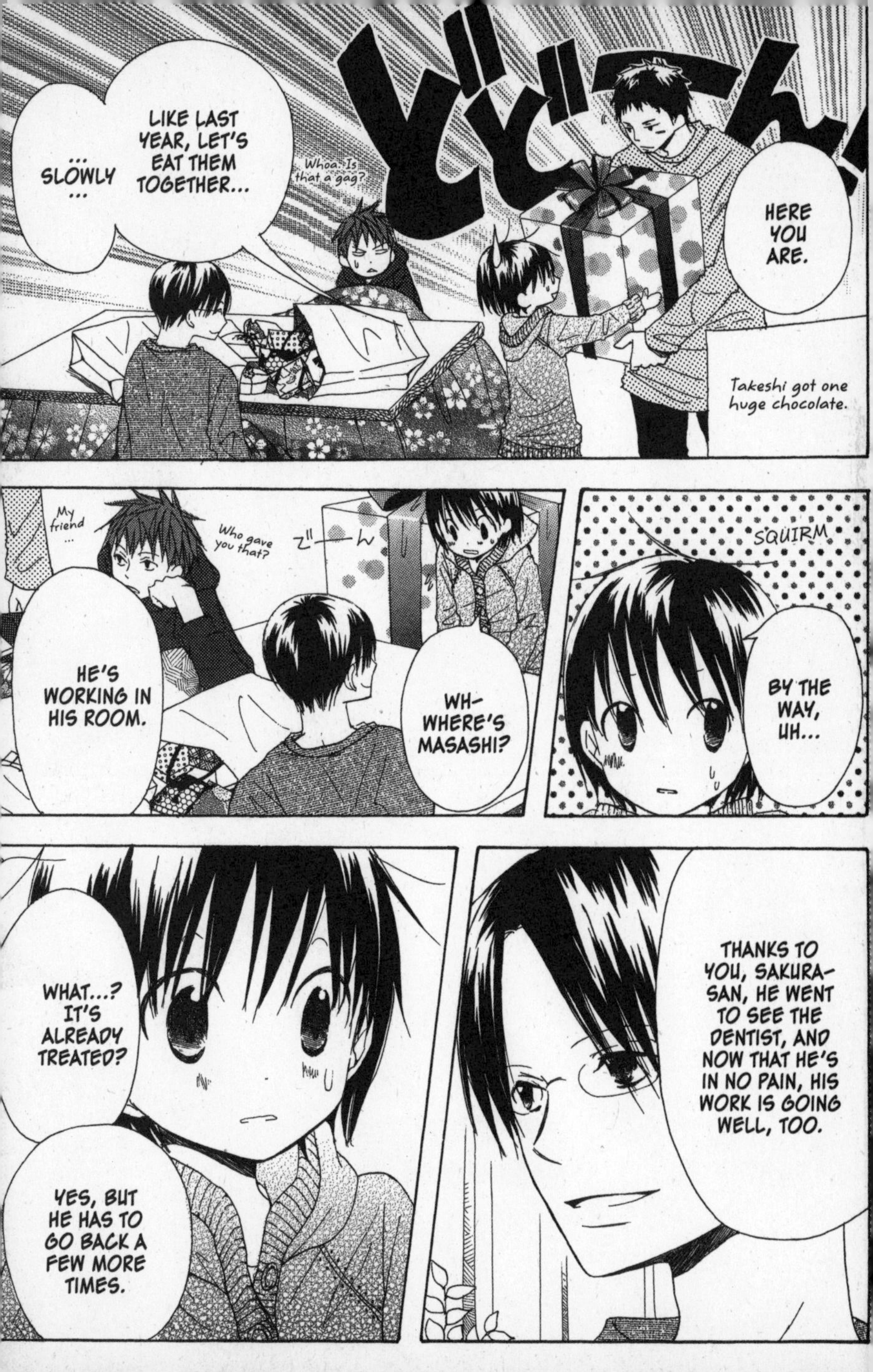
HERE YOU ARE.
Takeshi got one huge chocolate.
Whoa. Is that a gag?
LIKE LAST YEAR, LET'S EAT THEM TOGETHER...
...SLOWLY...
SQUIRM
BY THE WAY, UH...
WH-WHERE'S MASASHI?
Who gave you that?
My friend...
HE'S WORKING IN HIS ROOM.
THANKS TO YOU, SAKURA-SAN, HE WENT TO SEE THE DENTIST, AND NOW THAT HE'S IN NO PAIN, HIS WORK IS GOING WELL, TOO.
WHAT...? IT'S ALREADY TREATED?
YES, BUT HE HAS TO GO BACK A FEW MORE TIMES.

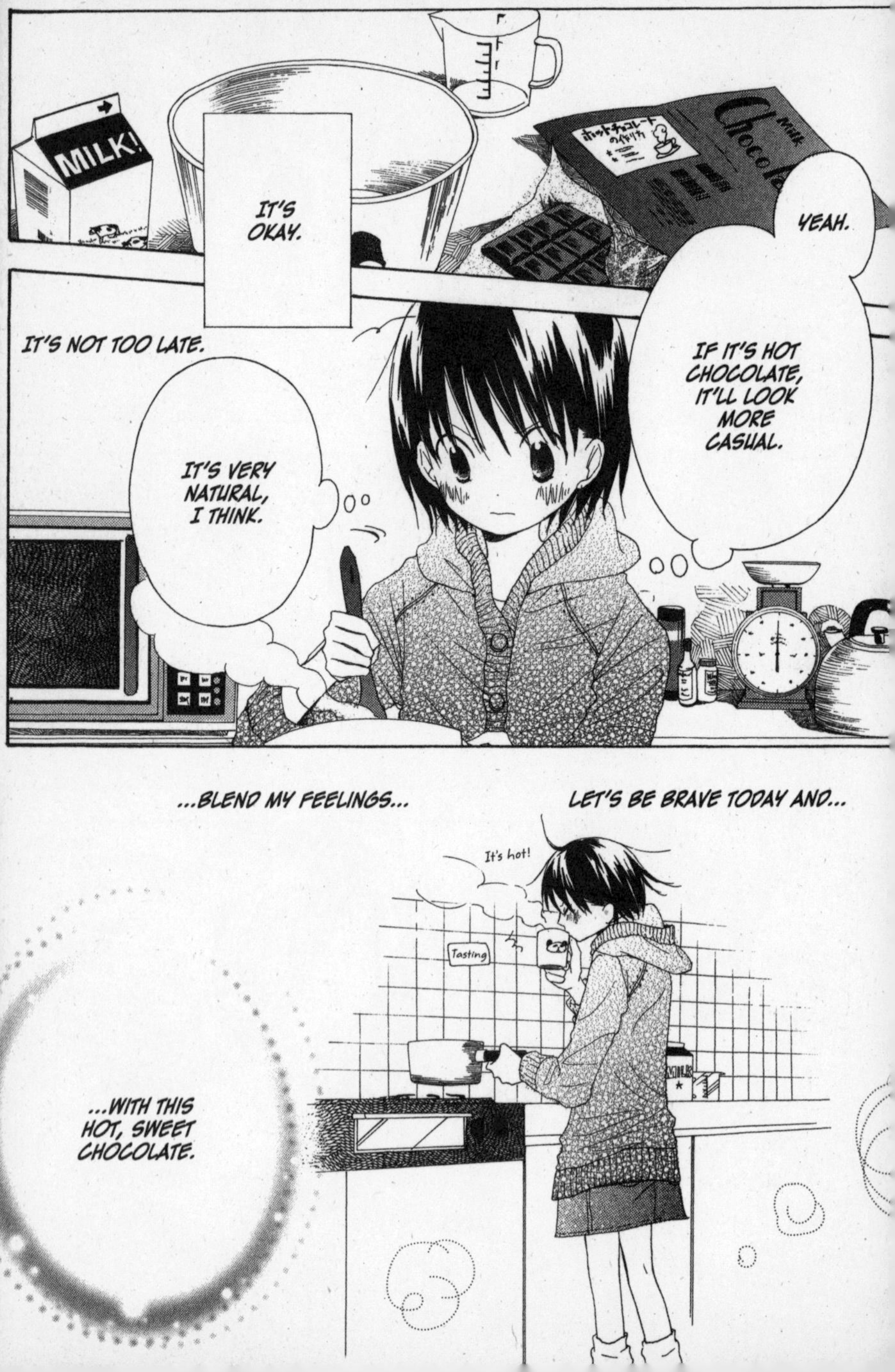
MILK!
YEAH.
IT'S OKAY.
IF IT'S HOT CHOCOLATE, IT'LL LOOK MORE CASUAL.
IT'S NOT TOO LATE.
IT'S VERY NATURAL, I THINK.
LET'S BE BRAVE TODAY AND...
...BLEND MY FEELINGS...
It's hot!
Tasting
...WITH THIS HOT, SWEET CHOCOLATE.

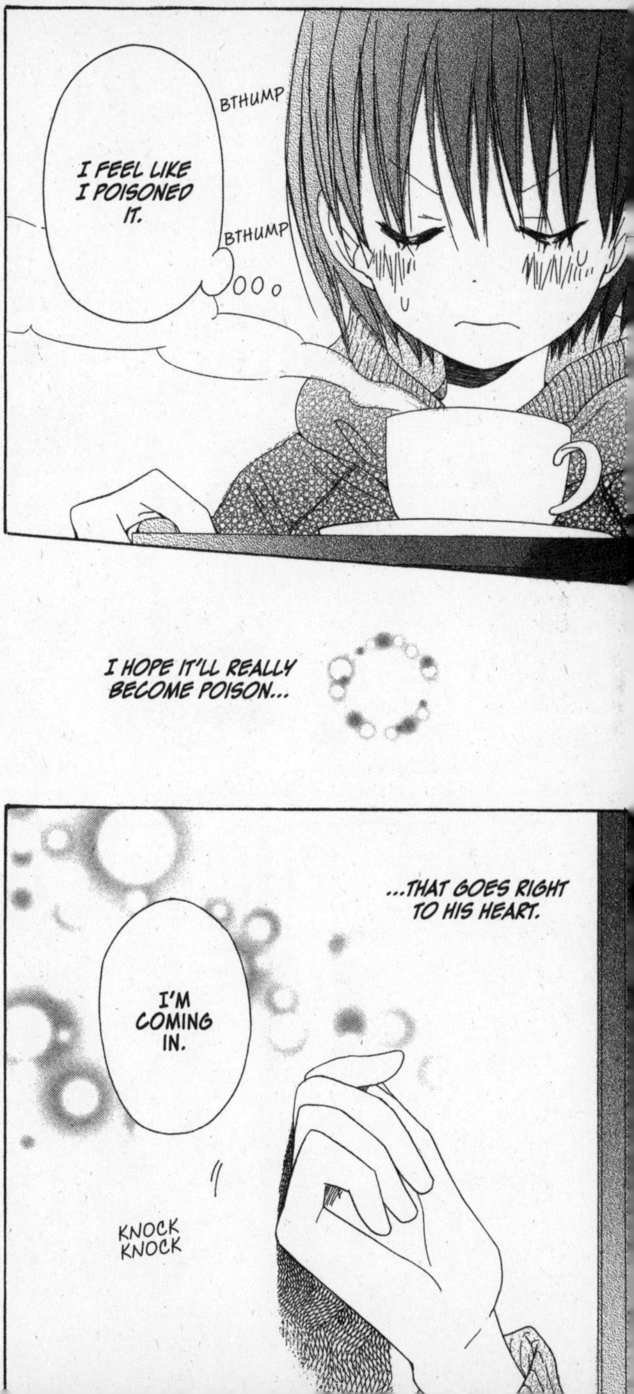
BTHUMP
BTHUMP
I FEEL LIKE I POISONED IT.
I HOPE IT'LL REALLY BECOME POISON...
...THAT GOES RIGHT TO HIS HEART.
I'M COMING IN.
KNOCK KNOCK

6

At last, this is the last column. I hope you enjoyed Me & My Brothers volume 5. I used children versions of the characters for the bonus manga because it's easy to draw. I just wanted to draw Takeshi as the Tortoise. Takeshi didn't get many votes for the character contest that was held in the magazine, but he's my favorite. I have to love him, if nobody else will. I'd like to show you the results of the contest in the next volume. Please don't tell me that you're not interested.

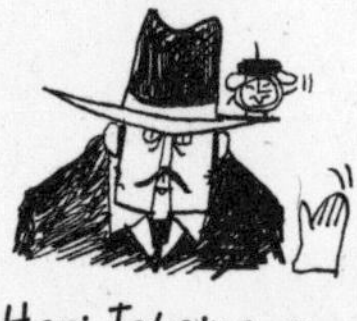

Hari Tokeino

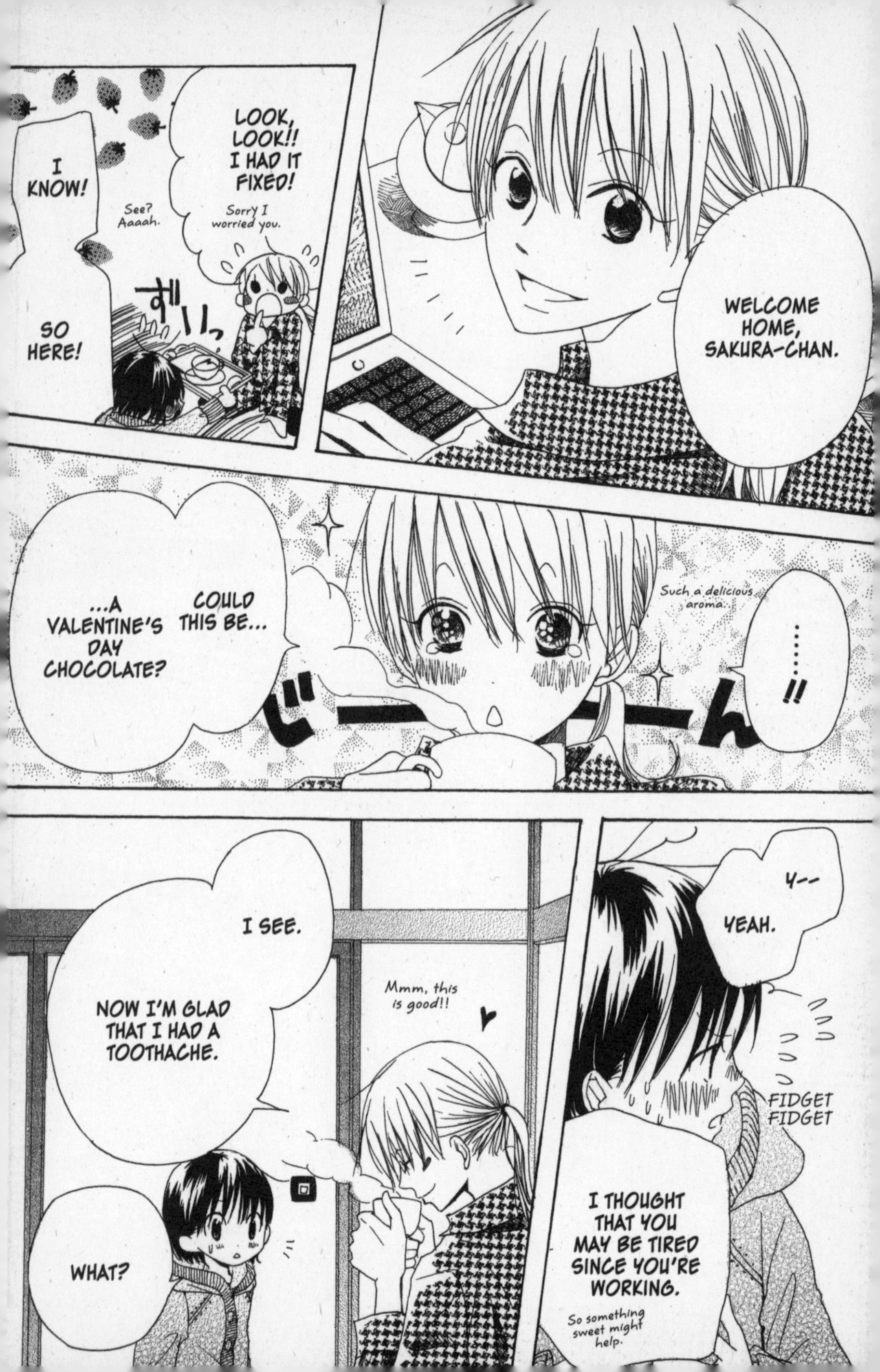

WELCOME HOME, SAKURA-CHAN.
LOOK, LOOK!! I HAD IT FIXED!
Sorry I worried you.
See? Aaaah.
I KNOW!
SO HERE!
......!!
Such a delicious aroma.
COULD THIS BE...
...A VALENTINE'S DAY CHOCOLATE?
Y--
YEAH.
FIDGET FIDGET
I THOUGHT THAT YOU MAY BE TIRED SINCE YOU'RE WORKING.
So something sweet might help.
I SEE.
NOW I'M GLAD THAT I HAD A TOOTHACHE.
Mmm, this is good!!
WHAT?

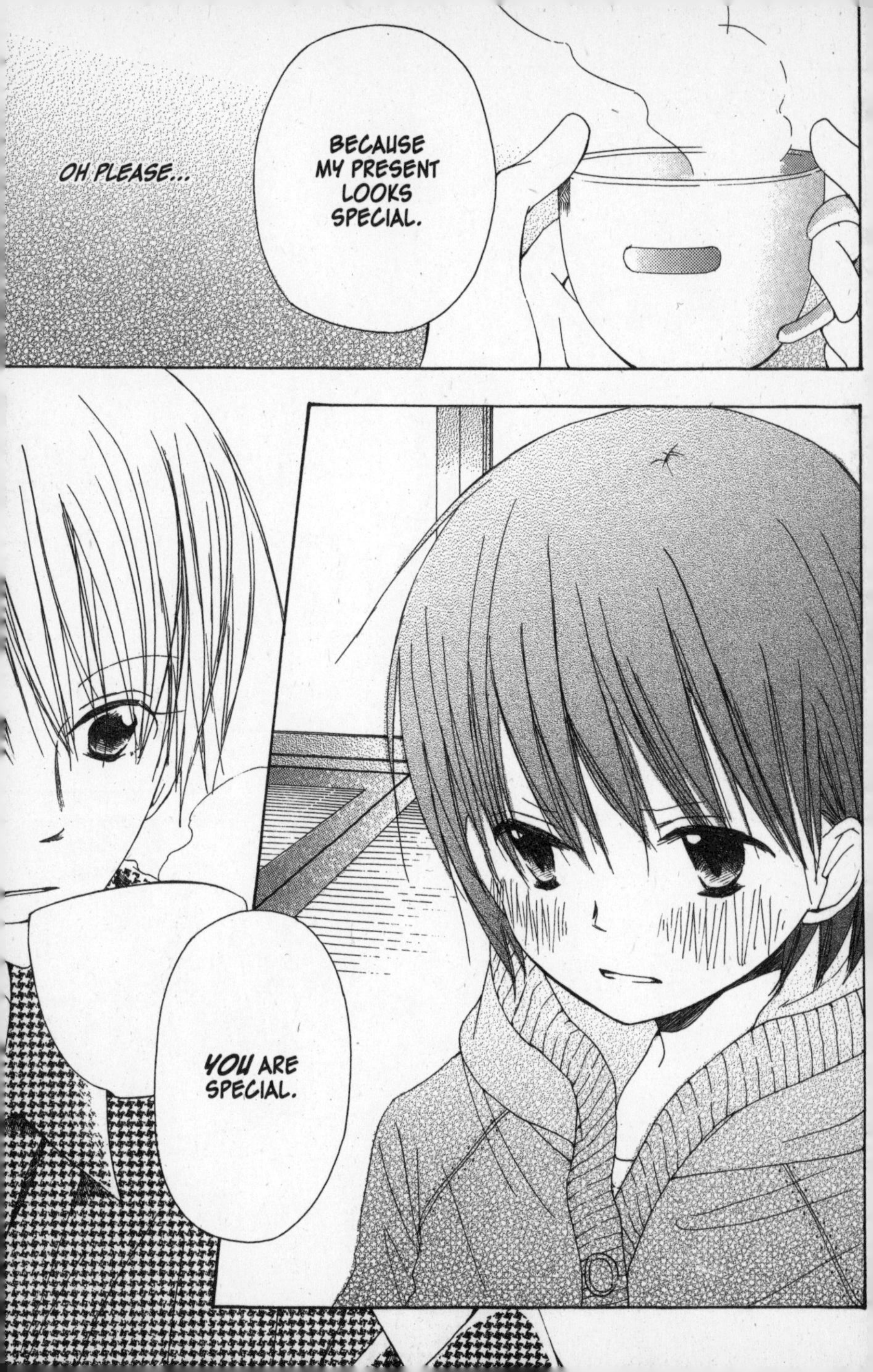
BECAUSE MY PRESENT LOOKS SPECIAL.
OH PLEASE...
YOU ARE SPECIAL.

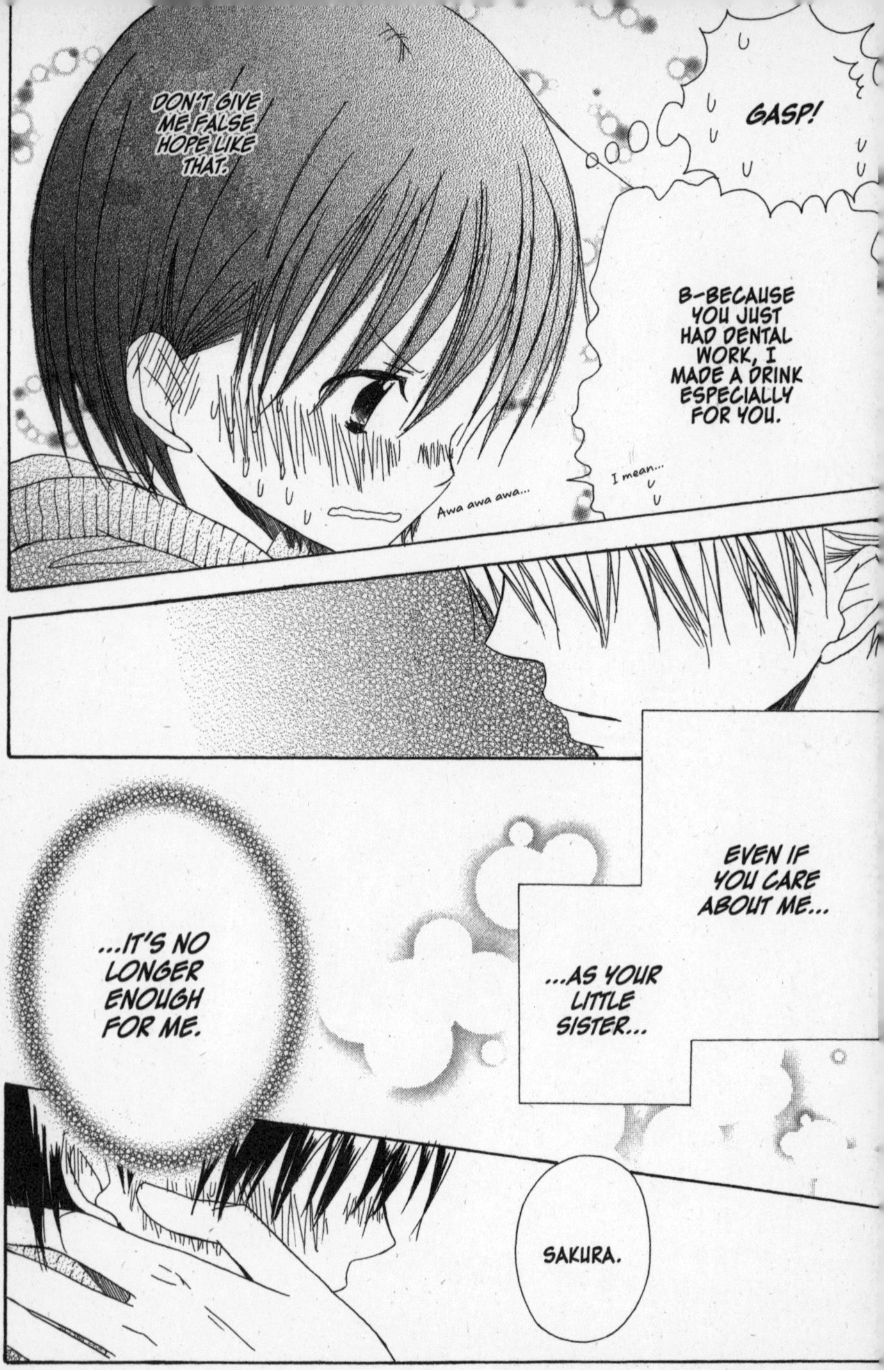
GASP!
B-BECAUSE YOU JUST HAD DENTAL WORK, I MADE A DRINK ESPECIALLY FOR YOU.
I mean...
Awa awa awa...
DON'T GIVE ME FALSE HOPE LIKE THAT.
EVEN IF YOU CARE ABOUT ME...
...AS YOUR LITTLE SISTER...
...IT'S NO LONGER ENOUGH FOR ME.
SAKURA.

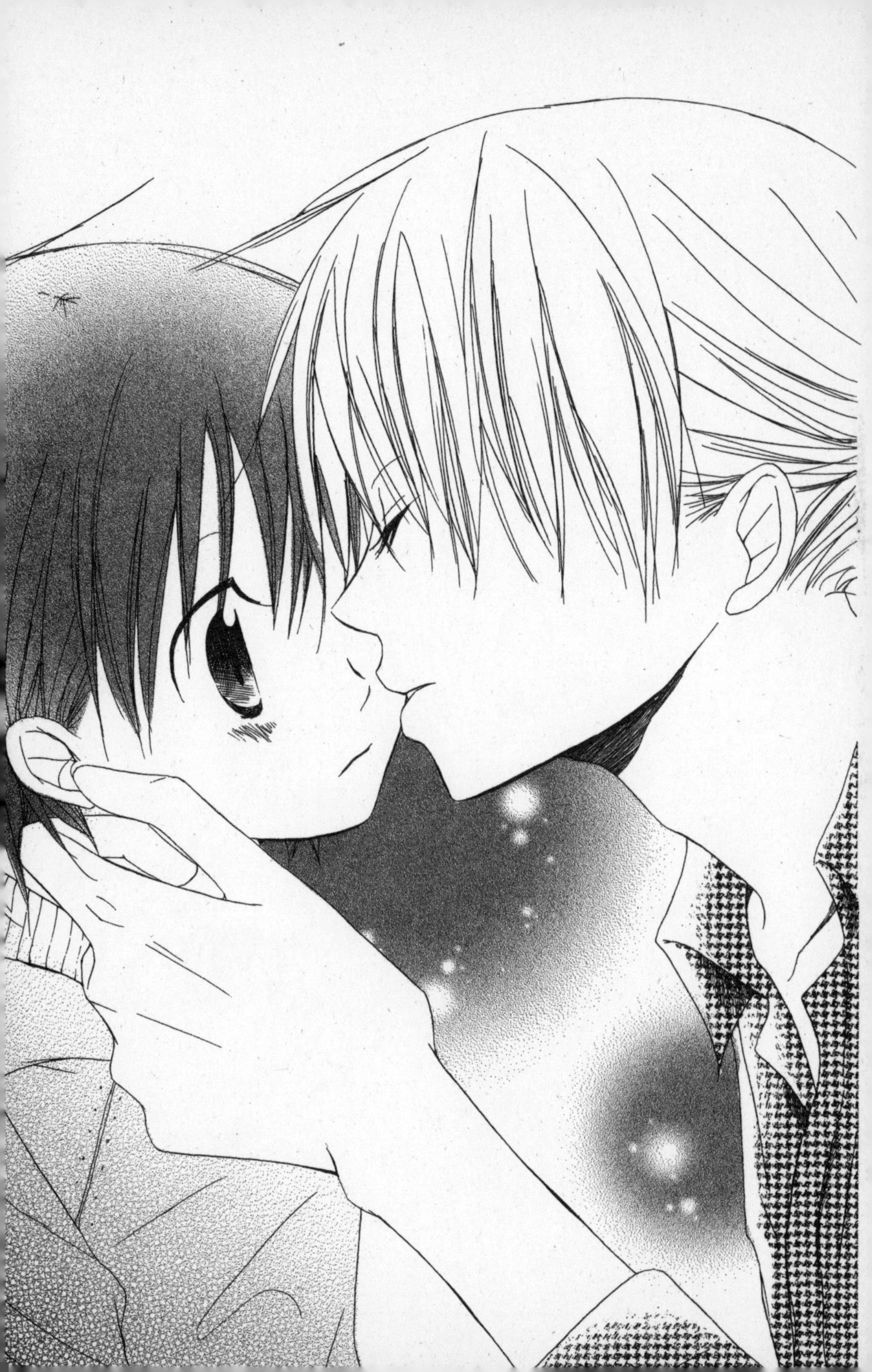

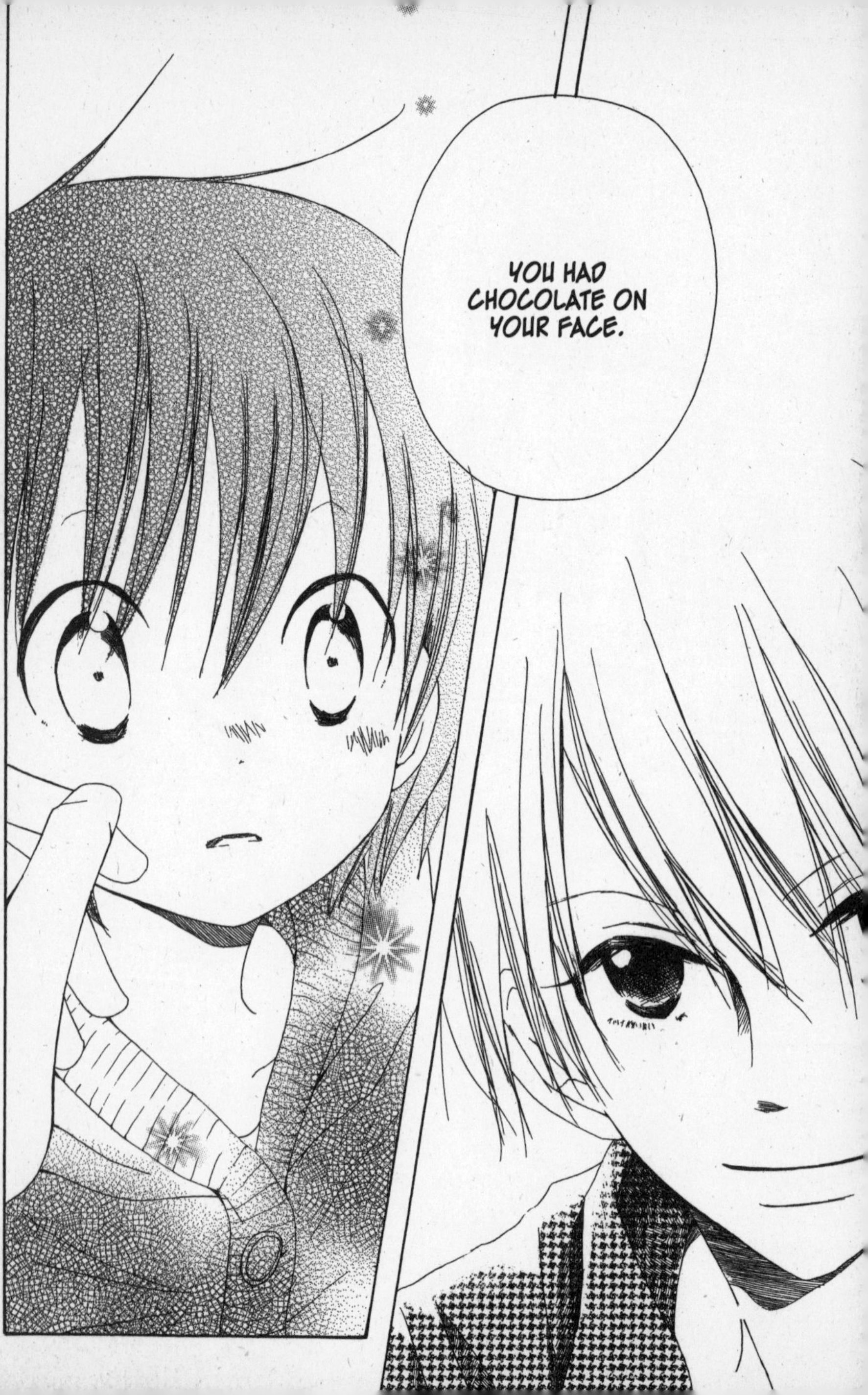
YOU HAD CHOCOLATE ON YOUR FACE.

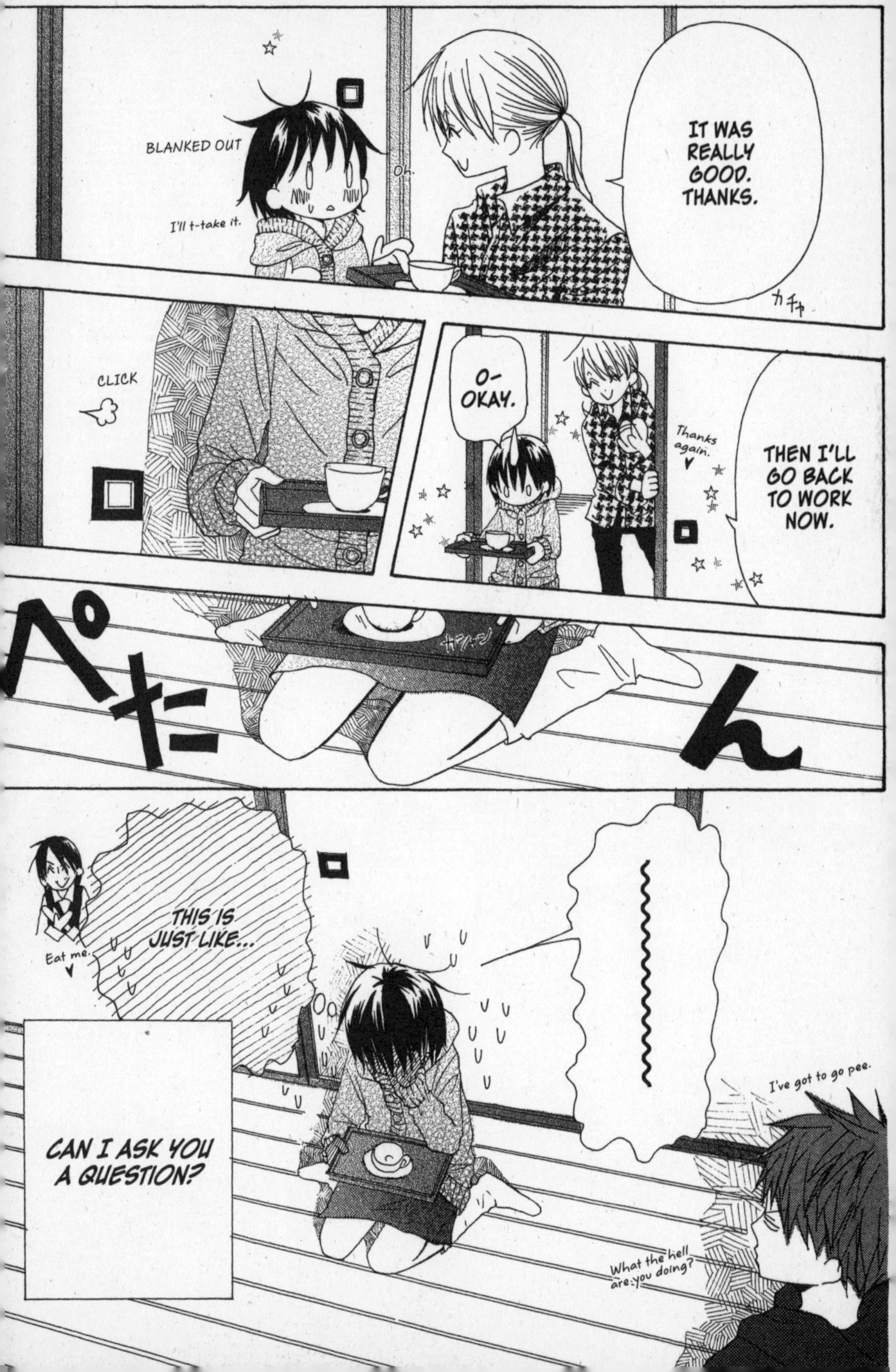
IT WAS REALLY GOOD. THANKS.
カチャ
Oh.
BLANKED OUT
I'll t-take it.
THEN I'LL GO BACK TO WORK NOW.
Thanks again.
O-OKAY.
CLICK
ペたーん
I've got to go pee.
What the hell are you doing?
THIS IS JUST LIKE...
Eat me.
CAN I ASK YOU A QUESTION?

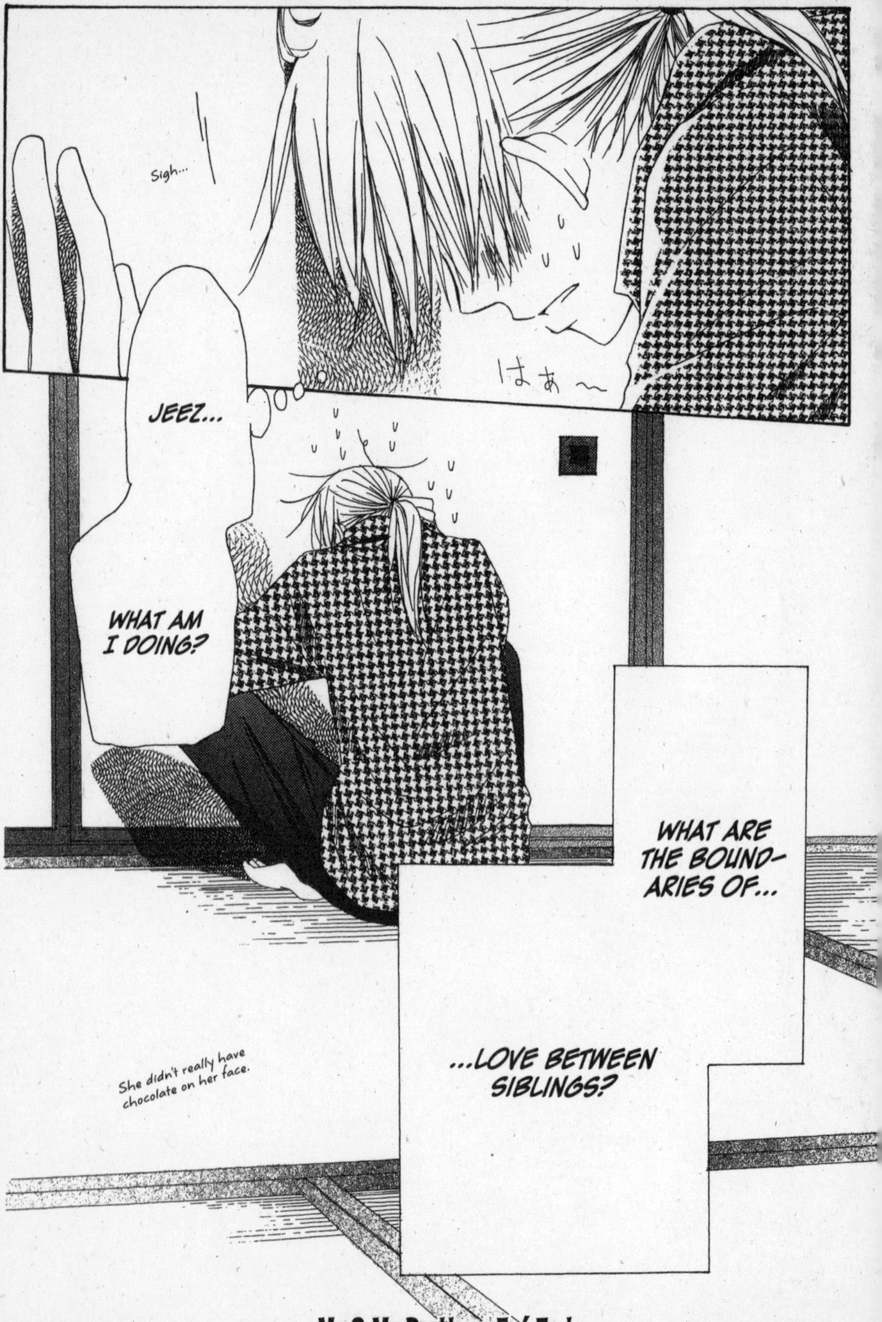
はあ～
Sigh...
JEEZ...
WHAT AM I DOING?
WHAT ARE THE BOUND-ARIES OF...
...LOVE BETWEEN SIBLINGS?
She didn't really have chocolate on her face.

Me & My Brothers 5 / End

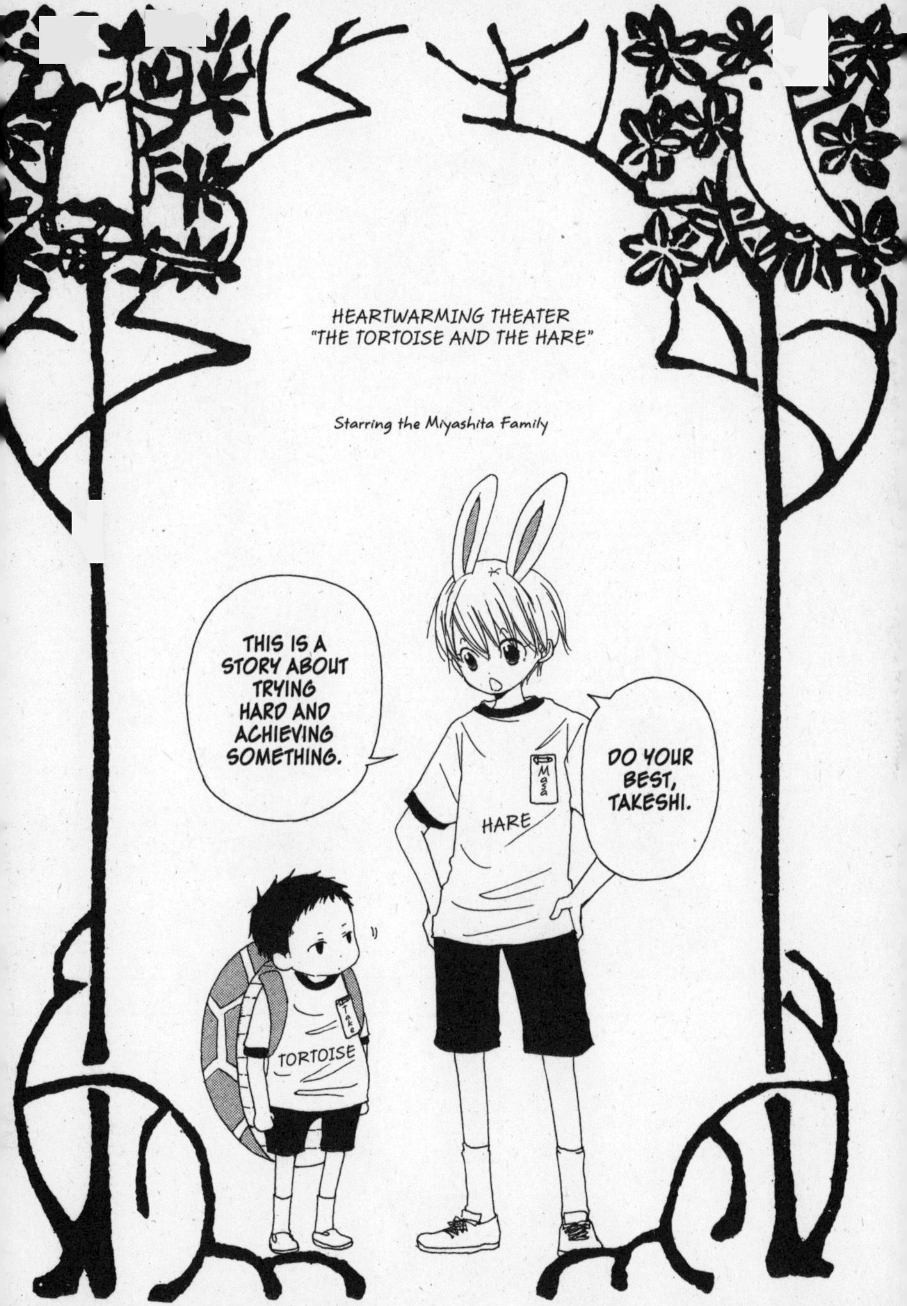
HEARTWARMING THEATER
"THE TORTOISE AND THE HARE"
Starring the Miyashita Family
THIS IS A STORY ABOUT TRYING HARD AND ACHIEVING SOMETHING.
DO YOUR BEST, TAKESHI.
Masa
HARE
Take
TORTOISE

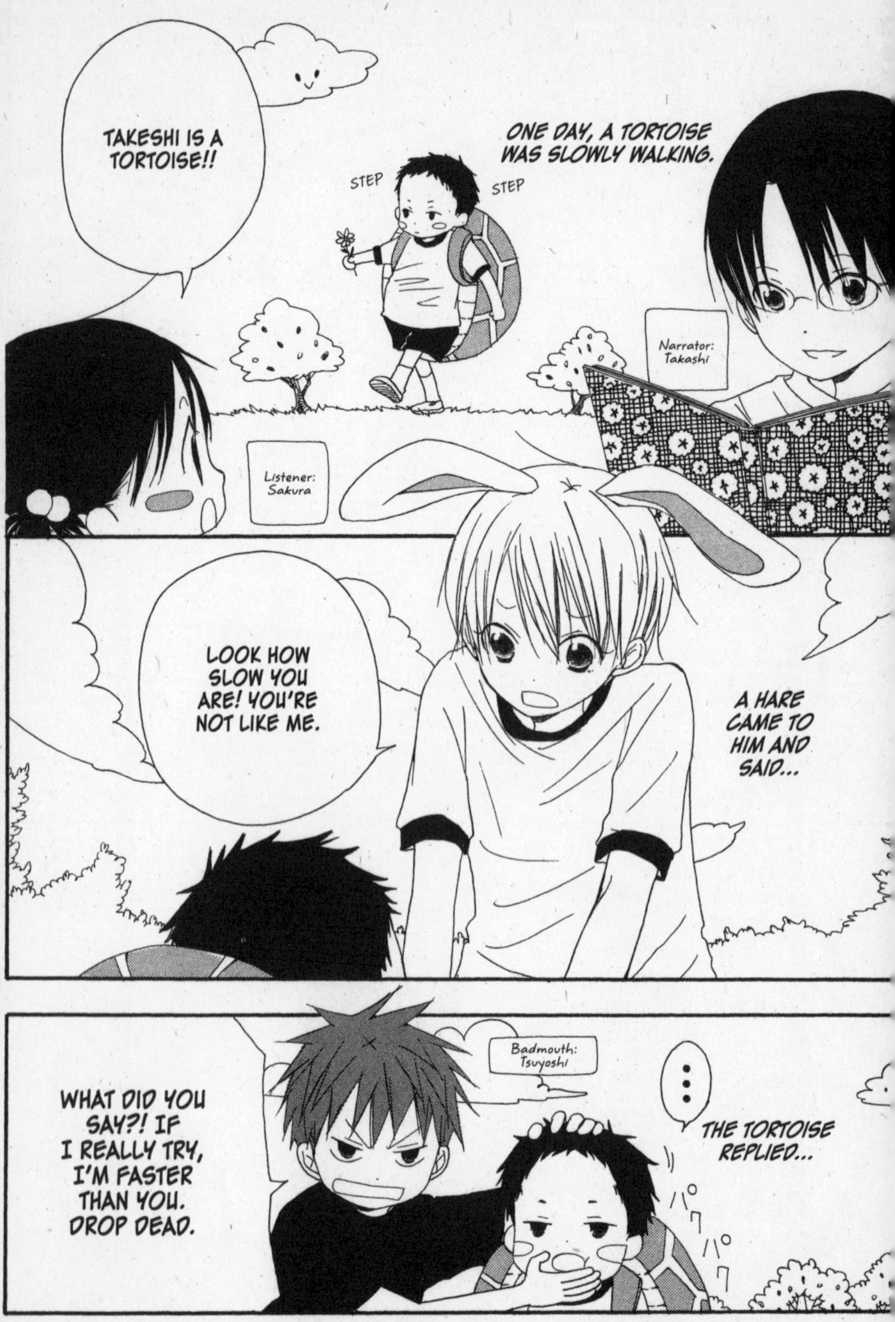
ONE DAY, A TORTOISE WAS SLOWLY WALKING.
Narrator: Takashi
STEP
STEP
TAKESHI IS A TORTOISE!!
Listener: Sakura
A HARE CAME TO HIM AND SAID...
LOOK HOW SLOW YOU ARE! YOU'RE NOT LIKE ME.
THE TORTOISE REPLIED...
...
Badmouth: Tsuyoshi
パク パク
WHAT DID YOU SAY?! IF I REALLY TRY, I'M FASTER THAN YOU. DROP DEAD.

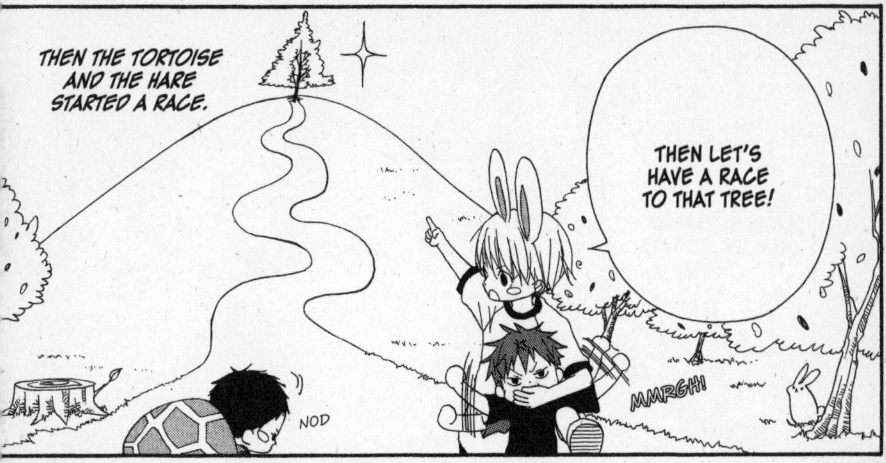
THEN LET'S HAVE A RACE TO THAT TREE!
THEN THE TORTOISE AND THE HARE STARTED A RACE.
MMRGH!
NOD
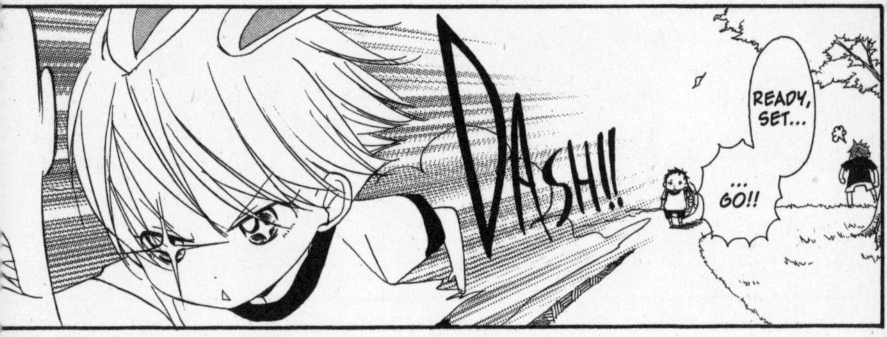
READY, SET...
... GO!!
DASH!!
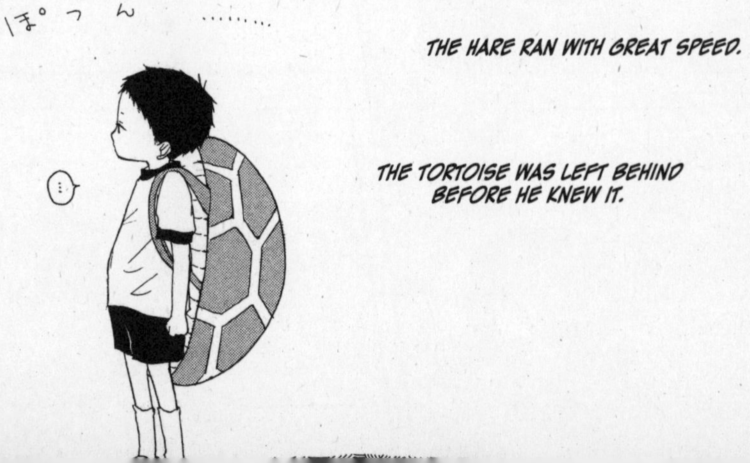
THE HARE RAN WITH GREAT SPEED.
THE TORTOISE WAS LEFT BEHIND BEFORE HE KNEW IT.
ぽつん
....
...

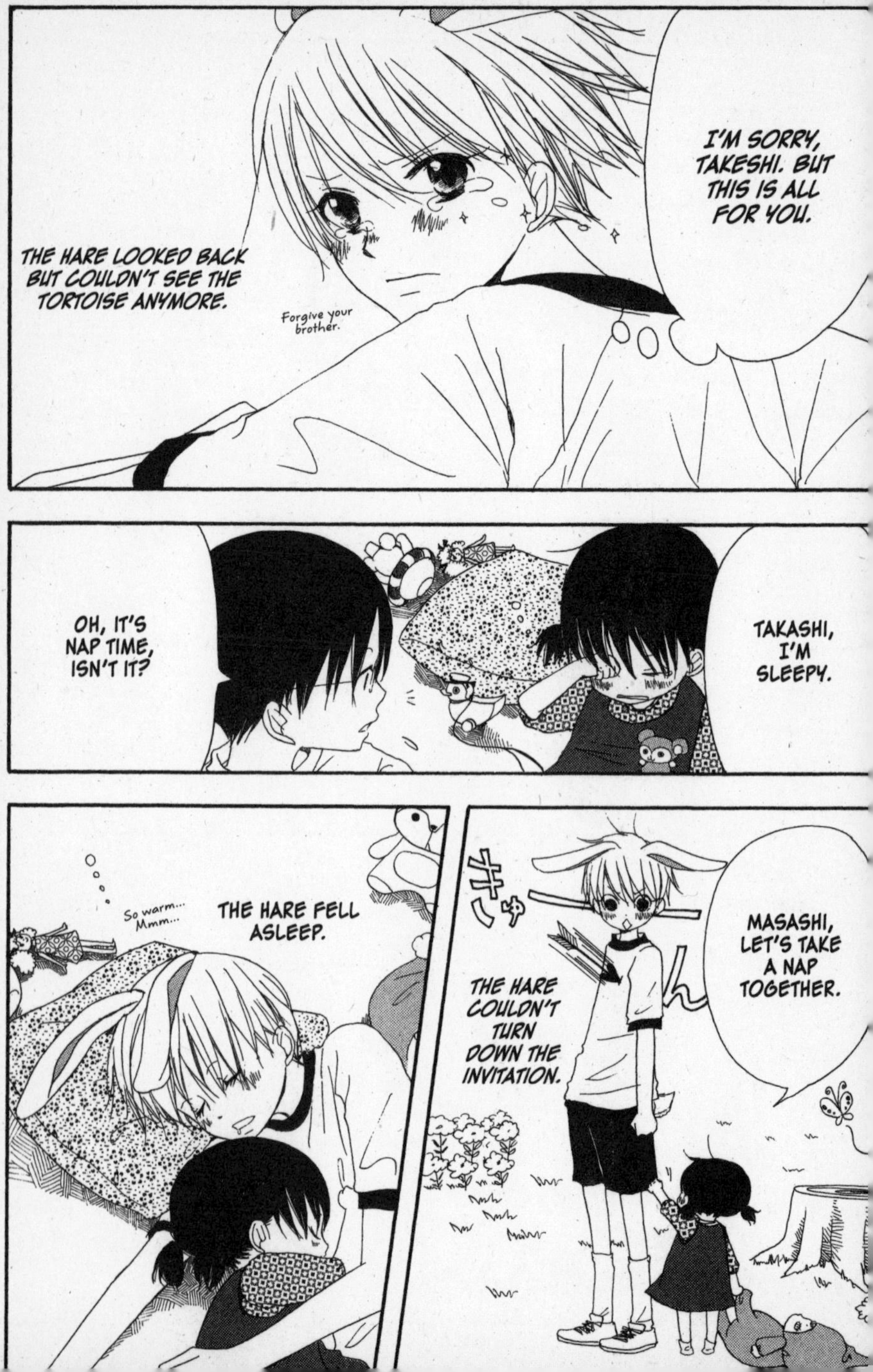
I'M SORRY, TAKESHI. BUT THIS IS ALL FOR YOU.
THE HARE LOOKED BACK BUT COULDN'T SEE THE TORTOISE ANYMORE.
Forgive your brother.
TAKASHI, I'M SLEEPY.
OH, IT'S NAP TIME, ISN'T IT?
MASASHI, LET'S TAKE A NAP TOGETHER.
キュん
THE HARE COULDN'T TURN DOWN THE INVITATION.
So warm... Mmm...
THE HARE FELL ASLEEP.

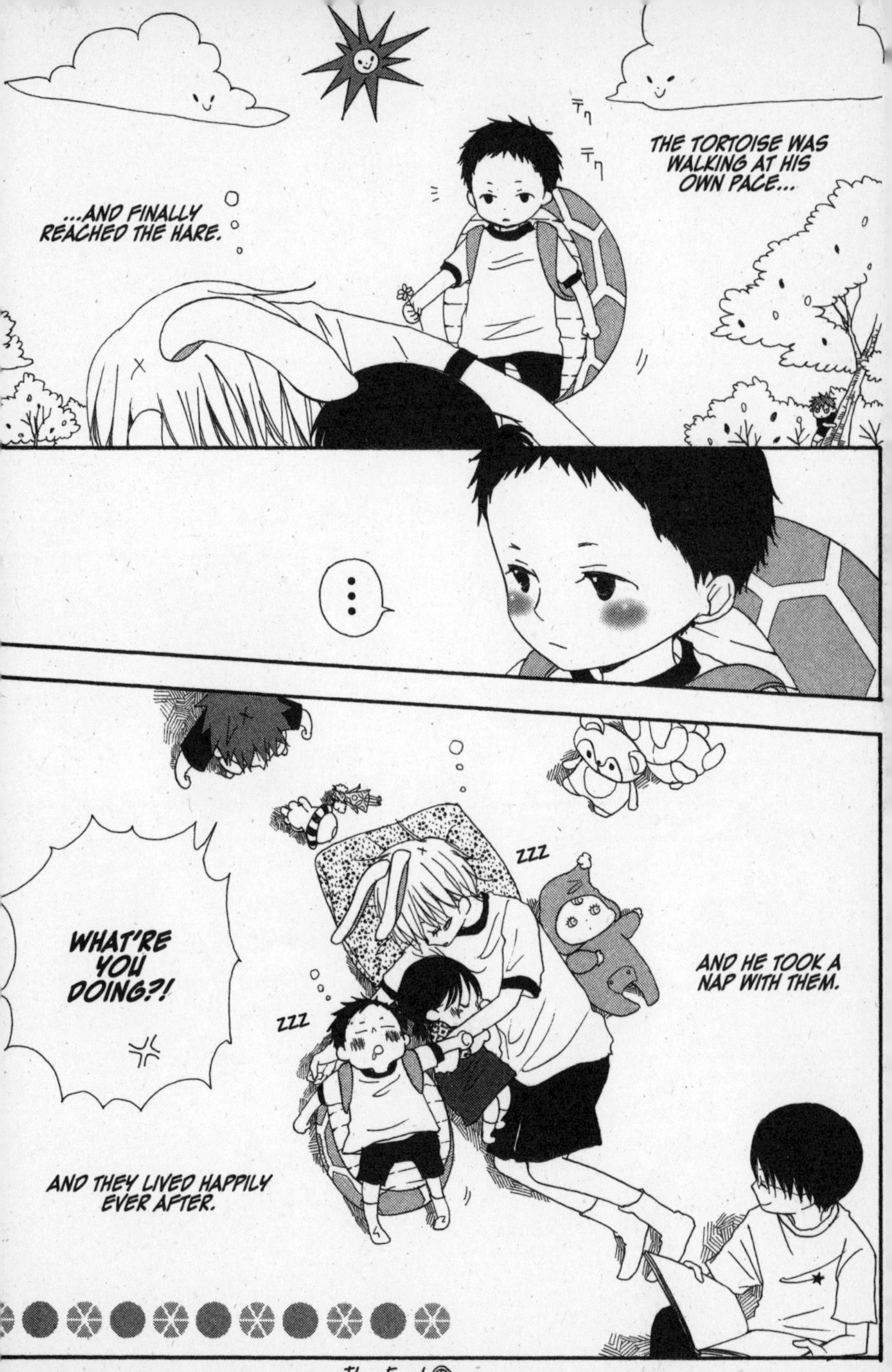
THE TORTOISE WAS WALKING AT HIS OWN PACE...
...AND FINALLY REACHED THE HARE.
...
AND HE TOOK A NAP WITH THEM.
ZZZ
WHAT'RE YOU DOING?!
ZZZ
AND THEY LIVED HAPPILY EVER AFTER.

The End

Next Time in...

Me & My Brothers

WHEN TSUYOSHI COMES HOME ALL BEAT UP, MASASHI AND SAKURA CAN'T HELP BUT WONDER WHAT HAPPENED. THEY PLAY DETECTIVE AND FOLLOW HIM TO THE HOSPITAL WHERE THEY FIND HIM HELPING OUT A BOY WHOSE IDENTITY IS UNKNOWN. THE MIYASHITA FAMILY SOON FINDS ITSELF HOUSING AND FEEDING THE BOY... WILL THAT BE ENOUGH DISTRACTION FOR MASASHI AND SAKURA TO GET OVER WHAT HAPPENED ON VALENTINE'S DAY?

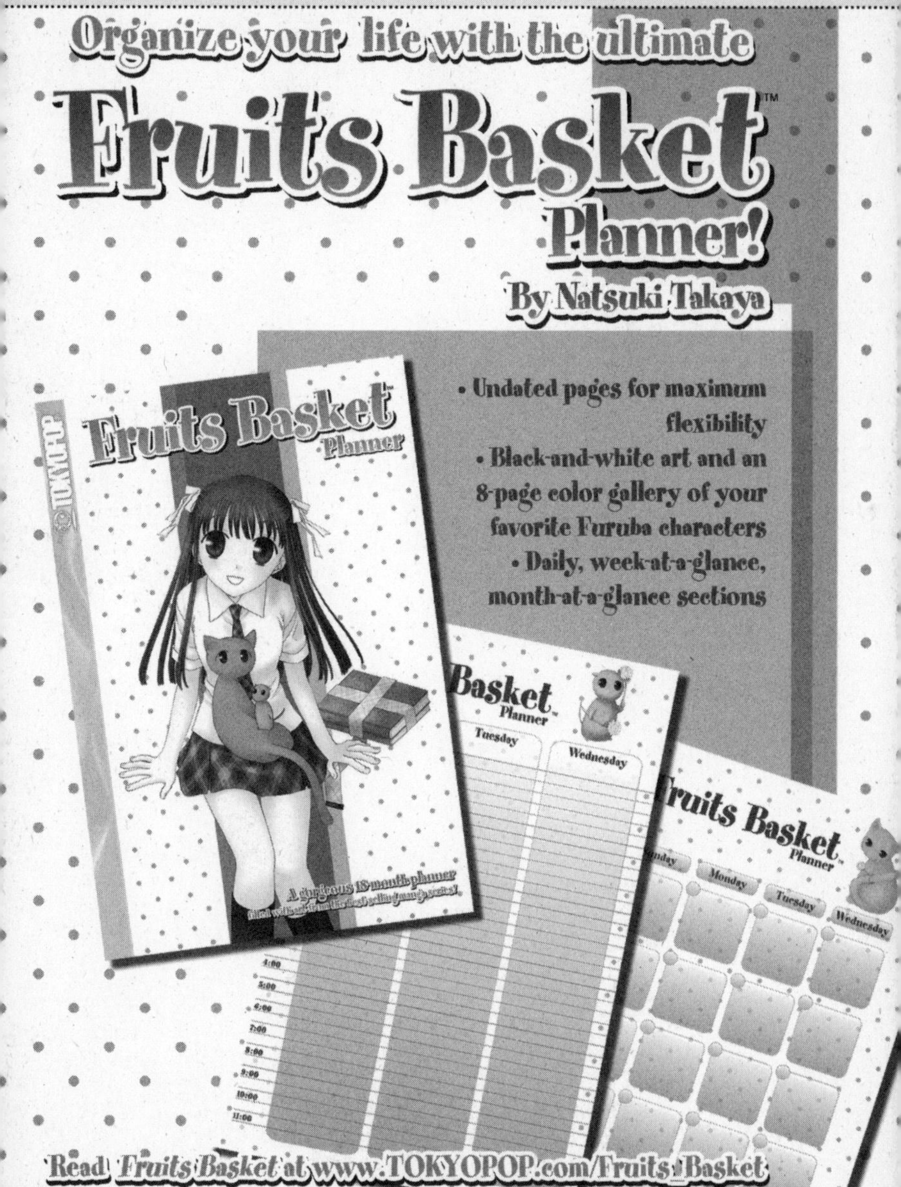
Organize your life with the ultimate
Fruits Basket™
Planner!
By Natsuki Takaya
• Undated pages for maximum flexibility
• Black-and-white art and an 8-page color gallery of your favorite Furuba characters
• Daily, week-at-a-glance, month-at-a-glance sections
Fruits Basket Planner
TOKYOPOP
Basket Planner
Tuesday
Wednesday
Fruits Basket Planner
Monday
Tuesday
Wednesday
4:00
5:00
6:00
7:00
8:00
9:00
10:00
11:00
Read Fruits Basket at www.TOKYOPOP.com/Fruits_Basket
© 1998 Natsuki Takaya / HAKUSENSHA, Inc.

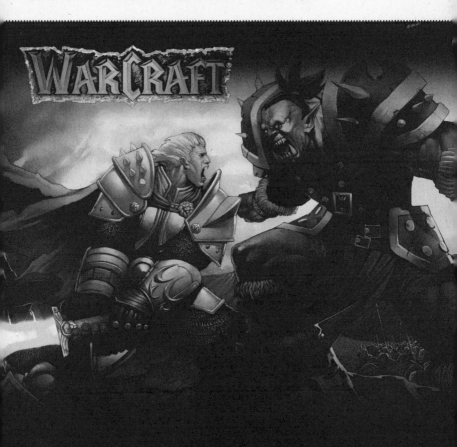

STOP!

This is the back of the book.
You wouldn't want to spoil a great ending!

This book is printed "manga-style," in the authentic Japanese right-to-left format. Since none of the artwork has been flipped or altered, readers get to experience the story just as the creator intended. You've been asking for it, so TOKYOPOP® delivered: authentic, hot-off-the-press, and far more fun!

DIRECTIONS

If this is your first time reading manga-style, here's a quick guide to help you understand how it works.

It's easy... just start in the top right panel and follow the numbers. Have fun, and look for more 100% authentic manga from TOKYOPOP®!